More Advance Praise for *Collusion*

"Nomi Prins is that rare combination of real-world expertise, scholarly method, and a brilliant writing style. Here, she goes beyond the tired complaints about central bank money printing to show that manipulation of markets by the central bankers is far more complex and pervasive than labels like 'easy money' can convey. Collusion is brilliant and timely. It's a 'must-read' for savers, students, journalists, and public officials."

—James Rickards, bestselling author of
Currency Wars and *The Death of Money*

"Nomi Prins spent years embedded behind enemy lines with the corporate criminals who caused the economic crisis of 2008 and whose executives continue to reap record profits while gambling with the futures of millions of families. She could have joined in the grand theft and lived the highlife. Instead, she switched sides and has emerged as one of the fiercest critics of crony capitalism and its sustained attacks against poor and working people. This is the book that the financial elites don't want you to read."

—Jeremy Scahill, Academy Award nominee, bestselling author of
Blackwater, and cofounder of The Intercept

"The US doesn't have a financial press. It has something better—Nomi Prins. Prins shows that the financial corruption of today exceeds that of the Roaring 1920s, because today the Federal Reserve and US Treasury are leading participants in the corruption. Read this book to understand the central bank conspiracy against the world economy."

—Paul Craig Roberts, former *Wall Street Journal* editor and
assistant secretary of the US Treasury

"Central Banks, led by the Federal Reserve, are the opioids for private banks addicted to being reckless with other people's money. Prins, drawing from her previous work in Wall Street firms and her present field research around the world, says, 'We are headed for another epic fall.' Taxpayers, workers, and consumers who will suffer from another bailout all better read this clear, concise, compelling book."

—Ralph Nader, consumer advocate and author of
Breaking Through Power: It's Easier Than We Think

"Scarier than Stephen King horror fiction. Prins, a refugee from Goldman Sachs, tells the truth on her fellow banksters and their abuse of the scary uber-power they wield when they take control of money-printing machinery of the world's central banks. Astonishingly, she got deep inside these secretive power chambers—and came out alive with truly fascinating tales of the blood diamonds of global finance. I particularly enjoyed, if you can use that word, her exposure of the cruelty and cupidity of the banking potentates who suffocated Greece to please the gods of Markets and Mammon."
—Greg Palast, author of *The Best Democracy Money Can Buy*

"[An] unflinching, troubling exposé...well worth a close read by anyone looking to understand the roots of the last crash and prepare for the next."
—*Publishers Weekly*

"A somber, important warning that's likely to cause readers to wonder about the safety of their assets, if not fear for the near-term future."
—Kirkus Reviews

COLLU$ION

Also by Nomi Prins

All the Presidents' Bankers
It Takes a Pillage
Black Tuesday
Jacked
Other People's Money

COLLU$ION

HOW CENTRAL BANKERS
RIGGED THE WORLD

NOMI
PRINS

NATION
BOOKS
New York

Nation Books
116 East 16th Street, 8th Floor
New York, NY 10003
www.nationbooks.org
@NationBooks

Printed in the United States of America

First Edition: May 2018

Published by Nation Books, an imprint of Perseus Books, LLC, a subsidiary of Hachette Book Group, Inc.

Nation Books is a co-publishing venture of the Nation Institute and Perseus Books.

The Hachette Speakers Bureau provides a wide range of authors for speaking events. To find out more, go to www.hachettespeakersbureau.com or call (866) 376-6591.

The publisher is not responsible for websites (or their content) that are not owned by the publisher.

Companion song: "You and Me" by Danny McGaw

A catalog record for this book is available from the Library of Congress.

ISBNs: 978-1-56858-562-8 (hardcover); 978-1-56858-563-5 (e-book)

LSC-C

10 9 8 7 6 5 4 3

Dedicated to
the citizens of the world

CONTENTS

CHARACTERS: The Conjurers of Money

Shinzo Abe: Japan's prime minister since December 2012. He had occupied the post in 2006–2007 but resigned because of health issues. After that, Japan was governed by five prime ministers, none of whom stayed in charge for more than sixteen months. Abe's second term as prime minister was marked by his decision to make economic policy a priority. His economic strategy consisted of three points: monetary expansion, flexible fiscal policy, and structural reform aimed at long-term investments, and is referred to as "Abenomics."

Tarō Asō: Japan's deputy prime minister and finance minister from December 2012 to present. He served as Japan's prime minister from September 2008 to September 2009.

Ben S. Bernanke ("Helicopter Ben"): Succeeded Alan Greenspan as the chairman of the board of governors at the Federal Reserve System for two terms from 2006 to February 2014. He was responsible for leading the monetary policy actions in response to the international financial crisis.

Mark Joseph Carney: Governor of the Bank of England from July 2013 to present. He was governor of the Bank of Canada from February 2008 through June 2013. Earlier in his career, he worked for Goldman Sachs for thirteen years in London, New York, Toronto, and Tokyo.

Agustín Carstens: Governor of Banco de México from 2010 to October 2017. He served as Mexico's finance minister from December 2006 until December 2009. He was deputy managing director of the International Monetary Fund from 2003 to 2006. He was runner-up for IMF president to Christine Lagarde. He assumed the role of Bank for International Settlements general manager from October 2017 to present.

Vítor Constâncio: Vice president of the ECB from 2010 to present. He was governor of the Bank of Portugal from 1985 to 1986 and from 2000 to 2010.

Mario Draghi ("Super Mario"): President of the European Central Bank from November 2011, when he succeeded Jean-Claude Trichet. Draghi was governor of the Bank of Italy from December 2005 to 2011 and vice chairman and managing director at Goldman Sachs International from 2002 to 2005. Draghi's

ECB presidency has been marked by zero and negative interest rates and major quantitative easing measures. His policies have come under scrutiny in Europe, because Europe has not demonstrated any significant signs of real recovery.

Toshihiko Fukui: Governor of the Bank of Japan from 2003 to 2008, incorporating forty years of service there.

Timothy F. Geithner: US Treasury secretary from January 2009 to January 2013. He was president of the Federal Reserve Bank of New York from 2003 to 2009.

Ilan Goldfajn: Current chairman of the Central Bank of Brazil in the provisional government of Michel Temer. He worked at the IMF from 1996 to 1999 and was director of the Central Bank of Brazil between 2000 and 2003. He was chief economist at Banco Itaú Unibanco, the largest private bank in Brazil.

Hu Jintao: General secretary of the Central Committee of the Communist Party of China from November 2002 to November 2012 and president of the People's Republic of China from 2003 to 2012, when he retired and was replaced by Xi Jinping. He led China during the 2008 financial crisis, and his team was responsible for maintaining high growth during that period.

Lou Jiwei: Chinese minister of finance from March 2013 until November 7, 2016. He was the chairman and CEO of China Investment Corporation, the sovereign wealth fund responsible for dealing with some of China's foreign exchange reserves.

Haruhiko Kuroda: The thirty-first governor of the Bank of Japan; he has occupied the post since March 2013. Before that, he was the president of the Asian Development Bank from February 2005 to 2013. Kuroda is a key figure in applying Prime Minister Abe's economic policy; he was responsible for leading Japan into the negative interest rates zone.

Christine Lagarde: Managing director of the International Monetary Fund (IMF) from July 2011 to present. She won the slot against governor of the Bank of Mexico, Agustín Carstens. Lagarde had worked for the French government since 2005, in the posts of minister of agriculture and fisheries and minister of finance and economy. She was chairwoman of the G20 when France was in charge of its presidency in 2011.

Joaquim Vieira Ferreira Levy: A naval engineer with a PhD in economics from the University of Chicago. He was secretary of Brazil's National Treasury during the first Lula da Silva government and minister of finance in 2015 in the Rousseff government. He was director of Brazil's second-largest commercial bank, Bradesco, until appointed minister of finance in late 2014. When he left the Rousseff government, he took a finance director position at the World Bank.

Jacob (Jack) Lew: Replaced Tim Geithner as US secretary of the Treasury for Obama's second term. He occupied the post between February 2013 and January 2017. Before that, Lew served as White House chief of staff from 2012 to

2013. He is a member of the Democratic Party and served in both the Clinton and Obama administrations.

Li Keqiang: China's seventh and current premier, in office from March 2013 through the present. Before that, he was the first vice premier in Hu Jintao's government. Premier Li Keqiang, and his vice premiers, as well as former finance minister Lou Jiwei and People's Bank of China governor Zhou Xiaochuan, are broadly considered pro-business economic reformers.

Luiz Inácio Lula da Silva: President of Brazil from 2003 until 2011 (reelected in 2006). He was the founder of the leftist Workers Party. In early 2016 he temporarily assumed the position of chief of staff of the presidency of the republic at the end of Rousseff's government. He was convicted and sentenced for several charges of corruption in the context of Operation Car Wash.

Guido Mantega: Coined the term "currency wars"; he was the most controversial minister of finance of Brazil through the second government of Lula and first government of Rousseff. He is considered responsible for the takeoff of Brazil in international markets of assets, commodities, and investments and the decline of the Brazilian economy.

Guillermo Ortiz Martínez: Former governor of Banco de México from 1998 to 2009. From 1994 to 1997, he served as the secretary of finance and public credit under the Zedillo administration. He was chairman of the board of the Bank for International Settlements from March 2009 to December 2009, and has been on the advisory board for the Globalization and Monetary Policy Institute at the Federal Reserve Bank of Dallas from 2008 to present.

Henrique de Campos Meirelles: Chairman of Brazil's central bank from 2003 to 2011. Since May 2016 he has been minister of finance of the provisional government of Michel Temer. He holds a degree in civil engineering from the University of São Paulo. Before running the Central Bank of Brazil (BCB), among other things, he was president of FleetBoston's (formerly BankBoston) Corporate and Global Bank in the United States.

Shoichi Nakagawa: Japan's minister of finance from September 2008 to February 2009. He died in October 2009.

Enrique Peña Nieto: President of Mexico and member of the Mexican PRI party from December 2012 to present.

Lucas Papademos: Governor of the Bank of Greece from 1994 to 2002, when he assumed the post of European Central Bank vice president, until 2010. In 2011, in the middle of the Greek debt crisis, Papademos assumed the post of Greek prime minister.

Henry (Hank) M. Paulson: The seventy-fourth secretary of the Treasury of the United States, serving from July 2006 to January 2009. Before that, Paulson was

Goldman Sachs's CEO from 1999 to 2006. After leaving the Treasury, Paulson founded the Paulson Institute to promote sustainable growth cooperation initiatives between the United States and China.

Dilma Vana Rousseff: President of Brazil from 2011 until 2016 (reelected in 2014); she was removed after an irregular impeachment process. She worked in the government of President Luiz Inácio Lula da Silva as minister of mines and energy from 2003 to 2005 and chief of staff from 2005 to 2010. During that time, she was chairwoman of the board of directors of Petrobras.

Wolfgang Schäuble: German conservative politician from the Christian Democratic Union, Angela Merkel's party. Schäuble served as finance minister from 2009 to October 2017. He served as federal minister of the interior from 2005 to 2009. Schäuble was a strident defender of the European Union project inside Germany.

Masaaki Shirakawa: Succeeded Fukui as the governor of the Bank of Japan, a position he occupied from April 2008 to March 2013. During Shirakawa's term, the BOJ restarted the quantitative easing measures that were created and used by Japan from 2001 to 2006.

Dominique Strauss-Kahn: Former politician from the French Socialist Party. He was the managing director of the IMF from November 2007 to May 2011, when he resigned as a result of sexual assault accusations. He was in charge of the French Ministry of Economy and Finance from 1997 to 1999. During his term, the IMF called for a stronger role for the special drawing rights (SDR) as a possible alternative to the US dollar's position as a reserve currency.

Michel Miguel Elias Temer Lulia: Acting president of Brazil since May 2016 and confirmed as provisional president after the removal of Rousseff. Previously, he served as vice president of Brazil for Rousseff's two terms. He is the honorary president of the Brazilian Democratic Movement Party, a party considered center.

Alexandre Antônio Tombini: Former governor of the Central Bank of Brazil (BCB) during Rousseff's government. He is an economist and had considerable influence as president of the BCB, experiencing some friction with different finance ministers during his tenure.

Jean-Claude Trichet: President of the executive board at the European Central Bank from November 2003 to October 2011. Before that, he ran the French Treasury for six years and was governor of the Banque de France for ten, from 1993 to 2003.

Axel Weber: The president of the German Bundesbank from April 2004 to April 2011, when he resigned one year before the end of his term. He was elected a member of the governing council of the European Central Bank in 2004.

Wen Jiabao: China's sixth premier, served as the head of the government for ten years, or two terms, from 2003 to 2013. He was the central figure in the establishment of China's economic policy during that period, especially measures to confront the global financial crisis.

Xi Jinping: General secretary of the Central Committee of the Communist Party of China, president of the People's Republic of China, and chairman of China's Central Military Commission from November 2012 to present.

Janet Yellen: The fifteenth chair of the board of the Federal Reserve System, acting since February 2014 for a four-year mandate. Yellen was an economics professor at the University of California, Berkeley. She succeeded Chairman Ben S. Bernanke after being his vice chair from 2010 to 2014. Before that, she served as president and chief executive officer of the Federal Reserve Bank of San Francisco. Wall Street considered Yellen a "dove" who largely maintained the policies of Ben Bernanke. Trump selected Vice Governor Jerome Powell to succeed her in November 2017, for a term starting in February 2018.

Yi Gang: Yi Gang became deputy governor of monetary policy of the People's Bank of China in 2007. At the PBOC, he served in multiple positions since joining in 1997, including as deputy secretary general of the Monetary Policy Committee from 1997 to 2002. He served as former director of the State Administration of Foreign Exchange from 2009 through January 2016. He earned his PhD from the University of Illinois.

Zhou Xiaochuan: Governor of the People's Bank of China from 2002. In 2009, at a pivotal moment of financial instability, Zhou gave a speech titled "Reform the International Monetary System" that questioned the role of the dollar as a reserve currency. He pressed for and achieved the yuan's inclusion in the IMF special drawing rights basket.

AUTHOR'S NOTE

To research this book, I set out on a global expedition. I visited Mexico City, Guadalajara, Monterrey, Rio de Janeiro, São Paulo, Brasília, Porto Alegre, Beijing, Shanghai, Tokyo, London, Berlin, and many cities throughout the United States. I navigated high-speed railways through China's countryside, witnessed anti-impeachment demonstrations in Brazil, sipped coffee with students, farmers, and small business owners throughout Mexico, and traversed the offices and halls of the US Congress.

The journey included my return to China, where I had first visited as a young banker working for the now-defunct investment bank Lehman Brothers. Financial instruments were less complex in the late 1980s and early 1990s. But it was a time when the role of finance was rapidly changing. So was the nature of the global economy and the risk imposed upon it by bankers. They altered it, trade by trade, bet by bet.

At the time, I was working on the futures and options desk while moving from my master's to PhD coursework in statistics. I held a purist attitude about analytics (the math behind financial instruments) in contrast with the cocky, salesperson mentality of other colleagues pushing financial products. In my early twenties, I'd argue with the salespeople I worked with, one in particular, about the numbers and who got credit for what new analytical approach. Taking credit, whether or not it was yours to take, was part of the Wall Street survival tool kit. I was never particularly good at that part.

To quell the bickering, management decided to send me and that salesperson on a road trip together—around Asia. If we didn't kill each other, in the process we'd sell some products or, at least, open accounts. I'd explain the math; the salesperson would sell the products. He was a hothead, but in the end, after various near-death experiences, including our driver's rush against oncoming traffic to get us to the airport in the Philippines, we reached a truce and garnered some business for Lehman in Asia.

I didn't realize it then, but the "product" we were trying to sell to the Chinese contained both financial and political underpinnings, as so many do. The People's

Bank of China held more reserves in US Treasury bonds than any other central bank. We introduced them to one of our products called "Term TED Spreads." We would sell them US Treasury bonds and they would short, or sell back, a "strip" of exchange-traded futures and thereby lock in what was called a Treasury Eurodollar (or TED) spread. It was supposed to represent the way the market viewed the integrity of US government credit against that of LIBOR,[1] a rate set by a consortium of major banks. LIBOR would later be criminally manipulated by big banks in the lead-up to the financial crisis of 2007–2008.

Lehman profited from selling both the bonds and the futures. Term TED Spreads was a basic product, but its mechanics were similar to the more complex ones to come. The early nineties represented a simple time, from a central bank perspective. The power of central banks over markets and economies was contained. Though I didn't know it then, I would be working with and analyzing central banks for the better part of the next three decades.

I left Lehman shortly after that trip and took a position at Bear Stearns in London at which I created the financial analytics department. During my time there, the euro premiered as the official currency of the Eurozone. The Asian crisis struck. Bill Clinton was impeached. The Glass-Steagall Act, which had prohibited bank deposits from being used to fuel speculative activities within big banks, was repealed. Increasingly complex derivatives were sold to the portfolios of any entity with enough cash or credit to buy them, even if that credit came from the sellers of those derivatives.

Returning to New York in 2000, I worked as a managing director at Goldman Sachs, where I was responsible for the analytics underlying a rapidly evolving product, credit derivatives. I also ran a swat team that "hunted" for "white elephant" transactions tailored especially for major financial clients and corporations. The internal pressures within the firm regarding that "hunt" were intense. Wall Street had become less focused on client risk as products became more complicated and lucrative. One senior manager advised me that, if I wanted to get ahead at Goldman, I had to make upper management my clients, not the external customers. That was a pivotal moment for me; though a steady stream of internal politics at Goldman, on Wall Street, and in the corporate world at large is a constant presence, to have it so plainly spelled out stopped me cold. It was the kind of moment from which there is no turning back. It was friendly advice as well, but it just didn't sit well with me.

Shortly after, the entire country was shattered by the events of 9/11. We each have our stories from those days, where we were, what went through our minds, how it changed us as people, as a nation. For me, those tense moments walking up Broadway away from Wall Street with the acrid, debris-filled smoke of the Twin Towers in the air, was a last straw. I left Goldman Sachs. Partly because life was too short. Partly out of disgust at how citizens everywhere had become collateral damage, and later hostages, to the banking system. Since then, I've dedicated my life to exposing the intersections of money and power and deciphering the impact of the relationships between governments and central and private bankers on the citizens of the world.

In 2004, I explored those post-1970s alliances in my first book, *Other People's Money: The Corporate Mugging of America*. In that thesis, I warned of the calamities that would ensue as a result of credit derivatives, then a tiny blip on the banking and business media radar. Although other analysts eventually reached similar conclusions, I was one of the first "insiders" who explained when, why, and how this crisis would unfold. What happened following the repeal of the bipartisan-passed 1933 Glass-Steagall Act in 1999 was unavoidable. As long as people's deposits remained fodder for reckless speculation, I wrote, the world was at risk. Indeed, a few years later, the US economy collapsed, taking down markets and economies around the globe. Some people said banks weren't to blame, people who couldn't afford their mortgages were. But that's not a logical conclusion if you do the math and know how banks create and sell mortgages.

The financial crisis began three years after my book came out and escalated through 2008. Those events led to my next book, *It Takes a Pillage: Behind the Bonuses, Bailouts, and Backroom Deals from Washington to Wall Street*. The book tapped into the psyche of Wall Street, revealing how the very structure of the financial system hinged on traders flocking to the next big bet, regardless of the stakes. In addition, the *same* people and families kept popping up, cycling through Wall Street and Washington. They influenced the economy beneath them from their loftier heights of status, private money, and public office, dismantling laws that stood in their way and finding loopholes in others. Private banks normalized market manipulation. Central banks made it an art form, with no limits.

The big banks, with their strong personal and legacy connections to the government and the backing of central banks, particularly the Fed in the United States, thrived through economic and geopolitical conflict. Their bloodlines and family connections spanned a century. In my book *All the Presidents' Bankers: The Hidden Alliances that Drive American Power*, I dug deeper. The project took me to presidential libraries across the country. I perused documents untouched for decades—or ever—that supported one conclusion: *relationships matter*.

Whether central bankers proclaim to support or oppose each other matters. In *Collusion*, I expose these international relationships and the power grab of central bankers at the Fed, European Central Bank, Bank of Japan, and other central banks that have fabricated or "conjured" money to fund banking activities at the people's expense. Since the financial crisis, these illusionists have created money, altered the nature of the financial system, and orchestrated a de facto heist that enables the most powerful banks and central bankers to run the world.

The concept for *Collusion* cohered in my mind after I was invited to address the Federal Reserve, the International Monetary Fund (IMF), and the World Bank in June 2015. Because I had been vocal about labeling recent central bank policies "insane," at first I thought the invitation was a mistake; I even asked as much of the Fed office that invited me. Their response was, "We are looking forward to what you have to say."

In the well-appointed and historic boardroom where the Federal Open Market Committee (FOMC) sets monetary policy, I was to address a roomful of international central bankers in the morning kick-off session of the three-day global conference. The boardroom was situated upstairs from the portrait of Carter Glass, who helped steer President Woodrow Wilson's proposal for the Federal Reserve System that culminated in the Federal Reserve Act of 1913 through Washington. In 1919, Glass became Wilson's Treasury secretary, succeeding William G. McAdoo in the role.[2] Glass in memoriam watched over the atrium where we had our group photograph taken that morning to commemorate the occasion. The central bankers hailed from the same institutions that routinely met at G7 and G20 and other multinational central bank gatherings around the world. My host placed me at the front of the room.

Chair of the Federal Reserve Janet Yellen opened the event, indicating the banking system was better but some instability still lurked. She was followed by an assistant Treasury secretary who touted the accomplishments of the Obama administration in combatting financial risk with the Dodd-Frank Act (which didn't actually break up the banks). Cardinal Theodore McCarrick, fresh from a meeting with the pope, reminded everyone of their responsibility to help the poor.

Then it was my turn. I explained why years of supporting a private banking system of recidivist felons with no strings attached couldn't possibly lend itself as a panacea for financial or economic stability. "You have the power to do better," I told the central bankers. But the real question is, "Do you have the will?" For what began as an "emergency" monetary policy had morphed into an ongoing norm and provoked a shake-up of the world economic order.

Over the days of that conference and ever since, multiple global central bankers (including from the Fed and IMF) have thanked me privately for my honesty. Yet their policies have barely changed at all. No significant regulations have been introduced to fix the structural problems behind the last financial crisis. Banks and the markets have been subsidized by quantitative easing and conjured-money policy. Central banks have colluded to provide global artificial money and subsidies as they see fit rather than to actualize authentic, long-term, tangible growth and stability or require anything in return from the big banks they helped the most.

Whether the broad population knows it or not, this collusion among the most elite central banks has run rampant and deep. Worse, central bankers have no exit strategy for their policies, no great unwind plan, despite repeatedly throwing out words that indicate they do. It's like pushing a huge snowball to the edge of a cliff and hoping the cliff will morph into a valley before the snowball plunges and destroys whatever is in its way below.

Which means we are headed for another epic fall. The question is not if, but when.

INTRODUCTION

It is not the responsibility of the Federal Reserve—nor would it be appropriate—to protect lenders and investors from the consequences of their decisions.

—Ben Bernanke, Federal Reserve chairman, 2007

The 2007–2008 US financial crisis was the consequence of a loosely regulated banking system in which power was concentrated in the hands of too limited a cast of speculators. Since the crisis, G7 central banks have pumped money into private banks through an unconventional monetary policy process called quantitative easing (QE). QE is an overtly complex term that entails a central bank manufacturing electronic money and then injecting it into banks and financial markets in return for purchasing bonds or securities (or stocks). The result of this maneuver is to lift the money supply within the financial system, reduce interest rates (or the cost of borrowing money, disproportionally in favor of the bigger banks and corporations), and boost the value of those securities. The whole codependent cycle is what I call a "conjured-money" scheme, wherein the cost of money is rendered abnormally cheap.

Speculation raged in the wake of this abundant cheap capital much as a global casino would be abuzz if everyone gambled using someone else's money. Yet bank lending did not grow, nor did wages or prosperity, for most of the world's population. Instead, central bankers created asset bubbles through their artificial stimulation of banks and markets. When these bubbles pop, the fragile financial system and economic world underlying them could be thrown into an economic depression. That's why central banks are so desperate to collude.

Enabling certain banks to become "too big to fail" was the catastrophic mistake of the very body supposed to keep this from happening, the Federal Reserve. The Fed happens to be the arbiter of bank mergers—and it has never seen a merger it didn't like. Legislation to deter "too big to fail" had been in existence since 1933. In the wake of the Great Crash of 1929, a popular bipartisan act called the Glass-Steagall Act restricted banks from using federally insured customer deposits as collateral for

1

large-scale speculation and asset creation. Banks that were engaged in both of these types of practices, or commercial banking and investment banking, were required to pick a side. Either service deposits and loans, or create securities and merge companies and speculate. By virtue of having to choose, they became smaller. Big bank bailouts became unnecessary. But that act was repealed in 1999 under President Clinton. As a result, banks went on a buying spree. The larger ones gobbled up the smaller ones. Along the way, their size and loose regulations gave them the confidence and impetus to engage in riskier practices. Ultimately, they became so big and complex that they could create toxic assets and provide financing to their customers to buy them, all at once.

That's how the subprime mortgage problem became a decade-long financial crisis that required multiple central banks to contain it. Big banks could buy up mortgages, turn them into more complex securities, and either sell them to global customers, including pension funds, localities, and insurance companies, or lend substantive money to investment banks and hedge funds that engaged in trading these securities. The Fed allowed all of this to happen.

Massive leveraging (or betting with huge sums of borrowed money) within the securities those big banks created and sold exacerbated the risk to which they exposed the world. Eight years after the crisis began, the Big Six US banks—JPMorgan Chase, Citigroup, Wells Fargo, Bank of America, Goldman Sachs, and Morgan Stanley—collectively held 43 percent more deposits, 84 percent more assets, and triple the amount of cash they held before. The Fed has allowed the biggest banks on Wall Street to essentially double the risk that devastated the system in 2008.

But in the banks' moment of peril, the Fed unleashed a global policy of injecting fabricated money into the worldwide financial system. This flood of cheap money resulted in the subsequent issuance of trillions of dollars of debt, pushing the global level of debt to $325 trillion, more than *three times* global GDP.[1] By mid-2017, the total assets held by the G3 central banks—the US Fed, the European Central Bank (ECB), and the Bank of Japan (BOJ)—through conjured-money QE programs had hit more than $13.5 trillion.[2] The figure was equivalent to 17 percent of currency-adjusted global GDP.

To garner support for their multi-trillion-dollar QE strategies, the G3 central bank leaders peddled the notion that they were helping the general economy. That couldn't have been further from the truth. There was no direct channel, no law, no requirement to divert the Fed's cheap money into helping real people. This was because borrowing and subsequent investing in the real economy required funds from private banks, and not from central banks directly. That's how the monetary system was set up. And private banks were under no obligation to do anything with this cheap money they didn't want to do.

Central bank money crafters realized early on that simply adjusting benchmark interest rates in their countries was no longer effective without quantitative easing. They had to wax unconventional with monetary policy. And then they had to collude to spread their programs globally. They concocted and plowed cash into their respective banking systems.

Specifically, the largest private banks, including JPMorgan Chase, Deutsche Bank, and HSBC, that inhaled this cheap money were not required to increase their lending to the Main Street economy as a condition of the availability of that money. Instead, the banks hoarded the cash. US banks colluded with the Fed to get that cash by stashing their bonds as "excess reserves" (more reserves for emergencies than regulations required) on the Fed's books. And, because of the Emergency Economic Stabilization Act of 2008, they received 0.25 percent interest per year from the Fed on those reserves, too. Wall Street used its easy access to cheap money to increase speculation in derivatives and other complex securities. They used it to buy back their own shares, thus effectively manipulating their own stock—in broad daylight and with explicit approval from the Fed. In turn these banks dialed back their lending to small and midsized businesses, which hampered their growth potential.

The danger with having a system rely on so much conjured capital is that when central bankers stop manifesting it, it could go into shock; markets could plunge, credit seize, and a new crisis emerge. That's why central banks are walking the tightrope between altering their policies and doing nothing to alter them, thereby continuing them by default, with no exit plan.

Sir Isaac Newton's third law of motion states: for every action there is an equal and opposite reaction. This principle doesn't hold linearly at the intersection of money and politics, but it's illuminating when cross-examined. Relationships must be untangled, geography collapsed, and time compacted to grasp the true causes and effects of money in politics.

After the monetary system faces the sober reality of a real shock, the truth is that it may never truly return to its prior state. The system morphs into something new. *Collusion* chronicles the ascent and interaction of the world's elite central bankers, who accumulated unprecedented power and influence over the world economy following the financial crisis of 2007–2008. It tells the tale of how these undemocratically selected officials have irrevocably transformed the very system they are sworn to protect.

At the onset of the crisis, the Fed colluded with other central banks to decrease the cost of money. Their fabricated money didn't come from taxes, revenues, profits, or growth. The Fed did so by exercising its emergency powers under the Federal

Reserve Act of 1913 to do *whatever* it deemed necessary to contain the crisis. Or so it said.

The Fed was established through legislation passed in December 1913 under Democratic president Woodrow Wilson, following a series of bipartisan negotiations orchestrated by Virginia congressman Carter Glass. Development of a US central banking system had begun several years earlier, with the efforts of former Senate banking committee leader Nelson Aldrich, the Republican senator from Rhode Island who convened a select team of private bankers in secret at a club designed by and for the wealthiest members of US society, at Jekyll Island, Georgia. They proposed a central bank that would back private banks in the event of a financial crisis such as the Panic of 1907. The Fed that emerged became the last resort for private US banks that needed liquidity[3] or, later, fabricated "money" to operate when credit was tight or unavailable. Secondarily, the Fed was tasked with maintaining stability, low inflation, and full employment through setting monetary policy, or the level of rates—and by whatever means necessary.

Fast-forward about a century. By late 2008, the Fed had gone into overdrive carving out a role as America's sub-superpower. The central bank adopted an imperial position in the global central bank hierarchy, unleashing a series of power plays among other central banks.

The Fed pushed its strategies globally. It saw no other option. So entangled and codependent were the big US and global banks that the only way to keep the money flowing into the banking system was to enlist the help of allies the world over. The international monetary system of interest rates, currency movements, and debt creation had become so intertwined with the US banking system that "saving" the latter meant co-opting the former. The major G7 central banks followed the Fed for two reasons: geopolitics and fear. They feared a deeper and more prolonged liquidity crisis if they didn't do the Fed's bidding.

Central bankers determine the value of money by setting interest rate levels directly and make additional adjustments by purchasing bonds. The more bonds they purchase, the lower they can keep interest rates because they manufacture demand, which pushes up bond prices, which, by the nature of bond math, pushes down interest rates. They influence, or try to influence, the worth of currencies by buying and selling them locally and internationally. These bankers tend to cycle through various public and private posts domestically and on the world stage of the global monetary system network.

SHIFTING MONETARY SYSTEMS: DEVELOPED TO DEVELOPING NATIONS

Emerging from the ravages of the financial crisis, developing countries challenged the status quo of US- and European-led money policies. They developed new economic, trade, and diplomatic alliances to seek refuge from the Fed and the US dollar. That was in stark contrast to prevailing monetary policy history.

The World Wars of the twentieth century had spawned a US-led monetary structure that came to dominate markets and geopolitics. In 1944, self-interested financial leaders convened at Bretton Woods to craft a monetary system centered on US and European currencies and interests. While Europe rebuilt its war-torn cities, the United States capitalized on its superpower role, and developing countries were overshadowed.

In contrast, the twenty-first century gave rise to a *financial* world war. Conjured money was the weapon of choice. Fabricated funds went toward subsidizing the private banking system and buying government debt, corporate debt, and stocks. By providing the grease that kept money flowing, central bankers superseded governments—they set the cost of money and provided the confidence in ongoing liquidity—the world was their battlefield.

On the surface, the International Monetary Fund (IMF) was established by the United States and Europe (with olive branches extended to other countries) to fund postwar development. But, in practice, both the IMF and the International Bank for Reconstruction and Development (part of the World Bank Group and commonly referred to as the World Bank) fortified the economic and political power of the core US-Europe alliance. The power of this entity increased after the most recent financial crisis, as did its growing embrace of emerging economies, including China and Russia.

Leaders of developed and developing countries embarked on a paradigm shift. The world would gradually be divided between those who depended on Fed policies and those who had been harmed by them. Gatherings and conferences of central bank leaders would become focal points and outlets for criticism against the systemic risk, low growth, and poverty being spawned.

The global financial system elites meet up in swanky locations. They take each other's calls and tend to avoid mere mortals (some have not driven their own cars in decades). In practice, they *operate* in such a way so as to continually grow and retain their power. The modern outsized influence of these nondemocratic private-public banking institutions and individual leaders eclipses that of governments and has become an indispensable backdrop to markets and capital flows. Theirs is a natural process of greasing the wheels of banks and markets. Except it's not. By following the money and power alliances to their source, a more compelling story emerges, one of collusion, forced collaboration, and a changing monetary and financial system hierarchy.

In 2009, the world was coming to terms with how massive the global financial crisis was. The American financial system was broken. The international monetary system was breaking. It was unclear how far that "developing disaster" would extend. Central bankers are not elected by voters. Yet they play at government. They promote policies under the auspices of stabilizing prices, achieving full employment, and maintaining (a somewhat arbitrary level of) inflation. Since the financial crisis, they have ushered in an unprecedented period of artificial intervention.

Before the crisis, central bankers exhibited gross negligence of their regulatory responsibilities to contain bank risk and fraud. In an effort to minimize the fallout, they lavished extreme monetary intervention on the biggest banks and markets in which they operated. What started as a rescue mission for the biggest US banks in the form of liquidity "lifelines" metastasized and became global.

This in turn caused other countries to reexamine their positions in the international financial hierarchy relative to the United States. Non-Western nations such as China and Russia had no interest in becoming casualties of another US-led crisis and came to understand that dependency on the US dollar put them at risk. Emerging market nations began to gravitate toward China for refuge, seeking a way to maintain trade while diffusing exposure to the risks of the US.

Classic monetary policy sets rates and credit conditions in "pursuit of maximum employment, stable prices, and moderate long-term interest rates."[4] But after the financial crisis, zero percent interest rate money remained manna for stock and real estate markets. What began as self-described "emergency measures" by the Fed became the new normal. Like Dr. Frankenstein, the Fed had created something with implications far beyond what it understood.

Wall Street was nourished by this monster. Foreign capital slithered around the world like a ravenous snake in search of prey. Speculation, short-term profit, and central bank encouragement allowed for global collaboration and ultimately unsustainable markets. All this created the *illusion* of economic stability.

The financial crisis of 2007–2008 converted central bankers into a new class of power brokers. Their behavior ran roughshod over the very notion of free markets because they rendered markets sustained through artificial means. Central banks re-redefined the balance of power in the international order. In developed countries, they launched a strain of financial warfare whereby they backed governments, implicitly forcing austerity on weaker countries. In developing countries, they advocated austerity for their own populations.

In the decade that followed, US debt rose from about $9 trillion in 2007 to $20 trillion in 2017.[5] The debt-to-GDP ratio nearly quadrupled, from 40 percent to 105 percent. The Fed held the equivalent of almost one-third of this amount as "reserves" on its books. This was effectively debt created by the US Department of the Treasury, bought by big banks, and returned to the Fed to earn interest for those banks. It did nothing to support the real, or foundational, economy. And without a solid foundation, you don't have a solid economy.

Something had to give—people's patience. The Fed's rising influence and power to create money—but not financial security or economic prosperity—prompted major shifts in voter preferences. Large-scale moves toward nationalism were met with bitter battles to maintain globalism. Superpower realignments and fresh alliances were activated with a zeal not seen since the wake of World War II. The Fed's fabricated-money strategy left other central banks with a choice: collusion or consequences.

THE POWER GAME

Classically, central banks hold reserves in case of emergencies, set interest rates, and allocate funds to calm or restructure the world after panics or wars. The more recent role they have assumed is one of securing the entire financial system and influencing the economic trajectory of entire sovereign nations. This is the antithesis of democratic rule. Such a monetary oligarchy operates beyond democratic norms and limits.

The scope of their activities, and the sheer level of international coordination and its results, was unthinkable before 2008. Never before has money been so cheap—for so long. Never before has there been no imagined alternative to artificial capital. Never before have certain elite central bankers sought to control all others. Never before have central bankers attempted to dominate the world monetarily and economically—and been able to do it.

Much of the twentieth century belonged to Wall Street. The twenty-first century now belongs to the central banks. Historically, every bubble has been followed by a bust. Central banks have created an artificial money bubble, specifically crafted for the purpose of lavishing banks and markets with cheap capital. Though the Fed began to signal a reduction in the size of its book in mid-2017, by miniscule percentages, reducing it substantively in practice has significant ramifications. These include catalyzing a rise in rates and therefore the cost of debt denominated in dollars around the world. That could impair the ability of emerging markets (EMs) that borrowed money in US dollars to repay their debts. In turn, these actions could lead to corporate bond defaults for companies, forcing major job loss or wage reductions in order to remain afloat.

A handful of officials control the fates of billions of people. The more these officials rely on artificial money, the greater their power. G7 central bankers, such as Fed leader Ben Bernanke, followed by Janet Yellen, ECB head Mario Draghi, and BOJ head Haruhiko Kuroda, sought to subsidize their banking systems and markets through unprecedented intervention.

This situation belies an integrated network of a new, influential breed of central bankers. Lurking behind their actions is a monumental yet subtle shift. The rise of the Fed's power and that of its allies *catalyzed* irrevocable changes that have provoked the increase in non-G7 central bank powers, such as that of the People's Bank of China, and instability in major emerging market nations such as Mexico and Brazil.

POWER OF THE UNELECTED

From public or private posts, central bank governors are usually appointed by government offices or officials on the basis of ideology and personal relationships. In the United States, there is a pretense of public choice, and then Congress votes on the candidate. In practice, however, no candidate for governor of the Fed has ever been rejected by Congress, so de facto the US president selects that individual. For purposes of job security, central bankers can either stay aligned with the president or they stay above ideological politics. But they don't have to. They are free to decide monetary policy as they see fit, without transparency or accountability.

In countries like China, Brazil, and Mexico, the president or minister of finance appoints the central bank governor. The selection is fraught with political undertones, even though some presidents stress that the central bank operates independently of the government. In the case of the multinational central and development banks that shape monetary policy, such as the IMF, the World Bank, and the Bank for International Settlements (BIS, or "the central bank of central banks"), leaders are chosen by member countries. Thereafter, they are selected and appointed by former members. It's a rotating, exclusive club.

SUPPLYING DOLLARS, INCREASING INEQUALITY

Beginning in 2008, the Fed provided US dollar liquidity to international markets by doubling its foreign exchange swap lines with the Bank of Canada, Bank of England, Bank of Japan, National Bank of Denmark, European Central Bank, Bank of Norway, Reserve Bank of Australia, Bank of Sweden, and Swiss National Bank, from $290 billion to $620 billion. This was the central bank equivalent of "the House" providing extra money to the gamblers at nearly no cost, so they could keep placing wagers until their spate of bad luck dissipated.

When these carefully crafted (think: artisanal) subsidies, called "currency swaps," were first used by central banks in the 1960s, the dollar was weakening as other countries hit post–World War II production strides. In that environment, the Fed offered $20 billion of currency swaps in dollars, an amount worth $160 billion today. The idea was to furnish foreign banks with US dollars with which to engage in trade and financial transactions with US banks. That amount was one-quarter of the figure on offer by the Fed in 2008. Currency swaps weren't the only provision of money on the menu, nor were they enough to satiate the imperiled financial system, starving for more dollars.

By September 30, 2008, markets had devoured these currency swaps, pushing the value of the king dollar relative to other main currencies back on top. The global financial crisis was caused by US banks and their negligent-at-best regulator, the Fed. Yet, the dollar exhibited its most acute appreciation since being allowed to "float" after the gold standard was abolished in 1971. This happened by virtue of the Fed's crafting just enough dollars to keep the system going, but not enough to drive down demand for the dollar. The Fed was the perfect drug dealer, keeping its customers always wanting a little bit more.

The dollar's rise was attributed to traditional reasons: it was a "safe-haven" currency, there was a shortage of demand, and traders were "unwinding" or getting out of trades that had bet on a weaker dollar. All that was true. But the biggest factor was the Fed's choreography.

Starting in 2012, the Fed portrayed the desire, but not the action, to retreat from its policies of providing liquidity to world markets and major banks. The US central bank offered a gamut of benchmarks, from inflation to unemployment, as necessary conditions to shift to tightening rate policy. But it feared negative repercussions of a major policy shift. So, the Fed's goalposts stayed in constant flux.

Global citizens saw no significant upgrade in their personal financial conditions. To the contrary, the majority of wages stagnated after 2008. Between 2012 and 2015, developing country wage growth slowed from 2.5 percent to 1.7 percent. Among developed G20 countries, it rose from 0.2 percent in 2012 to 1.7 percent in 2015, but most of that increase went to the top 10 percent of the population.

Despite central banks' claims of spurring economic growth with their methods, the wealth gap between the rich and the poor remained near record levels. In November 2016, the Organisation for Economic Co-operation and Development (OECD) announced that, although the richest 10 percent had rapidly bounced back, long-term unemployment, low-quality jobs, and greater job insecurity had disproportionately hit low-income households. According to the OECD's study of thirty-five member countries, "By 2013/14, incomes at the bottom of the distribution were still well below pre-crisis levels while top and middle incomes had recovered much of the ground lost during the crisis."[6]

Since 2009, central bank leaders in developing nations, from Brazil to China, and in struggling developed nations, have warned the public about the false sense of security this cycle of government debt creation and central bank debt possession provides. On June 29, 2014, Jaime Caruana, governor of the Bank of Spain and head of the BIS, noted, "Ever rising public debt cannot shore up confidence. Nor can a prolonged extension of ultra-low interest rates. Low rates can certainly increase risk-taking, but it is not evident that this will turn into productive investment...if they persist too long, ultra-low rates could validate and entrench a highly undesirable type of equilibrium—one of high debt, low interest rates and anemic growth."[7]

The Bank for International Settlements was established in Basel, Switzerland, in 1931 during the Great Depression. This was a time when people had lost confidence in their banks and their ability to extract money when they needed to. The BIS was to sit above all the world's central banks and monitor global behavior to thwart crises and stimulate coordination. In practice, because all the elite central bankers were involved, it was a central bank club more than a monitor. Even the BIS, in strange irony, has become critical of zero interest rate policy as an economic cure-all. In its words, "Globally, interest rates have been extraordinarily low for an exceptionally long time. . . . Such low rates are the remarkable symptom of a broader malaise in the global economy." The conclusion of the BIS report minced no words. It pronounced an epic shift. "Global financial markets remain dependent on central banks."

Dependent is a strong word. Yet a more accurate way to depict the situation had emerged. The biggest central banks had *become* the market.

The only policy intentionally propping up the entire global financial system is that of cheap money. According to the BIS, "Since the global financial crisis, banks and bond investors have increased the outstanding US dollar credit to non-bank borrowers outside the United States from $6 trillion to $9 trillion."[8]

The Fed exacerbated a cheap-money addiction through its obtuse and often impromptu messaging, releasing disparate statements to tease or test markets. It behaved like an encroaching army: it colluded with allies but left no options on how to oppose its orders.

The symbiotic relationships among central banks, major governments, and private banks are nothing new. What *is* new is the extent to which the Fed's collusive monetary policies first elevated and then diminished the status of Western central bank leaders relative to Eastern ones. The overriding reach of the Fed had the unintended consequence of opening the United States to the loss of its political superpower status. If the Fed raised rates too high or too quickly, it would cause a global crash, the ultimate proof of the policy's ineffectiveness at fostering long-lasting economic stability.

Until the middle of 2015, the IMF had been mindful not to be too openly critical of the Fed. The time had finally come; when faced with the threat of the Fed raising rates and damaging already weakened emerging market currencies and potential debt payments, its managing director, Christine Lagarde, became emboldened to do so. She cautioned the United States and the world about the side effects of the Fed's cheap-money policy, pointing to the problems that could arise if the Fed raised rates too quickly or by too much.[9] Meanwhile, the IMF worked with the Chinese government and central bank to add the yuan to the "basket" of currencies backing the "IMF currency," or special drawing rights (SDR) basket. This was in allegiance to the rising power of China and diversification of the global monetary system away from the US dollar.

The G20, relatively dormant on the issue of monetary policy since its creation in 1999, rose to prominence in the year following the financial crisis. In 2016, the global forum for governments and central bank governors comprising the twenty major economies convened in China for the first time. The move boosted a major US rival and reaffirmed its rising spot as a prominent economic and diplomatic contender. It punctuated and portended the trend of growing tension among developed and developing states.

The countries I explore in *Collusion* represent the main pivot points of the world's post-crisis political-financial shift. Mexico was caught between its tight relationship with the United States and its growing desire for independence; Brazil, the largest Latin American economy, was deepening its associations with China but grappling with its United States–centric tendencies. China used the financial crisis to elevate its diplomatic and trade hegemony, globally. Japan was caught in the crosshairs of its old US alliance and fresh opportunities with Europe and its former foe, China. For Europe, certain elite leaders embraced United States–backed monetary policy, but the resulting internal political-economic turmoil would tear apart its structure. They represent case studies of the dual machinations of central bankers domestically and on the world stage.

MEXICO

In Mexico, the financial crisis and the Fed's reaction to it presented a domestic conundrum. The Central Bank of Mexico, or Banco de México, had to decide whether and when to play follow-the-leader with Fed policy. On the surface, the United States' southern neighbor had no choice because of trading relationships. The governors of Banco de México over that period, Guillermo Ortiz and then Agustín Carstens, were well situated globally because of their US relationships. However, they were also caught in the vortex of following the Fed or paying homage to their country's domestic economic needs.

Both men were critical of US monetary policy and the risk the US banking system imposed on the world. Carstens, the more politically leveraged of the two, was nominated along with France's Christine Lagarde for the second-most-powerful central bank post in the world, the head of the IMF. He lost. His US allies did not support him. The decision was one that could have altered the nature of the relationships between the United States and Latin America. Chapter 1 explores the growing rift between

Mexico's US allegiance and independence. The adversarial relationship of President Donald Trump with Mexico affects not just the economies of both countries but also their central bank coordination. Carstens resigned his post as central bank governor after Trump became president, opting for a more international platform as general manager of the BIS instead.

BRAZIL

In the wake of the financial crisis, Brazil burst onto the international stage with a determination that it had not exhibited before. The Latin American powerhouse led the charge to adopt an alternative to a financial and monetary system centered around the US dollar. The BRICS[10] alliance afforded Brazil sizable financial and political benefits, because China and India were destined to contribute more than 40 percent to global economic expansion through 2020 versus the US contribution of just 10 percent.[11]

The story of Brazil in Chapter 2 probes the impact of the Fed's policy on a country that once had relatively little impact on the international stage from a monetary policy perspective. In the global struggle for supremacy between the United States and China, Brazil emerged as a leading financial and trading battleground.

CHINA

To artificially stimulate its markets and banks, the People's Bank of China (PBOC) adopted a variety of money-conjuring techniques. The Chinese central bank emerged as a primary critic of the Fed, its superpower rival. Raw disdain for the Fed's policies catapulted China onto the global stage as a currency alternative and economic partner for emerging market nations. In October 2016, the yuan was accepted into the IMF's SDR basket of currencies, receiving the third-largest weight, behind the dollar and the euro. This represented a seismic shift from the IMF's former adherence to G7 currencies.

As the United States exuded an increasingly anti-China attitude publicly, China forged other trade and economic alliances. These were accelerated by China's reactions to the Trump administration. China's story in Chapter 3 highlights the evolution of the PBOC and renminbi against the backdrop of ongoing political jockeying between Beijing and Washington.[12] It illuminates the reimagining of the existing global monetary system behind this superpower battle.

JAPAN

When Haruhiko Kuroda, governor of the Bank of Japan, came to power, he executed the largest conjured-money play in the world. The BOJ's quantitative and qualitative easing (QQE), which began in 2013, augmented a negative interest rate policy with large-scale purchases of Japanese government bonds (JGBs).

The real story behind such actions, told in Chapter 4, is one of collusion between Japan's government and its central bank. As with Mexico and Brazil, balancing the domestic economic situation and US demands created tension. Japan chose to follow the United States from a monetary standpoint but quietly arranged monetary alliances with its neighbor and historical rival, China. In the process, the Bank of Japan amassed a larger ratio of assets to GDP in Japan than any other country in the world. In early 2016, Kuroda led the BOJ into negative interest rate policy (NIRP). From 2013 to 2017, the BOJ expanded its balance sheet from a figure equivalent to 35 percent of Japanese GDP to 94 percent. It bought 80 trillion yen (over $600 billion) of securities monthly to keep rates negative.

EUROPE

Finger pointing between central bankers and governments exploded during the financial crisis and its aftermath. The inherent economic stability that resulted ignited a battle between the ECB and the German Bundesbank, the area's strongest central bank before the euro existed. Wolfgang Schäuble, German finance minister, has been the main critic of the ECB. To curtail market "contagion" in the Eurozone, ECB head Mario Draghi repeatedly invoked quantitative easing with even more creativity and enthusiasm than the Fed.[13]

For her part, German chancellor Angela Merkel was politically cautious on Draghi's policy amid a period of uncertainty about her own political future. Political instability infused with conjured-money policy reshaped EU internal power dynamics. Real growth remained anemic. Youth unemployment reached all-time highs. Greece had to pay for more austerity-linked debt with money it didn't have. Voters removed or reduced support for old political leaderships. The refugee crisis placed extra political pressure on an already unstable union, pushing voters to the right and ignoring the instability caused by money-conjuring policies.

Central banks in Europe and the troika—the European Commission (EC), the ECB, and the IMF, and the officials who led them[14]—exacerbated the instability and growing inequality in Europe. This was a leading cause of the fractured environment that crucified Greece, promoted Brexit, and gave rise to greater potential cracks in the wall of the EU project. It was a sign of a voting pattern traversing Europe, emphasizing the north-west versus south-east divide, invoking nationalism, and weakening the European Union as a whole, as discussed in Chapters 5 and 6.

What began as a monetary policy commitment to copy the Fed and foster banking liquidity under the guise of promoting growth revealed the disconnect between the money conjurers and ordinary citizens. Citizens were not taking it quietly. They were aware that something was amiss and didn't know whom to blame besides establishment politicians because they did not realize the extent of the influence of establishment central bankers upon them.

We have arrived at a new—unstable—normal. There's no hard stop, no external force or organization to dial back the artificial lubrication of the banking system and financial markets. Yet, "QE infinity" isn't a solution to real economic growth. It is financial chicanery that can lead to worse problems, ranging from asset bubbles to the inability of pension and life insurance funds to source less risky long-term assets such as government bonds that pay enough interest to meet their liabilities. Low rates hamper savers from reaping adequate interest, which forces them into riskier investments just to grow their nest eggs. Higher rates, however, would constrain the artificially concocted liquidity in the system.

The issue isn't whether this money-conjuring game can continue. It is that central banks have no plan B in the event of another crisis. As collusion continues, the Fed continuously reaffirms itself as having succeeded in restoring the economy and stabilizing the banking system. Janet Yellen declared in June 2017 that the dangers of another crisis would hopefully not occur in "our lifetimes."[15]

A decade earlier, her predecessor, Ben Bernanke, got it wrong as well, having declared in May 2007, "We do not expect significant spillovers from the subprime market to the rest of the economy or to the financial system. The vast majority of mortgages, including even subprime mortgages, continue to perform well."[16]

Quantitative easing has resulted in the issuance of trillions of dollars of debt and historically high levels of debt-to-GDP. According to the McKinsey Global Institute, total global debt grew by $57 trillion, and no major economy decreased its debt-to-GDP ratio since 2007.[17]

By late 2017, the Fed, ECB, and BOJ held about $14 trillion of this debt on their books. The first decade of the "new normal" began and ended with the hubris of the Federal Reserve's leadership. It is underscored by global markets and banks that have become dependent on central bank liquidity, too-big-to-fail banks that are bigger than before, and epic debt. Central bankers are "talking up" economies to prove their own effectiveness. This projected illusion of strength is predicated on manufactured money and the masking of structural, systemic flaws. No significant changes have been made in core developed nations to foster real growth and foundational stability. And that means—a more vicious crisis is building.

1

MEXICO: There's No Wall Against US Financial Crises

We're in round one or two. This is a fifteen-round fight.

—Guillermo Ortiz, governor of the Central Bank
of Mexico, World Economic Forum in Davos,
Switzerland, January 23, 2008

In early 2008, Mexico boasted a large and thriving economy. After five years of steady growth, GDP had reached over $1.1 trillion by 2008 from $770.2 billion in 2002.[1]

As a gateway to Latin America, Mexico seemed destined to be a US subsidiary, not a partner. So it was doubly ironic when the United States "sneezed," as it were. The recklessness of the US banking system and insufficient oversight by its key regulator, the Federal Reserve, caused a US financial crisis that temporarily inflicted a "cold" on one of its top three trading partners.

Having suffered several crises over the previous decades, Mexico had attempted to strengthen its financial stability by crafting a diverse economy that boasted an ambitious population keen on expanding cultural, business, and technological prowess. Mexico was also well positioned with a bounty of natural resources. Both a burden and a curse, the country relied heavily on the United States economically. This would prove to be one of the principal challenges that its central bank, Banco de México, faced when trying to act independently of the Fed.

Balancing its domestic responsibilities with the demands of the Fed put a strain on Mexico's historic devotion to US policies. Both of Banco de México's successively serving governors, Guillermo Ortiz and Agustín Carstens, reacted in different ways to the push from the Fed and pull from their country.

Ortiz was a man of fortitude, though. He had navigated several Mexican economic crises, including as minister of finance during the 1994 peso crisis. At the time, the *New York Times* called Ortiz "a bulldog administrator—short on style but tough enough to take on anyone who crosses him."[2] Prior to that, he was chief negotiator for Mexico during NAFTA (North American Free Trade Agreement) discussions and an executive director at the IMF from 1984 to 1988.[3]

15

Ortiz served two consecutive six-year terms at the helm of Banco de México, from January 1998 to December 2009. His father was a soldier during the Mexican Revolution. The military family background affirmed Ortiz's stalwart personality.[4] He led the central bank with a steady hand. He played by the rules of procedure, mixed with lessons of past experiences. That understanding cemented his decisions while giving rise to political tensions when the central bank's monetary policy clashed with the government's fiscal one.

His successor, Carstens, had a slightly more global establishment background and disposition. He was well versed in the ways of the International Monetary Fund and maintained personal friendships with its leadership. Carstens was more Americanized than Ortiz and was an avid Chicago Cubs fan from his graduate years at the Milton Friedman school of economics, otherwise known as the University of Chicago.

The Fed's emergency money-conjuring policies stoked domestic power squabbles between the central bank and the government. Growth in Mexico's international reserves had enabled the central bank to withstand adverse moves in capital markets like the US financial crisis. But the aspirations of the two men varied. Ortiz was a product of the Mexican establishment; he understood its power dynamics and how to navigate its political channels. For his part, Carstens (a confident, corpulent, well-connected multinationalist) believed the central bank was more tied up with the United States than either would have liked.

HOW IT ALL BEGAN

On a frosty day in late January 2008, Banco de México[5] governor Guillermo Ortiz traveled to Davos, Switzerland, to address the World Economic Forum, a gathering of political-financial glitterati that included prominent politicians, central bankers, and private bankers. The topic was "The Power of Collaborative Innovation."[6] It was an optimistic banner given that financial innovation was about to breed financial crisis. Elite-speak often touts widespread collaboration, but the main power alliances call the shots. This exclusive gathering instigated the divide between emerging market countries and the United States.

The United States wasn't in full crisis mode yet. Even though it remained in denial, other nations could not ignore the subprime market and toxic assets built upon this shaky foundation that was about to self-destruct. If they knew, there was no other option but to watch and develop a defensive strategy for the future. This meeting in the Swiss Alps stoked nothing short of an embryonic mutiny against the world's major power.

Brazil was the nation chairing the G20 that year. At the Davos proceedings, Henrique Meirelles, head of Brazil's central bank, presciently announced that leaders should focus on restoring financial stability in the wake of the US subprime crisis.[7] Other officials concerned about the US banking system included European Central Bank president Jean-Claude Trichet and Malcolm Knight, chief executive officer at the Bank for International Settlements, the central bank of central banks. Though the looming crisis had not grabbed the public spotlight yet, impending system failure in the United States was already evident to these elites and any journalist paying attention.[8]

Nevertheless, everyone paid homage to the US financial system on the surface, even though beneath its veneer of success lay a cesspool of lurking financial dangers. But at one of the panels, Ortiz appeared to have other ideas. He was complimentary in characterizing the United States as "an innovator" in the financial markets. However, he took the opportunity to warn that such innovation was dangerous as well because "almost as a matter of definition, the market outpaces regulation."

His panel was hosted by US media personality Maria Bartiromo.[9] When asked to comment on credit freezes spanning the global markets, Ortiz quipped, "Well, I can say: 'This time, it wasn't us.'"[10] Indeed, it was the US Fed failing to do its job properly.

In Mexico, concerns of an impending crisis were mounting. The United States could afford to act nonchalant. Mexico could not. Ortiz claimed that regulators "didn't understand" the complexity of various financial instruments.[11] He was right. But like other Latin American counterparts who voiced concerns or left rates high when the Fed didn't, his stance would dampen his career trajectory and was largely disregarded by the major money conjurers. Yet, by breaking away from some of his larger fellow moneymakers, Ortiz sealed not just his professional fate but also in many ways that of Mexico's economy.

Conditions in Mexico had already stumbled as a result of the economic recession that brewed in the United States since late 2007. In January 2008, the Hacienda y Crédito Público, Mexico's Treasury Department, lowered its 2008 forecast to 2.8 percent from 3.7 percent growth in GDP. "That the U.S. downturn will affect us—there can be no doubt," Mauricio Gonzalez, president of Mexico-based analysis firm Grupo Economistas Asociados, told USA Today.[12]

Despite warnings of overheating financial innovation, there was a long-standing partnership between the Mexican central bank and the US Federal Reserve System. Shortly after the leadership gathering at Davos, the Mexican central bank head ascended to a high level of elite status: in February 2008, Ortiz was appointed to the advisory board for the Globalization and Monetary Policy Institute at the Federal Reserve Bank of Dallas, a group studying the impact of globalization on US monetary policy. The Dallas Fed had a tradition of such exchanges with Mexico's central bank leaders, by virtue of the geography and because Mexican bankers were often connected to US elites. Their alliances ran through academic institutions, American boards of directors, and government relationships.

Ortiz's appointment was a culmination of decades of collaboration with his US counterparts. "I have known Guillermo Ortiz for over 30 years," said John B. Taylor, advisory board chairman and Mary and Robert Raymond Professor of Economics at Stanford University. "He brings unparalleled skills, experience and knowledge about central banking and its global dimensions."[13] Legacy connections proved critical in driving coordinated monetary policy.

Ortiz's personal ties with the United States were extensive. He had received his PhD at Stanford University. In 1999, he became a member of the Group of Thirty, an elite economic and monetary affairs consultancy group comprising the public and private sectors and academia and based in Washington, DC.

Ortiz sensed the magnitude of shocks to befall the US banking system before US president George W. Bush, Treasury secretary Hank Paulson, or Fed chairman Ben Bernanke did. Bernanke, a so-called expert on Depression-era economics and crashes in America, was readying a massive monetary intervention to eclipse that of the Great Depression of the 1930s. It would signal the birth of major collusive and conjured-money policy across oceans and borders.

On February 4, 2008, the White House submitted its budget to Congress. Bush proposed a $150 billion stimulus package and the highest military budget since World War II.[14] He told Mexico's president Felipe Calderón that his spending plans would also help Mexico's economy.[15] The United States needed Mexico to stay strong as its own center crumbled. In the age of globalization, stability mattered. What transpired on one side of the border was just as important as that on the other.

Calderón took his cue from President Bush. On March 3, 2008, he announced a Mex$60 billion (US$5.6 billion[16]) stimulus package of tax breaks, utility rate discounts, and other spending programs to help Mexico weather the US slowdown.[17] He assured businesspeople at the National Palace in Mexico City that his plan would "help make medium-term growth more dynamic." His words soothed the impresarios seated in the historic locale, where Mexico's leaders had assembled since the days of the Aztecs.

As events unfolded, so did financial chaos. It turned out that Bush was preparing for a monsoon with a $5 umbrella. Two weeks later, Bear Stearns, a New York–based investment bank in operation for eighty-five years, collapsed. The bank had leveraged too many complex securities stuffed with subprime mortgages. One CEO in particular who would benefit from Bear's downfall was Jamie Dimon, a Class A board director at the NY Federal Reserve board.

On March 16, 2008, JPMorgan Chase got a $30 billion bailout from the Fed in the form of a guarantee to purchase Bear Stearns (my former firm). That figure was five times the Mexican stimulus amount. It was a sign of worse to follow. In a March 18, 2008, press release, the Fed noted, "Financial markets remain under considerable stress, and the tightening of credit conditions and the deepening of the housing contraction are likely to weigh on economic growth over the next few quarters."[18] That understatement opened the door for emergency monetary policies and greenlighted the blueprint for central bank collusion later on. The financial crisis was brewing, big Wall Street banks were frantically selling their worst assets to the least sophisticated investors. The Fed was slowly reducing rates in anticipation of a liquidity squeeze. The world noticed.

About a month later, on April 22, 2008, the three NAFTA leaders, US president George W. Bush, Canadian prime minister Stephen Harper, and Mexican president Calderón, gathered in New Orleans to discuss the impact on Mexico of the impending financial crisis. As President George W. Bush's numbers plummeted to the lowest of his administration, he told his counterparts, "Now is not the time to renegotiate NAFTA." Bush emphasized, "Now is the time to strengthen free trade."[19] He believed the three were stronger together and that, with the banking system buckling, strength was definitely in order.

Harper, seeing the light at the end of the tunnel with the Bush administration, said Canada would consider a renegotiation of NAFTA—but with the next US president. He took the opportunity to say that his government would not want to restrict NAFTA's major trade cornerstones. For Canada, that meant oil—it was the largest single supplier of oil to the American economy.

Calderón concurred: "This is the time to strengthen and reinvigorate this free trade agreement among our three countries.... We talked a lot about the NAFTA, and of course we agreed that this is not the time to even think about amending it or canceling it."[20]

During the press conference, a reporter asked Bush how deep and how long the US economic recession would be and how it would affect Mexico.[21] His response was, "I—we're not in a recession, we're in a slowdown.... I'm probably the most concerned about the slowdown.... That's why we passed...a significant pro-growth economic package."

Calderón had also passed a growth package in Mexico. As Bush said, "The President is plenty capable of handling reform.... And he'll do what he thinks is right for the country of Mexico."[22] The United States didn't interfere much with Mexico, as long as it stayed in line with what the United States wanted it to do. In the eyes of American policymakers, if Mexico was to succeed, it would be because of the US government. However, if it was to fail, it would be because it remained obstinate to US guidance.

LEADING TO CRISIS, FIGHTING INFLATION

By mid-2008, Mexico, Latin America's second-largest economy after Brazil, faced a problem of its own: inflation.[23] Usually, rising prices solicited one monetary policy remedy, that of raising rates. Making it more expensive to buy things in turn reduces demand and decreases prices.

That's exactly what Ortiz proposed. Banco de México increased its benchmark overnight interest rate on June 21, 2008, from 7.5 percent to 7.75 percent.[24] As a rate move, it was an insignificant increment. Its deeper meaning was more substantial, however: it was the first such move by Banco de México governor Ortiz since October 2007.[25] Concerned about runaway prices caused by a world food supply crisis, Ortiz raised the bank's key interest rate mere days *after* President Calderón publicly pressured him to *cut* borrowing costs to boost growth, per Fed policy.[26]

Ortiz further raised rates to 8.25 percent by August 15, 2008.[27] The move helped the peso strengthen to a near six-year high versus the US dollar.[28] It demonstrated a degree of independence from Mexico's central bank leaders in contrast to the Federal Reserve's headquarters at the Eccles Building in Washington. Mexico was deviating its monetary policy from the Fed's. The US central bank had cut its federal funds rate to 2 percent from 5.25 percent the prior September.[29]

The decision would return to haunt Ortiz. The act of raising rates, even a little, flew in the face of the Fed's new protocol of flooding the financial system with cheap money in the guise of "stabilizing" its shaky economy and looming credit crisis. The key rules in this artisans of money game were the unwritten ones—international collusion on monetary policy, especially by a "friendly" neighbor, was to exhibit a united front. Dissention in the ranks had consequences.

It was natural for Ortiz to weigh international etiquette against national need and pick the latter. Yet his rate-hike decision lay in contrast to the wishes of President Calderón,[30] who did *not* want to raise rates but rather wanted to follow US policy. Three days earlier, Calderón had chosen a different path to provide relief, freezing food prices on 150 staple food items.[31]

The rate hike pitted former friends—Calderón and Ortiz—against each other. Ortiz wanted to keep Mexico's central bank independent of politicians and was dead set on anti-inflation measures in an autonomous manner. Calderón wanted to follow the Fed's lead.

CREDIT SQUEEZES AND US BAILOUTS HIT MEXICO

By August 2008, Mexico faced a double whammy: a credit crunch at the hands of US banks operating there, and increasing volatility in the foreign exchange market. Ortiz took decisive action. Banco de México altered its auction mechanism—in place since May 2003—to prevent worried banks from stockpiling reserves with the central bank and instead encouraging them to loosen up and allow for domestic capital flow.[32] If the Mexican peso depreciated by more than 2 percent on any day, various mechanisms unleashed the auctioning of reserves to prevent a "free fall." A strong peso signified foreign investor confidence. (It also meant exports would be more expensive, which would mean less money to Mexico from US tourism or business flows.) The preemptive move occurred a week before financial Armageddon.

On September 14, 2008, US Treasury secretary Hank Paulson, Fed chair Ben Bernanke, and NY Fed president Timothy Geithner pressed Bank of America to purchase Merrill Lynch (run by Paulson's Goldman Sachs protégé John Thain) for $50 billion.[33] On September 15, Lehman Brothers declared bankruptcy for reasons similar to Bear Stearns's. On September 16, insurance giant and Wall Street guarantor AIG received an $85 billion federal bailout. The government·gift indirectly saved the group of big Wall Street banks with tight political connections, including Goldman Sachs and JPMorgan Chase.

The Fed's unprecedented intervention in the private sector coupled with the demise of Lehman Brothers caused a death in liquidity that ran southward like a mudslide. The contagion barely even blinked for the $700 billion bank bailout package passed by the US Congress on October 3. Ultimately, the Fed would cut rates to zero on December 16, 2008. The era of limitless cheap money had arrived.

Stakes and tempers rose. At the National Association for Business Economics 50th Annual Meeting on October 7, 2008, Bernanke tried desperately to diffuse the damage the United States was causing, but for which it was taking no responsibility, by offering the world US dollars. "To address dollar funding pressures worldwide," he said, "we have significantly expanded reciprocal currency arrangements (so-called swap agreements) with foreign central banks...which helps to improve the functioning of dollar funding markets globally."[34] The swaps were with South Korea, Singapore, and Mexico. Bernanke proliferating dollars throughout the world demonstrated his overall confidence in the dollar. Beyond the need to keep up with dollar demand as the major world reserve currency was a play for survival. If his central banking colleagues around the globe believed in the dollar, they would believe in the crafting of money. Mexico, connected as ever to that scheme, had to believe—its economy depended on it.

By that time, Mexico had spent a tenth of its foreign exchange reserves defending the peso. The cost of credit was soaring for local Mexican companies.[35] Several large firms began selling pesos to cover their hedges on the exchange rate, making matters worse. Mexico hadn't experienced such currency depreciation since the "tequila crisis" in the early 1990s,[36] when the rapid devaluation of the peso to US dollar caused massive capital flight from Mexico by foreign investors seeking a shield from volatility in the country. According to the *Economist*, "The peso's slide was exacerbated by the unwinding of derivatives contracts that had been profitable while the currency was steady."[37]

The siesta was over quickly. Mexico was no longer independent from the crisis and its currency was unraveling fast. In August 2008, the peso stood at 10 per dollar—its strongest level since 2002. By October 2008, it had bled 30 percent of its value, plunging to a level of 13.2 per dollar.[38] That was just the beginning.

FOUR FATEFUL DAYS

The rest of Latin America fared no better. On October 8, 2008, stocks in Colombia crumbled 5.9 percent; Argentina's major index shed 4.3 percent. Stocks in Brazil shed 3.1 percent.[39]

Mexico's Foreign Exchange Commission[40] accelerated its intervention. This was noteworthy. Since its establishment in 1994, when the Foreign Exchange Commission allowed the central bank to begin floating the peso, the commission had executed only minor interventions.[41] By late October, the peso was down 18 percent against the dollar from the start of the year.[42] The US subprime crisis had become Mexico's currency crisis.

The Fed was in its own crisis mode. It cut rates half a point and cited "intensification" of the crisis as its reasoning. It would not operate alone in response to the US banking catastrophe. The Fed knew it would take an international full-court press. So Bernanke urged five other central banks to cut rates, too.

The Bank of England cut its rate by a half point. So did the Canadian, Swiss, and Swedish central banks. The Bank of Japan expressed support but because its rates were already so low took no further action. It was the Fed's eighth cut since September 2007.[43] When Alan Greenspan ran the Fed, he was dubbed the maestro.[44] Bernanke, on the other hand, was the consummate magician. He provided the illusion of competence in his orchestration of global monetary policy collusion—so long as no one looked behind the curtain.

The joint cuts by that group of central banks were exceptional and rare, and these orchestrated efforts foreshadowed global collusion beyond prevailing imagination.

Ortiz had to act fast. In Mexico City, he and the secretary of finance and public credit, Agustín Carstens, called a press conference at the presidential palace to calm national nerves.[45] Ortiz opened the event. Carstens sat pensively to his right.[46]

Ortiz announced Banco de México would sell US dollars into the market through two types of "extraordinary" auctions. These indirectly helped the Fed in its liquidity drive. US dollars would be sold directly into the market to meet demand for this "safe-haven" currency. If all went right, selling dollars would prevent further deterioration of the peso. The first type of auction totaled $11 billion between October 10 and October 23.[47] The second was to reduce exchange rate volatility.[48] In all, Mexico sold $15.18 billion worth of US dollars in late 2008 alone. Mexico would not only act in the spirit of confidence with the United States but also sell its currency.

Mexico was leaking money on diminished trade and capital outflows. Poverty began rising significantly after 2007 as food prices jumped.[49] The underemployment rate rose by 3.5 percentage points between the second quarter of 2008 and second quarter of 2009, from 6.5 percent to 10 percent.[50] From September to October of 2008, Mexican stocks shed 21 percent.[51]

In the world of high finance, what cures the markets does not always offer relief to real people. However, Ortiz's actions did soothe Mexican markets. He calmed international investors to retain foreign capital. (In 2010, the BIS would call Ortiz's moves "stabilizing" for tempering the foreign exchange market during late 2008.)[52] Then Ortiz flew to Washington, DC. He was hell-bent on saving the system, despite the perception that Mexico and other Latin American countries were shielded from the worst of the US crisis or that they were not integral players when it came to solving problems.

On the morning of October 9, 2008, Ortiz and Bernanke conducted a thirty-minute closed-door meeting at the Eccles Building, which housed the Fed's chambers.[53] The *Wall Street Journal* reported, "Mr. Ortiz declined to discuss details of the discussions, but the fact that officials in Washington are talking to foreign officials such as Mr. Ortiz suggests they are open to learning from other countries' experiences—even as the current crisis roiled those very nations."[54]

That these two individuals were meeting was in itself significant. Either Ortiz was consulting with Bernanke, or the other way around, but it was a departure from the norm. Ortiz had more experience with crisis than the Fed chairman, though Bernanke, a self-titled "student of the Great Depression," would never give him credit for his opinions. Bernanke mentioned Ortiz and the Bank of Mexico just once, in a sentence fragment unrelated to the crisis, in his memoirs of the crisis period, *The Courage to Act*[55] (he did not mention Ortiz's successor, Agustín Carstens, at all). During the crisis, Ortiz was an important, underrated figure critical to the United States. Had Ortiz completely failed in Mexico, the situation north of the border could have been catastrophic. Bernanke needed to secure his friends, as any military commander would.

While Ortiz was in Washington, a normally optimistic Calderón, who had run for office on an "employment" pledge, gave a somber nationally televised speech to announce his $4.3 billion spending plan. His plan, he assured, was "not a financial rescue." (His statements reflected those of Brazil's President Lula and its central bank head, Henrique Meirelles.) He promised to focus on "strengthening the motors of our economy," on emergency infrastructure plans (roads, schools, houses), oil, and small businesses.[56] He emphasized sustaining Mexico's "main street" economy.

In paternalistic tones, Calderón underscored the central bank's strength. "Unlike in the past, when a lack of dollars led us into terrible crises," he said, "today we have foreign reserves of more than $90 billion and we practically have our external debt paid through the next year and a half."[57] Regardless of those reserves, the peso was feeling the heat.

On October 10, 2008, the Bretton Woods Committee's International Council hosted its annual Luncheon for World Financial Leaders at the prestigious Willard hotel in Washington. Keynote speaker former US Treasury secretary Larry Summers gave a talk titled "Renewing the Bretton Woods Compact." He outlined the elements he felt were important to a successful financial rescue package.[58]

The United States amplified its control over the existing system during the crisis US banks caused. This arrogance would rip that system apart. Other countries, such as China, uninvolved in the crafting of Bretton Woods hierarchy, saw opportunity in a new financial order.

For his part, Ortiz observed a glaring absence of political leadership. He cautioned that central banks should be proactive, but not overstep their role. "Central banks have been thrown into a role they should not be playing. They are not political actors—and do not have the legitimacy to act in this capacity."[59] Little did he know.

Central bank leaders clashed over what to do about the escalating global crisis, alternating between blaming each other and seeking solutions. The Dow posted its worst week ever, falling more than 1,874 points, or 18 percent.[60]

Early Saturday morning, October 11, President Bush, in the Rose Garden flanked by Treasury secretary Henry Paulson, announced, "We're in this together." He said the G7 nations had agreed to a plan of action that would help "systemically important financial institutions and prevent their failure."[61]

The next day, while the Fed was approving the mega-acquisition of Wachovia by Wells Fargo, Ortiz and Dallas Federal Reserve Bank president Richard Fisher sat among a group of central bank heads at the Institute of International Finance (IIF) conference in Washington. They discussed the crisis and its consequences for the global economy.[62] Confidence in the international monetary system was fading fast.

Ortiz stressed, "It's better to err on the side of doing too much rather than doing too little."[63] He admonished the US government and his US counterparts for their handling of the US banking system. It was imperative to stop its bloodletting because the wounded animal to the north had the propensity to starve the south to save itself. "Do whatever it takes to restore confidence," he warned from experience. "Once you lose it, it's very difficult to get it back."[64] Meetings with Bernanke and the Fed likely had not been as conducive as Ortiz would have liked, hence the harsh tone. He couldn't cross the top dog at the water bowl, but he could bark loud enough to get attention.

While Calderón deployed government stimulus, Ortiz returned to Mexico to craft market intervention techniques to both replicate and defend against those of the Fed. The Fed, meanwhile, opened copious lines of credit to demonstrate its commitment to "large well-managed emerging markets" that were bearing the brunt of financial collapse.[65]

By that time, it was clear to the world's top central bankers and finance ministers that the US Fed had placed them in a precarious position. No one was happy about it. The painful irony was that they had to take direction from the Fed in order to exit the crisis that the Fed's enabling of Wall Street speculation had caused. Mexico, too, was forced to take part of the financial crisis on the chin.

On October 19, 2008, at a Bank of Mexico conference, Ortiz spoke beside the IMF first deputy managing director and former vice chairman of JPMorgan Investment Bank, John Lipsky, a man sporting a sizable mustache to accent his elite résumé. Regarding implications for emerging markets (EMs), Lipsky said, "Structural improvements—and the improvement in the management of fiscal and monetary policies—bolstered the resilience of most large emerging market economies to external shocks, allowing them more perspective on their response to the crisis."[66]

But Ortiz knew the system was stacked against emerging markets. That was the way the IMF functioned. It wasn't personal, it was business. The idea was to use crisis to press structural reforms, which meant more open markets to exactly this sort of chaos was no antidote. His country had experienced this countless times. Latin America was ground zero for the IMF's financial experimentation.

Bernanke was in over his head. Fortunately for him, he ran the most powerful central bank in the world. So, he diverted attention to problems of other nations. Mexico's anemic condition rose to prominence on his agenda because it was the most connected to the United States. On October 20, 2008, Bernanke stressed the need for global coordination with his allies. For the conjurer, the appearance of synchronized efforts was as powerful in fostering confidence as results.

Bernanke touted coordination as if the world was a willing partner rather than hostile participant. Speaking before Congress, he said, "The United States consulted with other countries, many of whom have announced similar actions. Given the global nature of the financial system, international consultation and cooperation on actions to address the crisis are important for restoring confidence and stability."[67] Though the latter was true, it was the US (and European) banking system that lay in disarray. The king money magician was deflecting culpability for Wall Street's recklessness by blaming the world for reacting to crisis with crisis.

GIVE A BANK A DOLLAR, THEY'RE GONNA WANT TRILLIONS MORE

The United States and Mexico were both very concerned over one another before and after that October period. The Fed began to take notice. On October 28, 2008, at a Federal Open Market Committee meeting, Nathan Sheets, director of the board's Division of International Finance, addressed the issue of ongoing market operations and the swap proposals the Fed was conducting, noting, "Our interdependencies with Mexico are particularly pronounced."[68]

The question was whether there would be a broader effect on US banks if their global outposts suffered in a sort of secondary shock basis. In that case, it might come down to preserving the big US banks with Mexican subsidiaries. As Sheets added, "If the Bank of Mexico or the Mexican authorities move to address tensions in their financial system, the standard that has been set by several Federal Reserve actions...my feeling is that Banamex, owned by Citi[group], would have the same access to these kinds of facilities as other Mexican institutions."[69]

In his dual capacity as vice chair of the FOMC, Tim Geithner concurred. It wasn't Geithner's first Mexican rodeo either. He had served in the Clinton administration during the 1993 NAFTA negotiations, which opened a new age for trade in North America. And during the first peso crisis, when the Mexican peso was hit by speculation from international bankers, he was deputy assistant Treasury secretary for international monetary and financial policy (in January 1999 under Treasury secretary later turned Citigroup executive Robert Rubin).[70]

Geithner corrected Sheets. The United States *might* back US bank subsidiaries in Mexico "if a weak US institution in Mexico faces substantial needs in Mexico."[71] In other words, the United States would call the shots on Mexico's banking system as it pertained to US mega-banks. It could provide stimulus to US banks with international subsidiaries.[72]

In the world of conjured money, US banks in foreign lands, like military outposts, could count on Fed support. Citigroup had massive exposure to Mexico—$35.0 billion by December 31, 2008.[73]

To further supplement its falling foreign reserves, Banco de México agreed to a $30 billion foreign currency swap line with the Fed on October 29, 2008. Just as artisans are vocationally skilled in designing hand crafts, these central bankers crafted facilities to dispense money on the fly. It was the first time the Fed lent money to emerging market countries to prevent a global dollar shortage.[74]

The Fed established more swap "facilities" to support US dollar liquidity in amounts of up to $30 billion each with the Banco Central do Brasil, Banco de México, the Bank of Korea, and the Monetary Authority of Singapore.[75] The purpose was to mitigate difficulties in obtaining US dollars in countries with solid economic fundamentals.[76]

The IMF, rising in prominence as a result of the crisis, established a Short-Term Liquidity Facility to help member states, mostly those from emerging countries.[77] Even the most elitist of the elite hit panic mode. "Exceptional times call for an exceptional response," IMF head Dominique Strauss-Kahn proclaimed on October 29, 2008.[78]

Meanwhile, in San Salvador, El Salvador, Latin American leaders joined leaders of Spain and Portugal for the Ibero-American summit. United Nations secretary-general Ban Ki-moon issued an ominous video greeting: "A global financial crisis endangers our work. Prices for food and fuel have escalated, and trade talks are stalled."[79] While the United States focused on its banks, the rest of the world focused on keeping people from starving.

Faces around the room were ashen. When he rose to speak, Calderón said, "Our first goal is to avoid an increase in extreme poverty." He added, "The drop in employment and the rise in fuel prices could push new millions into poverty in just a year." Inflation in Mexico had nearly doubled to 5.80 percent since 2007.[80] Loan defaults and the amount of past-due loans were mounting quickly.

To help facilitate liquidity in its own country, Banco de México executed a Fed QE move. The central bank announced a program to repurchase up to Mex$150 billion (or US$18 billion) of debt securities issued by the IPAB (Instituto para la Protección del Ahorro Bancario, the Bank Savings Protection Institute).[81] It implemented a Mex$50 billion auction of interest rate swaps for investors to switch long-term for short-term debt. This was their version of quantitative easing, similar to actions taken during the 1994 peso crisis.[82] Banco de México described them as "measures designed to foster a more orderly functioning of financial markets."[83] Still, Ortiz proceeded with care.

HISTORY REPEATS ITSELF

The pandemonium in 2008 wasn't the first time US banks and monetary policies hampered Mexico's economic stability. By the early 1990s, big US banks like Bank-America, Chase Manhattan, Chemical Bank, Citicorp, Goldman Sachs, and JP Morgan accounted for 74 percent of US–Latin American exposure, or $40.4 billion.[84] If the credit worthiness of the region fell, so would the profitability of these giant banks.

Into that debt haze, the Clinton administration signed NAFTA on December 8, 1993. The first victors were banks. The *Los Angeles Times* concluded, "Banking will be among the first industries opened to foreign competition under NAFTA." Prior to NAFTA, foreign banks had been barred from operating subsidiaries in Mexico for fifty-five years.[85]

By January 30, 1995, Mexico's central bank reserves had shrunk to $2 billion from $24.4 billion the prior year. At the request of former Goldman Sachs co-CEO turned secretary of the Treasury Robert Rubin, President Bill Clinton invoked his emergency powers. He extended a $20 billion loan to Mexico from the Treasury Department's Exchange Stabilization Fund so that it could repay its debts to US banks. US banks were *saved*.

Citicorp posted an historic $3.5 billion profit for 1995. As a result of the US bailout, Mexico ultimately underwent a $135 billion bailout of its own banks in the late 1990s. Many local Mexican banks were sold to foreign banks. According to the US State Department, at the time, "The implementation of NAFTA opened the Mexican financial services market to US and Canadian firms. Foreign institutions hold more than 70 percent of banking assets and banking institutions from the US and Canada have a strong market presence."[86]

The share in total assets of foreign-controlled banks rose from 24 percent in 1998 to nearly 50 percent by the end of 2000 and to over 70 percent after the purchase of Banamex by Citigroup in 2001.[87] In February 2010, Mexican president Ernesto Zedillo joined Citigroup's board of directors.[88]

By 2015, five foreign banks, led by Citigroup/Banamex, owned 64 percent of Mexican financial assets, more external bank ownership than in any other country. The top five banks held 72 percent of the country's total financial assets. Only one—Banorte—was local.[89] Foreign banks in Mexico, armed with cheap money, could afford to be less accountable for speculative activities. Citigroup was also an important bank for Mexican elites.

THE PRE-THANKSGIVING SUMMITS OF STATUS QUO BATTLES

The G20 subgroup of developing and emerging central bank governors assembled in São Paulo, Brazil, on November 8–9, 2008, to address their fears. It was a week before the full G20 event in Washington. They released a routine joint statement. However, packed in the final communiqué was a bold message, the kernel of an alternative monetary system solution. The group still wanted to reform rather than banish the old system, but this was a start:

> The Bretton Woods Institutions must be comprehensively reformed so that they can more adequately reflect changing economic weights in the world economy and be more responsive to future challenges. Emerging and developing economies should have greater voice and representation in these institutions.[90]

The declaration sparked power struggles. For Mexico, it opened the door for competition between France's Christine Lagarde and Mexico's Agustín Carstens over the second-most important global monetary policy slot, head of the IMF. Emerging countries found glaring fault in the divide between old institutions and their domestic and global interests.

The IMF had never been led by a non-European member, just as the World Bank had never appointed a non-American president. These were Western demo-cratic institutions, yet they were supposed to work primarily with the developing world. The opportunity to allow a leader from outside Washington or Wall Street signified hope and change in the power structure of Western and developed nations relative to emerging market ones.

The G20 emerging nations subgroup had no sympathy for the advanced nations that had inflicted crisis and economic hardship upon them. The final communiqué from that Meeting of Ministers and Governors in São Paulo in November worried, "Advanced economies, where the crisis came into being, are slowing markedly and some are already close to or in recession." The group expressed support for a stron-ger IMF watching over developed economies, stressing, "We believe that the IMF must enhance its early warning capabilities with due regard to systemically impor-tant economies, in order to anticipate stresses and identify at an early stage vulner-abilities, systemic weaknesses and spillover risks across financial markets that can endanger both the international financial system and the global economy."[91]

Mexico was ground zero for this clash because of its proximity to the world's most developed economy. The developing countries saw opportunity in establish-ing a unified voice to consider alternatives to the Bretton Woods system. If they were not to be given a real seat at the table, they would eventually build another one altogether.

Though he did not attend that São Paulo meeting, the year marked Ortiz's tenth anniversary as a G20 governor. He had attended his first G20 meeting in 1999.[92] Ortiz knew the financial landscape well, understanding Mexico's place in it and the balance of collusion and independence.

A week later, the main G20 Summit on Financial Markets and the World Economy opened in Washington, DC. The atmosphere was tense, hostile even. The broader DC assembly neglected to address the purposefully agitated language of the São Paolo statement as well as its focus on advanced economies' sabotage of develop-ing ones.[93]

In DC, Calderón, not Ortiz, spoke on behalf of Mexico, in more tempered tones than Ortiz would have. "The international financial institutions must adopt a much more active role," he stressed, "supporting emerging and less developed countries so that the impact on economic activity and poverty is minimized."[94]

Ortiz was across the Atlantic, in Europe, attending the Fifth ECB Central Banking Conference in Frankfurt, Germany. The two-day conference focused on the topic "The Euro at Ten: Lessons and Challenges." He joined Bernanke and ECB head Jean-Claude Trichet on a panel to discuss international interdependency and monetary policy during the recent crisis.[95]

Ortiz remarked that "emerging markets must be cautious and they cannot engage in a persistent fiscal expansion."[96] It was—and remains—typical US dogma to press developing countries for open financial borders regardless of risk. It meant less control over their own economic destiny and more reliance on the whims of the major central banks during financial crises and exaggerated monetary interventions. The more the Banco de México attempted to separate from the Fed, the more it was drawn in. That seemed to be the case with many global central banks—but Mexico had the additional burden of geography.

A December 2008 *New York Times* article titled "When the US Sneezes, Mexico Catches Cold" noted, "But this recession, it is the profligate United States pulling down fiscally disciplined Mexico."[97] It was a distinct shift from prior crises.

Still, Banco de México's 2008 year-end report waxed pessimistic. "Deterioration and uncertainty about both financial markets and the outlook for the US and the rest of the world economies negatively affected the Mexican economy and its financial markets…risks of a downward adjustment in economic growth for 2009 have increased considerably."[98] The Mexican Stock Market Index had shed 23.6 percent of its value over 2008.[99]

To quell the hemorrhaging, Ortiz called for more auctions through December 2008. He later published a paper with the Brookings Institution (in July 2016) explaining that these were established "to provide liquidity to the foreign exchange market and restore its proper functioning, an absence of which threatened to preclude corporations from meeting their US dollar obligations."[100]

The world was bailing out the United States. The US government and the Fed were bailing out Wall Street.

Despite slumping markets, Mexico's GDP for 2008 achieved a 1.4 percent growth rate.[101] The figure represented a third of Mexico's January 2008 forecast of 3.25–3.75 percent. It was worse up north. During the final quarter of 2008, the US economy posted its largest contraction in twenty-six years. US GDP fell 3.8 percent, adjusted for inflation.[102] That was alarming for Mexico, with 80 percent of its exports sold to the United States.[103] Mexico feared financial shocks from the market, but the ripple effects could be catastrophic if not contained.

GLOBAL CRISIS BENEFICIARY: THE DOLLAR

As a sign of the insanity of money-conjuring policy, the US dollar rose relative to the peso in late 2008—even though the Fed was cutting rates to zero, and Mexico's rates had risen to 8.25 percent by the end of 2008.[104] In a normal world, higher interest rates translate to stronger exchanges rates. External capital is always seeking the highest returns for the least amount of risk. High interest rates provide high returns and therefore attract more capital, which strengthens a country's economy and therefore its currency. However, this wasn't a normal world. It was a panicked one, and in panic, the safe-haven currency reigns supreme, even if it's the one causing the panic.

Bank analysts offered their perspectives on this phenomenon. The dollar's rebound "is a sign of real panic and risk aversion," Kathleen Stephansen, head of global economic research for Credit Suisse in New York, told the *New York Times* on October 22.[105] Rising US dollar strength, or "panic behavior," as Alberto Bernal, head of emerging markets research at Bulltick Capital Markets, called it, "has nothing to do with Mexico and everything to do with the US."[106]

Yet it was Mexico that suffered. By the end of 2008, 37,500 jobs in the formal sector of Mexico's economy were lost.[107] In the informal sector, a job pool equal to nearly half of the formal sector, numbers were far higher.[108]

NEW US PRESIDENT, SAME FED POLICIES

With the financial crisis in full throttle, Barack Obama was inaugurated as the forty-fourth US president on January 20, 2009. Six days later, Tim Geithner was sworn in as his Treasury secretary, sliding over from his New York Fed president slot, where he supported bailouts and neglected proper Wall Street bank regulation.[109] Under his watch, national debt would jump from $10.6 trillion to $16.5 trillion. At least a third of that rise went straight to the Fed in the form of bank reserves, more money than would ever reach those suffering on Main Street.

The change of US presidents and political parties did not provoke a similar change in the Fed chair spot: Bernanke remained captain of the money-conjuring ship. *Time* magazine named him Person of the Year in 2009, and the Fed continued to craft money from thin air. On inauguration day, the Fed offered $150 billion to US banks in the form of eighty-four-day credit through its Term Auction Facility.[110] Two weeks later, another $150 billion auction in twenty-eight-day credit followed.[111]

The Fed busily coordinated multi-trillion-dollar global central bank efforts to keep the US financial system and its European counterparts artificially solvent and capital markets primed. In contrast, in 2008 the US government fashioned a mere $152 billion economic stimulus package for the "people."

Mexico followed suit—but with comparatively less grandiosity. On January 7, 2009, Calderón introduced a $150 million economic stimulus package to prevent layoffs (a tiny sum compared to the amount of Banco de México money made available to buy bonds from struggling banks). Then minister of finance Agustín Carstens predicted zero growth. Ortiz characterized that forecast as optimistic in an economic clash of Mexico's current and future central bank heads. Banco de México predicted a contraction of between 0.8 percent and 1.8 percent and 450,000 formal job losses for 2009.[112]

Ortiz was fighting a losing battle against the Fed on rates. He finally relented and announced the first cut on January 16, 2009, of 50 basis points, from 8.25 to 7.75. During the first seven months of 2009, he slashed the overnight rate from 8.25 percent to 4.50 percent[113] in an attempt to stimulate the economy. The actions were politically motivated, too. The decision to imitate US monetary policy boosted Ortiz's career.

As a nod to Mexico, Ortiz was promoted from board member to chairman of the BIS on January 12, 2009, succeeding Jean-Pierre Roth.[114] Ortiz had joined the board in 2006 along with top central bankers the world over, including the People's Bank of China governor Zhou Xiaochuan and ECB president Jean-Claude Trichet. In keeping with BIS protocol, directors were elected based on relationships. Ortiz and Carstens were governors of central banks the BIS had close relationships with through its representative offices in Mexico City and Hong Kong. Ortiz's three-year term as chairman began March 1, 2009.[115]

Bernanke sharpened his tack of blaming the world for US bank–instigated economic weakness. As he told a US Senate subcommittee on February 24, 2009, "In contrast to the first half of last year, when robust foreign demand for US goods and services provided some offset to weakness in domestic spending, exports slumped in the second half as our major trading partners fell into recession and some measures of global growth turned negative for the first time in more than 25 years."[116] In addition to his skills at conjuring money, he proved adept at conjuring denial.

Complementing the Fed's money-fabrication strategies, from October 2008 to February 2009, Banco de México pumped $28 billion into the markets.[117] The central bank supported the Mexican peso by selling $17.9 billion US dollars of its reserves.[118] In February 2009 alone, it initiated six interventions, pumping a total of $1.83 billion into the market through direct sales to market participants to reduce foreign speculation.[119]

However, those actions didn't halt its declining economy. Exports fell in the first quarter of 2009 by 26 percent owing to the US economic downturn.[120] The peso was imperiled. Mexico was considered a risky bet compared to the United States. The peso hit its then-lowest point since 1990 of 15.45 pesos per dollar.[121] Mexican banks were losing the confidence of international investors, and markets were bleeding foreign capital. Yet, cheap-money collusion by the Fed, reluctantly replicated by Ortiz, could only go so far.

As the *Wall Street Journal* observed in March 2009, "Seeking a port in the global storm, investors have piled out of historically less reliable IOUs issued by national treasuries around the globe and into US Treasury bonds." The *Journal* lamented, "Mexico is *numero uno* on the victim list."[122]

In May 2009, at the Reuters Latin American Investment Summit in Mexico City, Ortiz noted, "There is a sensation that we have probably touched bottom in this crisis....I think that we have firm signs that we will see a better second half compared to what we saw in the first half."[123] His central bank had already loaned $3.22 billion of the $4 billion it auctioned the prior month and activated a $30 billion swap line with the Fed. Ortiz needed that bottom to be secured in order to save face domestically.

Smack in the middle of the economic crisis, on July 5, 2009, Mexico held midterm congressional elections. Results reflected economic fears. The Institutional Revolutionary Party (PRI) won 241 of the 500 seats in play, up from 106. President Calderón's National Action Party (PAN) placed second with 147 seats, losing 59 seats.[124] The PAN became the minority party, receiving less than 30 percent of the vote. In 2006, an estimated 42 million people lived in poverty in Mexico. Toward the end of Calderón's term, that number had leapt to 53 million (of a population of 114 million).[125] It wasn't the result he had bargained for before the US financial crisis.

To combat the brewing credit crunch in Mexico, Ortiz tapped his international connections.[126] He had served on the IMF Committee on Governance Reform from September 2008 to 2009, the only Latin American leader on the nine-person committee.[127] He now turned to the IMF for help. It offered an investor and geopolitical confidence boost, approving a $47 billion line of credit to Mexico on April 17, 2009.[128]

Internally, the Mexican economy remained in jeopardy. Money was flowing out. Mexico's unemployment shot to a fourteen-year high of 6.4 percent in August 2009 before dipping back to 5.9 percent in October 2009. The figure belied a severe job problem in the manufacturing industry, mostly located along the US-Mexico border.[129]

The idea of austerity or spending cuts reared its head. In tandem with its US and EU counterparts, Mexico's elite decided the working class should contribute its fair share to the local economy. Like other financial alchemists before him, Ortiz now supported this fiscal position. At a press conference at the Mexican senate in September 2009, he remarked, "It obviously has costs, but the greatest cost for a country would be not doing anything." The package combined tax increases and government spending cuts.[130] If central bankers were subsidizing the banks that crashed the economy, the working class would pay the price to rebuild it.

The Fed, determined to disperse culpability for the crisis, did Mexico no favors. Instead, in its 2009 third-quarter statement, the Fed poured salt on Mexico's wounds: "Reminiscent of pre-Tequila tensions is the vast amount of foreign reserves the central bank is spending trying to contain peso pressures. Since the peso weakness began in October, the central bank has provided almost $20 billion in liquidity to ease peso volatility. Evidence of capital flight also materialized in the cost of the country's debt. The premium Mexico pays relative to comparable US instruments more than tripled last fall."[131]

ORTIZ'S DAYS WERE NUMBERED

Ortiz's ongoing public criticism of inadequate US banking regulation was a thorn in Calderón's side—the president preferred to maintain the country's relationship with the United States free of accusatory language. Yet, he wasn't stopping but increasing his call to normalcy.

At a Stanford University roundtable on October 24, 2009, moderated by veteran US TV host Charlie Rose, Ortiz urged more transparency in banking, given that "the amounts of money involved are so huge." When the financial sector "becomes disconnected from the real world," he said, the economy "turns into a betting game....If we have to use taxpayers' money to make these bets, there's something very wrong."[132] That was exactly the case.

Four days later, in its quarterly inflation report released October 28, Banco de México cited the combination of decreased consumer spending and a dry spell in tourism as having cost Mexico $2.3 billion in 2009.[133] GDP contracted by 7 percent for 2009.[134] Capital outflows and bank losses were exacerbated by Mexico's high degree of foreign bank ownership (the highest of any country in the world) and the Fed's turning the screws.

Ortiz sounded the alarm across the most prestigious of academic networks. In a Yale University speech in November 2009, Ortiz was adamant. Complex securities and derivatives were too much for current regulators to handle. He explained to the audience that "OTC [over-the-counter] derivatives were also used in what turned out to be mere speculative trades."[135] The main banking regulator was the US Fed. It was also the central bank that subsequently called the shots for Mexico, and ultimately the world.

A year after the developing nations subcomponent of the G20 had issued their statement stressing the need for a different post–Bretton Woods monetary system, Ortiz was on a roll. He urged a new financial order, one in which developing countries had more of a say in their own destinies than developing ones. He said, "One of the outcomes of the current crisis has been the recognition that the G10 economies have lost some of their clout in favor of other countries and regions." He wanted it back.

"This, together with the failure of some of these countries to regulate and supervise their own financial institutions," he said, "has raised the question of their ability to continue leading international policy coordination and to establish principles and standards for best practices and regulations. The result has been the acceptance of the idea that international efforts should be led and coordinated by a wider and more representative set of countries, the G20."[136]

This recognition was one of the most momentous shifts in the expansion of power beyond the core G20 in the early days after the crisis. The United States was responsible for paving the way to a rejection of the old monetary system. Through its irresponsible regulatory and subsequent monetary policy behavior, other countries had put the United States on notice. An elite outsider, Ortiz called the elite insiders out on their right to run international policy.

But it was official: Ortiz had gone too far for Mexico's president.

THE ASCENSION OF AGUSTÍN CARSTENS

Ortiz's six-year term was up at the end of 2009. On December 9 of that year, Calderón nominated Agustín Guillermo Carstens to take his spot.[137]

Carstens began serving on January 1, 2010. He brought with him an arsenal of US alliances and stellar connections.[138] He had received his MA and PhD from the University of Chicago, with its free market doctrine. From 2003 to 2006, Carstens served as deputy manager of the IMF.[139] He had chaired the IMF and World Bank Joint Development Committee from March 2007 to October 2009. He even had personal ties to the main US-Mexico bank, Citigroup-Banamex (Banamex Financial Group was purchased by Citigroup in August 2001 for $12.5 billion). His wife, Catherine, had been chief economist for the Futures and Options division of Euro American Capital Corp., an offshore subsidiary of Banamex, the first Mexican bank to offer and trade derivatives.

Ortiz's perceived ousting was publicly controversial because many believed that Mexico needed continuity during the financial chaos. By that time, the crisis looked to be receding, but Ortiz had become too much of a wildcard in the artisanal money stakes. Carstens was likely to be more of a yes man—under Calderón's lead. With his establishment background, he would be a point person of the Fed and offer a gateway to Washington Beltway economic leaders. Carstens was also considered more of a "rank-and-file" Wall Street guy. Ortiz, on the other hand, chose to believe in the "autonomy" of Banco de México from the government, which was supposed to be its mandate. Like Ortiz, Carstens came from the minister of finance position, a sign that true independence between the central bank and government wasn't going to happen.

As for Ortiz, he moved to the private sector. He served as chairman of the board of Grupo Financiero Banorte from March 2010 to December 2014 and chairman of its advisory board from 2015. In October 2015, he became chairman of the Brazilian bank BTG Pactual Casa de Bolsa Mexico. Where he once straddled the reform gap between the BIS and IMF, he now served to bridge the gap between two of the largest banks in Latin America.

That revolving door was as normal in Mexico as it was in the United States. Ortiz would continue a tradition of Latin American leaders transitioning into private banking, prestigious academic institutions, and intergovernmental arenas that offered them huge sums of money.

FOREIGN MONEY FLOWS AND CURRENCY WARS

The Mexican economy stabilized, growing by 5.5 percent in 2010, its fastest annual growth rate in ten years[140] and one of the highest in the OECD.[141]

Carstens guided Banco de México through a low-rate policy, as expected. The by-product of Mexico clawing back from its worst recession since 1932 was peso appreciation. Yet, that currency strength opened up another can of worms: fear that too much of a rise in the peso could have an undesirable impact on Mexican exports, rendering them too expensive and cutting into demand.[142]

By the evening of October 24, 2010, Ortiz, now on the outside looking in— warned of a currency war that for Mexico arrived in the form of the peso overheating, not devaluing. In the game of global currencies, through a mix of monetary policy, economic strength, and speculative bets, there are always winners and losers. As *Financial Times* reporter Adam Thompson noted, "While most people in Mexico were using their Sunday to unwind, Ortiz was telling an audience at the Mexico Business Summit in Toluca, just outside the capital, that the ease of investing in Mexico was increasing the risk of an overvalued currency."[143]

Attracting foreign capital, which could increase the currency's value, was both a badge of honor and a competitive sport in Latin America. Mexico's main rival for foreign money, Brazil, boasted a much higher benchmark rate of 10.75 percent compared to Mexico's rate of 4.5 percent. Both levels had the capacity to lure foreign investors seeking higher returns than the zero rates offered in the United States and Europe. This cheap money was easy to come by—and even easier to lose. That fear complicated the game of attracting foreign capital but didn't end it, by any means.

Still, a headstrong Carstens took an opposite tack from developing countries such as Brazil and Colombia. They began imposing levies and ending tax exemptions on foreign capital in a bid to temper hot money speculation. He, in contrast, following University of Chicago theories of free market capitalism, openly criticized such seemingly isolationist moves.

In an October 27, 2010, interview, Carstens told Mexico's Radio Formula that currency wars are "very destructive."[144] At a press conference in Mexico City that day, he reported that employment exceeded pre-crisis levels.[145] Yet he signaled there might be more rate cuts to attempt to help the peso decline to a more comfortable level. In practice, it was a monetary policy head fake; he would impose no cuts until December 2015.

Meanwhile, the Fed and ECB had slashed rates. The Fed was planning to pump hundreds of billions of dollars into the markets (or, as it said, "the economy"). The move bothered Carstens for the same reasons it had Ortiz. He told reporters on November 17, 2010, "This could generate the risk of generating bubbles in emerging economies. When these burst they generally cause a lot of volatility."[146] Carstens was well aware that in the new interconnected world of central banking, what the Fed did would soon affect his policymaking ability. It would also significantly impact the Mexican economy and people.

In November 2010, China chimed in and criticized the Fed's second round of QE as it threatened to "shock" emerging markets with "hot money." Brazilian finance minister Guido Mantega compared it to "throwing money from a helicopter."[147] Hence, "Helicopter Ben" became Ben Bernanke's money-conjuring nickname.

In the end, though, Carstens's US allegiance won. He concluded Mexico would benefit if the Fed's monetary stimulus boosted US economic growth. "It's an understandable measure, and up to some point even desirable," he said. "If I were in Ben Bernanke's shoes, I would do the same."[148] Carstens had made his decision. He was all in with the Fed.

ZOOMING HOT MONEY

By 2011, foreign inflows to Mexico had almost doubled over the prior year to Mex$70.4 billion (US$5.78 billion) as international investors anticipated the Fed would pump more liquidity into the US economy (read: its banking system) and continue zero interest rate policies. That meant US rates would stay low. Investors sought greater returns elsewhere.

Meanwhile, Mexico's central bank head's status was elevated globally. On January 10, 2011, the board of directors of the BIS elected Carstens as a board member.[149] Carstens saw this as an opportunity. He had climbed the ranks of the IMF. The BIS served as the next step in a career that extended beyond the Mexican central bank. And in that role, he would likely seek to render the BIS an even more powerful global entity.

A few months later, at the G20 and IMF assembly of finance ministers and central bank governors in Washington on April 14–15, 2011, Carstens touted Mexico's recovery: "There have been some mixed figures about the US economy, we still are optimistic about the evolution of the Mexican economy."[150]

Yet, despite it being a foreign capital magnet, the Mexican economy itself grew only 3.9 percent in 2011, the weakest pace in two and a half years. The services sector dipped, and a renewed global slowdown emanating from Europe dampened exports.[151] Indeed, Mexico looked like a beacon of financial light compared to what was going on across the Atlantic. Portugal had to cut a €78 billion bailout deal with the EU/IMF.[152] Greece received notice for a second bailout of $155 billion (€109 billion) in order to prevent contagion in Europe.[153]

Similar to the leader before him, Carstens's star power was ascending. In May 2011, he was rumored to be in the running to replace a scandal-plagued Dominique Strauss-Kahn as managing director of the IMF. "It would be appropriate to have a non-European because a pair of fresh eyes could see European problems with greater objectivity," Carstens told *El País* on a visit to Spain as part of his strategic international lobbying campaign for the exclusive position.

"I think emerging countries have been faithful partners in the international economy in recent years and we should be recognized," Carstens said.[154] It was a subtler attempt to enter the world's higher echelons than Ortiz had executed. From there, Carstens could navigate a tighter Latin America–emerging market partnership but remain on par with the Fed and its global allies.

In May 2011, at the United States–Mexico Chamber of Commerce Annual Gala in Washington, DC, Ben Bernanke and Carstens were both awarded the Good Neighbor Award. Carstens pressed Mexico's case (and his own), beaming, "For the first time in several years the Mexican economy in 2011 will grow at a faster rate than Brazil's."[155]

On June 13, 2011, the IMF released its official statement of consideration for the nominations of Agustín Carstens and Christine Lagarde for the post of IMF managing director.[156] Battle lines were drawn. Carstens met with Tim Geithner—if he could get US financial leadership to back him, he had a far greater probability of gaining the position.

The United States, with nearly 17 percent of the voting power, didn't need Carstens in that position enough, though, and supported Lagarde. Venezuela, Bolivia, Peru, Panama, Uruguay, Mexico, Paraguay, Belize, Honduras, Guatemala, the Dominican Republic, Nicaragua, and Colombia backed Carstens's bid for the IMF helm. So did Australia and Canada. But Brazil broke ranks, backing Lagarde.[157]

About two weeks later, Carstens was named runner-up for the IMF post. Even though Mexico was a top three trading partner, the United States was not about to step in the way of France's Christine Lagarde and the institution's sixty-five-year history. China, India, Brazil—all emerging powers—voted against Mexico's bid for the IMF. The *Wall Street Journal* observed that Carstens, the Chicago Cubs fan, knew the odds had him as a long shot.[158] "I think also someone coming from the outside would speak their mind more frankly and I think that would be an advantage,"

Carstens had said. But Europe was facing a sovereign debt crisis and it wanted a European at the helm of the IMF in case it needed help.

Undaunted, Carstens traveled to New York City in September 2011 to attend the Bloomberg Markets 50 Summit. "The balance of risks in Mexico still calls for a relatively neutral monetary policy, which is precisely where we stand today," he told the summit. "There may be circumstances in the future that call for lower rates."[159] The Wall Street crowd, business executives, and various leaders did not only see a banker from Mexico—they saw one of their own.

Carstens met with William Dudley at the New York Federal Reserve for a working lunch and meeting afterward.[160] That month, he was named Central Bank Governor of the Americas for the Year 2011 by *Emerging Markets* magazine. Later that year in Miami, Florida, he received a Bravo Award 2011 by *Latin Trade* magazine.

Then Mexico's currency took a turn for the worse. The peso fell 14 percent from August to late September, hitting 13.56 per dollar.[161] This slump was in part attributed to speculation that Mexico would follow Brazil in cutting its key rate. Putting it into context at the Fed's annual late-August Jackson Hole central bankers gathering, Carstens noted his concern about a US slowdown, but not about rate comparison in Latin America.

The rivalry between Mexico and Brazil, the rock stars of the emerging markets, intensified. The battle lines were drawn around legacy relationships and geography. Mexico had proximity to the United States, whereas Brazil had regional dominance and major trade relations with China. Private investors saw opportunities in playing both sides of this monetary combat, and currency speculators were equally happy to take bets on how the regional political relationships would impact exchange rates.

Respective national banks also sought to take advantage of shifting geopolitics and investor appetites by competitively offering their services. The next president of Mexico would offer significant reforms, a different approach to cartel violence, and an opportunity for financial innovation. Elections on both sides of the border had investors eager to bet on the outcome. The Mexican economy, where the risks were known compared to some of the other emerging market countries, was an outpost of the American marketplace.

FASTER GROWTH AND A NEW PRESIDENT

According to the Organisation for Economic Co-operation and Development, Latin America was expected to grow 4.1 percent in 2012. Mexico was blossoming again while Europe was flailing.

The year 2012 brought another US presidential election and a debt and identity crisis in Europe. There was also a general election in Mexico. As a July 2012 *New*

York Times op-ed pointed out, "If ever there were an election preordained as a result of economic performance, it would be Mexico's election."[162] Centrist PRI leader Enrique Peña Nieto won handily (Calderón by law could not run for a second term anyway, but his party was trounced). Peña Nieto had been the governor of the state of Mexico from 2005 to 2011 and had worked for President Zedillo during the Clinton years. Peña Nieto was a lot like Obama—young, charismatic, he had a lovely wife. But his party, like the others, was riddled with corruption, and, as with Calderón, the election invited voting controversy. As his minister of finance and public credit, he appointed Luis Videgaray Caso, an MIT graduate and his confidant since 2005.

The Fed remained cautious on Mexico. In July 2012, Fed governor Elizabeth A. Duke visited Mexico City to discuss central bank cooperation in times of crisis. She observed, "Though Mexico's recovery in the second half of 2009 was strong, it had less momentum and considerable economic slack remained in the country. As such, the Bank of Mexico did not consider it necessary to raise policy rates during its recovery period, unlike many other Latin American central banks."[163] Mexico had passed the good neighbor monetary policy test. Other Latin American central banks had deviated from the Fed's cheap-money policy to attend to inflation. In contrast, Mexico had toed the line, the collusion blueprint.

At the same event, Carstens supported the Fed's artisanal-money coordination policy. He stated, "These turbulent episodes showed that international coordination in implementing policies is more productive and efficient than unilateral implementatioh...in times of crisis the benefits of coordinated action are more than evident."[164]

Mexico now proved comparatively beneficial to the United States as European debt problems grew. The peso was again dropping relative to the dollar though. The depreciation lowered the price of Mexican exports to the United States and raised the cost of its imports.[165] Brazil and China were forging a stronger economic alliance with each other. The United States needed Mexico in its corner.

Because of that, the Fed announced another money-crafting measure on September 13, 2012. Nearly four years after the crisis, US banks still couldn't sell their toxic mortgage assets. So the Fed jumped into action by purchasing $40 billion worth of them per month.[166]

When asked for his comments on the measure by Reuters, Carstens responded in solidarity: "We welcome the measures because for Mexico the most important issue is to have a strong US economy." He added, "If monetary policy can do something to strengthen the economy of the United States, then obviously that will end up helping us as well....We agree with the policies adopted."[167] A sharp slowdown in the United States would hurt growth south of the border.

With the European debt crisis intensifying, talk of a double-dip recession spooked markets, central banks, private banks, and the general population. It was a

US election year and Obama wanted to take credit for "saving" the economy, which meant the economy had to preserve its state of "recovery." Sure enough, underscored by the Fed's money-conjuring policy, Obama easily retained his position as leader of the free world against Republican challenger Mitt Romney. Bernanke kept his post until 2014. His eventual successor and former Clinton adviser, Janet Yellen, would advocate his policies.

Meanwhile, Europe entered double-dip-recession mode despite, or perhaps because of, actions of the troika (the IMF, ECB, and EC). Anti-austerity measures blanketed Southern Europe. Portugal, Spain, Italy, and most notably Greece became grounds for widespread protest and strikes.

Latin America provided a breath of fresh air for speculators and conjured-money flow. While Europe faltered, Mexico roared. As the *International Business Times* reported on December 11, 2012, "Quietly, steadily and without much of the glitz and attention afforded its northern neighbor, the Mexican stock market has been on a tear this year."[168]

SEEKING SOLUTIONS

In the midst of Mexico's lukewarm economic rebound, on March 8, 2013, Banco de México cut its key rate by 0.5 percentage points to a record-low 4 percent. It was the first cut since 2009. After a nervous global market reaction to the cut, the bank assured the markets the cut was not part of an overall easing cycle for the future.

In Banco de México's inflation report, the biggest concern was growing global risk. "The slowdown of the Mexican economy, which had been observed since the second half of 2012, intensified. This loss of dynamism derives from a series of adverse shocks, both domestic and external, which have amplified the slack in the economy."[169]

Subsequently, in its September and October meetings, Banco de México lowered rates by 25 basis points at each meeting.[170] Mexico began 2013 with rates at 4.5 percent and ended with them at 3.5 percent. Mexico's 2013 economic growth was just 1.3 percent.[171] Calming markets and projecting assertive action was all that stood between confidence and crisis. Carstens was not about to be the one who let the ship take on water.

But a series of economic problems plagued Mexico. In April 2013, overdue consumer debts hit their highest level since the 2008 global financial economic crisis.[172] That wasn't all. Mexico's GDP suffered a surprise contraction of 0.7 percent in the second quarter versus the previous quarter. It was suddenly hitting its worst year since 2009.[173]

Facing an approval rating slumping along with the economy, in May 2013, President Peña Nieto announced a fiscal reform package. In theory, the funds would help struggling small and medium-sized businesses, which numbered about five million in Mexico at the time.[174] The idea was to ignite the economy from the ground up. Carstens estimated the reform could add an ambitious half a percentage point to growth within two or three years.

Just six months earlier he had praised the Fed's latest QE plan, Carstens was now irritated about the situation, not just for himself and Mexico but for emerging markets. In the middle of August 2013, he spoke at the Federal Reserve Bank of Kansas City, where he excoriated the Fed's QE methods and lack of a clear exit plan as potentially causing further turmoil.

"In advanced economies," he said, "it would be desirable for them to implement a gradual and predictable exit from unconventional policies. Better communication by the Fed, to speak in one voice, would be very important at this time as well. Advanced economies' central banks should also mind the spillover effects of their actions. Otherwise the lingering crisis will be reactivated, but probably with new actors. In the case of emerging market economies, they need basically to strengthen their economic fundamentals."[175]

On October 14, 2013, Banco de México celebrated its twentieth year of political independence from the Mexican government, which allowed it to set price stability for the economy, technically absent of intervening politicians.[176] At the corresponding conference "Central Bank Independence—Progress and Challenges" held in Mexico City, Bernanke addressed the crowd—via prerecorded video—to celebrate. ECB head Jean-Claude Trichet was also in attendance.

Bernanke acknowledged Carstens's efforts during the global financial crisis and wished him well in his work stabilizing the Mexican economy. Using words unlike those in former finger-pointing Fed reports, he complimented Carstens for mirroring Fed policy. "The strong links between our economies have led to close cooperation between our central banks. An example is the bilateral currency swap arrangement between the Federal Reserve and the Bank of Mexico that was set up during the global financial crisis...one of fourteen that the Fed established with foreign central banks around the world [that] alleviate dollar funding pressures, reduce interbank borrowing rates, and calm market fears during some of the worst phases of the crisis."[177] Bernanke never hesitated to praise himself for coordinating global central banks.

Five days later, Manuel Sánchez, deputy governor of the Banco de México, addressed the United States–Mexico Chamber of Commerce in New York City. He underscored the downside of the Fed's actions: "Until last April, these policies constituted an important factor behind substantial capital flows directed to emerging markets in the search for higher yields."[178] The unprecedented nature of Fed policies was affecting the emerging markets in general, and Mexico in particular.

The Fed didn't just "save" the US financial system, it altered the flow of capital everywhere. The resultant obsession for seeking higher-yielding securities always had a dire flipside—"hot" or speculative capital rushed out of emerging countries at the worst possible moments.

BANCO DE MÉXICO FURTHER EMBRACES CHEAP MONEY

For Mexico, no real growth occurred during the first half of 2014. By June 6, 2014, Banco de México cut rates again from 3.5 percent to a record-low 3 percent.[179] The domestic economy faced several trouble spots. GDP growth remained under 3 percent despite more positive forecasts, and income from exports suffered from the drop in commodity prices.[180] Year-over-year, retail sales fell 1.7 percent. Consumer confidence declined.[181] While the financial media heralded the road to recovery on Wall Street, the financial situation for Mexico seemed to be anything but stabilizing.

Foreign money, on the other hand, remained abundant owing to cheap-money policy. As a result, major foreign bank conglomerates decided to lend more to the local economy. In September 2014, Citi-Banamex announced a four-year $1.5 billion investment program. Peña Nieto, Citigroup CEO Michael Corbat, and the chairman of the board of Banamex and co-president of Citigroup Manuel Medina Mora championed the project.

Manuel Medina Mora said, "These investment programs are a reflection of the commitment that those of us who are part of Banamex have with Mexico. . . . It is a privilege to be the National Bank of Mexico."[182] As of July 2014, Banamex made up 13 percent of loans to Mexican companies versus the 32 percent that Banamex and Citigroup extended in 2000.[183] Banamex also promised to expand lending to small and medium-sized enterprises (SMEs) to $4 billion, plus support public and private energy sector projects with $10 billion of credits, debt, and capital issuances.[184] From 2009 through 2014, loans to SMEs grew at a real average rate of 12 percent per year.[185]

But, by late 2014, with the peso and oil prices falling, many loans were placed on hold. Medina Mora announced his departure from Citigroup effective 2015. Much controversy surrounded him, stemming from a corruption and fraud case involving Banamex and services company Oceanografía.[186] Mexican regulators fined the Citigroup unit of Banamex another $2.2 million.[187] The symbiotic connection of central banks, private banks, and US banks all blended into one dirty tequila sunrise.

TO FOLLOW OR NOT TO FOLLOW

Though Mexico was struggling economically, the US economy appeared rosy on the surface, inflaming fears through the Wall Street corridor of a Fed rate hike. Carstens again expressed his allegiance to US monetary policy at the Tech, the country's ultra-prestigious Mexico Autonomous Institute of Technology, in Mexico City: "Given an imminent increase in US interest rates, there's a high probability that rates in Mexico will also have to be raised this year."[188] The suddenly hawkish Carstens was wrong about the imminence but correct about the increase.

Latin American economic growth stalled further because of more drastic drops in the price of oil and local currencies relative to the dollar. Oil was a major contributor to the economic engine in Mexico. Falling oil prices meant a shock to the system. It appeared as if central banks had hit a wall in their power to manifest market enthusiasm. The world was proving more difficult for the Fed, its key allies, Banco de México, and others to navigate—or control. But that didn't mean the Fed was going to throw in the towel on collusion.

Carstens was selected to be chairman of IMF's policy advisory committee for a three-year term effective March 23, 2015.[189] It was a consolation prize after Lagarde nabbed the top spot at the IMF. It did, however, recognize Carstens's unique connections to the United States and his global stature. He was the first Latin American to hold that title, and the post reflected the extent to which Mexico was politically and financially integral to the United States in the artisanal money era.

Yet, Carstens remained a man standing on the outside of the United States looking in. He was shunned by the Western financial leaders to whom he had shown consistent allegiance. The fact that he was rejected by the Bretton Woods system would not be lost on the central banker. He still had navigated Latin America politically to hedge his other power aspirations. By April 2015, he was even more worried about the state of emerging economies. The cracks in the wall of financial stability were widening.

While at an event held by the Peterson Institute for International Economics in Washington, DC, Carstens criticized the long-term impact of Fed policy because "recovery of the world economy...still depends heavily on the monetary policy stances in main advanced economies [AEs] that are not sustainable over the medium and long term." He added that recovery had been slow and was "vulnerable to setbacks."

Despite years of questionable results, he noted, "the only stabilization policy instrument left was monetary policy, and therefore the main central banks have adopted, at different times, speeds and with varied modalities, unprecedented expansionary monetary policies."[190]

Carstens was playing both sides. He wanted to echo the Fed's policies so that Mexico could benefit from its association with the United States. However, the central banker also knew that his country had to compete with large Latin American economies like Brazil for foreign capital.

Mexico and Brazil represented 62 percent of the GDP of Latin America, and 55 percent of its population and its land. Both countries struggled under high foreign-denominated debt. Both nations' currencies were down relative to the US dollar. Both had systemic issues of corruption, though Brazil's were worse. Weaker growth in the region was an outcome of the volatility surrounding the Fed's manipulation of global monetary policy, which had altered the cost and availability of cheap money for speculators and bankers, but not regular citizens.

On March 11, Banco de México announced it would offer $52 million a day at auctions to sell US dollars. The maneuver was made to support the peso by an additional $200 million on days when the peso weakened by 1.5 percent from the previous trading session rate.[191]

Throughout Mexico, concern grew that any tightening policy could further hamper the peso by strengthening the dollar. To support the currency, Mexico's central bank decided on July 30, 2015, to increase its daily dollar auction from $52 million to $200 million.[192]

Finally, Banco de México sent the message that if peso volatility continued, it could act independently of the Fed. "If necessary, we can raise interest rates at any moment," Carstens said.[193] He was stepping out of the Fed's shadow, while keeping one foot in it. He did not want to follow Ortiz's path of diverging with his fellow conjurers too far. To step out of the shadow completely was paradoxically to be left in complete darkness.

Although tightening monetary policy was an uncharacteristic move by Banco de México, especially in a weak economy, supporting the level of the peso reigned crucial. The weak peso was hurting Mexican exporters and farmers.

Some fund managers thought a US rate hike could trigger big flows out of Mexico. "The actions of the Fed are not going to be the only thing that determines monetary policy going forward for the Bank of Mexico," Carstens assured reporters. Late in the game, he became determined to flex his independence. "The Bank of Mexico, at some point, has to send a signal that it is worried about the value of its currency," he said, "because this also affects the will of people to hold assets in the national currency."[194]

Carstens stood resolute. Peso-denominated bonds had fallen 8.4 percent in value in US dollars terms since the start of the year, significantly more than in the rest of the region.[195] Banco de México revised its annual growth target to between 1.7 and 2.5 percent, from 2 to 3 percent, citing weaker-than-expected exports despite an anemic peso and a slump in domestic oil output.

As in the past, emerging countries still coveted foreign capital to survive economic turmoil without relying on internal commerce. This was a double-edged sword. After slumping during the first quarter of 2015, the Mexican economy picked up in the second quarter. The services sector offset lackluster industrial output hit by shaky exports and lower oil prices.[196] But still, commodity price drops, a China growth slowdown, and fears of a rate increase plagued markets that summer.

Carstens reacted as Ortiz had in 2009, performing some artisanal money magic of his own. On July 30, 2015, he announced a currency injection of Mex\$8.6 billion over the next two months. "If the peso needs the reinforcement of higher rates, we will raise them independently of what the Fed is going to do," he announced again. "We could raise rates in August, we don't have certainty that it will happen in August. It could be at any moment." The peso extended interim gains following his comments.[197]

The amount of corporate and bank debt issued since the Fed embarked on its zero interest rate and QE policy ballooned. The total size of the emerging market nonfinancial corporate bond market had doubled to \$2.4 trillion in 2014 versus its size in 2009.[198] Plus, the volume of nonperforming loans and general debt payment burdens had also risen on US dollar strength.

That meant emerging market banks, particularly those exposed to high degrees of foreign currency lending, were in trouble. By August 2015, Mexican public companies started showing greater amounts of debt due to peso depreciation. There was a 22 percent debt value increase for the top fifty companies trading on the BMV (Mexican Stock Exchange).[199]

In contrast to the Latin American debt crises of the 1980s and 1990s, loans and bonds were now not just extended by private US banks but also subsidized by the Fed. Systemic risk had been elevated by the money conjurers. Yet, midlevel Mexican companies had trouble gaining access to credit.[200] On August 24, 2015, the Dow dropped 1,000 points in early trading, an historic first. It shed 588 points that day—the worst one-day loss since August 2011.[201] Shocks on Wall Street meant aftershocks in Mexico.

THE FED RAISES RATES: MEXICO BLINKS

On December 16, 2015, the wait was over. It was the first time in nine years of nearly zero percent interest rates that the Fed raised fed funds rates—by a quarter of a point, from zero to 0.25–0.5 percent. No FOMC member disagreed. The next day, Banco de México followed suit. It increased its interbank rate by a quarter point to 3.25 percent. Carstens had kept his word.

There was no pretense of independence. Banco de México admitted its first rate hike since August 2008 was "mainly in response" to the Fed's decision.[202] The rate had averaged 5.38 percent from 2005 until 2016, reaching an all-time high of 9.25 percent in October of 2005 and a low of 3 percent in June of 2013.[203]

In an interview with Reuters afterward, Carstens explained the move, in lieu of his previously stated intention that the Fed's actions would not determine those of his central bank. "We are facing opposing forces," Carstens said. On one side, inflation expectations were well anchored, but the peso's deep losses could still "ultimately have some impact on prices, especially for tradable goods."[204]

Domestic necessity had reared its head for Banco de México. "This year has been the worst ever for emerging markets in terms of capital inflows," Carstens declared at the December 2015 World Affairs Council of Atlanta at the Atlanta Fed's headquarters. "Low interest rates in advanced countries like the United States for a while sent capital flowing into emerging markets in search of higher returns. Now, the flow of money has slowed thanks to a stronger US economy and slowing emerging economies," Carstens said. "Some investors move lots of capital quickly from one nation to another, and this volatility can push down the value of local currencies."[205]

The Fed's pre-Christmas rate hike riled markets worldwide. There was a palpable fear that the cheap-money party could be over. The trickier problem was that such anxiety could trigger a credit squeeze that could hurt emerging market countries. Cheap money that had been pumped into those countries could exit faster, leaving chaos behind. It was a damned if you do, damned if you don't scenario for the Fed—with major global implications.

Emerging market central bankers were in a fight against the cheap-money clock. Speculators were squeezing the last drop out of high returns while conjured-money policy lasted. They were worried. In a speech in Paris on January 12, 2016, at the Farewell Symposium for BIS chairman and Banque de France head Christian Noyer, IMF head Christine Lagarde cautioned, "Emerging and developing economies are now receiving up to $1.5 trillion of capital inflows per year. And it has become more difficult to prevent liquidity shocks from doing serious harm to an economy."[206]

At the same symposium, Carstens expressed his concerns: "Given the way that international capital flows have been intermediated and the presence of relatively thinner financial markets in emerging market economies, the unwinding of monetary policies in advanced economies could trigger portfolio adjustments that might be quite destabilizing."[207]

Carsten's words, like those of Ortiz eight years earlier, were prophetic. The peso dove despite Banco de México's action. On January 22, 2016, a CNN headline blared "1 Mexican peso is now worth 5 cents." Luis Videgaray, Mexico's finance minister, called the peso "clearly undervalued" as it fell to 19 pesos per dollar. "It is in the line of fire of market volatility since it is the most widely traded emerging market currency."[208]

Panic mounted because of one tiny rate hike. International speculators weighed their thoughts on which Latin American currency would do better in the environment. Yet by February 5, 2016, net inflows increased to their highest level in three months. Even in the midst of a weakening peso, international investors flocked to Mexican government bonds.

Carstens waxed optimistic, "Mexico's economy should grow slightly more than 2.5 percent in 2016."[209] Mexico's citizens did not share his enthusiasm. Mexico's minimum wage remained one of the lowest in the region.[210] Its working poor percentage had risen from 32.9 in the third quarter of 2008 to 41.4 by the first quarter of 2015. By January 2016, crude oil prices had fallen to their lowest level since 2003. Remittances from Mexicans abroad overtook oil revenues for the first time since tracking began in 1995.[211] The central banker reaction and the actual conditions for *el pueblo* told two very different stories. Reality, as it often does, met the illusion of persistence in Mexico.

Even though the Fed didn't raise rates in February 2016, Carstens executed a quintessential anti–currency war move. He raised rates *again* on February 17—by 50 basis points. No one saw the move coming. The peso, which had declined steadily from 10 to 19 to the dollar between 2008 and mid-February 2016 (and by 18 percent during 2015), strengthened to 17.92 to the dollar as of March 8, 2016.

As Carstens explained on March 11, 2016, "Our monetary policy will above all be led by...the exchange rate, the monetary policy relative to the United States and the inflationary pressures that could occur due to the economic cycle in Mexico."[212]

Mexico had invoked independent monetary policy successfully. The move boosted the peso and helped retain foreign capital in Mexican banks. This direct action also kept Mexico from having to sell US Treasuries to bolster its reserves, which helped the Fed keep rates low.

MEXICO—UNITED STATES TRADE

Mexico buys more US products than any other nation except Canada; nearly five million US jobs depended on trade with Mexico.[213] A lower peso would throw a wrench in trade on all sides and impact jobs.

It remained important that the United States and Mexico stick together. It was in the United States' strategic interest to keep China from engaging too much with Mexico. The Mexican relationship with China was meager compared to its ties with the United States, or even the relations shared between Brazil and China. This allowed potential and significant room for expansion.

By February 2016, Banco de México had already auctioned $3.5 billion for 2016,[214] on top of the $24.5 billion in 2015 it auctioned to defend the peso.[215] On April 16, 2016, Carstens was in a bind. He announced, "We will not be shy about using our interest rates."[216] He was done waiting on the Fed and thought raising rates would be a cheaper way to protect the peso regardless of what the Fed did.

Still, the markets were surprised by another Banco de México 50-basis-point rate hike on June 30, 2016. The decision occurred a week after the United Kingdom vote to leave the European Union, or Brexit. It lay in opposition to the Fed keeping its rate unchanged. The peso was one of the currencies most damaged by the Brexit vote, hitting a low of 19.52 pesos per dollar.

At the Kansas Fed's annual gathering in Jackson Hole, Wyoming, in late August 2016, Carstens disturbed the power status of the core central bankers assembled there. "We are sort of reaching the limits. In many countries monetary policy activism has run its course."[217]

Carstens had laid down the gauntlet. The world was on a path to irrevocable change that resulted from a financial crisis met by collusion in a conjured-money policy. That shift would not end until a new financial order, trade and diplomatic alliances, and monetary system were erected.

Academics and former government officials took notice of the internal identity battles being fought over monetary independence versus global allegiance. Dr. Alejandro Poiré, a man with an impressive résumé in public service, had graduated from ITAM (Mexico Autonomous Institute of Technology), a select university where other notable elites had studied, including Agustín Carstens.[218] Having earned his PhD in political science from Harvard University, his political career traversed President Calderón's administration during the crisis. He became dean of the School of Government and Public Policy of the prestigious Tecnológico de Monterrey in Mexico City.[219]

Regarding the relationship between the United States and Mexico after the financial crisis, Dr. Poiré noted, "It's not an ordinary case of a small country depending on cash inflows from sales of basic goods or oil exports from a large country. It's substantially different because many things produced in the United States have Mexican input and vice versa."

This situation rendered monetary and fiscal policy independence less clear-cut than it had been historically. "Independence as a principle on which to make decisions is probably risky in and of itself," Poiré explained. "But we aren't just going to toe the line of Wall Street or the Fed or Washington." Instead, he continued, "the kind of independent monetary authority we want to have is one of a highly open international economy that can react forcedly to changes in an external situation."

THE WRITING ON THE WALL

During the 2016 US presidential election, Republican candidate Donald J. Trump campaigned on the promise to construct a "great wall" along the United States and Mexican border—and to make Mexico pay for it. His stance on the issue helped catapult him into the White House. By casting illegal Mexican immigrants as "murderers and rapists" and blaming Mexico (and China) for stealing US jobs, Trump galvanized economically anxious voters who were disgusted with the political establishment.

Mexican president Peña Nieto lost public support because he was not more forceful against Trump, instead inviting him to Mexico. Mexican leaders, skilled in diplomacy and the complexity of national relationships, would not soon forget this gesture.

Trump's November victory crushed the peso and dampened Mexico's growth forecasts. In December 2016, Banco de México reestimated 2017 GDP growth at 1.6 percent—half the 3.18 percent estimated at the beginning of 2016.[220]

Upon returning from the Asia-Pacific Economic Cooperation (APEC) summit in Lima, Peru, in November 2016, two weeks after Trump was elected US president, Mexico's economy minister Ildefonso Guajardo had made it clear: if the United States turned its back on free trade, he would open the door to China. "If one power exits a space, you can bet another will step in," he told a group of reporters in Mexico City.

Guajardo said Mexico would weigh the benefits of the China-backed Regional Comprehensive Economic Partnership (RCEP), a trade pact that excludes the United States, in order for Mexico to "have a means of integrating itself with the Asia-Pacific (region)."[221] Chinese president Xi Jinping had also attended that APEC meeting, where he proclaimed "here we are" on free trade. He vowed to keep opening China's economy to other countries.

Carstens foresaw a different kind of shadow casting itself over Mexico from the north. It was not just the possible leadership shift in the United States but also what that said about the population's perspective on Mexico. He was not shy about voicing his fears. The US president-elect was a danger of such magnitude that he could become a "horror film for Mexico," Carstens told a group of executives in Guadalajara, Mexico, just before Christmas. "Right now we have seen the short films," he continued, according to Spanish newspaper *El País*, "but beginning on January 20 the film is going to run."[222]

He had a choice: fight for an elusive independence or move on. Carstens had narrowly missed his opportunity to run the IMF and alter the course of geopolitics and global monetary policy from that post. But his international influence capacity was not gone—merely delayed.

On December 1, Carstens announced he was stepping down from his post effective July 2017 and that he would begin a five-year term as head of the BIS on October 1, 2017. The news shocked Mexico and sent the peso down to 20.8 to the dollar. Carstens's term was not supposed to end until 2021. He told a news conference, "In no way should my departure be read as a reaction on my part to an economic situation or any misunderstanding with the finance ministry or the federal government."[223] But the suddenness of his decision stoked the rumor mill that the situation wasn't so simple. His sharp criticisms of Trump made it seem likely he would follow a similar path to Lagarde's, promoting non–United States alliances the world over.

The BIS's stated mission, penned in 1931, is "to serve central banks in their pursuit of monetary and financial stability, to foster international cooperation in these areas, and to act as a bank for central banks." Historically, the BIS not only supported the prevailing monetary system but also the world's power hierarchy behind it. With Carstens at its helm, the emphasis on a more equitable influence split among developing, developed, and "transitioning"—as, for instance, China characterized itself—nations could gain steam. A shift that was a decade in the making.

As with many pronouncements of the monetary elite, things would not go exactly as scheduled. Because of the difficulty the government faced in replacing Carstens, he agreed to stay on past his original resignation date and to join the BIS on October 1, 2017.

NEW YEAR, SAME TRUMP

On the morning of January 26, 2017, President Trump goaded Mexico by tweeting, "If Mexico is unwilling to pay for the badly needed wall, then it would be better to cancel the upcoming meeting."[224] In response, Peña Nieto tweeted that he would cancel his visit to the United States the following week.[225] The result of this Twitter spat constituted a break with custom. In the modern era of the US presidency, the new administration's first invitation is extended to the leader of a neighboring NAFTA country—Canada or Mexico. In 2009, Mexican president Felipe Calderón was the first foreign leader to visit incoming President Obama.[226]

Insulted by the cancelation, Trump tweeted, "Mexico has taken advantage of the US for long enough. Massive trade deficits & little help on the very weak border must change, NOW!"[227] This marked the start of an adversarial era between the two neighbors. The period started with the US financial crisis, evoked overreaching Fed policy, and provoked economic fragility that gave way to nationalism and would hurt both countries.

Carstens kept his eye on the ball. A week later, he stated, "To some extent monetary policy has definitely been taken to its limits—I would say so for sure. I would certainly advocate for going back to a regime that is more in line with what we consider to be a 'normal monetary policy.'" But there were risks even in that cleanup strategy. He warned, "The exit from the ultra-loose monetary policy of the past years has to be very gradual and it must not put at risk the progress which was achieved so far."[228]

Mexico did not crumble. Nor did Carstens. The Fed raised rates twice by mid-2017, on March 16 and June 15, by 25 basis points each. On June 22, Banco de

México raised rates by 25 points to 7 percent, the highest level in eight years and the seventh hike in as many meetings. Perhaps outpacing Fed rate hikes was Carstens's way of asserting his independence.[229]

And Trump waffled on the trade agreement issue. "You know I was really ready and psyched to terminate NAFTA," he said on April 26, 2017. "I'm not looking to hurt Canada and I'm not looking to hurt Mexico. They're two countries I really like. So they asked to renegotiate, and I said yes."[230]

His son-in-law and chief adviser, Jared Kushner, had been spending time with Mexican leaders and saw the benefit from a US economic and trade perspective of continuing a solid relationship with Mexico, but the administration remained adamant.[231] Negotiations for reworking NAFTA were set for December 2017. However, Mexico would take no chances in this rapidly changing global hierarchy, forging new and better relationships with China, Japan, and Europe as by-products of an increasingly isolationist Trump administration and US position.

Mexico was not alone. Given its roller-coaster ride through US monetary decisions and its own litany of scandals, Brazil would do the same.

2

BRAZIL: National Politics Meets the Federal Reserve Meets China

QE creates excessive liquidity that flows over to countries like Brazil. Definitely, for Brazil it does create a problem and Brazil will present proposals in that regard to several countries—the US and China—to reach a different agreement not to generate so many distortions.

—Henrique Meirelles, head of the Central Bank of Brazil,
November 4, 2010

Whereas Mexico's lot in the aftermath of the 2008 financial crisis was to walk a fine line between independence and cooperation with the United States, Brazil's economic and political woes, as complex and chaotic as they were, required a more precarious balancing act to navigate. They also largely revolved around one major player. Henrique Meirelles operated in the shadows of multiple presidents and possessed a footprint that spanned the world. Once head of the Central Bank of Brazil (BCB) and later minister of finance, he was Brazil's most powerful monetary and economic policy architect at the onset of the twenty-first century. Meirelles was also the most constant force through more than a decade and a half of economic ups and downs and financial and political scandals that made soap operas looks like kids' cartoon shows.

It was on January 1, 2003, that President Luiz Inácio Lula da Silva (or "Lula") appointed hawkish, Harvard-educated Henrique Meirelles to run the Banco Central do Brasil.[1] Before his appointment, Meirelles had built a solid international financial career at FleetBoston (formerly BankBoston), where through twenty-eight years of work he had become president of that merged bank's (BankBoston and Fleet Financial group) corporate and global bank.

Meirelles was a man of quiet fortitude, firm and discreet. He operated close to the vest, domestically and internationally. He attained elite status within Brazil but also had solid ties to Washington, DC, and President George W. Bush's Treasury secretary Hank Paulson. Trained as a civil engineer, his career spanned the public and private sectors. Meirelles received a degree in civil engineering from the Poly technic School of the University of São Paulo (USP) and an MBA from the Coppead Institute of the Federal University of Rio de Janeiro (UFRJ) and attended the Advanced Management Program (AMP) at Harvard Business School.[2]

Throughout the years, Meirelles maintained a position at the epicenter of Brazil's political and monetary saga. His career was a study of well-timed patience and opportunism. His power metastasized through his influence over the path and fabrication of money and his international connections. Around Meirelles's ascent as a money conjurer and arbiter, then, everything changed, yet ultimately nothing changed at all.

For decades, Brazil had been a monetary policy maverick compared to the rest of the world—by necessity. Since the military dictatorship of the 1980s, Brazil stood out in Latin America for its monetary policies being tied to the economy.[3] Levels of exchange rates were used as tools to calm public criticism and insulate the country from currency fluctuations.

The *B* in the BRICS[4] nations bloc, Brazil was of acute interest to the Western (US and European) financial establishment and to the rising Chinese-led Eastern bloc. The BRICS nations, at the time they formed their geo-economic bloc, aggregated regional powers in size, economic performance, and diplomatic influence to counterbalance, in a coordinated way, US hegemony. Brazil took on a major role in that global shift.

OUTSIDE THE VORTEX OF THE US FINANCIAL CRISIS

At first, during the crisis, Meirelles did not blindly follow the Fed's money-conjuring policies. Instead, he was forced by circumstances to balance domestic requirements against those of external monetary doves espousing cheap money as a cure-all for economic woes.

The strain surrounding these actions pitted Brazilian central bankers against finance ministers in a series of domestic squabbles that became known as "Battleships," a term coined by André Singer, a Brazilian political scientist from the leftist Workers Party, signifying political-monetary conflicts between central bank and minister of finance leaders.

These disagreements led to governments toppling. They played out in dramatic detail in the national press. Monetary policy decisions had the effect of swaying Brazil from one end of global alliances to another and back again. Meirelles was the central character in that tug-of-war: monetarily, economically, politically—domestically and globally.

Prying open territories for productive or speculative investment was a core US financial policy since the early twentieth century. At an August 9, 2006, meeting with US ambassador Clifford Sobel regarding the foreign business environment, Meirelles promised to use his leverage "behind the scenes" to foster a "more welcoming investment climate" for US business interests in Brazil in return for US support for his central bank power base.

The implication of this request was immense. Meirelles asking the US Treasury secretary to pressure Lula for BCB independence was brazen. Imagine if the Fed chairman chose to enlist the help of China's minister of finance to pressure the US president to increase the Fed's independence.

According to WikiLeaks documents, though, Meirelles argued that US Treasury secretary Henry Paulson "in particular would be able credibly to make that point" to Lula and finance minister Guido Mantega.[5] Paulson and Meirelles were kindred spirits. They shared the same prestigious alma mater, Harvard, and later, in 2012, Meirelles would become a board member of the environmental organization Paulson co-chaired, the Latin America Conservation Council (LACC), a self-described *do*, not *think*, tank of global elite.[6]

In the two years following that conversation, the focus of foreign bankers on Brazil skyrocketed. Major US banks, notably Paulson's old firm, Goldman Sachs, scrambled to hire staff in Brazil to boost their ground operations there.[7]

That foreign attention was rewarded. On April 30, 2008, US rating agency Standard & Poor's bestowed an investment-grade rating on Brazil,[8] enabling US pension funds, previously confined to investment-grade limits, to allocate money to Brazilian securities directly as well as to private equity or hedge funds plying money in Brazilian markets and enterprises. US broker presence in Brazil increased by 60 percent during the lead-up to the financial crisis, from 2006 to 2008.[9]

Despite the merriment caused by the S&P rating and a US-friendly BCB chief, though, US subprime crisis clouds were steadily forming: liquidity in the US credit markets dried up because of the Bear Stearns collapse in March 2008. Contagion to other markets because of the glut of toxic assets that US banks had dispersed globally was imminent.

Yet in April 2008, President Lula brushed off the impact of that brewing storm: "There [in the United States], it is a tsunami; here, if it comes, you will get one small wave that one can not even surf," he said.[10]

Within Brazil's presidential residence building, dubbed ostentatiously despite its austere Cold War–esque design the Palácio da Alvorada,[11] Lula remained unconcerned that US liquidity problems could spill over into Brazil. In fact, in contrast to directives from Fed chairman Ben Bernanke, before the July 25, 2008, monthly Monetary Policy Committee (Copom) meeting of the BCB board of directors in Brasília, Lula urged Meirelles to accelerate the pace of raising rates in order to keep capital flows in Brazil. "Do what needs to be done," he told him.[12]

Lula's views also resulted from the opinions of minister of finance Guido Mantega, who, though usually more a dove, during this period converged with Meirelles's
hawkishness on rates.[13] Since 2006, Lula had organized his government around conflicts between right-wing BCB chairman (Meirelles) and left-wing Workers Party
minister of finance (Mantega). Like a Brazilian Franklin Delano Roosevelt who
worked both sides of American politics, he vacillated between using Meirelles or
Mantega to justify government actions relative to public opinion.[14]

Such rate hikes sent two messages: first, that the BCB preferred inflation control to economic growth stimulation through cheaper money; and, second, the BCB
wanted to continue to accommodate foreign capital inflows seeking higher returns.

Less than two months later, the financial world crumbled. Lehman Brothers
went belly up on September 15, crippling the US banking system. The US government and Fed reacted by subsidizing private banks (in particular, the Big Six US
banks that were key toxic asset creators). The Fed fashioned an historic bailout program that invoked zero interest rate policy (ZIRP), initiated a strategy of quantitative
easing by which the central bank fabricated money to purchase government bonds
and other securities, and created massive lending programs for banks with relaxed
collateral rules. The Fed coerced central banks worldwide to adopt similar strategies.
The G7 central banks opted in; some G20 central banks, like the BCB, did not.

The combination of the crisis and the response of central banks reflected a paradigm shift. Remedies showcased as ameliorating economic fallout instead bolstered
private banks in epic ways at the expense of funding real growth in mainstream
economies or forcing banks to do so. This led to realignments in the prevailing financial order. In Brazil, this shift caused a political move to the right that would portend
many other such swings the world over, including in the United Kingdom and the
United States.

During the fall of 2008, the Brazilian stock market (Bovespa) bounced up and
down like a yo-yo reacting to each external central bank intervention. After falling
on Lehman's collapse, it spiked on September 19 amid rumors of a US bailout. On
September 30, it was boosted by a liquidity injection courtesy of six main central
banks—Bank of Japan, the Federal Reserve, the European Central Bank, Bank of
Canada, Bank of England, and the Swiss National Bank.

It leapt on confirmation of a European financial system bailout on October 13.
On November 24, it rose on news of an extra US bailout capital injection of $20
billion for Citigroup, a bank with strong historic tentacles in Brazil, Mexico, and
throughout Latin America.[15] But these were interim spikes. The index lost half its
value from May to October 2008 as foreign capital fled to home countries, devastating local markets, people, and firms in its wake.

Major central banks took advantage of the financial crisis to fabricate money and support key private banks under the guise of helping mainstream economies. Peripheral financial agents rushed to determine which countries would be the recipients of this resulting "hot money." The BRICS countries proved enticing to Western speculators because they had not been hammered by the subprime crisis as had the United States and Europe. China offered a large domestic consumer base and cheap labor force but political disparities. Brazil offered a wide interest rate differential owing to its high rates and, it seemed at first, its solid affinity with the West.

Generally, during a global financial crisis, the primary concern of emergent countries like Brazil flips from attracting capital to stopping capital flight. The name of the game is to keep money where it is and build proverbial dams to contain outward flows.

Meanwhile, the US financial crisis spread like malignant cancer, killing healthy economies along the way. Liquidity concerns finally manifested within the halls of Brazil's identical government buildings. On December 3, 2008, Lula switched gears and pressed Meirelles for rate reductions (in keeping with US policy to keep the wheels of its financial system greased). In a public ceremony in Brasília, he claimed rates were "above what common sense indicates that we should have."[16]

On December 16, the US Fed cut rates to zero.[17] Still, credit crunches hampered global markets. Brazil suffered a small recession in 2009 (with GDP at −0.2 percent). Lula was facing the demise of his rosy economy at the hands of US bankers and of his monetary policy bend at the hands of the Fed. Even car factories in the ABCD[18] region in São Paulo, where he had worked as a young labor union leader, were cutting jobs.

With the onset of recession, Mantega was able to strengthen his position relative to Meirelles. There was a political reason for that: Lula needed to sustain economic growth to support the 2010 presidential election of his protégé, chief of staff and former energy minister Dilma Rousseff.[19] Mantega reasoned that adopting lower rates could be effective in that regard.[20] Meirelles promised to reduce the SELIC (the Special System for Settlement and Custody) key rate at the January 20, 2009, meeting. Though he dismissed claims that he caved to the whims of Lula and Mantega, his actions indicated otherwise.

NO RISK, REALLY?

The "balance of power" battle between fiscal and monetary policy advocates raged on. But when it was politically expedient, Meirelles turned dovish himself. He began chopping rates on January 29, 2009, eventually cutting the benchmark rate to 8.75 percent by March 2010 and to 7.25 percent by October 2012 (the lowest point since the BCB's inflation target was adopted in 1999). Thus he temporarily adhered to the Fed's policy.

Brazil's currency, the real, held its own in the face of worldwide financial chaos. At the beginning of 2009, before the real began to be crushed relative to the US dollar in the second quarter, major Brazilian banks such as Itaú Unibanco Bank, Bradesco Bank, Bank of Brazil, and BTG Pactual Investment Bank took advantage of the real's strength (some later called it an overvaluation) and the crippled state of foreign banks. They bought the Brazilian operations or shares in foreign banks operating in Brazil. Branches of Swiss Bank, Union Bank of Switzerland (UBS), and the Portuguese Banco Espirito Santo were among the most attractive targets.

The phenomenon had precedent. In May 2006, Bank of America Corporation agreed to sell its BankBoston (Meirelles's old company) operations in Brazil to Banco Itaú, Brazil's second-largest private bank.[21] The deal resulted in Bank of America gaining about 7.4 percent of the equity of Itaú and becoming a board member. Other Brazilian banks bought the Brazilian operations of foreign banks like HSBC and Citigroup. In November 2008, Itaú Unibanco Bank announced its purchase of beleaguered American International Group's (AIG) 50 percent share in Brazilian insurer Unibanco AIG Seguros.[22] Top-tier investment bank BTG Pactual made several foreign acquisitions between 2009 and 2013 in South America, the United States, Switzerland, and Italy.[23]

To commemorate the first anniversary of the financial crisis in September 2009, Brazilian newspaper *Folha de São Paulo* asked Meirelles about the stability of Brazil's banks in the crisis "aftermath."[24] Meirelles assured the press that the dangers of another systemic crisis that could harm Brazilian companies with US dollar and derivatives exposure had passed. He echoed then-prevalent Fed sentiment promoting the idea of central bank collusion, "The concert of actions solved the problem of liquidity." In the twenty-first century, G7 and central bank alliances were the financial equivalent of post–World War II ones.

When asked whether the real's appreciation would create new excesses in the derivatives market, Meirelles exuded an optimistic, free market defense, befitting his days at Harvard. "Recent losses taught a dramatic lesson, not only in Brazil, but worldwide," he said. "Today no one would take the kind of risk that was assumed before." But he defended his decision early in the crisis to wait until January 12, 2009, to reduce rates in contrast to other central banks' moves: "Credit markets were still dysfunctional…inflation expectations were still very high. A rate cut would only generate more volatility and insecurity."[25]

On the pervasive issue of bank spreads (the difference between the rates at which banks take money from the BCB and the rates they charge for lending it out), Meirelles also bowed to free markets: "The main factor that will lead to the fall of 'spreads' is increased stability and competition." If other banks lowered their spreads, he reasoned, Brazilian banks would, too. Eventually.

But toward the end of the year, with growing pressure on his actions in light of oncoming recession, Meirelles switched gears. He slashed rates from 13.75 percent to 8.75 percent between January and December 2009.

CURRENCY WARS

Whether because of those rates cuts, expansion of credit for the middle and lower classes, exemption from various sectors of the economy, or freezing of some industry taxes, the economy did recover and grow. Rather than shaking hands over a shared leadership victory, Mantega and Meirelles sparred over policy more frequently, blaming each other for Brazil's remaining problems, including high public debt, low wages, and a fiscal deficit, and clashing over how to address them.

On April 16, 2010, Mantega voiced his concerns that Meirelles would turn around and raise rates to curb inflation and cool off the pace of the "strong" economic recovery. He considered Meirelles's projections of 7 percent GDP growth "exaggerated."[26] He was wrong. Brazil enjoyed 7.5 percent GDP growth in 2010, which is why Lula ended his second term with more than 80 percent of popular support. Meirelles ignored Mantega's concerns, choosing instead to embrace a combination of inflation fighting and foreign capital attracting that came from higher rates.

The BCB switched gears again and raised the SELIC to 9.5 percent on April 27, 2010.[27] Unlike US markets, which had reacted affirmatively to zero percent interest rates because they made it easy for big speculators to bet on the markets and for big companies to borrow money cheaply with which to buy their own shares, the Brazilian stock market fluctuated in its reaction to rate hikes, tending to react favorably because rate hikes signified the central bank was at least trying to combat inflation in the country.

Rates returned to historic highs throughout 2010 as Meirelles continued raising rates to 10.75 percent. Consistent with his hawkish nature, he used inflation rate growth (from 4.3 percent in 2009 to 5.9 percent in 2010) to anchor his rate hike policy, even though inflation remained within the BCB's target band of 2.5–6.5 percent during that period. The result was that these comparatively high rates attracted foreign capital flows seeking greater returns relative to what was available in their home, mostly G7, countries.

At the time, an expansion of credit to families allowed them to partake in the economic upturn. Almost the entire middle class bought new cars and traveled abroad for the first time. The idea of "doing Miami" to buy American products on the cheap because of the favorable exchange rate became common. Never had

Brazilian families traveled so much and purchased so many new automobiles. This was the main reason for Lula's expansion of the economy and high approval.

Until the autumn of 2010, the BCB refrained from intervening in the local currency market because public sentiment about monetary policy and the economy itself were pointed upward. But that feeling was short-lived. During September 2010, as both became shakier, the BCB changed its strategy and intervened by as much as $1.5 billion in a single day, averaging $1 billion a day for two weeks—or ten times its prior daily average—to contain the new problem of overvaluation of the real resulting from excessive foreign capital flows and speculation.

It was Mantega who famously coined the term "currency war" and called global attention to the brewing conflict that underpinned these capital and trade flows. He used the term to describe how other central banks were lowering or manipulating exchange rates to give their own economies an advantage from a trade perspective, rendering their exports comparatively cheaper. On September 27, 2010, he proclaimed, "We're in the midst of an international currency war…this threatens us because it takes away our competitiveness."[28] According to Mantega, if you weren't fighting the war, you were already losing it. Brazil's currency was appreciating, making its exports more expensive, which contributed to Brazil's worst trade balance in eight years.[29]

The real continued to appreciate throughout 2010. The positive by-product of that was the rising stock market. Mantega positioned himself and the government to take credit for that. Indeed, he claimed the market "owes its progress to Lula" in response to rumors that the government's new financial tax on foreign exchange transactions was enacted to mitigate real appreciation.[30]

Whereas Meirelles had raised interest rates, which subsequently attracted capital inflows, Mantega countered by imposing a new tax to fight real overvaluation. The Credit, Exchange and Insurance Tax (IOF) applied not only to international transactions but also to domestic credit operations, especially credit cards. But this measure failed to temper the appreciation of the real versus the US dollar. The strong real hampered exports' competitiveness.[31] Mantega believed the extra foreign tax would curtail real overvaluation. It didn't really, but some economists claimed it would have been worse without this measure.

THE BEST OF TIMES

The October 31, 2010, presidential election was set to take place amid the Brazilian economy's recovery from the US financial crisis shock and early 2009 recession. The country was headed to close out 2010 with 7.5 percent GDP growth. It was a stellar year.

Plus, Brazil remained in foreign capital attraction mode. Its private equity and hedge fund industry had garnered increasing international interest.[32] Brazil's hedge funds had already grown by 23 percent in 2010 compared to 2009. Private equity assets reached $36 billion in 2009 from $6 billion in 2005.[33] The notion that the crisis was over was widely promoted by the Fed, and yet cheap conjured-money remained policy and meant more capital oozing in. Even pension funds, which had gotten burned when the stock markets tanked in 2008 and 2009, were again seeking risky investments, pre-crisis lessons unlearned.

The National Bank of Economic and Social Development (BNDES), Brazil's development bank, joined the party to stimulate national speculation activities, plowing $1.1 billion into local private equity funds. As a result, in 2010, private equity funds reflected a higher proportion of GDP for Brazil than they did in most other emerging markets.

This meant more battleship fights over rates and hot money loomed. In a November 13, 2010, interview at the Seoul G20 Summit, shortly after Dilma Rousseff was elected president, Mantega jumped the gun—and over Meirelles—to confirm that the BCB would cut the SELIC in 2011. "How much it will fall, I don't know," he said, "but I can assure you it will fall."[34]

Mantega and Rousseff had taken some similar positions as ministers under Lula, but they were ideologically distinct. Mantega was a Workers' Party economist who had helped write the economic programs of Lula's campaigns in the 1990s, and he became Brazil's first minister of finance since its Constitution (1988) to the leave government without taking a job in the private sector. Mantega and Rousseff's joint thinking was that if the BCB cut rates, it would increase local liquidity and lending and decrease the strength of the real, which would benefit Brazil currency-war style.

Mantega vowed Rousseff would seek a balanced budget by the end of her term in 2014 along with a reduction in net debt-to-GDP from 41 percent to 30 percent. He cited her plans to reduce federal spending and subsidies to the state development bank, a part of a deal with the BCB for lower rates in return for austerity measures. Mantega knew that without something in return, it would be impossible to convince the BCB to cut rates. His decision was to offer austerity—even if austerity would hurt the middle and lower classes.[35] But he was smart and put "the blame" for austerity on the planning minister.

Rousseff had been elected over rival Jose Serra from the right-wing Brazilian Social-Democracy Party (PSDB) by a vote of 56.05 percent to 43.95 percent. As her vice president, Rousseff selected Michel Temer, head of the PMDB, as part of the first formal deal between her Workers' Party (PT) and the Brazilian Democratic Movement Party (PMDB).

Against Lula's wishes, Rousseff changed the guard at the BCB. Inflation hawk Henrique Meirelles got the boot. The dove Alexandre Tombini became chairman on January 1, 2011, when Rousseff took office.

In Tombini, Rousseff chose an economist from outside the financial markets in a bid to block critics' cries about eroding BCB autonomy. Career public servant and former senior adviser to the executive board at the Brazilian representative office of the International Monetary Fund, Alexandre Tombini fit the bill because he was the architect of Brazil's inflation target system and thus was respected by the financial markets. In addition, he had domestic and international perspective, having graduated with a degree in economics from the University of Brasília (UnB) in 1984 and earned his PhD in economics from the University of Illinois at Urbana-Champaign (an orthodox but pragmatic economics department).

After being ousted from his position, Meirelles received at least twelve job offers from the private sector, among them the presidencies of Barclays and Goldman Sachs in Brazil. He chose a position at J & F.[36] From 2012 to 2016, Meirelles assumed the chairmanship of the advisory board of J & F, the holding company for the Batista brothers, Wesley and Joesley, which included the infamous José Batista Sobrinho, or JBS.

The BCB routinely fought for autonomy relative to the Brazilian government. When Meirelles's contrarian policy of hiking rates into 2009 caused a recession, the BCB lost symbolic power. Thus, in 2011, Tombini began his tenure forced to accept a deal with Mantega[37] and President Rousseff whereby he would cut rates in exchange for promoting fiscal austerity.

The ideological battle around the simple mechanics of raising or lowering rates was about more than direction. It waged over the thorny issue of how to treat foreign money flows in a way that was best for Brazil. For, in Brazil, as in many developing nations, inflation often reared its head as a fierce and fickle beast, pitting politicians and central bankers against each other and battering a nation in the crossfire.

Rousseff's choice signified that Brazil would follow the United States and Europe and embrace lower interest rates.[38] Meirelles was accused of keeping Brazil's interest rates too high for too long. Private banks in Brazil, which had benefited from higher rates, were sad to see him go. He would not forget his displacement. The switch showed Rousseff distancing herself from her mentor, Lula. Regardless, it seemed the BCB would act in concert with other major central G7 banks. But what worked for them wouldn't necessarily work for Brazil.

CAPITAL CONTROLS

In early 2011, because the flow of speculative foreign capital financed with conjured money that spewed into Brazil concerned Mantega, he launched a personal crusade for jurisdiction over foreign capital controls.[39] "We oppose any guidelines, frameworks or 'codes of conduct' that attempt to constrain, directly or indirectly, policy responses of countries facing surges in volatile capital inflows," he told the IMF's steering committee on April 16, 2011.

What he really wanted to do was keep a lid on capital flow volatility. But neither the IMF nor any major country agreed with him. To the United States, especially, loose financial borders meant a country was on the path to becoming "developed"— the financial equivalent of nirvana. Combined with zero- to low-cost Western money, it was a policy of neoliberalism on steroids.

As foreign speculators stormed into Brazil in pursuit of quick returns, through quick bets on purchases of private equity firms or otherwise, at first new BCB head Tombini greeted them with open arms and loose regulations. American private equity (PE) funds bought chunks of Brazilian ones. In September 2011, US PE giant Blackstone paid $200 million for a 40 percent stake in Pátria Investimentos.[40] JP-Morgan Chase's hedge fund, HighBridge, bought a majority stake in Gávea Investimentos, a $6 billion Brazilian fund owned by Armínio Fraga, BCB chairman before Meirelles (during Fernando Henrique Cardoso's presidency).

Rousseff's election marked the end of Meirelles's long reign at the BCB. With Tombini at the helm, BCB fully switched gears to rate reduction mode in line with the big Western central banks. (Meirelles had cut rates at a point, too, but against his will and always while threatening to raise them again.) On September 1, 2011, the BCB cut rates to 12 percent (from 12.5 percent). Rates hit a low on October 11 of 7.25 percent. It took six months—until April 18, 2013—before they rose again (to 7.5 percent). Tombini had earned his nickname "Pombini," Portuguese for dove.[41]

In the United States, the Fed deployed aggressive quantitative easing measures, buying billions of dollars of government and mortgage bonds in exchange for adding liquidity, or cheap money, to the market and big banks. The ECB responded to the Greek and other local crises with similar measures. But this global embrace of zero interest rate policy (ZIRP) and later negative interest rate policy (NIRP) presented an international conundrum to banks in developed countries that didn't pursue the same policies. For, if every central bank on Earth chose that same path, financial giants in core markets couldn't extract mega-returns from developing ones. Emergent "safe" markets with relatively high interest rates were required to protect the wealth of the speculator class from core countries. Asset bubbles bolstered by conjured money grew everywhere. In places like Brazil, they were increasingly reliant on foreign flow.

There was another problem that affected the local population and businesses. Private banks in Brazil weren't lending cheaper money to regular customers. Credit restriction was causing difficulties across domestic business and class lines as well as anger toward the private banks. As a result of this tension, on May 26, 2011, the Federation of Industries of São Paulo and Unified Workers' Central labor force union added their voices to the chorus of groups demanding changes in private banking lending policy. The union called for a "reduction in the spread of banks"[42] and a reduction of benchmark interest rates. It endorsed BCB proposals of increased purchases of US dollars (or foreign exchange [FX] swap reverses) to protect private companies against future strengthening of the real.

Big private Brazilian banks like Itaú and Bradesco were reticent about reducing their lending rates. Their lending policies were based on the higher rates of the past, not the lower ones of the present. So, banks charged higher spreads, or greater interest rates, on loans relative to prevailing central bank interest rates, rendering the cost of getting credit higher for consumers. The BCB and government were equally unhappy. Private banks were using cheaper money to increase their profits, but not help the local economy. Their obstinacy reduced Tombini's power over credit supply and caused him great angst in terms of personal political capital in fighting for credit spread reduction to help ordinary citizen borrowers.[43]

To assuage his growing number of critics, Tombini stressed that reducing banking spreads was a "government priority."[44] From a regulatory perspective, however, just like in the United States, there was no way to force banks to lower their rates and expand their borrower base. The matter highlighted the power of private banks over politics. A month later, Mantega joined the public outcry, calling the prevailing level of spreads "absurd."[45]

This went on, to an extent, regardless of who was in power, with lending rates for some borrowers reaching as high as 400 percent per year.[46] But some concessions were made along the way. On April 10, 2012, Mantega met with Murilo Portugal, president of the Brazilian Federation of Banks (Febraban), to reason with him on the matter.[47] Portugal was having none of it. He countered, "We need to reduce the *costs* of financial institutions so the 'banking spread' and hence interest rates can be reduced."[48] To him, that meant reductions in reserve requirements, taxation for social contributions, and looser regulations for pension funds. He wouldn't capitulate to Mantega without holding a ransom over his head.

Mantega was incensed private banks were trying to "throw the bill back to the government."[49] Banks held firm. They presented twenty different proposals to the government for how they would agree to reduce their lending rates. Portugal also wanted a reduction in compulsory reserve levels that stood at 55 percent of deposits, "a slice above the level practiced in the rest of the world."[50]

Reducing reserve requirements (RRR) was another money-conjuring ploy enacted by various central banks, notably the People's Bank of China. Requiring private banks to hold less capital in reserve in the event of a financial emergency meant that banks were able to keep more of that capital on hand. The assumption was that banks would then lend whatever they didn't keep in reserve at their respective central banks. In practice, though, big global banks simply used extra funds for speculative purposes.

A day before Labor Day in Brazil, on April 30, 2012, in a speech broadcast on every open TV channel, Rousseff added her voice to the call for private banks to reduce rates. "It is unacceptable that Brazil," she said, "which has one of the most solid and profitable financial systems, continues with one of the highest interest rates in the world."[51]

Her government exerted muscle where alliances were strongest—over public banks—to decrease rates in an effort to evoke a similar response from private banks.[52] Public banks such as Bank of Brazil and Federal Savings Bank complied. The largest regional state-owned banks did also, mainly in the states governed by the Workers' Party.

The Brazilian government and BCB's battle with the private financial system over providing easier credit to the population echoed the situation in the United States, where zero-cost money had not induced private banks to extend parallel largesse. Rousseff chastised the "perverse logic" of private banks: "The Selic rate is low, inflation remains stable, but the rates on overdrafts and credit cards are not coming down."

She praised public banks for the concern they showed for Brazil's people. "Federal Savings Bank and Bank of Brazil chose the path of good example and healthy market competition, proving that it is possible to lower the interest charged on loans to their customers, cards, overdraft including payroll loans." She urged consumers to support the companies offering "better conditions," to press private banks to change their business strategy. She was digging her own political grave.

In Brazil, the three main state-owned banks were very important. They represented three of the top five banks in the country.[53] The Bank of Brazil is the biggest Brazilian bank, strong because of its presence in small cities and the influence of its public employees. Other federal banks in the top five are the Brazilian Development and Social Bank, a main source of investment funding, and the Federal Savings Bank, the most important actor in housing loans.

In Brazil's private sector, there are two main banks, Itaú Unibanco Bank and Bradesco Bank. The first resulted from a merger that occurred between 2008 and 2010 that was approved by Meirelles. Itaú Unibanco kept its distance from the Workers' Party government and supported Marina Silva during the 2014 election. Bradesco Bank was the closest private bank to Rousseff's government because of its business presence in low-income classes and Joaquim Levy's participation. Levy had been secretary of Treasury between 2003 and 2006 in Lula's government.

On May 30, 2012, the BCB cut rates by another half point to a record low of 8.5 percent.[54] The vote, led by Tombini, reflected the assumption that inflation risk was "limited" and global "fragility" was having a "disinflationary" impact in Brazil.

Private banks eventually relented. They had waited to see whether public banks would compete with them, or just threaten to, and were sufficiently afraid of losing business to somewhat alter their ways. On December 17, 2012, Febraban president Portugal announced, "We have a responsibility to improve the efficiency of banks and the quality of our services and continue to reduce costs."[55]

Meanwhile, Mantega intensified his fight to curb foreign speculators. On October 13, 2012, he chastised the IMF's support of free-flowing capital without accounting for its sources. His views echoed those of executive directors from Argentina and India. He said, "We reaffirm the need for a more balanced approach within the IMF on how to limit excessive short-term capital flows."[56] No one was listening.

The IMF played both sides in adopting its related policy statement. It noted that "full liberalization" was *not* "an appropriate goal for all countries at all times," *but* "countries with extensive and long-standing measures to limit capital flows are likely to benefit from further liberalization in an orderly manner." In other words, despite concerns, opening borders for cheap capital remained its mantra. It was a blow to Mantega and a victory for unfettered capital flows in the era of conjured money.

Still, at the end of the year, Mantega told Brazil's key economic newspaper *Valor Econômico* that the one-year anniversary of Brazil's new economic policy (lower rates and bank spreads) was a "period of structural change."[57]

Despite being low for Brazil, its relatively high interest rates still attracted historical levels of foreign speculative capital, overvalued the real, and hurt the "competitiveness of Brazilian production." Yet, he asserted, "the era of easy, risk-free gain" is over.[58]

Prophetically, his message contained warnings. First, because the era of easy money emanating from the West and Japan was far from over. Second, a reduction in interest rates and depreciation in the real could cause losses to the same export sectors that had borrowed abroad and replaced domestic products with imported ones and could also hurt those parts of the financial sector that relied on higher rates for their profits. Conjured-money policy outside of Brazil was inadvertently causing more problems for the future than helping solve present ones.

INFLATION RISING

No sooner had bank spreads fallen than inflation rose, partly because of climate change. In early 2013, a deep drought plagued Brazil (its worst in half a century), putting upward pressure on electricity and food prices.[59] This precarious state of affairs put Mantega, in his office in the P block of the Esplanade of Ministries, in a quandary. He had two choices. The first—act as if inflation wasn't happening. The second—avoid focusing on rising inflation. He opted for the second.

He told Reuters on February 7, 2013, "The trend is for inflation to fall."[60] His comments were the polar opposite of Tombini's seemingly uncharacteristic hawkish views.[61] (A small group of Tombini's supporters was quick to tell Reuters that he was often misunderstood and was in fact more conservative in terms of monetary policy than his reputation indicated.)[62] Brazilian political and central banking policies were at odds. Tombini realized Mantega would not attain the fiscal objectives he had promised the BCB.[63] And so, an acute epoch of every man for himself began. So were the seeds sown of a political shift that would shock Brazil and reverberate throughout the world. Tombini wanted to raise rates to combat inflation—a stance on which international traders made bets favoring him. On March 14, 2013, Goldman Sachs economist Alberto Ramos forecast a possible increase in the SELIC by April or May.[64]

The media inflamed the tense situation. During her April 10 morning show on Globo (an almost monopolistic Brazilian TV channel), TV star Ana Maria Braga sported a tomato necklace, signifying how expensive tomatoes had become.[65] Six days later, the BCB switched course and began a rate-hiking trend to contain inflation. This was also a month after Tombini addressed a Goldman-sponsored event in São Paulo that portended the hikes.

And yet, though inflation rampaged, the BCB's April 16 minutes revealed ambiguity over exactly how to address it.[66] Since 2012, taming the real had been an acceptable factor to explain increasing inflation (though not enough to solve Brazil's current account problems). Less politically tolerable was citing contributing factors such as a tight labor market and higher wages. Blaming robust employment for inflation would entail curbing the labor force, which was not a popular leftist platform. The BCB minutes wisely shied away from mentioning employment being too high.

From there, policies shifted regarding the treatment of external capital flows into Brazil. If the Fed, as rumored, ended ZIRP or "tapered" QE, Brazil would have to pay more interest to attract the hot money upon which its economy had become dependent. It was a financial catch-22; permitting such inflows had driven currency overvaluation.

Money flow was a double-edged sword. Though it might prove harder to control future foreign capital outflows, external capital was needed to close the balance of payments. Foreign capital won. On June 4, 2013, the government announced it would cut the IOF tax rate on credit, bond, securities, and derivative transactions to make it easier for foreign money to enter (a reversal of the earlier position).[67] Mantega continued to fear extensive capital outflows combined with a reduction of inflows if the Fed were to "taper" its QE policies, as was rumored, which could hurt

Brazil. So, two weeks later, the tax on currency exchange transactions by foreign investors for funds entering Brazil's exchanges and markets was also removed as a measure to keep capital in.[68]

Since Tombini had taken the helm of the BCB in January 2011, annual inflation had shot up to more than 6 percent, the top of the BCB's target range.[69] By June 2013, utility price hikes demoralized the population. With an increase of twenty cents in bus fares in the city of São Paulo as a final straw, a wave of social media–organized street protests swept the country. Citizens staged anti-Rousseff demonstrations against FIFA's World Cup event and protested other seemingly unnecessary expenditures they deemed unwise uses of dwindling national funds for the purpose of showing off internationally.

The protests gained national prominence, and participants from varied ideological positions made various demands. Dilma Rousseff was only one target of these demonstrations. Protestors spanned from the Far Left to anarchists, members of the center-right, evangelicals, groups calling for the return of the monarchy, neo-Nazis, and the famous black-blocks, who were responsible for the most aggressive demonstrations and vandalism.

Massive protests broke out against raising bus tariffs in São Paulo and the rest of Brazil's major cities. State police reacted violently, which generated solidarity protests throughout Brazil. Other protests targeted poor quality in public services like health and education, popularizing such terms as "for a FIFA standard public health system" and "for a FIFA standard public security." The references to the federal government's support of the costly World Cup was clear. Since 1988, Brazil has had a Unified System of Health (SUS), free health care coverage for every Brazilian citizen, sustained by the federal government. But because it did not provide the best service in terms of quality, people criticized subsidizing the World Cup over hospitals.

Regarding inflation, there was enough blame to go around. Some economists, notably the revered Werner Baer, Tombini's former economics professor at the University of Illinois, believed Tombini had been betrayed by Mantega, who hadn't controlled spending and borrowing in tandem with low rates, which would have boosted investment. Though Tombini started raising rates in April 2013 to fight inflation despite a weak economy—absent the government's role of curbing spending—hikes were not enough to curtail inflation. Plus, higher rates choked credit, further hurting the economy.

By late August, Brazil faced a potential currency crisis. During the Rousseff years, current account results grew a bit worse each year, culminating in total disaster in 2014. In 2013, there were current account problems, almost zero GDP growth, and massive demonstrations against corruption. The real was dropping. Fast. Wanting a weaker currency was one thing; having one crushed by foreign speculation was another. Brazil wasn't alone in its concern about the strong US dollar. Emerging market central banks began draining billions of dollars in reserves to prop up currencies against the dollar, even with no US rate hike materializing.

For Brazil, the method differed. By defending the real in the futures instead of spot foreign exchange (FX) market (eight times as large and more liquid), the BCB could avoid touching its $375 billion reserves as other central banks were doing.[70] It could sell dollar and buy real contracts and settle the difference later. Companies that had to pay interest on debt in dollars but received profits in real were most active in those contracts. To reduce volatility, the BCB offered them the ability to access extra dollars later if needed.

By November 11, 2013, the BCB had raised rates back to 10 percent, reflecting not just a rate hike to thwart growing inflation but a slap in the face to Rousseff's prior support of the old BCB policy of cutting rates. It was the sixth hike that year.[71]

Brazil's economy deteriorated as the US economy improved. That trend of bifurcating economies between developing and developed countries in the past would have signified just another global financial cycle and Brazil's relative position in it. When emerging economies overheat because of massive capital inflows from developed nations, there is no internal majority pushing for restrictive financial measures because the money is generally welcomed.[72] When that capital leaves for greener pastures, the emerging country is left with a hole to fill.

In Brazil, the ongoing ideological battle of wills and elites over monetary policy raged internally. But externally, they were pressured by the presence of epic global central bank intervention that caused a deluge of capital flows from G7 countries seeking higher yields through a coordinated, unprecedented fabrication of capital. This had unnaturally fueled excessive speculative inflows from dominant to recessive countries, from those that controlled monetary policy or created the most artisanal money to those that reacted to it.

MORE PROMISES, WORSE RESULTS: HEADING TOWARD 2014

When she sought the presidency, Rousseff railed against austerity as part of her platform of promises. In November 2012, she had spoken at an Ibero-American leaders' summit in Cadiz, Spain, criticizing austerity as a solution for the economic crisis in Spain.[73] "Policies that only stress austerity are showing their limitations," she had said. "Exaggerated and simultaneous fiscal consolidation in every country is not the best response to the global crisis and could make it worse, leading to worse recession."

Given Brazil's economic condition in 2013, though, that anti-austerity sentiment she once espoused died a quick death. By the fall of 2013, Brazil's financial system was in distress. It had gone from foreign investor darling to demon with lightning speed because of the alleged recovery of the United States and its Pacific Alliance partners. On September 27, 2013, the *Economist* wrote the first of many scathing analyses of Brazil titled "Has Brazil Blown It?"[74] The piece attacked Rousseff, who, the editors deemed, had "created new problems by interfering far more than the pragmatic Lula."

The *Economist* further argued that Rousseff "has scared investors away from infrastructure projects and undermined Brazil's hard-won reputation for macroeconomic rectitude by publicly chivvying the Central Bank chief into slashing interest rates. As a result, rates are now having to rise more than they otherwise might to curb persistent inflation."

The criticism underscored the power and logic gap in conjuring money: it was fine for elite countries with big banks and central banks to cut rates, not for others.

In early January 2014, Brazil's former BCB head Henrique Meirelles, who went on to become president of the Advisory Council of J & F Investments in 2012 (the holding company of JBS, Brazil's largest food company, funded by BNDES during Lula's and Rousseff's governments and central to 2017 bribery charges against President Michel Temer), was dismayed. To him, it was important to correct failed "creative" economic policies, like those adopted after his tenure.

"Historical experience," he wrote in *Folha de São Paulo,* "shows that the best way is to adopt policies that have worked in many countries, including Brazil."[75] It was his way of justifying the high rates he had sought. His comments were a direct attack against Mantega's, Rousseff's, and Tombini's cheap-money policies, and they sealed the beginning of Rousseff's defeat. This money conjurer and US ally attacked her publicly, signaling harder days to come. The moment underscored the fateful bet that the PT and Rousseff had made against Meirelles when she kicked him out of the BCB.

By September 2014, Brazil posted the worst current account deficit since 2001.[76] It occurred during an anxiety-filled presidential election and intense disputes among Rousseff, the winner; PSDB pro-austerity neoliberal candidate Aécio Neves, who came in second; and the Brazilian Socialist Party candidate and Itaú Bank favorite Marina Silva, who placed third.

The markets became increasingly erratic. The real depreciated by 12.69 percent through 2014 even as the SELIC was raised by 1.75 percent. Gasoline and diesel prices increased by 3 percent and 5 percent, respectively, despite a 60 percent reduction in global oil prices, causing pain to average drivers.

On October 29, 2014, the BCB raised rates from 11 percent to 11.25 percent.[77] Other major central banks remained in low-rate mode. Politically, Tombini made it clear that Rousseff would not control monetary policy anymore. Yet inflation would not be tamed. By December 2, the BCB's Monetary Policy Committee voted unanimously to raise rates to 11.75 percent.[78]

GROWING SHADOWS OF POLITICAL DISCONTENT

On January 1, 2015, while Brazilians were nursing New Year's Eve hangovers, Brasília, the capital, witnessed the swearing-in ceremony for President Dilma Rousseff, reelected on October 26, 2014, for her second term. She narrowly defeated Aécio Neves (of the right-wing PSDB) with 51.64 percent to 48.36 percent of the vote. She vowed to kick-start the economy, tackle corruption, and make budget cuts.

It had been an arduous reelection campaign. Reacting to pressures to cut spending and dismissing Mantega during an open press conference with journalists, Rousseff had a plan.[79] She selected a new, more hawkish minister of finance, Joaquim Levy. He was a keen austerity proponent, boasting a PhD from the University of Chicago and a long career at institutions like the IMF, the Inter-American Development Bank, the European Central Bank, and Bradesco Asset Management.

Facing a choice between the social support base of the Left and the need to promise tolerance for the financial markets and international sentiment, Rousseff went with the latter.

Embryonic in June 2013, antigovernment demonstrations blossomed after Rousseff's second victory. They were compounded by the problem of leverage, or taking on too much debt during good times without considering the consequences of unwinding.

At first, starting in the late 2000s and into the 2010s, as Brazil's firms took on more foreign debt, they were subsidized by the government, which borrowed at 14.25 percent and lent to them at 2 percent. A January 2015 IMF paper characterized this "Bon(d)anza" as reminiscent of past Latin American debt crises, but this time corporate rather than sovereign bonds were managed by foreign banks.[80] In addition, the real was getting crushed in the markets, rendering foreign interest payments even more expensive to make for Brazilian companies.

On January 24, 2015, the left-leaning and once-dovish Tombini completely crossed over to the "other side." With his reputation on the line as inflation rose above target limits, he did what other money conjurers around the world were doing: he overstepped his monetary policy role to advocate fiscal austerity to tame inflation. This was an unpopular idea because historically in Brazil these two areas of economic influence were distinct and theoretically separate. This was an unprecedented bid to combine power over both elements, rendering them more political than practical in the process.

"A consistent fiscal policy implemented rigorously ultimately helps inflation converging to the target,"[81] he said in an interview at the World Economic Forum in Davos, Switzerland. Fiscal austerity and tight monetary policy jointly implemented during a deep recession, however, was not a strategy that had proven effective, nor one used by Brazil before. But these were desperate times. World policy was becoming Brazil's policy, or at least Brazil's elite were now accepting it as so.

By early 2015, Petrobras, the country's flagship oil company, was mired in domestic scandal and its foreign investors were livid. Lawsuits for billions of dollars of losses resulting from having been "misinformed" about Petrobras's true condition stacked up. On February 24, 2015, Moody's cut Petrobras's rating to junk, pushing its bond prices to record lows. In New York, US judge Jed Rakoff consolidated lawsuits against Petrobras and its bankers—Citigroup Global Markets, JPMorgan Securities, and Morgan Stanley[82]—into a large class-action suit.[83]

A month later, on March 24, the BCB ceased sales of FX swaps in the futures market to support the real. The real sank to a twelve-year low.[84] In 2013, the BCB had auctioned $1 billion of dollar loans and $500 million of FX swaps weekly. By 2015, it offered just $100 million a day in swap auctions. However, the swap program was never about simply supporting the real. It was designed to protect local companies that were too indebted in foreign currency. Tombini hoped companies would have enough time to adjust their balance sheets for the new exchange rate situation, despite the fiscal costs of the FX swap program.

He badly miscalculated the extent to which large foreign debts would weigh down Brazilian companies booking profits in real and making interest payments in dollars or other currencies.

THE RISE AND CRASH OF PETROBRAS

Beyond the real dropping and inflation rising, another scandal now snaked into multiple sectors and government areas: rampant corruption and fraud at state-run oil giant Petrobras. During 2014, Petrobras common stock market value dropped by 37.9 percent and its preferred stock by 37.6 percent.

Between January 2003 and March 2010, Rousseff had been the chair of the Petrobras board. In 2015, as the newly reelected president, she had to deflect weekly diatribes from her own minister of finance and BCB head in the midst of investigations into criminal practices at Petrobras and a tanking economy. Brazilian newspapers were relentless in their condemnation of everything she had done or might do.

With oil prices diving and scandal escalating, Petrobras needed money to make interest payments. The firm owed $135 billion in loans and bonds to international investors, and the budget cuts it was proposing were comparatively shallow. Fortunately for Petrobras and indicative of superpower realignments, China came to the rescue. On April 1, 2015, Petrobras signed a $3.5 billion financing agreement with the China Development Bank, part of a broader cooperation agreement with China.[85] (Petrobras got another $10 billion lifeline from China in early 2016.)[86]

On May 19, finance minister Levy supported José Serra's Law Project about private concessions in the pre-salt area, which was discovered off Brazil's coast in 2006 and had the capacity to produce thousands of barrels of oil a day and which had been a Petrobras monopoly since 2010. The project removed Petrobras monopoly obligations, which theoretically would allow the influx of foreign companies to gain access to what would have been Brazilian-controlled oil supplies.[87] It was argued that Petrobras's costs would be reduced and its revenues would increase with the dispensation of the pre-salt exploration monopoly. Levy's action was meant to pressure Petrobras and support Serra's initiative.

Serra had lost the presidential election to Rousseff in 2010. Now her finance minister and former opponent were locking arms. If Serra's Law Project was approved, it presented an opportunity for international financial agents to acquire parts of Petrobras again. Given the ties among US banks, financial markets, and US big oil companies, that represented a great prospect. (On February 24, 2016, the Brazilian senate approved Serra's project through an inside deal over the protests of Workers' Party senators.)

THE UNITED STATES–CHINA TRADE WARS

China and Latin America grew closer during the twenty-first century, particularly during the period of cheap money initiated by the US financial crisis. Trade between the two regions increased twenty-five-fold, from barely $10 billion in 2000 to $270 billion in 2012.[88] In 2014, China assumed the position of Brazil's top trading partner, followed by the United States and Argentina.

In 2015, despite the slowing Chinese economy, external funding from state-run China Development Bank (CDB) and the Export-Import Bank of China hit a near-record $29 billion—triple the 2014 amount and more than the 2015 funding from the World Bank and Inter-American Development Bank combined.

A total of $35 billion of multilateral financing platforms reached Latin America, $20 billion of which came from the China–Latin America Industrial Investment Fund, $10 billion from the CDB for Latin American infrastructure, and $5 billion from the China–Latin America Cooperation Fund. About 95 percent of the loans from Chinese government banks to Latin America went to Argentina, Brazil, Ecuador, and Venezuela. US banks were lending corporations cheap money, but the Chinese were settling in for the long haul.

On June 11, 2015, during a meeting in Brussels with Alexis Tsipras, the prime minister of Greece, Rousseff tried to soften the blow of her new austerity policies, noting that austerity in Brazil was not like that in Greece, because of Brazil's $370 billion in reserves. "We make an adjustment, but we do not have a structural imbalance," she explained. "We have a financial system without any bubble."[89] Brazilians are excused for laughing out loud at that statement. The bubble was caused by a surge of outside capital dictating internal policies. It would not pop without causing pain to its population. In the meantime, as a contingency of the federal budget, public expenses were cut, social programs were reduced, infrastructure programs were interrupted, and airports and ports were given the most minor of concessions.

According to Rousseff, the high inflation was "atypical," the result of currency adjustments, drought, and rising US interest rates. (Though the Fed had not raised rates yet, Brazil's markets were reacting to the mere threat of higher US rates.)

Finance Minister Levy remained focused on economic and budgetary policy. A few weeks later, in an interview with *El País* regarding inflation and his decision to cut spending more, Levy said, "Market prices are behaving a little better. To the extent that the central bank was vigilant, this increase does not become a process."[90]

He was inferring that Brazil was not dealing with an inflationary process but a "moment" that had resulted from a combination of administered price "readjust" and political crisis. He was technically right, but his argument rendered the act of raising rates to fight inflation unnecessary. In his mind, the dust would clear, inflation would drop, Brazilians would embrace spending cuts, and scandals would cease. Or, Brazil would stop being Brazil.

This wasn't the first time that Brazil's economy witnessed deep recession coupled with steep inflation, but it was the first time that Brazil reacted so extremely to external artisanal money policies.

On July 9, 2015, the IMF (which had forecast a 0.3 percent expansion that January) predicted Brazil's economy would shrink by 1.5 percent in 2015 as global demand for commodities, particularly from China, waned.[91] Rousseff pressed for more spending cuts and tax hikes, echoing Europe's approach to dealing with Southern Europe, a recipe destined to elevate hardship for Brazilians. Brazil was experiencing its worst unemployment since 2010 (6.9 percent),[92] the largest twelve-month accumulated inflation rate since 2003 (8.89 percent),[93] and the highest consumer default rate growth since 2012 (16.4 percent). In mid-2015, Brazil's gross debt-to-GDP rose to 65 percent from 51 percent in late 2011.

Rousseff attempted more damage control against growing criticism of her austerity programs. In a September 7 Independence Day speech broadcast over social media platforms, including her Facebook page, she admitted the government had made mistakes, noting, "Difficulties and challenges were caused by a long period during which the government understood it should spend whatever it took to secure employment and worker income by continuing investments and social programs."[94] She added, "Now we have to reassess all of these measures and reduce those that must be reduced."

A week later, the government announced more budget cuts and new taxes.[95] Proposed tax changes included a tax on checks, the abolition of tax benefits for exported manufactured goods, and adjustments on equity interest. Citizens would pay the price for government corruption and mismanagement. Payments of benefits such as scholarships in Brazil and abroad and transfers to universities and federal institutions were delayed.

In September 2015, Brazil's unemployment rate shot to 7.5 percent from 4.3 percent in December 2014, the lowest measured unemployment rate in Brazilian history.

S&P's rating downgrade of Brazil on September 5 shined light on the unpopular austerity measures.[96] For Rousseff, the combination of alleged corruption while she chaired Petrobras and the economic recession crushed her popularity to a record low and increased calls for her impeachment. Levy had entered office on a promise to maintain Brazil's investment-grade rating. Rousseff's support for his austerity plans were spun as a way to maintain the investment grade, but they had not achieved that goal.

Brazil's real was the worst-performing EM currency in 2015, dropping by 30 percent. Brazil's Ibovespa stock index fell by 35 percent in dollar terms, exhibiting the fourth-worst performance of ninety-three global benchmarks tracked by Bloomberg.

Brazil officially entered recession in Q2.15, with GDP falling by 2.6 percent. The Petrobras scandal and investigations into inappropriate connections between industrial CEOs and the government, plummeting commodities prices, and a general EM sell-off by hot money speculators only exacerbated matters.

Tombini pursued a highly contractionary monetary policy, while other central banks maintained zero or near zero interest rates, to contain inflation after Rousseff's reelection. Because inflation didn't come from real excessive demand, though, the policy only deepened the unemployment problem without making a dent in the inflation caused by massive real devaluation and the adjustment of administered prices.[97]

Rate hikes had been a way to demonstrate the BCB's autonomy (and rebuild its credibility with private speculators seeking returns) after Rousseff's pressure to reduce rates during her first term. But they had a harsh, unanticipated domestic effect.

Other Latin American central banks were adopting cheap-money policies to encourage growth in the style of true currency wars and Fed-led policies. In Chile, for example, currency depreciation since 2013, despite above-target inflation, was intentional.[98] Brazil went in the opposite direction of neighbors like Bolivia and Paraguay. Tombini stood in contrast to his Latin American neighbors and the rest of the developed world's major countries.

Compared to the other BRICS nations, Brazil fared worse before and after the US financial crisis. Its average GDP growth between 2002 and 2009 was 3.5 percent, and between 2011 and 2014, it was 2.2 percent.[99] In comparison, South Africa's was 3.3 percent and 2.2 percent, Russia's was 6.6 percent and 1.5 percent, China's was 10.9 percent and 8 percent, and India's was 6.9 percent and 5.5 percent, respectively. Regionally, only Mexico fared worse, with 1.8 percent and 2.5 percent levels. Brazil's unemployment rate, which had fallen below 5 percent in 2014, rose to 7.5 percent by November 2015. Wages that had once risen alongside inflation were falling.

Corporate debt issuance in dollars increased as the real sank. Intercompany loans had tripled from $67 billion to $206 billion between Q1 2009 and Q1 2015. Plus, outstanding Brazilian offshore dollar loans tripled from $34 billion to $107 billion.[100] For households, debt as a portion of income had also risen, making it harder for people to pay for new items or save for the future.

The BCB was stuck in a domestic conundrum. It couldn't cut rates to stimulate growth without stoking more inflation and real devaluation, yet high rates caused more inflation, defaults, and credit squeezes. Brazil's dollar-denominated debt was more expensive to service as a result.[101]

So, Tombini joined the austerity game. It played well internationally if not domestically. On October 8, 2015, he addressed the International Finance Institute in Lima, Peru, saying that fiscal adjustment (spending cuts) was occurring at a slower rate than expected and that "non-economic domestic factors" had increased volatility.[102] He sought to evade blame for a situation that would tank Rousseff.

Even Lula jumped into the fray to take Rousseff's side regarding austerity. On October 29, he said, "The priority zero—if we want to start to govern this country is to create conditions to approve the measures that Dilma sent to the National Congress so that she can definitely finish the fiscal adjust."[103] It would be a page-turn in the government's propaganda machine, but more surprises loomed on the horizon. On November 24, the senate leader Delcídio do Amaral was arrested for allegedly interfering in Petrobras investigations.[104]

In 2015, industrial production fell 8.1 percent.[105] By the end of November 2015, Brazil's inflation exceeded 10 percent for the first time in twelve years. The government froze certain discretionary spending on November 30, putting Brazil at risk of a government shutdown. The BCB had already raised borrowing costs to the highest levels in a decade, having doubled the benchmark interest rate from 7.25 percent in March 2013 to 14.25 percent by late 2015. That made no dent in double-digit inflation.

On December 1, 2015, Goldman Sachs warned of "outright depression" in Brazil following a 1.7 percent contraction during the second quarter of 2015.[106]

Calls for President Rousseff's resignation intensified as the Brazilian economy cratered. Her opponents accused her of using public bank funds to fudge the budget deficit during her second election year, a practice known as *pedaladas fiscais*. She and scores of Brazilians considered it part of a mounting coup or *golpe*.

House of Representatives president Eduardo Cunha started the impeachment process against Rousseff on December 2, 2015. Six days later, Rousseff's vice president, Michel Temer, executed a Judas move, publicizing a letter accusing Rousseff of having no confidence in him or his party.[107] He complained that she made him look like a "decorative" vice president rather than an active one.

Despite the mocking in the media that eschewed, Temer would have the last laugh—or second-to-last laugh, anyway. If Rousseff was tarred with scandal, he could be tarred with the same scandal.

Christmas brought no presents to Brazil. Rousseff's officials were jumping ship. On December 18, Levy left the government to become financial director at the World Bank (the number two spot under its president), spelling the economic end of Dilma's government. Levy's departure meant the government had lost control over the country's economic, fiscal, and monetary policy.[108]

Just before Christmas, on December 21, Rousseff's newly appointed minister of finance, Nelson Barbosa, a heterodox economist with a PhD from the New School in New York City, announced Petrobras didn't need a government injection.[109] He believed rising oil prices could solve its problems. The next day, Brazil's antitrust authority, CADE, opened investigations into contract rigging associated with the twenty-one companies and fifty-nine execs already under criminal probe.

Petrobras's problems hampered Brazil on multiple levels, beyond political scandal and the estimated $30 billion in indirect-effect GDP losses.[110] Owing to funding issues and regulatory requirements associated with the investigations, Petrobras stopped payments to other Brazilian firms, sending some into bankruptcy and others to the brink. Associated sectors were imperiled, including the navy and steel and construction sectors.

Petrobras was downgraded to junk by S&P on February 18, Moody's on February 24, and Fitch on May 11, 2016. Around the same time, Fitch downgraded seven Brazilian state companies to junk, all from the energy sector.[111] The banking sector fell under investigation for a myriad of crimes. Falling revenues plus higher costs resulting from greater debt burdens caused more trouble. Pension funds were increasingly underfunded, which intensified local population and political unrest.[112]

HAPPY 2016 (OR NOT)

The new year of 2016 kicked off with more bad news. Brazilian Christmas retail sales were the worst since 2005.[113] Rising debt, defaults, bankruptcies, jobs losses, lawsuits, and currency devaluation added to the dire picture.

The IMF concluded that Brazil wouldn't see growth until at least 2018, marking the first time in over a century Brazil would fail to expand for that long.[114] It forecast Brazil's 2016 GDP to shrink by 3.5 percent, after having contracted by 3.8 percent in 2015. This was also the first time since 1901 that Brazil had back-to-back recessions deeper than 3 percent. The prospect pressurized the BCB's first 2016 meeting. On one hand, financial markets expected another increase of 0.5 percent in rates (any more dovish measure would be considered a resumption of Rousseff's power over the BCB). On the other, entrepreneurs and workers criticized the idea of an increase.

In early January 2016, Tombini repeated his culpability dodge: "This has to do with political issues," he said,[115] thus deflecting responsibility for high rates and related instability to the government, which had not yet approved full fiscal adjust. He pressed Rousseff for more fiscal adjustment. Tombini said the BCB was deploying several remedies, including a "sizeable amount of international reserves, keeping a solid financial system... providing FX hedging instruments to the economy, and tightening monetary policy."

He did not consider depreciation in the real "a source of distress" and noted the Brazilian economy was less exposed to exchange rate risks because of its high reserve levels and the FX swap program instituted during the Fed's "taper tantrum" threat. He alluded that the labor market was adapting to the "economic slowdown," though "the presence of wage rigidities makes disinflation more challenging," meaning he hoped wages would sink. He vowed the BCB would maintain current rate policy for a "sufficiently prolonged period" to reach its inflation target by the end of 2016. Tombini knew he would lose either way. So, on January 20, 2016, he kept the benchmark rate unchanged at 14.25 percent.[116] A month later, on February 17, S&P further downgraded Brazil to junk status. The external fears about Brazil's scandals were compounded by its economic descent. But Brazil had some powerful external allies, an old one and a new one, jockeying for position.

BRAZIL'S FUTURE: THE UNITED STATES OR CHINA?

Beyond the political ground wars whipsawing Brazilians lay a critical battle between the East and the West for the soul of Brazil's international position. The US government, by not issuing any public statement in support of Rousseff's government, accentuated its desire to have her out. The issues were not about whether Brazil's political or financial landscape should be rid of corruption (in the United States, similar corruption in the form of kickbacks to politicians from the private sector was legalized in the form of campaign contributions) but of hegemony.

Geopolitical and geo-economic maneuvering reigned over monetary policy considerations. In the aftermath of the financial crisis, Lula's and Rousseff's governments crafted stronger ties with China relative to ties with the United States.

Rousseff supported the BRICS development bank, newly formed in 2014, to stand up to US-led Western equivalents, such as the IMF and World Bank. Trade between China and Latin America shot up from $10 billion in 2000 to $270 billion in 2012. Sino-Brazilian trade leapt from $6.5 billion in 2003 to $83.3 billion in 2012.[117] As of 2014, China was Brazil's top trade partner, followed by the United States and Argentina.

In February 2016, Brazilian senators met with a Chinese delegation to discuss the proposed bilateral agreement to build the R$40 billion (US$10 billion) Bi-Oceanic Central railway. It was to be an on-land road linking one coast to the other, from the Atlantic in Brazil to the Pacific in Peru, to provide more efficient routes for key products such as iron, soybeans, oil, chickens, and lithium to be exported to China. The Chinese delegation included chairman of Hsin Chong Construction Group, Lin Zhouyan.[118]

The South Port and Railway East-West Integration (Bi-Oceanic railway) was set to be financed, built, and operated by the China–Latin America Industrial Fund (CLAI Fund) and China Railway No.10 Engineering Group (CREC). The investment was to be made in conjunction with the Bahia Mining Company (Bamin) and the Bahia state government; Bahia was the second-most-important state, governed by Rousseff's Workers' Party.[119]

The United States was alarmed. Latin America has been the "backyard" of the United States since the Monroe Doctrine. The American government did not relish the prospect of seeing the continent's resources funneled to Asia. Because Rousseff's government was open to doing all sorts of deals with China, the United States would side with her opposition, albeit quietly at first—through the National Security Agency levying spying allegations against Rousseff and other foreign leaders.

China's worry was that its stake and future with Brazil could be imperiled without Rousseff. A new government could backtrack or nullify existing arrangements, meaning a loss of jobs but a gain in favor with the United States. Certain banks and businesses wanted Rousseff out for precisely the latter reason.

Rousseff's quandaries paved an avenue back to tighter US alliance and neoliberal policies, such as privatization, the lifting of capital controls that had limited certain hot money flows, and development projects that extracted profits rather than fostered collaboration for mutual benefit.

QE PUSHED US SPECULATORS INTO BRAZIL

Conditions were getting uglier. On March 4, 2016, federal police stormed Lula's home to take him in for questioning. Three investigations about Lula's connections with companies prosecuted in Operation Car Wash (OAS and Odebrecht) officially started on March 17, 2014, but became more prominent over the years.[120] In

Portuguese, *Operação Lava Jato,* or car wash, meant doing a thorough cleaning of Brazilian politics, a joint operation of the judiciary, prosecutors, and federal police, at the national level, against corruption in all spheres of government.

In a defensive move to protect her former mentor, Rousseff appointed Lula as her chief of staff on March 16, 2016.[121] According to the Brazilian constitution, ministers of state can be judged only by the supreme court. And Operation Car Wash was known to move slowly in the upper court.

It was a risky bet that was nearly blocked by Gilmar Mendes, a Justice official who had lunched with Serra—Rousseff's opponent in the 2010 election yet also one of the top officials investigated in the Car Wash operation—hours before deciding the case. Yet, all the drama drove the real and markets higher. In investors' minds, an end to Rousseff's reign and her leftist agenda was a preferable alternative to installing her opposition party's own equally scandal-plagued leader Michel Temer, a man tarred by Car Wash investigations for allegedly taking bribes and around whom bribery scandals in connection with JBS would continue to swirl through his presidency later.[122]

Every time it looked like curtains for Rousseff, the stock market rallied and foreign flows increased, just as they had during the height of the money-conjuring period. Two kinds of capital streamed in to the country: money betting on a quick turnaround and money sticking around for the long haul.

In April 2016, at his office in Brasília, Joao Barroso, senior adviser at Brazil's central bank (BCB), considered the effect of capital inflows on Brazil as connected to the Fed's artisanal money policies. According to his original analysis, over 54 percent of capital inflows from the United States to Brazil were caused *directly* by QE. Most of that capital flowed into Brazil's bond market, because rates there were so much higher than in the rest of Latin America.[123]

Barroso also estimated that up to 65 percent of total US portfolio flows to major Latin American countries were directly caused by the Fed's QE, isolating out all other factors. But, as he noted, "though these flows are small relative to the Fed's $4.5 trillion balance sheet, they are considerably large relative to the recipient economies."[124]

Throughout Latin America, US capital had coursed more into equity markets than into bonds. Speculative capital, funded near zero thanks to the Fed, craved higher returns. When Brazil showed less political and economic risk, the capital stuck around. As in the United States, investors weren't interested in long-term infrastructure projects but in short-term returns.

But in late 2015 and early 2016, the effects of political problems began to overwhelm those of Fed-stimulated cheap-money flows and masked the extra problem of leverage, or taking on too much debt during the good times without considering the consequences of unwinding it. More foreign debt saddled Brazil's corporations, which, as noted, the government subsidized by borrowing at 14.25 percent and lending to them at 2 percent—an unsustainable gap with which to run a country. But that was the lot that Brazil faced, given its difficulties manufacturing cheap liquidity compared to the developed countries that lent its companies money.

And that's why Barroso considered coordinating global and local monetary policy a difficult task. Beyond the big four central banks (of the US, Europe, Japan, and China), he said, "It's a game theory problem—everybody does their best for their country individually yet must balance the gains of coordination." Partly for this reason, Brazil turned to new alliances to augment its economic fortunes and secure its future. Yet, excess coordination pressures, when they don't help local economies, create major fractures.

The effect of the Fed's QE on Brazil was also related to proximity and good old-fashioned opportunism. The United States drove more capital flow globally, but that capital could retract on currency devaluation compared to the longer-term investment capital coming from China.

Brazil's secretary of international affairs Luis Balduino and Erivaldo Alfredo Gomes, undersecretary of Economic and Financial Institutions and International Cooperation at the Ministry of Finance, key figures in the Rousseff government, worked on Brazil's relationships with the New Development Bank (NDB; the new name of the BRICS bank established on July 15, 2014).

According to Balduino, the NDB sought to be viewed as a "serious" player in the development space, which, since the Bretton Woods agreement after World War II, had been dominated by the US and European World Bank and IMF. The NDB would "contribute to the $1 trillion financing gap that the G20 said needs to be filled," he stated. In the new power wars, the goal of fresh alliances and institutions like the NDB was to fund environmentally sustainable projects, which, because they were not based on old energy or reliant on oil and fossil fuels, extended collaborations beyond the old paradigm of the United States dollar and petrodollar. The shift that the mere existence of the NDB represented was historic.

In April 2016, in São Paulo, former finance minister Luiz Bresser-Pereira, who had helped design Brady bonds during the Latin American debt crisis of the 1980s, discussed his theory of "New Developmentalism." The theory states that when emerging countries rely more on local capital flows than on foreign speculation, they are more stable economically.[125]

According to Bresser, imperialism still existed. The US system impeded stability and autonomy in developing countries. The reality, he said, is that "countries like

Brazil don't really need foreign money or finance." Instead, they must develop more domestic finance and investment opportunities, which would also alleviate currency crises and wars.

He considered economies to be nationalistic: the world is still divided into nation-states that compete more than cooperate, which threatens social progress in general. Rather than being spent on people, cheap money constantly seeks to expand itself. The cheaper the money, Bresser argued, the more it can be used to help people. Yet, in practice, that didn't occur, especially in the developed world. Instead, fabricated money was used as a weapon in financial warfare. It altered domestic and international power structures by furnishing capital to the G7 nations and their banks so that they could speculate globally, especially in developing countries, in markets rather than in direct economic investment that benefited populations.

In the spring of 2016, beyond the "reality TV" aspect of the politics, as former president Lula called them in his interview with Glenn Greenwald of the *Intercept*,[126] something larger was at stake: a power struggle between the elites of the West and China.

TEMER'S "COUP"

Despite national protests and various hair-raising events—such as when the interim president of the House of Representatives, Waldir Maranhão, took over in the absence of Eduardo Cunha and tried to annul the impeachment process, which by that time was already in the senate[127]—impeachment of Rousseff barreled ahead. A Senate vote on May 12, 2016, concluded with her suspension and a decision to move toward impeachment.[128] Rousseff would fight the accusations of budgetary crimes, but it wasn't just Congress she was battling, it was the entire money-conjuring regime. They wanted her out.

Upon taking over as interim leader on May 13, 2016, former vice president Temer was quick to implement austerity. He vowed to cut government spending and audit social welfare programs for the poor to kick-start Brazil's economy.[129] Rousseff's old rival Serra became minister of foreign relations in the Temer government (serving in that position through April 2017), and he became responsible for global trade, too. In Brazil, unlike in the United States, the foreign minister has a dual responsibility for both diplomacy and foreign trade.

THE RETURN OF MEIRELLES

The harshest austerity measures were unveiled by Temer's newly appointed finance minister, none other than former BCB head Henrique Meirelles.

That decision made, speculation mounted over who from the two big private banks would win the central bank helm.[130] On May 17, 2016, Meirelles nominated

Itaú Unibanco Holding's chief economist Ilan Goldfajn to head Brazil's central bank.[131] Born in Israel, Goldfajn had many US and international ties. He had received his undergraduate and master's degrees in Brazil and earned his PhD in economics from the Massachusetts Institute of Technology in the United States. He had worked as an economist at the IMF and as an assistant professor at Brandeis University in New York.[132] He was a consultant for international entities (such as the World Bank, the IMF, and the United Nations), the Brazilian government, and the private sector.

Less than a month after assembling an interim cabinet, three of Temer's government ministers—the minister of planning, minister of transparency, and minister of tourism Henrique Alves—were fired. They were stained by allegations from Operation Car Wash.[133]

Temer, to the delight of foreign banks, spoke of privatizing public companies in the communication, postal services, airports, and smaller banks sectors. He considered removing Petrobras's exclusivity over pre-salt, which had benefited Chinese companies, and handing it over to other foreign oil companies—American and European ones.[134]

That summer, the 2016 Olympics brought further desperation to the people of Brazil. Temer signed an emergency loan to the State of Rio de Janeiro to help finance its infrastructure—in return for the state selling off its public water supply and sanitation company.[135] When the games opened in August, Temer was so despised he did not show his face at the ceremonies. Instead, he appeared on a big screen to a loud chorus of boos, with people watching worldwide.[136]

On August 17, 2016, Brazil's unemployment rate hit a four-year high of 13.3 percent from 6.5 percent at the end of 2014.[137] Meirelles responded by calling for austerity measures and pension reforms.[138] It was an unpopular move that would constrict an already anemic economy, yet it pushed the stock market up further. Within the new government, there was also disagreement over the real. Interim foreign minister Jose Serra warned against excessive appreciation, whereas Meirelles, true to neoliberal form, signaled less currency intervention to enable the real to float more freely.[139]

As head of the BCB, one of Meirelles's former aims had been to obtain more autonomy for the entity. Temer's interim government began constructing a constitutional amendment to underscore that very autonomy and give the BCB latitude to deploy *any means necessary* to meet its objectives, balancing financial stability with inflation targets.

"We call it operational autonomy," incoming central bank chief Ilan Goldfajn said. Goldfajn's former employer, Itaú Bank, had supported the bill since 2014. The spin was that an amendment would elevate international perception that the BCB operated independently of politics.

Meirelles's moves demonstrated a perfect domestic power circle—before Lula, he ran a major global division of FleetBoston, then he was head of the BCB, then he returned to the private sector, and now he was the main arbiter of monetary *and* fiscal policy in Brazil. All of these positions rested on his ties to the United States, including his JBS position, because Joesley Batista wanted to increase his business in the United States.[140] Meirelles left JBS as soon as he was nominated for the minister of finance position, moving directly from his JBS office into the Planalto Palace.

Goldman Sachs economist Alberto Ramos said the government's new "dream team" would "bring to the Temer administration a team of respected, well trained technocrats with very rich and valuable experience in both the private and public sectors."[141]

Under a photo of Meirelles depicted as a god bathed in white light flying with arms stretched skyward above the population, popular economic website Arena do Dinheiro (Money Arena) ran a piece called "Meet the Man Who Will Save the Economy of Brazil."[142] Brazil "is free to resume growth through liberalism, economic orthodoxy, confidence and transparency with the population with entrepreneurs and investors [with] friend of the market, Meirelles."

El País dubbed him "the favorite of the financial market crisis for Brazil," a man who "rocks the husky heart of the money men." Bloomberg called Meirelles "one of Brazil's most accomplished financial officials." "While lacking political charisma," Bloomberg noted, "the tall, balding and somber Meirelles, 70, is admired as well as ambitious and could position himself for a run at the presidency."[143]

On August 31, 2016, Rousseff's fate was sealed. She was officially impeached by the Senate in a 61-20 vote and lost her presidency.[144] Though it was the day of the final vote of the impeachment that suspended her from office, she had retained certain political rights. Now, she no longer had any power.[145]

And it was Michel Temer, not her, who boarded a plane to China, the country Rousseff had forged new alliances with, to attend his first G20 meeting. Those alliances would be caught in another money-conjuring vortex as global power battles between West and East continued to pivot around Brazil.

It had taken Meirelles only five years since his BCB ousting to achieve this victory over the two key elements of financial power in Brazil. He was again the country's chief artisan of money and was even in line to become Brazil's new president, a trifecta fait accompli. Brazil was again up for grabs with respect to alliances with either the United States or China.

The corruption scandals swirling around Temer's cabinet didn't stop, nor did they curb Meirelles's influence over economic and monetary policy. Even Speaker of the House of Representatives Eduardo Cunha (the bandleader of Rousseff's impeachment) was arrested on corruption charges in October 2016.[146]

As president, Temer made good on his promises of reform and austerity. On December 23, 2016, he levied what he dubbed "a great Christmas gift": a reform package that, among other things, increased the number of work hours in a day from eight to twelve and established a minimum retirement age of sixty-five regardless of the number of years worked. Meirelles said the government would not negotiate changes to its proposed minimum age of retirement of sixty-five years.[147] "In principle we don't have a plan B," he said.[148]

MEIRELLES THE HAWK BECOMES THE DOVE

In February 2017, all austerity measures aside, S&P maintained Brazil's junk status and negative outlook. (It had downgraded Brazil's long-term foreign and local currency sovereign rates to junk in September 2015 and February 2016.) The agency forecast low growth for the upcoming years and government debt rising toward 67 percent of GDP by 2019.[149] Meirelles downplayed these predictions, citing new structural reforms on the horizon. The markets responded enthusiastically to his statements and ignored economic concerns.

Meanwhile, the domestic scene became increasingly chaotic. In Espirito Santo, riots broke out while the police were not getting paid. Meirelles had directed fiscal policy that manifested as blood in the streets. In Rio Grande do Sul, under the government of José Ivo Sartori, ally of Michel Temer, and under Meirelles's guidelines, public research agencies and television stations were extinguished. Government employee wages were frozen, and the unemployment rate rose.

Yet Meirelles, with the confidence of a victor counting his spoils, declared the recession over multiple times.[150] It didn't matter that every major institute of economic research, including FGV (Fundação Getulio Vargas) and IPEA (Institute of Applied Economic Research), said the opposite.[151] On February 22, 2017, the BCB cut the SELIC rate by 75 basis points to 12.25 percent, the second cut in a row. With the official pronouncement of growth, Meirelles no longer needed to be a hawk. Nor did the BCB: "The reduction of interest rates in Brazil, which are among the highest in the world for a major economy, are seen as essential if Latin America's largest country is to recover from its worst recession in over a century," it noted.[152]

Temer was turning Brazil into a financial capital paradise, complete with extensive neoliberal fiscal policy and a twenty-year public spending cap proposal.[153] Meanwhile, Meirelles stood by his side. So did the central bank, set to enact the same policies that had led to such a rift between the elite beneficiaries of conjured-money policy and the population that suffered from it.

In the years since the US financial crisis, Brazil has gone from an internationally recognized regional power, respected for the strength of its economy, to a politically destabilized country with a weakened economy.

Responsibility for that decline was connected to multiparty economic elites and political hits and errors, as represented by Lula, Rousseff, and Temer. There was one common person who had worked with each of them: Henrique Meirelles, Brazil's conjurer of money. And as he sat in the government, his appointee in the BCB went about adopting the US Fed's strategy for economic stimulus, rendering money cheap. By May 31, 2017, the SELIC had been cut four times, from 13.75 percent to 10.25 percent, in contrast to Meirelles's former hawkishness.

On July 13, the parliament approved the 2018 federal budget proposal. The new minimum wage (as recommended by Meirelles) per month was set at R$979, or the equivalent of US$300. It was the smallest increase in the entire historical series. To compare it with other costs, consider that the average price for house or apartment rental in Brazil is R$1,000 per month.[154] Meirelles was also the main proponent of labor reforms that were punitive to workers, increasing hours and reducing guarantees of rest.[155]

The crisis Brazil faced, with no prospect of improvement until 2019 or 2020, was directly caused by the influence of Meirelles in Brazil's three most recent governments, first as chairman of the central bank, then as a government opponent working in the shadows with Washington, DC, and last as minister of finance. The relationship of Brazil with the Fed, IMF, China, and other global players was critically bound to the nation's disastrous economic and monetary policies that rendered it more of a passive participant on the global stage, albeit a pivotal one.

During the first G20 meeting held since Donald Trump became US president, in Hamburg in July 2017, Meirelles touted his accomplishments and Brazil's ameliorated condition: "We are managing in a very focused and concentrated way the economic agenda, the economy is going well, which is a more relevant aspect. The market has maintained relative stability. The labor reform is on the way. Pension reform should be discussed in the second half. In summary, we continue to work hard."[156] In reality, the unemployment rate was rising and economic activity was declining.[157]

On July 13, 2017, Meirelles's former boss Lula was convicted and sentenced to ten years in prison for graft.[158]

The SELIC hit 8.25 percent by September 2017, as Brazil's stock market rose in tandem. As for Meirelles: his bid for a trifecta loomed. Having run the central bank and the ministry of finance, in the fall of 2017, he began mounting his 2018 campaign for president.[159]

3

CHINA: Dragon Rising

The outbreak of the crisis and its spillover to the entire world reflect the inherent vulnerabilities and systemic risks in the existing international monetary system.

> —Dr. Zhou Xiaochuan, governor of the People's Bank of China,
> March 23, 2009

The twenty-first century rise of the People's Republic of China as an economic, monetary, and political superpower was accelerated by the US financial crisis and the Federal Reserve's collusion with G7 central banks to liquefy the financial system with conjured money.

China turned wary of the possibility of US economic contagion and publicly skeptical of the manner in which the US government enabled its banks to wreak global havoc as well as the links between cheap money, the US dollar's supremacy as the world's main reserve currency, and dangerous speculative asset bubbles. Concern and opportunity propelled China's geopolitical expansion in the 2010s following its economic expansion in the 2000s. The world's longest-serving G20 central bank head, Zhou Xiaochuan, who led China's central bank, the People's Bank of China (PBOC), was key to forging this destiny.

Zhou became governor of the PBOC in 2002. He was reappointed in 2007 and again in 2013. Zhou, born in 1948, the year the PBOC was established and the year before Mao Zedong proclaimed the establishment of the People's Republic of China (PRC), was the son of an early Communist Party member who mentored former Chinese president Jiang Zemin. Zhou trained academically as an engineer and was diplomatic in demeanor. His scholarly achievements provided him a similar gravitas in China to Ben Bernanke's in the US establishment.

On March 24, 2009, in a marquee speech, Zhou argued that the ongoing financial crisis was a by-product of loose regulations and US dollar dominance in the international monetary system. To diversify from the US dollar, he advocated moving the world, in general, and China, specifically, toward the IMF special drawing rights (SDRs) as a centrally managed global reserve currency.

Under Zhou's leadership, the PBOC provided extra liquidity to China's market by reducing reserve requirements (RRR) for Chinese banks. It adopted more market-friendly guidelines and transparency measures for the yuan to become a part of the IMF's SDR basket. Throughout China's march to greater influence on the global financial and monetary stage, Zhou engaged in constant public battles with the United States about the risks of US monetary policies.

There was something of the warrior Lao Tzu in his approach to pushing market reforms for the benefit of external consumption while pressing China's position as a superpower. Internally, Zhou orchestrated what he deemed best for China regardless of outside pressure. He spoke in reserved tones. For that very reason, his speeches often were misleading. Foreign politicians and press chided him and the PBOC for lack of transparency regarding its currency-related policies, but these US-led, often randomly dispensed criticisms rarely had numerical basis. In that regard, the PBOC was no different from any other central bank, including the Fed or the ECB.

President Jiang Zemin (1993–2003) first championed the notion of an ideal Chinese "socialist market economy."[1] In a 1997 speech addressed to Henry Kissinger and the late World Bank president Barber Conable, Jiang said, "The nonpublic sector is an important component of our socialist market economy."[2] Under his tutelage, and before Hu Jintao succeeded him as president, China became the fastest-growing economy in the world.[3] Zhou assumed his post on that wave of expansion and extended it to augment China's growing prominence in the superpower hierarchy, directly competing with the United States.

The US Fed assumed its role as global monetary policy coordinator as a result of the Bretton Woods agreement of 1944. But China began to play the long game after the financial crisis, disrupting US influence by increasing its own. This meant growing its economy, expanding its lending profile with countries that were formerly recipients of US debt, and forming fresh trade, currency, or other diplomatic partnerships with them by investing in long-term infrastructure and sustainable energy projects, and elevating its currency to one of the top five in the world. Even Japan, China's former foe and ally of the United States, chose to establish bilateral and multilateral agreements with China that were unheard of before the Fed began its collusion and money-conjuring scheme.

ZHOU'S INTUITION

During 2008, the Fed cut rates from 3.5 percent to 0–0.25 percent as the PBOC maintained rates at 7.5 percent until September 2008, when it cut rates to 7 percent and then further, landing at 5.8 percent in November.[4] Because of financial banking system turmoil during the first half of 2008, the US dollar fell against other major currencies. It even lost some of its luster as a safe-haven currency in late 2008, when the US-caused international financial crisis intensified and the Fed colluded to take global money-conjuring policy to unprecedented heights.

On March 6, 2008, ten days before the collapse of Bear Stearns, Zhou exhibited a moment of prescience.[5] Relying on his pragmatic and measured thinking as a trained engineer, he addressed a press conference on economic development and regulation held by the 11th National People's Congress (NPC) at the Great Hall of the People in Beijing. His assessment of the situation developing in the United States was prophetic.

Zhou saw an approaching boiling point and warned policymakers to be prepared for more fallout in the US banking system. Well before the broader US population became aware of it, and while US policymakers were pretending everything was fine, he told the gathering at the NPC, "The crisis has not yet run its course and it shouldn't be ignored."[6]

Yet, as the Fed entered a more aggressive money-conjuring mode toward the end of the year, Zhou reluctantly began decreasing rates, too, starting in September 2008. Five more reductions followed through December. Zhou pursued a gradual yuan valuation versus the US dollar (applauded by US policymakers) during the first half of 2008 as a way of controlling China's own rising inflation.[7] During the second half of 2008, he kept the yuan stable compared to the US dollar.

Zhou's deftness at his role—balancing what was good for China with caution for potential problems with external policies—took center stage. He understood the difference between the direct and indirect impacts of the escalating US subprime crisis on China.

"In terms of the direct impact," he said, "the proportion of subprime investments accounted for by Chinese financial institutions is relatively small, and they can handle it."[8] Indirect impact was another beast. As he opined, "The US economy may influence the global economy, for instance when it comes to trade, and...further effects." With the Fed poised to enter its longest period of zero interest rates ever, the PBOC's position on coordination or opposition was measured. "There's certainly room for interest rates to rise," said Zhou.

China needed to contain its domestic inflation, which required higher rates that lifted the value of the yuan. In the world of conjured money, this policy ran counter to the Fed's, yet in parallel with what the US government desperately wanted from China for trade purposes: a strong yuan that would render Chinese imports more expensive and US products more attractive price-wise.

On March 14, 2008, the yuan responded to the PBOC's policy of setting stronger exchange rate midpoints as a way to fight inflation (Chinese inflation had hit an eleven-year high of 8.7 percent in February 2008[9]). For two straight days, the PBOC elevated reference rates, pushing the yuan to 7.0875 against the dollar, its highest level since it abolished the fixed rate peg to the dollar in 2005.[10]

The renminbi (RMB) had been pegged at RMB 2.46 per US dollar for decades. During the 1970s, it was revalued until it hit RMB 1.50 per US dollar in 1980.[11] When China began opening its economy in the 1980s, the renminbi was devalued to lift the competitiveness of Chinese exports in an early form of currency wars. As its account balances improved, China adopted a higher peg of RMB 8.27 per US dollar from 1997 to 2005. On July 21, 2005, that peg was lifted. The yuan strengthened from July 2005 to July 2008. China reinstated the peg unofficially as the financial crisis intensified in July 2008.

Despite calamity within its own banking system, the United States was adamant about dictating the path of China's currency and financial policy. Just after the collapse of Bear Stearns, during his trip to China, Treasury secretary Hank Paulson, who later wrote a book touting his closeness with China, particularly during his days as the CEO and chairman of Goldman Sachs, noted that "a more flexible exchange rate is a more powerful tool in redirecting growth to domestic consumption."[12] He wanted China to look inward rather than compete.

China's reasons for being less protectionist had nothing to do with the United States but with internal inflation pressures due to rising food prices and its growing current account surplus. Yet Paulson chose to consider these items US related, or even US dictated. It was a power play combined with a pat on the back. The yuan gained 4 percent versus the dollar during the first quarter of 2008 compared with 6.86 percent in 2007.

Paulson was one of many US leaders obsessed with ruling China's currency policy and market reforms so as to open its capital borders to outside speculators, such as Brazil and other emerging nations were pressed to do. He tried to accomplish this change as a public servant, though he began this effort at Goldman Sachs, where he championed the firm's relationship with China for deal-making purposes. Like President Nixon, in whose administration Paulson had worked before he moved to Goldman Sachs, his visits to China sowed political and economic seeds.[13] "They've headed down the path to a market economy and capital markets are a very powerful force for good," he told the press in April 2008.

But like other US leaders, he had a blind spot for how the US banking system, compared to that of China (or of other countries), operated. He downplayed its propensity to cause financial destruction in the aftermath of the Bear Stearns collapse but before Lehman's and full-blown financial crisis. Instead, he pressed ahead with the ideologies of the Strategic Economic Dialogue initiative he began in 2006, to encourage China to liberalize its markets. As Paulson noted on a visit to China to speak with Chinese leaders on April 2, 2008, "The key is that, as they open up and they're the ones that create the regulatory structure,...the same rules will apply to all financial institutions."[14]

The US banking sector, including his former firm, would soon be bailed out by a combination of congressional funds and conjured-money policy. Paulson's concern about China's banking sector was misguided—it was the US banking system that would implode under a mélange of regulatory misses. In that wake, Chinese banks would ultimately rise in global stature. Paulson's brand of China-blaming was part of a bipartisan doctrine of similar diatribes, which China handled by attacking US monetary policy as it built up its own empire.

The Chinese government and the PBOC pressed yuan appreciation policy for its own purposes, not Paulson's or the United States'. By July 10, 2008, the yuan-dollar exchange rate hit 6.8464, its highest level since 2005.[15]

Unlike the more somber, "blank-faced," and reserved Hu Jintao, who cracked one joke (about hair dye) during his decade at the height of Chinese power,[16] Premier Wen Jiabao cultivated a friendly image with the upper echelons of Communist Party leadership and external leaders. His demeanor played well in international circles, enabling him to dispense uncomfortable truths about the subprime crisis, though for the most part they fell on deaf ears. In September 2008, at a meeting with Wall Street bankers, Wen underscored the rapid development of Chinese-US economic and trade relations as mutually beneficial to both countries and as contributing to global economic development, though the US subprime mortgage crisis triggered a financial upheaval.[17]

A few days later, at a World Economic Forum meeting, Wen warned, "The greatest challenge facing the international economy and finance is that the sub-prime mortgage crisis has affected some financial enterprises, even the physical economy, which resulted in the slowdown of global economy."[18] China had gotten caught in the storm of US regulatory and banking system recklessness and wasn't pleased about it.

As the financial crisis in the United States escalated, however, the PBOC found itself having to adhere more to the Fed's rate policy for liquidity reasons. On September 10, 2008, the PBOC reduced its benchmark loan interest rate and reserve requirement ratio for commercial banks by 0.27 percent to "foster economic growth." It was the first rate decrease since October 2005. The move reflected concern over the slowing economy and eased inflationary pressure.

The September 15, 2008, collapse of Lehman Brothers increased international instability. The Japanese yen benefited as "the" safe-haven currency, the largest reserve currency after the US dollar and the euro—which were both mired in banking problems—and exhibited its highest daily gain since 2002.[19] The Dow Jones Industrial Average (DJIA) experienced its biggest drop, 504 points, since the attacks on the World Trade Center on September 11, 2001.[20]

For the first time in ninety-five years, the Fed decided to accept equities as collateral for cash loans at one of its special credit facilities. It expanded its emergency lending avenues, while the ECB and Bank of England injected money into their codependent financial systems to keep them alive.

On September 29, 2008, the US House of Representatives rejected a proposed $700 billion rescue for banks, causing further upheaval.[21] The Standard & Poor's 500 stock index fell almost 9 percent, and the Dow Jones Industrial Average shed 778 points (almost 7 percent), to 10,365.45. The Nasdaq Composite fell 9.1 percent, its worst decline since the crash of 1987. Asian and European markets swan-dived.

A month later, the PBOC cut rates for the third time in six weeks, decreasing by 0.27 percent the one-year loan rate to 6.66 percent and one-year fixed deposits from 3.87 percent to 3.60 percent.[22] "China's economy is still facing relatively big downward pressure," the PBOC said. "At the same time, the overall level of domestic prices remains low, and real interest rates are still higher than the historical average."[23] China claimed it was little affected by the US financial crisis yet worried about global recession and the effect on its exports. That was not entirely accurate: the main concern in China was the effect the crisis would have on consumption and demand for Chinese products.

In November 2008, the PBOC cut its one-year lending and deposit rate by 1.04 percent, the largest reduction since the late-1990s Asian financial crisis. Its explanation echoed the Fed's, that the move was done "to implement a flexible monetary policy, to ensure the fluidity of the banking system, to ensure stable growth of credit and to demonstrate the positive role that monetary policy plays."[24] Zhou had temporarily shifted his discourse to both resonate with the Fed's strategy and emphasize the importance of his monetary policy.

It was clear to him and the Chinese government which country was hampering their growth and why. The PBOC noted, "China's economy has slowed significantly after the collapse of Lehman Brothers in September. Industrial growth slumped last month to a seven-year low while exports, imports, retail sales and fixed-asset investment all weakened."[25] Just before Christmas, the PBOC cut its key rates again in an effort, it said, to maintain economic growth and job levels. The one-year loan rate was cut by another 0.27 percentage point to 5.31 percent and the one-year fixed deposits decreased to 2.25 percent.[26]

YEAR OF THE OX

Throughout 2009, most developed countries' central banks dove deeper into money-conjuring mode. Emerging nations had to balance their domestic needs while succumbing to this directive, and the world economy saw no real recovery. Although the results of the Fed's policies did not boost US employment or growth rates, some

US banks declared considerable profits derived from the unrestricted use of cheaper money, while others remained at risk. To assign blame elsewhere for US economic problems, the US Treasury Department strongly criticized Chinese exchange rate policy and colluded with other developed countries to do the same.

Still, the US dollar suffered as the international community scrutinized its global role. In retaliation for the United States' accusations of currency manipulation, the Chinese government openly supported reform of the international monetary system and the role of the IMF and its special drawing rights as an alternative to the dollar. Emergent countries, the UN, and other international institutions also endorsed reconsideration of the structure of the international monetary system.

During the height of bank bailouts and cheap-money subsidies, and despite having presided over the NY Fed—the Wall Street "arm" of the Fed during the crisis incubation period—Tim Geithner labeled China the enemy. On January 23, 2009, during his Senate confirmation hearings, as the newly nominated Treasury secretary, Geithner said President Obama believed China was manipulating its currency[27] and that Obama would "use aggressively all the diplomatic avenues open to him to seek change in China's currency practices."[28] Those were financial fighting words. Geithner might have been a bit overzealous because the Obama administration declined to officially cite China for "manipulating" its currency,[29] but his public rhetoric kept the issue alive.

China was the largest foreign holder of US Treasury bonds, followed by Japan (until October 2016 when the two switched places).[30] As a result of Geithner's barbs, the price of long-term Treasury bonds dropped slightly, under expectations that Beijing would ease its purchases of US Treasury bonds in retaliation. But the reaction was brief, because China would only hurt the value of its portfolio of US Treasury bonds if it stopped buying US Treasuries. China's demand for US debt was a critical factor in keeping demand for it, and thus prices, up.

The Fed kept Treasury prices up and rates down through quantitative easing—or purchasing Treasury bonds. This had the effect of making the PBOC's stash of Treasury bonds rise in price as well. It presented a conundrum for China: selling Treasuries would reduce their portfolio value, but buying them was a tacit affirmation of US monetary policy. This was another reason Zhou led the charge for elevating the yuan as a reserve currency as a means to independence. The less reserves required to match US dollar volume, the more control China would have over its destiny.

At the end of Geithner's first visit to China in June 2009, *People's Daily*, the Chinese Communist Party's official newspaper, concluded, "After the US Treasurer's visit to China, it won't be hard to imagine someone saying, 'we know what happens when we buy US Treasury bonds. We won't be dancing around the US' baton.'"[31] It was hard to say whether China would become the United States' de facto ATM yet again,[32] but the writing was on the wall. China would not play nice with the United States while the United States remained critical of China, not while China was helping the United States by lending it money through buying its bonds.

On February 22, 2009, Hillary Clinton, the new US secretary of state, decided to end her trip around Asia by visiting Beijing. There, she met with Chinese president Hu Jintao, Chinese premier Wen Jiabao, and Chinese foreign minister Yang Jiechi. They discussed how to act jointly to foster global economic recovery. In an interview with Shanghai-based Dragon TV, Clinton presented herself as a team player. Now the United States needed China: "We are truly going to rise and fall together. Our economies are so intertwined, the Chinese know that to start exporting again to their biggest market the United States has to take some very drastic measures with this stimulus package, which means we have to incur more debt."[33] To Chinese leaders, Clinton exuded confidence in the integrity of US Treasury bonds to ensure Beijing would keep buying them.[34]

She had sung a different tune during the 2008 presidential campaign season when she had characterized the Chinese accumulation of US Treasury bonds and debt, in general, as a threat to national security: "It undermines our capacity to act in our own interest,"[35] Clinton said in response to a question after her address to the Council on Foreign Relations. "We can too easily be held hostage to the economic decisions being made in Beijing, Shanghai and Tokyo," she wrote to Paulson and Bernanke in 2007.[36]

On March 10, 2009, with the Dow in the basement, Fed chair Ben Bernanke spoke on systemic risk to the Council on Foreign Relations in Washington, DC. He echoed Clinton's refrain of rising and falling together, but he shifted culpability for the fallout of the Fed's inadequate US banking regulation onto the world. He characterized "global imbalances" that generated financial crises as the "joint responsibility of the United States and our trading partners."[37] The United States could do the crime, but the rest of the world was expected to do the time.

He listed four premises of the Fed's strategy to confront such crises, addressing the issue of "too big—or perhaps too interconnected—to fail," strengthening financial system infrastructure, reviewing regulatory policies and accounting rules so they "do not overly magnify the ups and downs in the financial system and the economy," and considering whether the creation of an authority charged with monitoring and addressing systemic risks would help protect the system from financial crises.[38] Technically, the latter was already one of the Fed's primary jobs.

Meanwhile, China was growing weary of suffering the consequences of US actions it could not influence. On March 13, at the close of the annual National People's Congress meeting in Beijing, Premier Wen Jiabao questioned the capacity of the United States to honor its financial promises. He noted that during the past few years the United States had depended on Chinese purchases of Treasury bonds to finance its budget deficit. "We have lent a huge amount of money to the United States,[...] I am a little bit worried. I request the US to maintain its good credit, to honor its promises, and to guarantee the safety of China's assets."[39] In a money-conjuring irony, the more debt the United States incurred in the wake of the financial crisis, and because the Fed policy was keeping Treasury prices high and rates low, the proportion of debt China held was lowered. The Fed would begin to own more debt than China through QE.

Because of the US-related decrease in exports and consequent job cuts, China worried about its yuan. Yet Wen Jiabao had to defend China's exchange rate policy against ongoing US criticism that demanded depreciation. He did so using actual numbers. "I don't think the [yuan] is depreciating. Since we reformed the exchange rate in July 2005, the yuan has appreciated 21 percent against the US dollar.[...] No other country can put pressure on our country to depreciate or appreciate the [yuan]." He added, "This is our independent decision and we will not be subject to any outside pressure on the appreciation or depreciation of renminbi."[40]

While serving during Hu Jintao's presidency, Wen Jiabao, former premier, was in charge of economic policies. He sought to rebalance China's growth to move toward a consumer-led model and away from investments and exports. He said, "Reform and opening up are the fundamental force that drives China's development and progress."[41]

Wen blamed the US financial system outright for the global recession—in response to Geithner's confirmation hearing rhetoric against China. According to the *Wall Street Journal*, the PBOC had stopped lending its Treasury holdings for fear the borrowers would go bankrupt.[42] It was an exaggerated depiction, but its point was clear.

China's government and central bank both espoused the dangers posed by the US-led global monetary system. On March 23, 2009, the PBOC released a critical document titled "Reform the International Monetary System" by Zhou.[43] It underscored the difficulty countries had honoring domestic monetary policy concerns while meeting the world's demand for reserve currencies, a situation known as the Triffin dilemma. The conflict, first identified by economist Robert Triffin in the 1960s, exists in monetary policy decision making regarding balancing short-term domestic and long-term international goals: countries whose currencies are global reserve currencies often need to provide an extra currency supply to meet international demand but in doing so could face an additional trade deficit as a result.[44]

The report made a monumental pronouncement. For the first time publicly, Zhou called for the inauguration of a supranational reserve currency related to the IMF's special drawing rights basket—to be managed by the IMF itself. Zhou's statement was a declaration of monetary policy warfare. He openly criticized the United States' inability to restore international liquidity in a definitive way and questioned the right of the US dollar to retain its position as the dominant world reserve currency. In the meantime, the Fed, for its part, was opening all sorts of avenues to provide banks liquidity.

Zhou advised: "The crisis again calls for creative reform of the existing international monetary system towards an international reserve currency with a stable value, rule-based issuance and manageable supply, so as to achieve the objective of safeguarding global economic and financial stability."[45] He was aware of the problems arising from global collusion in the pursuit of monetary policy, a situation into which the Fed had thrown the world.

He stressed, "The SDR has the features and potential to act as a super-sovereign reserve currency." The SDR was not a currency, per se, but the SDR basket could serve as a reserve or backup to any currency, just as reserves at the Fed and other central banks served as a backup to the US dollar. Zhou added, "Compared with separate management of reserves by individual countries, the centralized management of part of the global reserve by a trustworthy international institution with a reasonable return to encourage participation will be more effective in deterring speculation and stabilizing financial markets."

The idea of a collective currency had its downside. It aggregated the monetary powers of the major countries reflected by the SDR, but it also blended them in a more representational way, and it was a model that could extend to more currencies or even include gold. Moving toward a currency connected to the SDR basket would diffuse the US dollar's and US monetary policy's power, even as it lent power to the IMF, which was largely a US construct.

The next day, in retaliation for Zhou's antidollar campaign, President Obama, Bernanke, and Geithner united to vehemently reject the idea of a supranational reserve currency. This was about preserving US power over China. At a press conference, Obama emphasized, "I don't believe that there's a need for a global currency," adding, "The reason the dollar is strong right now is because investors consider the United States the strongest economy in the world with the most stable political system in the world."[46]

A week later, the G20 kicked off its second meeting in London to discuss solutions to the international crisis. In its pivotal "Leader's Statement," the group overrode the US objection to Zhou's suggestion. Leaders supported the IMF's capacity to provide international liquidity and establish a stable international monetary system. The statement was the first crack in the wall of the Bretton Woods Anglo-American-European construct. Yet it preserved and promoted the power base of one of its central entities, the IMF.

"The agreements we have reached today," the G20 statement read, "constitute an additional $1.1 trillion program of support to restore credit, growth and jobs in the world economy. Together with the measures we have each taken nationally, this constitutes a global plan for recovery on an unprecedented scale."[47]

About two months later two other cracks in the Bretton Woods wall came in quick succession from the BRIC nations.[48] On June 10, 2009, Brazil announced it would lend $10 billion to the IMF.[49] President Lula said he hoped it would influence future reforms of the multilateral organism in consideration of Brazil's prominent role. China and Russia announced loans to the IMF of $40 billion and $10 billion, respectively. Lula affirmed the importance of emergent countries in the wake of the US financial crisis: "The good news is that rich countries are in crisis and that emerging countries are making a huge contribution to save the economy and consequently, save the rich countries.... Wealthy countries are no longer the only ones that account for the world's production capacity and consumption."[50]

The second fracture resulted from the BRIC meeting in Yekaterinburg, Russia, on June 16, 2009. This first meeting of these four major developing nations did not include South Africa (which later made the group the BRICS nations). The meeting highlighted multilateralism and offered strong criticism of the world's financial situation, the crux of BRICS dogma.[51]

A week earlier, the chairman of China Construction Bank (CCB) Guo Shuqing called on the US government to issue bonds in yuan instead of US dollars. He affirmed plans to allow Chinese and foreign companies to settle bills in yuan rather than in dollars. The first chairman of a major Chinese bank to support wider use of the yuan, he concluded that "the US government and the World Bank can consider the issuing of renminbi bonds."[52]

Further moves away from the United States followed. On July 23, 2009, the Bank of Japan announced the first Tripartite Governor's Meeting of the PBOC, the BOJ, and the Bank of Korea (BOK) in Shenzen, China, to strengthen "mutual cooperation and communication and better safeguard economic and financial stability in the region."[53] A year later, these ASEAN-3 launched a multilateral currency swap agreement called the Chiang Mai Initiative to provide access to each other's currencies in the event of a credit crisis.

A month later, on August 13, the IMF announced the allocation of $250 billion in special drawing rights to be followed by another $33 billion.[54] The SDR basket's $283 billion total had increased in size tenfold as a consequence of the G20's April meeting in London.[55]

China would not rest until the yuan was part of the SDR basket. When the IMF was first established after World War II, the idea was to have a global currency, but the United States dismissed that notion and fought instead for the dollar to assume the distinction of being the world's main reserve currency. The shift to SDRs was a power play for the IMF. Pressing for the inclusion of the yuan was a power play for China.

Within a week, China became the first country to buy five-year bonds denominated in SDRs offered by the IMF. The symbiotic relationship between the IMF and China was an indirect attack on the power of the United States. China paid RMB 341.2 billion, or US$50 billion, as part of that strategy.[56]

Strengthening its international capital markets presence, for the first time on September 8, 2009, China issued $878 million worth of sovereign bonds denominated in renminbi in Hong Kong to offshore investors.[57] It was another step to converting the yuan into an international reserve currency. Since 2007, five state-owned Chinese banks had been doing that, including the Bank of China and the China Construction Bank, but only to domestic investors. This was a departure from them.

Battle lines were drawn. International central bankers leveled stronger, coordinated criticism of China's national currency policy. On October 4, 2009, at IMF meetings in Istanbul, the G7 finance ministers and central bankers demanded China strengthen its currency to correct imbalances in global trade. "We welcome China's continued commitment to move to a more flexible exchange rate, which should lead to continued appreciation of the Renminbi in effective terms."[58]

Chinese central bank vice governor Yi Gang responded that China's policy toward exchange rates would continue to emphasize stability. "Our exchange rate policy is very clear," he told Reuters.[59]

Because it foresaw a longer term in which to achieve its goals, the PBOC somewhat relented. In its 2009 Q3 monetary policy report, the central bank signaled it would work on yuan appreciation in the medium/long term and that the yuan's value would be referenced to a basket of currencies and leave aside its dollar peg. This would "enable market supply and demand to play a fundamental role in the yuan exchange-rate formation and to keep the exchange rate basically stable at an adaptive and equilibrium level."[60]

This happened to be in keeping with the Fed and ECB's money-conjuring policy. So, politically, China was choosing to placate the United States, on the one hand, while pushing its agenda forward with the IMF and other countries, on the other.

YEAR OF THE TIGER

While the central banks of developed countries maintained money-conjuring policies in 2010, the PBOC did the opposite. On January 6, it stated that it would "continue to implement appropriately easy monetary policy," but it would also raise three-month bill interest rates. The dual rate decision resulted from the PBOC finding itself caught up in that Triffin dilemma.

Meanwhile, US Treasury secretary Tim Geithner adopted a different, more conciliatory strategy regarding China's yuan policy. During a trip to India in early April 2010, in an interview with NDTV, Geithner said, "I am confident that China will decide it's in their interest to resume the move to a more flexible exchange rate that they began some years ago and suspended in the midst of the crisis."[61]

After India, Geithner traveled to Beijing. There, he had a private conversation with vice premier Wang Qishan. As *China Daily* wrote, "The decision to hold such a high-level encounter suggested that Washington and Beijing are trying to narrow their differences over currency that threaten to overshadow cooperation on the global economy, Iran's nuclear program and other issues."[62] The United States' sudden, more appeasing stance served as a way for the Obama administration to keep China out of Russia and counterbalance Japan's expansion.

Four days later, on April 12, at the biannual Nuclear Security Summit, held in Washington, DC, the currency topic arose. President Hu Jintao told Obama that China would follow its own course in reforming the yuan.[63] It was the first time the two had met since November 2009. Hu affirmed China's autonomy but confirmed, "China will firmly stick to a path of reforming the yuan exchange rate formation mechanism."

The Chinese government and the PBOC loosened the yuan's peg to the dollar on June 19, 2010, as promised.[64] The decision was viewed as a white flag in the spirit of alleviating China-US tensions regarding trade and exchange rate policy. As a result, the yuan hit its highest value in five years against the dollar. The move brought optimism to international markets, and stocks in London, Frankfurt, Paris, and New York rose. Chinese officials began traveling with key bankers to promote the use of the yuan in international trade and capital markets.

That summer, a growing chorus of global private banks promoted the idea that corporations use the yuan instead of the dollar in trade deals with China. The benefit was having more choices in their currency dealings, which meant they could evaluate which currency was more cost-effective or profit-producing rather than be confined to the major existing currencies. HSBC and Standard Charter offered financial incentives to companies opting for such trade deals. Throughout the developed world, these and US banks, such as Citigroup and JPMorgan, accompanied PBOC officials on roadshows to promote the Chinese renminbi.[65]

All of that focus on currency and trade levels served as a diversion from what was really important to China: becoming a superpower. To do so, it was imperative it maintain pressure on the current monetary system. On October 9, 2010, at the twenty-second meeting of the International and Monetary Financial Committee in Washington, DC, Zhou presented a detailed critique of the monetary policies of major countries such as the United States, United Kingdom, European Union, and

Japan.[66] According to him, they negatively affected the way emergent countries were supposed to deal with their own monetary policies. He lambasted money-conjuring policies. "Recovery in developed countries continues to rely heavily on unconventional stimulus policies, and private consumption and investment continue to be inhibited by high unemployment and insufficient credit."

He indirectly admonished US and Fed policy regarding handling of the aftermath of the financial crisis and the big US banks that had not been properly punished or restructured: "The countries concerned need to accelerate their disposition of toxic assets, restructure problem institutions, supplement bank capital, strengthen financial regulation, and rebuild sound financial systems." He said, "The continuation of extremely low interest rates and unconventional monetary policies by major reserve currency issuers have created stark challenges for emerging market countries." But the United States wasn't listening to such critiques, certainly not those from China.

Yet, around the world, central banks and finance ministers—implicitly or explicitly, depending on whether they hailed from G7 or G20 nations—became skeptical of the Fed's policies and thus began taking China's side on the matter. Brazil's minister of finance Guido Mantega voiced his concerns on October 8, 2010.[67] On November 8, Germany's finance minister Wolfgang Schäuble waxed so openly critical in an interview with the German newspaper *Spiegel*[68] that President Obama had to defend the Fed's second round of QE at the G20 summit in South Korea.[69]

On October 19, for the first time since December 2007, the PBOC raised rates by 25 basis points.[70] The yuan had risen 2.5 percent against the dollar since August, its fastest appreciation since the 2005 revaluation. This was the opposite of Fed policy—and was not necessarily intended to appease US currency demands. That November, China hit a record in exports. Its trade surplus relative to the United States exceeded $20 billion for the fifth time in six months. Inflation rose to its highest level in twenty-eight months, at 5.1 percent.[71]

In the United States, all continued as usual. Bernanke was reelected for a second term in the toughest chairman election in Fed history. In November 2010, the Fed began its second round of QE (QE2), purchasing $600 billion worth of US Treasury bonds in $75 billion per month increments. US unemployment had hovered above 9 percent all year, calling into question the effectiveness of US monetary policy to boost growth or job creation.

On Christmas Day, in a one-sentence announcement, the PBOC raised rates another 25 basis points.

YEAR OF THE RABBIT

China continued its attack on the status quo. On January 17, 2011, President Hu Jintao told the US press that an international monetary system dominated by the US dollar is "a product of the past."[72] Nevertheless, he believed it would take time for the yuan to be accepted as a global reserve currency.

Chinese banks, the third pillar of China's power triangle along with government and central banks, were increasing their global presence in lending. Between 2009 and 2010, two major state-controlled Chinese banks, the Export-Import Bank of China and China Development Bank, lent more than the World Bank to developing countries, about $110 billion versus the World Bank's $100 billion.[73]

On February 9, the PBOC raised rates for the third time in four months.[74] The move underscored concern over rising food and commodity prices in emergent countries. It came one week after the IMF's deputy director John Lipsky expressed concern about emergent economies' capacity to sustain growth even as many still had "expansionary" monetary policies. The cure is clear, he said: "Everybody is going to need to tighten monetary policy, reduce budgetary stimulus and continue with the process of structural reforms."[75] None of the world's major central banks adhered to that advice, with the exception of China. The structural reforms part, or austerity, was the way the IMF and World Bank dealt with developing countries, pushing austerity in times of need, constricting citizens instead of speculative opportunists.

On March 5, 2011, opening the annual National People's Congress in Beijing, Chinese premier Wen Jiabao addressed more than three thousand party delegates. He said the government expected an 8 percent growth rate in 2011 and aimed to keep inflation at 4 percent, because he recognized that prices were increasing quickly. "This problem concerns the people's well-being, bears on overall interests and affects social stability."[76] Inflation accelerated despite the rate hikes.

The strategy highlighted differences between China, which juxtaposed monetary policies with concerns over social responsibilities, and Western central banks, which seemed less concerned about people's protests or levying austerity measures. In the middle of 2011, Beijing, increasingly concerned about the social unrest that rising costs could cause, promised to assuage higher prices, such as of pork, a dietary staple, with government intervention.[77] The Western central banks, on the other hand, were cheerleading a supposed recovery in the United States despite prevailing economic anxiety. In Europe, austerity measures were being levied across the so-called PIIGS countries of Portugal, Italy, Ireland, Greece, and Spain, to make up for budget shortfalls.[78] Yet, these shortfalls were the direct results of the financial crisis and the European Central Bank supporting banks and investors through QE over social programs for people. In London, anti-austerity, antibank protestors smashed windows at multinational banks such as HSBC and Santander.[79]

On May 18, 2011, Dominique Strauss-Kahn resigned his position as head of the IMF under the clouds of a sexual assault scandal. In contention for the role of managing director was former French finance minister and international lawyer

Christine Lagarde. That was good news for China. In early June 2011, Lagarde visited China and spoke with several key officials there, including foreign minister Yang Jiechi, central bank governor Zhou Xiaochuan, finance minister Xie Xuren, and vice premier Wang Qishan.[80] Prior to her visit, she had traveled to India and Brazil, in keeping with her views on supporting emerging countries.

In Beijing, she told the press that it would be "very legitimate for Chinese representatives to be included at the highest level of the Fund's leadership." It was then that Lagarde and Zhou developed a friendly rapport based on mutual goals. She would have a strong ally in the East if she got the top IMF spot, and he would have an advocate for China in the IMF. In general, Lagarde was warmly received by the Chinese establishment as a supporter of China's initiatives to take a more prominent role on the global stage. In terms of forging an East-West alliance for the twenty-first century, she was one of the most instrumental world leaders.

On July 5, Lagarde was elected the eleventh managing director (and first female leader) of the IMF.[81] Her only competitor, Mexican central bank chief and prior IMF deputy managing director Agustín Carstens, was supported by Australia, Canada, and Mexico. China supported Lagarde, who supported the inclusion of the yuan in the SDR. So did the United States, which, despite Lagarde's support of China, stuck with the historical protocol of choosing a European leader over the emerging market candidate; also, as central banker, Carstens had focused more on inflation-related rather than money-conjuring policies.[82]

The following month, the yuan crossed the 6.40 line against the dollar for the first time in seventeen years.[83] Meanwhile, Europe was facing a growing debt crisis. The G7 held an emergency Eurozone meeting on August 7, 2011, to consider ways to provide liquidity to the region.[84]

With a possible return to crisis, nothing could be left to chance. The Fed announced it would keep rates at zero. The ECB intervened in Italy's and Spain's bond markets.[85] The Bank of England announced it would provide more stimulus if needed. The BOJ expressed concern about yen appreciation, and Switzerland announced an effort to contain an overvalued franc. They all worried about renewed global recession. In their post-meeting statement, the leaders promised they would "take all necessary measures to support financial stability and growth in a spirit of close cooperation and confidence."[86] Money-conjuring policy had not helped, yet it was the only item on the menu. China continued to stay out of that particular fray.

Still, the credit situation in Europe worsened. On September 25, Lagarde warned that the IMF's $384 billion emergency bailout fund was insufficient to support some countries' current economic situation in worst-case scenarios.[87]

Emerging countries called for solutions to the escalating Eurozone crisis. At the August IMF and World Bank meeting, Brazil's finance minister Guido Mantega had said that Europeans had a responsibility "to ensure that their actions stop contagion beyond the euro periphery."[88] PBOC governor Zhou had echoed this sentiment, stating, "The sovereign debt crisis in the euro area needs to be resolved promptly to stabilize market confidence."[89]

Now China was cast into the position of helper. Europe in need was an opportunity to take a more long-term tack toward a tighter alliance. Zhou told reporters that the timing of China's assistance to Europe depended on what the Europeans did next.[90] He thought the IMF should safeguard the long-term sources of funds to meet the needs of member states to tackle the crisis while promoting international diversification of the reserve currency system.[91] In that way, he was implicitly supporting the weaker European countries over the stronger ones and attacking the prevailing monetary system. Actions were being taken to forge tighter regional relationships, including with Vietnam, Pakistan, and Russia.[92]

On Christmas Day in Beijing, Chinese premier Wen Jiabao met with Japanese prime minister Yoshihiko Noda as part of the Japan–People's Republic of China Summit.[93] In an unexpected decision, the governments announced that both countries would promote direct trading of the yen and yuan, reducing their dependence on the US dollar in these transactions. The agreement was accompanied by one between Japanese and Chinese banks to establish a $154 million fund to co-invest in environmental technology and energy-efficiency businesses.

On New Year's Eve 2011, Zhou told Chinese news agency Caixin that China would maintain a "prudent" monetary path to ensure stability in 2012. He reaffirmed his compromise to "deepen financial reform, accelerate the development of financial markets, and strengthen and improve foreign-exchange management."[94] The performance of the yuan in 2011 was the best since 2009, which highlighted the commitment of the Chinese government to yuan stability and Zhou's plan to turn the yuan into an international reserve currency.

YEAR OF THE DRAGON

Money-conjuring policy had yielded no obvious results in global growth or stability. As a consequence of low economic activity, political and economic groups in Japan, Europe, and the United States divided into two camps: those that supported easy monetary policies and those that didn't.

But China—after three years of fiscal stimulus—was showing early signs of an economic slowdown as its use of the infrastructure it had constructed stalled.[95] The trade surplus diminished, and the Eurozone crisis caused speculators to shed emerging markets' assets.[96] Assets had fallen to $2.18 trillion on December 31, 2011, from $3.2 trillion on September 30, 2011. The steep quarterly drop was the first since 1998, during the Asian financial crisis. On January 13, 2012, China's foreign exchange reserves had decreased as investment from abroad moderated.

Thus it become more important for China to encourage external investment. On March 12, amid high volatility, capital outflows, and China's biggest global trade deficit in a decade, Zhou offered a carrot to external speculators saying, "We will allow and encourage market forces to play a bigger role, and the central bank's participation and intervention in the market will decrease in an orderly manner."[97]

The rest of the world, as economically dependent as it was on China's ongoing expansion, turned apprehensive. During the summer, for the first time since the 2008 crisis, the PBOC decided to cut rates in response to the reduction in economic activity.[98]

Zhou always tried to show the press his concern with "market forces," though some insiders thought that was his brand of marketing strategy. He was ambitious. Zhou was not only the chief monetary architect behind the yuan's internationalization project (for which global acceptance was essential) but historically supportive of China's social market ideology based on a mixture of state-owned enterprise and a desire for an open market economy. Despite that, he was committed to the Chinese way of doing things, supporting the party and the government.

While Zhou attempted to show that China was opening more toward external investors and capital flows, in the United States, at a lecture at George Washington University on March 20, 2012, Ben Bernanke took another swipe at China, its currency, and gold in one go. He explained that the problems regarding establishment of a monetary system based on the gold standard could be seen by analyzing the current Chinese dollar peg.[99]

Bernanke emphasized the flaws of a gold standard monetary system as exactly those faced by China. He both criticized China's peg to the dollar and associated it with the gold standard to show that China's problems would become the world's if things were done China's way—or if a gold standard was readopted. He wanted to keep the system as it was—not be the victim of a monetary system shake-up at the hands of China—by pointing out China's weaknesses and dependence on the United States. "If the Fed lowers interest rates and stimulates the US economy, that means also that essentially monetary policy becomes easier in China as well. Those low interest rates may not be appropriate for China," he said. "China may experience inflation because it's tied to US monetary policy."

Bernanke wanted to make it clear that the old system would never return. In reality, a renewed gold standard would usurp the Fed's power as the chief central bank of the world's dominant currency. "Since the gold standard determines the moncy supply, there's not much scope for the central bank to use monetary policy to stabilize the economy." Bernanke's real problem with gold, or any other standard, was that it diminished not the power of central banks in general but the power of *his* central bank.

On April 13, 2012, China expanded the yuan's trading band against the dollar, a measure indicating an attempt to diminish restrictions over its financial markets. The PBOC announced the yuan would be able to rise or fall 1 percent against the dollar on a daily basis, from a midpoint. Before that, the range of movement, established in 2007, was 0.5 percent.[100]

Three days later, the yuan fell the most in a single week versus the dollar.[101] The US government jumped to accuse Beijing of depreciating the yuan in order to hurt US manufacturers and contribute to a US trade deficit with China, which had risen 8 percent to $295 billion in 2011.

The United States believed that if the yuan exchange rate value was artificially lowered, the cost of buying exported goods from China was also lower, rendering China more competitive on the global market relative to the United States. (These accusations were disingenuous because the trade deficit had widened *before* this when the yuan value versus that of the dollar was higher.)

In early May 2012, Hillary Clinton, US secretary of state, and Tim Geithner, US secretary of the Treasury, traveled to Beijing. There they joined vice premier Wang Qishan and state councilor Dai Bingguo at the fourth joint meeting of the US-China Economic and Strategic Dialogue.[102] At those talks, Geithner said yuan appreciation was important to aid China in reshaping its economy and opening its markets. He was relentless, as if the entire future of the US economy was contingent upon minute differences in the dollar-yuan exchange rate. He stressed, "The United States has a strong interest in the success of these reforms, as does the rest of the world."[103]

Geithner praised the fact that the yuan had gained 13 percent over the last two years. Zhou, meanwhile, noted that market forces would prove whether the yuan was imbalanced, and if so, the market would have the power to correct it.[104] He was throwing US policy back at the United States.

The United States wanted it both ways: open markets and a strong yuan, regardless of whether those open markets would support it. At the same time, the Eurozone debt crisis brought greater political problems. Risk aversion drove the dollar index to its highest level since September 2010. The dollar was appreciating regardless of what the PBOC did.

The Chinese economic slowdown eventually reduced appreciation pressure on the yuan. As a result, on June 8, 2012, the PBOC announced its first interest rate cut since 2008.[105] The one-year lending rate was reduced 0.25 percent to 6.31 percent, and the one-year deposit rate to 3.25 percent. A month later, the PBOC cut the one-year lending rate to 6 percent.[106] To maximize the effect, it allowed banks to lend at 70 percent of that rate, down from 80 percent.

The Chinese government grew anxious. China's growth rate had fallen from the first quarter to 8.1 percent, the slowest economic activity since the summer of 2009.[107] However, inflation and potential asset bubbles remained concerns.

And although the yuan had steadfastly appreciated, that still wasn't enough for the United States, which maintained its public crusade against China's exchange rate policy. The Fed demanded monetary policy supremacy and collusion over conjuring money. The PBOC wanted to chart its own path.

In September 2012, the Fed embarked on its third round of quantitative easing (QE3). It claimed this was because of poor economic recovery, but major US banks were struggling under the scrutiny of their practices by prosecutors during the financial crisis. And it was an election year. The Fed tended to favor the party in power, though it theoretically operated as an independent entity. It also protected the biggest banks. Emergent countries saw this US monetary policy as irresponsible, fostering financial instability in the guise of promoting an economic recovery whose goal line kept changing.

On October 10, Zhou did not appear at the IMF meetings in Tokyo as expected—officially, because of a scheduling conflict but ostensibly because of the disputes between Japan and China over the islands in the East and South China Seas.[108] His deputy Yi Gang went instead. Rumors about Zhou's absence intensified after representatives from China's four major banks—the Industrial and Commercial Bank of China, Bank of China, China Construction Bank, and Agricultural Bank of China—chose not to attend the meetings either in protest of the territorial dispute.

Whenever things got complicated between China and Japan, the populations resumed their rivalry. In comparison, Japan and the United States had complementary economies and their central banks collaborated. A more prominent China could shift the balance of power in the region, resulting in loss of influence of Japan and, by extension, the United States.

On October 11, 2012, for the first time in nineteen years, the yuan rose to 6.28 per dollar as investors speculated on coming artisanal measures to revive economic growth in China.[109] It was the yuan's strongest level since China unified market exchanges in 1992. A month later, Zhou declared inflation was the main risk for China while again promising to transition to a more market-based economy with deeper financial reforms. "On the one hand, we need to maintain a healthy economy, but we also feel deeply that the People's Bank of China must push forward reforms and opening up."[110]

At the Caixin Summit on November 17, Zhou further explained his integrated philosophy.[111] "It is the central bank's job to maintain the health and stability of all key economic indicators while supporting the government's reform agenda...the risk of high inflation looms at all times, and the central bank should always be on guard against it."[112] By that time, China's inflation rate had fallen after the PBOC's two-year fight to return it to the 4 percent government target.

China continued poking holes in US and ECB money-conjuring policy. The PBOC's third-quarter report for 2012 noted "a by-product" of the Fed's third round of QE could be "excessive liquidity which could lead to large fluctuations in cross-border capital, price hikes of international commodities and eventually growing inflationary risks."[113]

On November 27, given mounting geopolitical tensions around the South China Sea, the US Treasury Department again accused China of maintaining the yuan as "significantly undervalued."[114] It represented a step backward in diplomatic relations. Although the yuan had appreciated 12.6 percent against the dollar since mid-2010, the Treasury insisted Beijing allow more flexibility in its exchange rate. "The available evidence suggests the [yuan] remains significantly undervalued, and further appreciation of the [yuan] against the dollar and other major currencies is warranted."[115]

The Chinese Embassy did not respond to the Treasury's comments. Chinese policymakers had always defended what they called the equilibrium of the yuan in relation to the economic activity level, which meant they believed (or affirmed believing) the yuan didn't have much room to appreciate. Facing their own losses, many US unions and lawmakers complained about the yuan's value and China's advantage in foreign markets.

The US Treasury refrained from officially labeling China as a currency manipulator as a way to minimize the importance of China's domestic intentions as well as its growing prominence on the world stage, which involved currency speculators and free market pressures on the currency as well. That worsened diplomatic tensions without any guaranteed remedy.

YEAR OF THE SNAKE

The weaker economic situation in China invigorated steps toward structural reforms. The incoming government—composed of Xi Jinping as president and Li Keqiang as premier—appeared at the Third Plenum in November 2013, pledging to allow market competition to influence the economy. "The focus of the restructuring of the economic system...is to allow the market [forces] to play a 'decisive role' in the allocation of resources," they said.[116]

Despite the shift in government leadership from Wen Jiabao to Li Keqiang on March 15, 2013, Zhou kept his spot as governor of the PBOC for a third term. According to the *Wall Street Journal*, "Even though he had passed the mandatory retirement age of 65[,] Zhou was at the zenith of his influence, as the new leaders embraced reforms that Mr. Zhou had been pushing for years, including letting the market set interest rates and removing barriers to the flow of capital into and out of China."[117] Zhou had proven himself resilient and politically savvy.

He had led the reform initiatives rendering China better adapted to market demands and had become well known by international market players. In 2011, *Euromoney* magazine had named Zhou the central bank governor of the year.[118] He was the only Chinese official to be part of the select Group of Thirty.[119] His consistent international reputation and alliances contributed to China's acquisition of superpower status.

Zhou pursued financial reform policies that liberalized the currency market. He broke the peg of the yuan to the US dollar, a step necessary to launch the yuan as a global currency. Keeping him at the helm of PBOC signified these reforms would continue.[120] During the year, the yuan overtook the euro as the second-most-used currency in international trade and finance, just behind the US dollar.

The 2012 US presidential campaign was marked by Mitt Romney accusing Barack Obama of *not* labeling China a currency manipulator.[121] When called to speak before the Senate on February 13, 2013, Jack Lew, Obama's new Treasury secretary, said he believed the yuan was "still undervalued" but sidestepped the question from Ohio Democrat senator Sherrod Brown of whether he would endorse the bill passed in 2011 that permitted the United States to slap duties on goods from countries with undervalued currencies.[122] Later, at the same hearing, Lew said that "addressing China's exchange rate would be a top priority" and that, if confirmed, he would "press China to move to a market-determined exchange rate, level the playing field for our workers and firms, and support a sustained shift to domestic consumption-led growth in China." He promised to work with Congress on the issue but still didn't endorse the bill. Obama won the election easily to assume his second term.

Ma Kai (vice premier), Lou Jiwei (minister of finance), and Zhou Xiaochuan (reappointed as governor) all assumed office on March 16, 2013. Five days later, China launched its most important economic reform program since the 1990s, after allies of former premier Zhu Rongji were put in charge of key economic agencies.[123] Zhu had been the architect of the economic reforms that prompted China's entrance into the World Trade Organization in December 2001 and he was attributed partial credit for China's economic success.

BRICS RISING

China was making strides internationally, too. On March 27, 2013, during a meeting in Durban, South Africa, the BRICS countries' leaders approved a $100 billion fund to confront currency crises, though they failed to reach a financing agreement for their development bank.[124] Russian prime minister Dmitry Medvedev said China would likely provide the largest amount of money for the foreign currency pool.

According to President Xi Jinping, the group "reached broad consensus" to "further unlock potential cooperation." Discussions about the associated development bank had begun a year before, when India proposed it amid criticisms that the World Bank and IMF were not fully committed to the economic and financial welfare of emergent countries.

On March 31, 2013, the yuan hit a nineteen-year high at 6.210 after the PBOC raised the daily reference to the strongest level in more than ten months.[125] Some analysts argued that Xi Jinping's first international visits as president drove the yuan's appreciation, especially because he was meeting the BRICS' and other emergent countries' leaders. The world stood eager for a non-US-based (or US-directed) development bank.

A few weeks later, the Obama administration announced it would monitor Japanese economic policies to ensure they were not devaluing the yen to increase competitiveness.[126] In the same report, the United States said China still undervalued its currency, though this was not characterized as an act of currency manipulation, legally. The US Treasury Department was adamant but refrained from using the term "currency manipulator," noting, "The available evidence suggests the renminbi remains significantly undervalued, intervention appears to have resumed, and further appreciation of the renminbi against the dollar is warranted."[127]

The US Business and Industry Council condemned the currency report and urged US president Obama to use tariffs to punish China for the yuan's manipulation, stating, "The Treasury Department's latest refusal to label China a currency manipulator once again demonstrates President Obama's deep-seated indifference to a major, ongoing threat to American manufacturing's competitiveness, and to the US economy's return to genuine health."[128]

Zhou had to placate US strife even though the yuan was hardly devalued from an historical perspective. On June 17, 2013, the yuan rose after the PBOC raised the reference rate to an historical record of 6.1598.[129] Governor Zhou told China Central Television that the PBOC would not intentionally depreciate the yuan to foster exports. China's industrial output growth compared to a year earlier slowed to 9.2 percent. Exports had increased, but more slowly, since the beginning of the year, and factory gate prices had fallen for the fifteenth month.

On October 9, President Obama officially nominated Janet Yellen to succeed Bernanke as chair of the Fed.[130] The Fed was pumping $85 billion a month into the economy through QE. It was no accident that Yellen was a key supporter of Bernanke's money-conjuring policies. (She was confirmed on January 6, 2014, and through December 2015 didn't hike rates one bit.)

October was a busy month for China in terms of outreach to other countries. The PBOC jumped into the money-conjuring fray and forged new relationships. On October 10, the PBOC and ECB established an historic bilateral currency swap agreement to purchase and repurchase yuan and euro from each other.[131] It would be valid for three years and reach a maximum of RMB 350 billion provided to the ECB and €45 billion provided to the PBOC. The ECB considered the agreement a step forward in growing bilateral trade and investment between the EU and China, and a means of stabilizing markets.

By December 2013, the yuan overtook the euro as the second-most-used currency in international trade and finance after the dollar.[132] In January 2012, it had been the fourth-most-used currency in global trade finance, and the euro was the second. The yuan represented an 8.66 percent share of letters of credit and collections in October 2013 compared with 6.64 percent for the euro. The US dollar represented an 81 percent share of letters of credit and collections in October, lower than in 2012, when it was 85 percent. During that period, the Japanese yen dropped one position, from the third-most-used currency to the fourth.

On the back of those developments, the yuan hit a twenty-year high. Investors concluded that Chinese policymakers were becoming more willing to adhere to market determinations.[133] As a result, according to Zhou, the PBOC would "establish a managed floating exchange-rate system based upon market supply and demand" and "basically exit from normal foreign-exchange market intervention." The moment had arrived to elevate the yuan to world reserve status.

YEAR OF THE HORSE

About three weeks before leaving office, Bernanke defended his epic QE program, claiming it had important effects on the economy. On January 16, 2014, in Washington, DC, he spoke at a forum sponsored by the Brookings Institution, the think tank that would become his employer.[134] He saw no immediate sign of asset price bubbles, none that would hamper money-conjuring policy, anyway. He said, "We don't think that financial stability concerns should at this point detract from the need for monetary policy accommodation which we are continuing to provide."[135]

Meanwhile, in Beijing, Zhou's read was different, as was his approach. The PBOC wasn't exactly buying bonds G7-QE style to flood the banking system with cheap money to speculate in the financial markets. But it was increasing the money supply available to banks so they could keep China's state-owned enterprises (SOEs) awash in conjured capital and to support massive infrastructure development projects that had reached overcapacity status.[136]

In China, conjured money went to building real things, whether they were needed or not, whereas for the rest of the G7, it tended to go into less tangible and more speculative uses. China was facing real economic concerns that had known effects in Brazil, Argentina, and Russia and that related to construction overcapacity internally. These were exacerbated by local currency devaluations from its major trading partner and rival, Japan. Since Japanese prime minister Shinzo Abe had been reelected on December 26, 2012, the yen had shed almost a fifth of its value relative to the US dollar, rendering the cost of its exports to the United States cheaper in dollar terms.[137]

As main trade rivals with Japan, both China and South Korea expressed concerns about that strong slide.[138] On the other hand, the United States welcomed it. At a Council on Foreign Relations event on January 16, 2014, in another part of Washington, DC, Treasury secretary Jack Lew said about Japan, "They need to get their domestic economy growing." He also warned, "Their long-term growth can't be rooted in a strategy that ultimately turns in any way towards reliance on an unfair advantage because of the exchange rate."[139] The United States wanted to keep other currencies from devaluing, but its stance on Japan, a money-conjuring collaborator, was much more conciliatory than it was on China.

And indeed, now, the yuan was falling. On February 28, 2014, the yuan exhibited a record daily drop. Investors speculated that the PBOC would widen its trading band, allowing more volatility in currency trading, as the Chinese economy grew more sluggish.[140] During February, the currency lost 1.3 percent of its value against the dollar, its biggest weekly drop since 2011.[141]

Zhou explained that those recent movements were simply the result of market influences. If anything, he argued, they demonstrated China gradually adapting its economy to this new, more liberalized framework. He emphasized, "We focus more on the medium-term trend, and the short-term trend doesn't necessarily represent the medium-term one."[142]

Meanwhile, Zhou assured an anxious world that China's economy could sustain growth between 7 percent and 8 percent.[143] But his external confidence didn't show up in China's currency. By March 20, the yuan fell to its lowest level in a year. That day, at her first news conference as head of the Fed, Janet Yellen said the Fed would *probably* end the quantitative easing program in the fall of 2014. That meant, technically, that the next step could be raising rates.[144] Her comments pushed bonds and stocks, accustomed to an abundance of cheap money, down and lifted the dollar up (which had the knock-on effect of causing the yuan to drop further against the dollar).

Sure enough, two weeks later, on May 13, Lew criticized China's devaluation path.[145] It was the US Treasury Department against the PBOC, round one hundred. He admonished that if China wanted to make the renminbi a world currency one day, it needed to demonstrate this intention by letting the currency freely float according to market movements. (Which it was.) The US government and the Fed could not conceive of their rate pronouncements and decisions as moving currencies as well, even though it takes two currencies to make an exchange rate.

CHINA AND RUSSIA

As a result of US hostility toward its policies and to diversify its economic footprint, China strengthened its ties with Russia. During key economic talks between the two nations on May 20, 2014, Russian president Vladimir Putin and Xi Jinping settled several critical trade and investment agreements.[146] One was an agreement between VTB, Russia's second-biggest bank, and Bank of China to pay each other in their domestic currencies. Russia's Gazprom signed a thirty-year $400 billion deal to supply gas to China, with payments in Russian rubles and yuan.

The Chinese-Russian agreement represented a commitment to confronting the US dollar's dominant position. According to Russian prime minister Dmitry Medvedev, the sanctions imposed by the European Union and the United States on Russia also incentivized the use of the ruble for trade and promoted its position as a future reserve currency.[147]

Business marched on ahead of politics. On July 9, the *Wall Street Journal* noted that American companies were conducting a record amount of business in yuan, looking to benefit from cost advantages over dollar transactions.[148] Payments made by US companies in yuan had quadrupled in 2014 over the prior year, reaching a record of 2.6 percent of the global yuan total. Transactions denominated in yuan still represented a tiny portion of the annual $500 billion in US-China trade, but companies and banks in both countries saw the yuan playing a larger future role.[149]

During the annual US-China Economic dialogue that month, on July 9–10, 2014, US and Chinese leaders reached an implicit agreement that China would intervene less in the currency markets.[150] The yuan had fallen 2.4 percent by then, as China's economic growth fell to an eighteen-month low in the first quarter.

As Zhou said, "We hope that the exchange rate can be kept basically stable, at a reasonable and balanced level through reforms." He noted that market supply and demand would play a bigger role in determining the exchange rate going forward.[151]

To sustain the yuan's internationalization progress, the PBOC had signed bilateral currency swap lines with more than twenty countries since 2009, including Switzerland, Brazil, Hong Kong, Indonesia, and South Korea. In contrast with

2012, when the yuan was fourteenth in the ranking of global payments by the Society for Worldwide Interbank Financial Telecommunication, it occupied seventh place in July 2014.

Zhou also had strong convictions about the role that gold could play in the monetary system. Because of the volatility of the yuan, the PBOC wanted better gold trading standards to avoid similar volatility in gold.[152] In its Q1 Monetary Policy Report, the PBOC stated, "Rules for gold lending business on the Shanghai Gold Exchange and the development of a gold leasing business [were] promoted. Rules on OTC gold trading and trading by commercial banks on behalf of clients were improved to prevent risks."[153] China's attraction to gold had waned somewhat, but holding it still represented a way to separate from the prevailing monetary system to the extent it could be added to some sort of a currency standard in the future. China's demand and that of its growing consumer base that operated in concert with government aims would continue.

The United States, European Union, and Japan remained in sync on money-conjuring policy, the latter two with the effect of shielding their currency policies from US wrath. As for China, the United States had little tolerance, consistently repeating the broken-record accusations of currency depreciation (through to the Trump administration).[154]

So, on October 10, 2014, US Treasury secretary Jack Lew again warned global policymakers against interfering in exchange rates for competitive advantage amid growing strength of the dollar and slowing world growth.[155] He asked that they "avoid persistent exchange-rate misalignments, refrain from competitive devaluation, and not target exchange rates for competitive purposes."[156]

His speech followed a 6.7 percent gain of the dollar against ten major currencies since late June. But the dollar had strengthened so much because the Fed was rumored to be entering a rate hike phase as other central banks intervened in their currencies. Lew dogmatically urged China to let the market set the value of the yuan (which it still was doing): "It is critical that Chinese leaders implement reforms that move the country toward a market-determined exchange rate and address financial-sector risks."[157]

In response to Lew, on October 10, PBOC deputy Yi Gang claimed that China had been constantly working toward a market-based yuan and that interventions over the currency had neared zero. "We are getting closer and closer toward our target of a market-based yuan rate; I am very confident that the yuan exchange rate is determined by market supply and demand."[158]

Elsewhere, there were Western alliances to be made. On October 11, the ECB said it would discuss whether to add the Chinese yuan to its foreign currency reserves.[159] Zhou was elated over the confidence vote. "It's good that more countries are willing to adopt the renminbi as a reserve currency as our economy grows and our financial reforms continue."[160]

Foreign conjecture had grown over Zhou's possible departure. There were rumors of internal political squabbles over his advocacy for market reform amid China's economic slowdown.[161] But his appearance on an elite panel alongside Janet Yellen and other prominent central bankers Sunday morning, October 12, at a G30 meeting in Washington served to squash them. Zhou consistently proved himself a consummate politician in deflecting US ire over China's policies, commanding global respect, and keeping his domestic government content. He wasn't going anywhere.

On October 28, the Fed announced an end to *growing* the QE program it had begun in November 2008. But with European growth stagnant, the G20 picked up the slack that might result from a slowdown in the Fed's global money conjuring. Leaders reunited in Cairns, Australia, and agreed to inject another $2 trillion into the global economy, which they said would create millions of jobs.[162] They also claimed progress on protecting the world financial system.

Meanwhile, with China's growth rate slowing to a more than five-year low that third quarter, on November 6, 2014, the PBOC unveiled its new tool to provide liquidity in lieu of a rate cut.[163] It pumped RMB 769.5 billion (US$126 billion) into China's lenders over two months through a medium-term lending facility, a kind of temporary bank that gave three-month loans to commercial lenders, reminiscent of the kind the Fed established for the US banking system in 2009. China, because of the recent economic slowdown, now had money-conjuring tendencies, too.

Two weeks later, on November 21, the PBOC also cut its one-year deposit rate to 2.75 percent from 3 percent.[164] "The Chinese economy is running within the proper range and positive signs have emerged in economic restructuring. However, high financing costs and obstructions still remain prominent problems for the real economy," said the PBOC. "Reducing high financing costs for enterprises, small and micro-firms in particular, is of great importance to stabilizing economic growth, job creation and the benefit of the people."

It was the first cut since 2012 after figures showed China's factory output contracting. As for the economy, President Xi told chief executives at the Asia-Pacific Economic Cooperation Summit that the risks faced by China were "not that scary" and that the government remained confident. He correctly remarked that even with China growing just 7 percent in the next year—its slowest pace in twenty-four years—it was still growing more than other economies.[165]

Xinhua, the state media, added support, underscoring the changing demographics in China's economic growth picture and its global financial market victories.

Alibaba, China's expansive version of Amazon, for instance, had set a record for the largest IPO in history in September 2014.[166]

But the economy was slipping. A month later, on December 10, new data revealed the slowest export growth for China in seven months.[167] In addition, five-year sovereign bond yields had risen the most since November 2013. In response, the PBOC intervened to set the strongest yuan reference rate since March 7.

Overall, though, the yuan fell 2.4 percent in 2014, the first annual decline since 2009. According to PBOC deputy governor Hu Xiaolian, the PBOC was pressing ahead with exchange rate liberalization and had withdrawn regular intervention. Therefore, any credit for the depreciation of the yuan belonged to speculators and was not the fault of the PBOC.

But beyond currency levels lay the more pressing matter of the distortion of the market by G7 central bank money-fabricating policies. As Zhou noted at the Tsinghua PBCSF Global Finance Forum in Hong Kong in December 2014, "Central bankers would have to rely on quantity-based monetary easing where price-based tools such as interest rates have reached the bottom. The three rounds of QE and Operation Twist[168] led to the largest expansion of the Fed's balance sheet since World War II, doubling to $4.5 trillion within the past five years."[169]

YEAR OF THE SHEEP

By 2015, emerging nations were struggling because of low commodities prices and China's reduction in demand. The nature of those effects differed across countries. Brazil, in particular, faced its worst days in years owing to a weak economy, currency depreciation, and political scandal. Russia was hurt by lower oil prices and sanctions, which dampened the ruble's value. Argentina had elected a president who promoted economic liberal reforms and a potential political inversion regarding Latin America's political and economic path. The global political turn to the right gained steam as people lost confidence in their sitting governments.

On May 9, 2015, a day before the seventieth anniversary of the World War II victory, Presidents Vladimir Putin and Xi Jinping again convened in Russia.[170] China was one of Russia's main trading partners. They signed two more joint declarations on financial cooperation two months after yuan-ruble futures began trading on the Moscow stock exchange. Russia's main bank, Sberbank, agreed to provide credit lines in both currencies to Chinese banks.

China's elite had fought against the prevailing monetary system since the financial crisis and embarked upon securing regional and international trade and economic alliances beyond the United States. Another element of China's ascension and independence was the New Development Bank (formerly the BRICS Development

Bank). The NDB opened its headquarters in Shanghai on July 21, 2015.[171] It was a momentous occasion, marking the first time a developing markets development bank was created by and for developing countries.

The first NDB president, K. V. Kamath, hailed from India. Its four vice presidents were appointed from the other countries: Xian Zhu from China as chief operations officer, Leslie Maasdorp from South Africa as chief financial officer, Paulo Nogueira Batista Jr. from Brazil as chief risk officer, and Vladimir Kazbekov from Russia as chief administration officer.

Shortly after the establishment of the NDB, in August 2015, the yuan underwent a 4 percent devaluation. The sharp decline followed a mini stock market crash: after having rallied by 150 percent over the prior year, the Chinese stock markets took a dive.[172] Since June 12, the Shanghai Stock shed about one-third in overall value, or $3 trillion worth of losses, causing about half of its fourteen hundred listed companies to file for trading halts to protect themselves from more losses.[173] The tenuous episode provoked a sense of panic throughout the speculator community, on fear of contagion or the onset of a global recession, as well as skepticism regarding China's attempts to fashion Shanghai as a major global market force along the lines of New York or London.

But movement on the yuan pressed forward despite the market volatility. On November 30, the IMF completed its five-year review of the special drawing rights basket and decided to include the renminbi.[174] The IMF had created the SDR as an international reserve currency asset in 1969 to supplement its member countries' official reserves. The value of the SDR, at the time of that decision, was based on a weighted basket of four major currencies—the US dollar, the euro (which replaced the deutschmark and French franc upon its 1999 creation), the Japanese yen, and the British pound sterling. The inclusion of the renminbi would take effect in October 2016, enabling the RMB to finally attain its status as an official international reserve currency, beside the US dollar, euro, British pound, and Japanese yen.

Two weeks later, on December 17, 2015, the China-Russia monetary alliance inched another step closer. Zhou and Central Bank of Russia governor Elvira Nabiullina signed a memorandum of understanding (MOU) and cooperation "to improve and deepen bilateral financial cooperation."[175] The momentous agreement was a direct outcome of the meeting that occurred in Beijing between Chinese premier Li Keqiang and Russian prime minister Dmitry Medvedev. It was a different kind of collusive move. According to the statement, "The goal of the MOU is to develop cooperation between the central banks in the spheres of mutual interests, including promoting local currency settlement; to continue cooperation in the areas of payments and bank cards; to facilitate the access of one party to issue local currency bonds on the territory of the other party; and to enhance cooperation in credit rating."

The two central banks shared a criticism of the US dollar as the main reserve currency and, by extension, the Fed as monetary policy leader. Although China and Russia had different ways of approaching this US power position, they agreed on the need for alternatives to the current international monetary system.

Meanwhile, the yuan continued declining relative to the dollar, which was good for China's trade, but not so good for US and China politics. The first half of December 2015 was characterized by a 1.3 percent devaluation in the yuan.[176]

Chinese exporters—as well as European and American importers—were happy. However, Chinese exporters were worried, especially if the yuan's level should translate into higher costs for imported raw materials and production. Into that weakness and uncertainty, the Fed's decision to raise rates by 25 basis points in December 2015 prompted US dollar gains. Initially.

The perception the Fed attempted to promote and the US media spread was that after seven years of "emergency measures" money-conjuring policy had proven effective. The US dollar rose on this notion. But the decision to adopt such a slight change in monetary policy showed caution regarding the US economic capacity to recover. Plus, a higher dollar might cause tremendous pain to countries whose private sectors were laden with dollar-denominated debt. Despite the fanfare, though, and the Fed's forecast of four more interest rate hikes during 2016, it would be the last increase for a year.

YEAR OF THE MONKEY

Chinese stocks took another plunge between January 4 and 7, 2016.[177] They were not alone. All of a sudden, turbulence returned. Stock markets had become dependent on the West's (and Japan's) money-conjuring policies, and the Fed's rate hike disrupted their party. It was unthinkable that the Fed's money conjuring could come to an end.

Emerging markets, particularly China, bore the brunt of that realization. Speculative capital raced for its home base, and China was not a home base. If the mini crash in the summer of 2015 in China's markets had taught foreign bettors anything, it was that financial markets could always get much worse before they got better. With the Fed in potential tightening mode, even slightly, money flow could become constricted, and that was not a bet they were prepared to take.

The yuan also took a dive.[178] This was not what the Fed had intended when it raised rates. Nor did it comport with US government initiatives to dictate China's rate and currency decisions. But China had to protect China. Zhou was well aware of his responsibilities to the People's Republic.

According to Chinese media, the devaluation was part of the effort to stabilize the yuan's international parity. Moreover, the IMF supported it.[179] The United States criticized the action because it rendered Chinese exports cheaper, but China asserted that exports were low because of the reduction of global demand. The battle had not died between the two superpowers.

The consequences were record losses in the offshore currency market. The yuan fell by 3.5 percent against the yen and by 0.8 percent against the euro. Chinese stock markets were suspended twice that first week of January. Japan's Nikkei fell 2.3 percent, and Hong Kong's Hang Seng dropped 2.8 percent.[180]

Headlines like "China's slowdown continues to drag, slowest since the global financial crisis" became Western lore, though within the copy beneath them there resided competing facts such as "China slowdown not as bad as feared."[181] Concern over liquidity drying up was not about a slowdown in economic growth but was fear that the global collusion to conjure cheap money would end. If a major participant stopped, what would happen to cheap capital flows? It was unclear which part of the world would take up the baton. The Fed could exit the money-conjuring game. But China was not in the game enough. All China had to do was prove it could be a player, and capital would flow eastward again. So, this time, without hesitation, that's what Zhou set out to do.

On January 11, 2016, PBOC chief economist Ma Jun agreed to an interview with Chinese newspapers and the *Financial Times* regarding the sharp depreciation of the RMB against the US dollar.[182] According to him, the Chinese exchange rate mechanism formation was not pegged to the dollar. He announced that "China will guide the market to form a yuan/dollar rate," anticipating a more flexible exchange policy.[183] It was the PBOC against the markets, defending its own power as much as the yuan's strength in the world.

However, the 1.5 percent yuan depreciation since the start of 2016 combined with the 4.7 percent weakening in 2015 sounded to China trade rivals as if China was entering a new "currency war" of competitive devaluations.

On January 19, the IMF released its World Economic Outlook global growth report. On the one hand, it boosted its forecast to an increase of 3.4 percent in 2016 from its estimated 3.1 percent in 2015. Forecasts regarding developed markets were positive, whereas emerging markets had problems that could be exacerbated by lower commodities and oil prices. The larger issue, though, was the shift in Fed policy and cheap money.

The report stated, "Prospects of a gradual increase in policy interest rates in the United States as well as bouts of financial volatility amid concerns about emerging market growth prospects have contributed to tighter external financial conditions, declining capital flows, and further currency depreciations in many emerging market economies."[184]

On January 21, in Davos, Fang Xinghai, vice chairman of the Chinese Securities Regulatory Commission, affirmed China was not trying to restore its economic growth by devaluing the renminbi. According to Fang, "A depreciation is not in the interests of China's rebalancing; a too deep currency fall would not be good for [domestic] consumption."[185]

Fearing global contagion more than currency devaluation for a moment, US secretary of the Treasury Jack Lew offered confidence in China's markets. He had "been following China very closely" and did not see "the situation today as being so dramatically different" from that at the end of 2015. He was basically trying to cover up the chaos that the slight Fed rate hike in December 2015 had caused markets and was extending an olive branch to China.

The following week, after reaching a thirteen-month low, the yuan recovered. China was trying to bolster confidence in the yuan after it fell 5.7 percent since August 2015. An editorial in China's *People's Daily* ironized it as George Soros's attempt to "declare war" on China's yuan and the Hong Kong dollar.[186] The January 27 piece accused Soros of attempting to bet against the yuan. A few days earlier, at the Davos World Economic Forum on January 21, 2016, Soros had told Bloomberg TV that a "hard landing" for the Chinese economy was "unavoidable." This tack was reminiscent of one that his funds had taken when he bet against Asian currencies in 1997. Soros told Bloomberg TV that he had bet against the S&P 500, Asian currencies, and commodity-linked economies.[187]

Despite a small recovery from the week's lows, Chinese shares recorded their biggest monthly fall in seven years. The Shanghai Composite Index had shed 22.6 percent of its value since early January, posting its worst month since October 2008. Things were looking very much like they had in the United States during the first leg of the financial crisis.

Given the precarious nature of the markets, Premier Li Keqiang called IMF head Christine Lagarde on the morning of January 28 to reassure her that China would use the yuan to promote exports and not provoke a currency war.[188] He promised to keep the yuan stable and improve communications about the currency with financial markets.[189]

On January 31, a money-conjuring injection from Japan proved an unlikely gift to China. Asian stocks rallied sharply after the BOJ's decision to further lower rates, pressing the yen to a six-week low. Crude oil prices stabilized, causing commodity-linked currencies to rise.[190] It appeared that the BOJ's moves, coupled with the Fed backing off on rate hikes, achieved stability.

Zhou wasn't going to adopt a wait-and-see mode. It was time for him to act, too. Enacting its own easing measure, the PBOC injected more than RMB 600 billion

(US$91.22 billion) into the markets in early February.[191] The PBOC had cut interest rates six times since November 2014, reduced the percentage of reserves banks must hold, and sold RMB 629 billion in December. The decision to inject more money hinged on the poor results of the Chinese economy in Q4 2015, which showed its weakest growth since the financial crisis.

As a result, a degree of normalcy returned and lingered for months. In that placidity, on May 20, 2016, the Chinese government conducted a series of new appointments. PBOC governor Zhou retained his position as the longest-serving central banker among major economies.[192] His focus turned to Europe, where an influx of refugees coupled with economic angst and hostility toward elites would soon cause a tear in the EU. A month later, the yuan hit a five-year low against the dollar as the US currency gained amid growing fears that Britain might leave the EU and economically destabilize the region as a result.[193]

THE NEW DEVELOPMENT BANK (BRICS DEVELOPMENT BANK)

China took advantage of G7 money-conjuring policy to expand its global footprint in much the same way the United States had done during the twentieth century. But its process was different. Whereas the United States expanded from a military perspective first, then by acquiring pieces of enterprise in emerging countries, China opted for long-term loan-based infrastructure partnerships. This contrasted with the method used by private US banks, which funneled in speculators seeking the flavor of the month or year and quick returns on capital, with the US government augmenting their businesses with military or political support. China's philosophy was to dispense capital over a greater horizon period, mostly to sustainable energy and other construction projects.

During 2015, funding to Latin America from the state-run China Development Bank and the Export-Import Bank of China hit a near record of $29 billion—nearly triple the 2014 amount. The sum eclipsed 2015 funding from the World Bank and Inter-American Development Bank combined.[194]

China's focus was on infrastructure that would benefit China, such as the $10 billion Bi-Oceanic railway financed through the China–Latin America Industrial Fund (CLAI Fund) and China Railway No. 10 Engineering Group (CREC) that would transport commodities from Rio de Janeiro to Peru's Pacific port of Arequipa.[195] China's own high-speed railway system was state-of-sustainable-energy-art.[196]

The New Development Bank (NDB) was part of China's overall strategy of collaborating with other emerging nations on development projects, spearheaded by BRICS for BRICS. The NDB signed its first loan agreement with the government of India to finance a $350 million project to develop and upgrade major district roads in Madhya Pradesh.[197]

The NDB plan was to raise $1.5 billion through issuing bonds between 2016 and 2018. To make those bonds most appealing to investors, the NDB secured an AAA rating from two Chinese credit rating firms.[198] The structure of the NDB and capital allocation to long-term projects was a far cry from the way G7 money-conjuring nations had rendered cheap capital available with no strings attached to big banks and their speculator clients and collaborators.

On April 10, 2016, at the annual conference of the Inter-American Development Bank in the Bahamas, Zhou noted that Latin America was incapable of resisting a global economic slowdown—without China's help, anyway. He emphasized cooperation and mutual coordination regarding trade and investment policies as well as the importance of both sides to each other: "In recent years, thanks to joint efforts, relations between China and the LAC [Latin American countries] have developed in multiple fields. In 2014, during a visit to the region, President Xi Jinping [had] set the ambitious goal of raising China-LAC trade volume to US$500 billion and China's direct investment volume to US$250 billion in ten years."[199]

China was the second-largest trading partner of Latin America. Thus, Zhou believed China should have flexibility in implementing its monetary policy.[200] He condemned the protectionism in trade that was beginning to form, and he called for countries to become more active in securing a global recovery. He routinely sought to focus attention on the problems of the international monetary system leaning too heavily on the US dollar and defended the expansion of the IMF's special drawing rights basket as a way to diversify from it.

According to the April 2016 IMF report on the regional outlook for Asia and the Pacific, the IMF was keen for China to take over the money-conjuring mantle if the United States abandoned it. It warned, "Further interest rate hikes by the Federal Reserve could lead to a further tightening of global liquidity and capital outflows from emerging Asia and other emerging market economies."[201]

Regarding China, however, it noted that "monetary accommodation (following a series of interest rate and reserve requirement cuts in 2015) and an easing bias to monetary policy as well as the announced on-budget fiscal stimulus should provide some offset."[202] The IMF actively wanted China to be a counterbalance to the United States and, yet, appeared to be advocating for it to deploy the same monetary policy strategy that the US Fed had adopted since late 2008.

In early June 2016, US Treasury secretary Jacob Lew gave an interview before speaking at the US-China Strategic and Economic Dialogue in Beijing. He stressed that China must improve monetary policy communication as it assumed a more relevant role in the global economy. Lew said that China's decision to devalue the yuan in August 2015 was "something that was confusing and not well communicated, and it gave rise to fears that China's economy was in a much weaker place than it actually appears to be or was perceived by policy makers to be."[203]

On June 24, in the wake of the Brexit vote,[204] Zhou told the IMF at the Michel Camdessus annual Central Banking Lecture series that the PBOC was aware of rising tensions regarding China's economic and monetary policy. But there were bigger fish to fry. Given the seismic shift that Brexit could possibly cause in the European Union and in the United Kingdom, and their currencies and trade agreements, he wanted to make it clear there was no place for repetitive, swirling accusations about China's policies. He affirmed, "We are paying close attention to international discussions on Chinese monetary policy and will adjust our policy in a dynamic way to meet the demand of China's economy, reform and development."[205]

As part of the official program of events, just before noon, Zhou had a candid conversation with Christine Lagarde.[206] She welcomed him with heartfelt praise in her introductory remarks.[207] She said he was "first and foremost" a "friend" she had known for a long time and that her respect and admiration for him has "only grown over time." She called Zhou a "central banker of the very best caliber" and "too modest" to take credit for all his accomplishments with respect to China. She praised China for its growing leadership in the financial arena and for leading the G20 with "wisdom, determination, and elegance."

Lagarde underscored that the inclusion of the Chinese currency in the SDR was a result of many years of hard work and that Zhou had "steered China's monetary policy throughout this impressive transformation." If China was a ship, she said, it would be "a large container ship" of "the new mega class." China accounted for the same share of global output as all the other EM countries combined, representing 30 percent of global investment and housing five of the world's biggest banks in terms of assets.

She commended his ability to combine a "global vision" with "Chinese wisdom" and noted that underneath his "very calm demeanor" was a "world-class intellect" and an "energetic personality with wide-ranging interests." She praised his being an avid player of badminton and tennis—which demand "stamina, agility, speed, precision and strategic skill," all of which "come very handy for a central banker." She lauded his deep appreciation for Western classical music and opera and even that he had coauthored a book titled *Journey of Musical Operas*. "Sharp, talented, well rounded, open-minded," he was a key player "in helping China navigate the next phase of its transformation." After the lecture, Lagarde presented Zhou the gift of a pair of badminton rackets.

Zhou, in turn, thanked Lagarde for her "comprehensive introduction," humbly deflecting her praise of him. He addressed the issue of the central bank's independence, noting that sometimes it fell under pressure because of its multiple aims,[208] which could create tension with other government agencies. "If a central bank has multiple objectives, it may be harder to be immune from the political reality," he said. "Ultimately the transition to a market economy will by and large be completed."[209] He vowed to focus on problems with systemic risk and China's shadow banks and to ensure traditional financial institutions maintained their prominent role in financing development.[210] In a transitioning economy such as China's (from centrally planned to market oriented), this needed to be taken into account. He noted that the PBOC's medium- to long-term goals were "financial stability," which had high priority, and to "promote reform and open up financial markets."

This was a significant moment. Zhou had been reluctant to point out philosophical differences between the PBOC and the government given their past alignment. The Western press had alluded to them, but China had not, nor had Zhou himself.

Lagarde and Zhou's warm relationship was genuine, largely resulting from their mutual respect and support for each other's goals. Lagarde advocated growing the power base of emerging countries within the IMF structure, and Zhou was grateful for a Western ally whom he could count on.[211] This personal alliance in a shifting global hierarchy underscored the role Lagarde played in reshaping superpowers and how much power the IMF wielded in the process.

On June 27, 2016, the yuan fell to a five-and-a-half-year low against the dollar as a result of Brexit—another political-economic opportunity for China, which caused more established currencies to rally as the British pound tanked. The PBOC tolerated the currency's weakening after the Brexit vote by setting a much weaker midpoint.

President Xi Jinping confirmed China's strength in the global turmoil on July 8, when he told a group of Chinese economists in Beijing that China's economic growth was "basically stable and in line with expectations."[212] He vowed that China would push ahead with "supply-side structural reform and continue to implement prudent monetary and proactive fiscal policies." He also cautioned that the transition from old to new economic growth engines would take time.

China wasn't just funding Latin American and African projects, pushing to enter the IMF's SDR basket, and increasing domestic stimulus but also inserting itself into European matters while the United States was in presidential election mode. While the United States focused on the political and media posturing between candidates, China tried to take over some of the US influence in Europe.

"Eurasian regions are facing opportunities as well as severe challenges such as terrorism and refugees, which require respect and cooperation from all sides," Chinese premier Li Keqiang said at a July 15, 2016, Asia-Europe summit in Mongolia. He took a shot at the United States, warning that world powers should not stir up regional conflicts. He implicitly wanted the United States to stay out of the conflicts surrounding the South China Sea and let China deal with them.[213]

Disputes had intensified around the area, through which about $5 trillion in maritime trade moved per year, including 80 percent of China's crude oil imports.[214] China lays claim to much of that space, and other Asian countries, such as the Philippines, Malaysia, Brunei, and Taiwan also have claims. The Philippines was concerned that China was building structures on an area called Scarborough Shoal, which China had seized in 2012, and had enlisted the United States to back it after The Hague declared some of China's artificial islands illegal in July 2016.[215]

The eleventh Asia-Europe Meeting (ASEM) summit had kicked off in Ulan Bator, Mongolia, on July 15, with fifty state leaders convening to discuss common issues, including antiterrorism, trade, and cultural exchange cooperation across Eurasia. Li noted Eurasia faced both "great opportunities and severe challenges" from terrorism and the refugee issue and that "all sides...[should] explore new paths to further promote Eurasian cooperation."[216]

He pledged China's commitment to address these challenges and to contribute to peace and prosperity in Eurasia and the whole world. Li used the forum to emphasize the positive performance of the Chinese economy during the first half of 2016, saying "vibrant, new business forms are booming and new growth momentum is accumulating."[217]

China's growth contribution to the world economy surpassed US figures. As of 2016, almost one-third of the world's GDP growth was due to China.[218] China's external direct investments hit $1 trillion for 2015, with $300 billion going to Asia. Its five largest banks' overseas loans had increased by $400 billion since 2010, hitting $677 billion in 2014. More growth was expected given the government's "go global" policies, internationalization of the renminbi, and grand regional development initiatives.

The Silk Road Economic Belt and 21st-Century Maritime Silk Road would develop new infrastructure connecting Asian, European, and African nations.[219] The related "One Belt, One Road" infrastructure initiative, with more than $1 trillion of projects, would also connect those continents and bordering seas, upgrading trade routes, roads, railways, ports, and maritime routes with diversified and sustainable development.[220]

By 2016, China had accounted for about one-half of regional growth and was the top trading partner of most major regional economies in East Asia and ASEAN.[221] During 1990–2016, the region grew about 6 percent per year, but so did its inequality.[222] One of the most equal economies in 1990, China's inequality came to be ranked higher than that of most other regions.

According to economist and Peking University professor Michael Pettis, inequality was the biggest issue keeping demand contained: "Even if China's middle class was growing, their demand as part of GDP was not growing as quickly."[223]

Meanwhile, total debt as a percentage of GDP rose. China needed a soft landing. Ironically, that meant that China's continued rise was based on optimizing the balance of crafted money and fiscal policy. As much as it wanted autonomy, it was caught in the money-conjuring mania.

During the July 24, 2016, G20 meeting in Chengdu, China, despite Japan's insistence they be a focus, Chinese exchange policies were not a main topic. Brexit was.[224] Even with an economic slowdown and a lower yuan, the finance ministers and central bankers seemed more worried about Brexit than Chinese policies. As an official at the summit told Reuters, "China's growth problems and exchange rate decline have not been much of an issue here. Japan with its concerns has been left a bit alone, no one wanted to join in."[225]

While the yuan had fallen 5 percent against a basket of currencies since the last G20 meeting, the yen had become stronger and faced more volatility; it was still considered a safe haven even with Japanese rates in negative territory. Japanese finance minister Tarō Asō agreed with US Treasury secretary Jack Lew on the need for structural exchange rate reform in China. Despite that, US criticism about the yuan decreased compared to that of other periods. Lew complimented China's improved transparency and noted market factors were indeed moving the yuan. With the European Union and United Kingdom suddenly more uncertain quantities, it made no sense for the United States to badger China.

The Fed's decision on July 31 to keep rates unchanged also sent the yuan lower. The move followed the PBOC's decision to strengthen its daily fixing by the most since June 23.[226] By early August, the PBOC reiterated plans to keep monetary policy "prudent" during the year, even though it faced calls for further monetary easing from researchers at China's top economic planner in order to help lower business costs and boost investment.[227] The PBOC offered multiple other tools to maintain high liquidity levels and keep reasonable credit growth instead.

The PBOC's methods included a half-point cut in the financial institutions' RMB deposit reserve ratio, the use of open market operations to facilitate medium-term lending facility (MLF), pledged supplementary lending (PSL), and other tools to provide liquidity. These were all derivations of tools in the Fed's artisanal money toolbox. The body vowed to continue to "promote the internationalization of the RMB and the yuan global acceptance significantly."[228]

The PBOC released a statement on August 15, 2016, urging investors not to focus too much on short-term conditions and affirming that the diverging pace of credit expansion did not mean a loss of strength of monetary policy.[229] The PBOC was concerned about corporate leverage and did not want to make changes in monetary policy again but was under pressure to be more clear and transparent in its communications.

Nevertheless, the decision-making process remained clouded. The PBOC was not totally disconnected from the central government, and Zhou was not the final voice of policy decisions. The bank still operated somewhat randomly. It had had no fixed schedule for policy decisions, did not publish votes or meeting minutes, and rarely provided scheduled press conferences. Zhou himself had already downplayed communication as a tool, but pressures from the IMF, which called for more transparency, provoked some changes in the central bank's attitude.

THE BREXIT EFFECT

Prospects for the first post-Brexit G20 meeting were bright for China. The September meeting was a major step toward a reorganization of European cooperation. Concerns about currency markets increased with Brexit in regard to volatility, a rise of protectionism, and more conjured-money policies, as was evident by the Bank of England cutting rates a few weeks after the Brexit vote.

The September 4–5, 2016, G20 Hangzhou meeting was the eleventh G20 meeting and the first to be held on Chinese soil. The schedule included sixty-six events held in twenty different cities in China. China also met with the other BRICS before the Hangzhou event. The goal was to rethink priorities of G20 economies and the way they have been solving the problems of global economic growth. The United States and China were at odds about which nation would reign over that growth.

In general, the United States and China continued to distrust each other through the 2016 US presidential election. The race pitted two candidates, Hillary Clinton and Donald J. Trump, neither of whom was especially warm to China, against each other. China's trajectory scared the United States, yet the two superpowers had to be pragmatic about finding common ground, if anything because their alliances were up for grabs. That's why China pressed for the yuan to be included in the SDR and Zhou tried to communicate his brand of monetary policy beyond his prior thresholds. Lagarde and the IMF required his transparency to maintain their own balancing act between the United States and China in the superpower realignment wars.

The PBOC increased its cash injections on September 14, 2016, to a five-month high. The move raised speculation that it was working to steady the Chinese financial markets à la Fed-type strategy.[230] The total amount of money provided was RMB 385 billion (US$57.7 billion). It was the highest addition since April. As a consequence, the yuan appreciated, motivated by the inclusion in IMF reserves. That wasn't all. On September 20, the PBOC announced that the Bank of China New York branch was approved to be the first yuan clearing bank in the United States.[231]

The moment for which Zhou had been angling for more than a decade had finally arrived. On October 1, 2016, the IMF, historically imbedded in Western monetary protocol, moved to include China's currency, the renminbi, in its special drawing rights basket of major reserve currencies. IMF leader Christine Lagarde characterized the decision as an "historical milestone" for the "international monetary system" and the "ongoing evolution of the global economy."[232] With its position in the SDR basket, China automatically assumed a more prominent role in global markets.

The PBOC proclaimed the inclusion "a milestone in the internationalization of the renminbi, and is an affirmation of the success of China's economic development and results of the reform and opening up of the financial sector."[233] Zhou's work had paid off. As he said on October 7, "We welcome relevant researches and discussions by the IMF on expanding the use of the SDR. China has already published its foreign reserves, balance of payments and international investment positions in both the US dollar and SDR, and the World Bank has also issued SDR-denominated bonds in China. China is willing to work with all relevant parties to promote the international monetary system reform, improve global economic governance, and maintain global financial stability."[234]

The United States, not supporting the inclusion to begin with, downplayed it. US Treasury secretary Jack Lew was condescending about the true impact—"being part of the SDR basket at the IMF is quite a ways away from being a global reserve currency," which to him would require from China more reforms and market liberalization.

Such minimizing of China's global position would not be up to Lew much longer. For China, the election of Donald J. Trump as US president on November 8, 2016, was a mixed blessing.

He had campaigned against China's "job-stealing" propensity, which resonated with his voters. Regardless of the rhetoric, as president, he would have to contend with the growth of China as an economic and political superpower and what opposing the multilateral trade agreements would ultimately mean for the hegemony of the United States and the dollar. The more China traded with other countries, the less it would trade with the United States, meaning the idea of Trump securing "better deals" would be unattainable simply because the United States would have reduced leverage. In addition, the more countries would trade with China, the more they would be cutting the United States out of the picture, bit by bit.

YEAR OF THE ROOSTER

On January 17, 2017, President Xi Jinping touted China's proactive approach on the world stage. In a keynote speech, referencing Charles Dickens's *A Tale of Two Cities*, he addressed three thousand elite businesspeople and politicians at the World Economic Forum in Davos.

He urged the world to "rise above the debate" over "fiscal stimulus or more monetary easing."[235] Innovation was the way forward. Protectionism was not. He defended the positive attributes of globalization. "Those who push for protectionism are shutting themselves inside a dark house. They have escaped the rain and clouds outside, but also missed the light and air." He added, "A trade war will only lead to suffering on both sides."[236]

It was an ambitious proclamation given the extent of central bank intervention that had taken place. His message followed eight years of China criticizing the Fed's cheap-money policy, which had inflated speculative bubbles but had not funded development projects to the extent that China had, regionally and globally.

China's policy of fiscal stimulus for its domestic economy would continue, but China was preparing for the grander phase—deploying money into lasting global development projects and the political, and possibly military, alignments that came with them. Xi did not mention President Trump by name, but his embrace of globalization and disdain for money being deployed into speculation in the financial markets rather than growth was clear. What the United States wouldn't do, China would.

On his third day in office, on January 23, 2017, President Trump made good on one of his key campaign promises. He issued a presidential memorandum followed by signing an executive order to "permanently withdraw" the United States from the Trans-Pacific Partnership agreement penned under the Obama administration.[237]

Because China hadn't been a part of that major agreement spanning twelve countries and 37.4 percent of global GDP to begin with,[238] the US exit meant China would have a freer rein in reinforcing and growing its other regional partnerships absent competition from the United States. China would have more latitude to pursue its broader free trade agreement, the Regional Comprehensive Economic Partnership (RCEP), which spanned sixteen countries, including Japan, almost one-third of global GDP, and almost half the world's population.[239] China stood ready to capitalize on linking with any countries Trump ostracized through nationalism, bombastic style, or broken bilateral agreements, such as Mexico.

President Trump's Treasury secretary, former Goldman Sachs partner Steven Mnuchin, repeatedly signaled wanting a strong US dollar, whereas President Trump wanted US trade to be more competitive, which meant a weaker dollar. That bipolarity characterized what would become the Trump administration's global economic policy.

On February 3, the PBOC raised short-term interest rates by a modest 10 basis points, which signaled the possible start of a tightening period.[240] China's export-import growth had rebounded to multiyear highs. The PBOC had repeatedly asked commercial lenders to curb new loans to temper any US-style lending frenzy and reduce financial leverage. It was being careful with China's future.[241]

According to a February 14 editorial by Caixin chief editor Hu Shulion, "The shift in tone indicated that while keeping its monetary policy stable, it will lean toward tightening it in order to curb the emergence of asset bubbles and to mitigate financial risks." He added, "A volatile international economic environment also poses challenges to China's monetary policy." US president Donald Trump's pledge to "revive US trade" made it harder to predict the Federal Reserve's future policy swings. Any move by the Fed has a strong effect on the yuan's exchange rate and China's capital outflows.[242]

China's growth was no longer slowing down. Its position in the world, and ability to finance it, was thus increasing. On April 22, 2017, Zhou addressed the annual spring meeting of the IMF and World Bank in Washington, DC. In his speech, he noted that "China's economic growth has stabilized" and its "GDP growth in 2016 reached 6.7 per cent, contributing 30 per cent of the global growth."[243] That figure can be compared to the US GDP growth of 1.6 percent and EU GDP growth of 1.8 percent.[244]

He used the platform to reinforce the threat he saw in asset bubbles and the need for prudent monetary and, implicitly, bank regulation policy. "Going forward," Zhou said, "the Chinese government will continue to maintain the soundness and consistency of macroeconomic policies. Monetary policy will remain prudent and neutral, striking a better balance between stabilizing growth and the task of deleveraging, preventing asset bubbles, and containing the accumulation of systemic risks."[245]

He professed his ongoing support for "the IMF's work on broadening the role of the SDR, and remarked that he expected more targeted and sustained efforts focused on addressing the inherent weaknesses in the existing international monetary system." It was nearing a decade since Zhou had first catapulted into prominence by criticizing the US dollar–centric monetary system in the wake of the US-caused financial crisis. His strides, with respect to his own influence and that of China's, would only increase as the United States conceded its spot on the world stage, whether it wanted to or not.

By the time the twelfth G20 summit kicked off in Hamburg on July 7–8, 2017, China had a solid read on President Trump and his protectionist stance, except when it came to military or territorial disputes. Thus, much of that meeting, though the US media focused on the relationship between Trump and Russian president Vladimir Putin, was really about the accelerated realignment of countries away from the United States. Isolationism is truly a one-way street. Absent a major war, from an economic standpoint, it makes enemies of friends and friends of enemies, depending on resulting realignments born of necessity. In the battle for economic survival and do-minion over the future of the global economy, one country's isolationism would prove another country's opportunity to forge new relationships with its former partners.

China was pragmatic. Its leaders understood Trump's role for his four years as president, and, in a way, his isolationist stance drove it to enhance its targeting of US allies for trade. Thus, China approached former US strategic partners like Germany and Saudi Arabia and forged more alliances with Russia. Russian president Vladimir Putin in turn began tending more toward agreements with Germany and China than with the United States. The world was becoming China-Russia-Germany-centric and was poised to continue on that path.

What began as a US bank–instigated financial crisis at the hands of an enabling Federal Reserve manifested in a superpower realignment further fueled by the election of "outsider" Donald Trump as US president. Those events catalyzed a major shift in the prevailing monetary system and superpower hierarchy, propelling China to a leadership role and Xi to epochal status. Trump's isolationist and protectionist policies only accelerated China's positioning. It will take decades to realize this shift completely, but looking back from the future, we will one day see clearly how those monetary and financial forces irrevocably altered world order.

Meanwhile, the ongoing escalation of war talk between the United States and North Korea, along with pressure that Trump placed upon China to pick a side, led the People's Bank of China to tell its banks to stop doing business with North Korea, from the standpoint of ceasing to open new accounts with North Korean custom-ers and winding down existing loans, in support of US economic sanctions against North Korea.[246] China did not go so far as to halt trade with North Korea, but it remained on alert for US directives as well as its own interests in the region.

As for the yuan, calls from inside the Chinese government, business commu-nity, and the People's Bank of China itself intensified to "free" the currency from central bank intervention. It was a further sign of the internal battle in China as to how to continue to strengthen its position in the global financial markets. In late September 2017, the China Finance 40 Forum, a prominent circle of national econo-mists, including ones from inside the People's Bank of China, released a paper advo-cating for a more free-floating policy regarding the yuan.[247] It was a clear sign that the yuan stood ready to take its place as a dominant reserve currency. Adopting such a policy would not mean no central bank intervention because, in practice, central banks existed to protect and defend their currencies, among their other tasks, but it did signal an enhanced internal drive to promote the yuan on the world stage, in a very public way.

In addition, after being the longest-serving major central bank leader, the reign of sixty-eight-year-old Zhou Xiaochuan was coming to an end as he considered his retirement.[248] He reigned through a period of three different Chinese presidents and three different US Federal Reserve chairs. Zhou had initiated that free-floating currency process by removing the official peg, or link, that the yuan had to the dollar. His successor would carry that torch.

Elsewhere in the region, Japan remained mired in a precarious allegiance balance between its US ally, its collaboration with China, and securing its own independent future in the rapidly changing global landscape.

4

JAPAN: Conjured-Money Incubator

There aren't any such things as a quantitative limit or anything, any numbers we can't overcome.

—Bank of Japan governor Haruhiko Kuroda, March 30, 2016

In the fall of 2008, as the US financial crisis gained steam, the Bank of Japan (BOJ) shadowed the Fed's policies, including introducing and expanding its supply of dollar funds for use by Japanese banks. The central bank was also cutting rates and increasing the amount of JGBs (Japanese government bonds) it bought in exchange for providing money to banks.[1]

Two BOJ governors presided over the early-crisis through post-crisis period. The first was soft-spoken Masaaki Shirakawa—a bird-watcher in his spare time.[2] He reigned from April 9, 2008, to March 19, 2013. The second was Haruhiko Kuroda, handpicked by prime minister Shinzo Abe for his dovishness. Kuroda took the helm on March 20, 2013, and proceeded to conjure money faster than any other central bank leader—including Ben Bernanke—ever had.

Shirakawa served under an array of six different prime ministers during a frenetic political period in Japan. The shifting of those bureaucratic deck chairs eventually landed Shinzo Abe in the prime minister post for a second run, and with that the end of his career at the BOJ.

Despite acting as central command for monetary policy, the strategies that the Fed perpetuated post-financial crisis were not created by the Fed. The Bank of Japan was the original G7 money conjurer, formulating an early version of quantitative easing in 2001.

In turn, Shirakawa was the major catalyst behind the creation of QE. Kuroda later followed in his tracks to become a long-time advocate of ultra-loose monetary policy.

Japan first used the QE method between 2001 and 2006 in response to a severe financial and banking crisis in the late 1990s.[3] The governor of the BOJ at the time was Masaru Hayami, under whose direction the BOJ first set rates to zero (in 1999) and thereafter introduced QE.[4] In his last speech about QE before leaving the BOJ in 2003, he said, "In March 2001 the Bank entered uncharted waters by adopting a quantitative easing framework. Commercial banks' current account deposits held at the Bank were adopted as a main target of money market operations, and ample liquidity has been provided."[5] The amount of liquidity provided under his tutelage would be eclipsed by post-crisis maneuvers.

Later research showed the program had little effect on Japan's consumer price index (CPI) or inflation levels, which it was designed to boost. But it helped financial institutions in need of cheap money.

Regardless, in November 2008, the Fed began its first version of quantitative easing (QE1), or large-scale asset purchases, as one of an array of money-conjuring techniques. Under QE1, the Fed created money to buy mortgage assets from ailing big banks.[6] According to the St. Louis Fed, one of the twelve banks comprising the US Federal Reserve System of which the Fed is the most powerful and central one,[7] "In a nutshell, QE entails unusually large purchases of assets by a central bank financed by money creation."[8] *Unusually* is the operative word.

THE POINT OF NO RETURN

On February 27, 2008, in his semiannual report to Congress, Bernanke expressed concerns over the US economic situation, the credit and job market, and housing price contraction.[9] He promised that the Fed would focus on reestablishing economic activity, leave inflation control as secondary, and keep reducing rates as it had been doing since August 2007.[10] Bernanke did so with cautious optimism. "Although the FOMC participants' economic projections envision an improving economic picture," he said, "it is important to recognize that downside risks to growth remain."[11]

The first shoe was about to drop for Japan. The fifth largest US investment bank, Bear Stearns, was nearing collapse. On March 16, 2008, Henry Paulson, US secretary of the Treasury, defended the Fed's decision to allow US banking behemoth JPMorgan Chase to buy Bear Stearns, one of Goldman Sachs's rivals, with government help. "Our financial institutions, our banks and investment banks are very strong," he said. "I'm convinced that they're going to come out of this situation very strong."[12] His words were prescient. Big banks did very well after the crisis.

The news propelled the yen to a thirteen-year high against the dollar, at ¥95.77.[13] Some traders saw this as an opportunity to buy dollars, while investors questioned the wisdom of keeping dollar-denominated assets at all. Japan was trapped in a tricky position: it was a main Asian superpower but dependent on the US economy and dollar movements.

In response, the BOJ flooded the banking system with $4.1 billion to promote liquidity. Japan's Nikkei 225 index rose 1.5 percent to 11,964 on the injection; but that was after an 8 percent decrease that pushed the index to its lowest level since 2005.

Fear of another episode reminiscent of the late-1990s banking crisis in Japan was palpable, and domestic disputes over how to avoid it intensified.[14] That period coincided with a major change in the leadership at the BOJ. Sitting BOJ chairman Toshihiko Fukui ended his term on March 19, 2008, after a forty-year tenure. An impasse over the next governor followed in which politics dictated the path of monetary policy. It was a matter of grave embarrassment to the government that it couldn't agree on a central bank leader, especially when the role and power of developed country central banks were so prominent.

Still, Japan's prime minister Yasuo Fukuda of the Liberal Democratic Party (a center-right to right-wing party) could not easily find a replacement who would be approved by the opposition party.[15] The party didn't like his suggestion of Koji Takami, a Ministry of Finance bureaucrat; they wanted to avoid government influence over the BOJ. In the end, they chose Masaaki Shirakawa because he was a career central banker and trusted enough by all parties. Many observers saw him as the mastermind behind the unorthodox policy of quantitative easing that the central bank had introduced in March 2001.[16]

Shirakawa was born in Fukuoka, Japan, on September 27, 1949, the year the Tokyo, Osaka, and Nagoya stock exchanges opened. He studied law as an undergraduate at the University of Tokyo. After graduating, he was hired by the BOJ in 1972. Inflation shot to 25 percent shortly afterward. The prevailing high-inflation period coupled with oil price shocks stuck with him. He became wary of asset bubbles and later the risks of the QE strategies that he would create.

In 1977, he received a master's in economics from the University of Chicago, known for its free market ideologies; this was the same year that World Bank chief economist Paul Romer and Obama adviser David Axelrod earned their undergraduate degrees there.[17] In 1995, he spent time in New York City as the BOJ's general manager for the Americas.

At the BOJ, he held a variety of monetary policy and financial stability positions, including executive director between 2002 and 2006, and was one of the key architects of the quantitative easing programs designed to combat the domestic banking crisis. After he left in July 2006, he taught at the Kyoto University School of Government until March 2008.[18] According to Reuters, "Those who have worked for Shirakawa describe him as a workaholic and a perfectionist. His few pleasures outside work include listening to the music of the Beatles and catching an occasional movie."[19]

Shirakawa assumed his role as the thirtieth governor of the BOJ on April 9, 2008. From the start, he was troubled about the extent to which credit conditions in Japan were already beginning to constrict, as they were in the United States. He kept the overnight call rate at 0.1 percent, but he made it clear, albeit cautiously, that he would take action to provide liquidity to the Japanese markets if he had to. "As with private-sector economic entities, complacency is the most dangerous risk for central banks," he said. "We need to be humble as numerous challenges await the global economy. My colleagues and I at the Bank of Japan will continue to come to grips with these challenges, working in cooperation with fellow central bankers, and financial supervisors and regulators. In finishing my remarks, I would like to request you in the private sector for your continued support and assistance, so that central banks can continue to progress."[20] As worried as he was about the environment, he believed that there could be no solution to its pressures without collaborating, or colluding, with other central banks.

On May 23, 2008, while addressing Japan's National Press Club, Shirakawa talked up the barrier between the health of Japan and the chaos from the United States. He said, "It seems that Japan's economy has become more resilient to negative shocks than in the past [and] is expected to return to a moderate growth path."[21] The world was getting more frenetic and Japan could not sit by idly and wait for a financial bomb to drop.

By August 2008, the BOJ emphasized it "would implement appropriate policies in an accordingly flexible manner."[22] It hadn't taken long to go from publicly expressing confidence in the Japanese economy to adopting the Fed's policies of injecting money into its financial system.

The September 16, 2008, collapse of Lehman Brothers catapulted the yen up against the dollar, as a safe haven, causing it to log its highest daily gain since 2002.[23] Meanwhile, the Dow experienced its biggest fall since September 11, 2001.

The US government decided not to save Lehman Brothers from bankruptcy. Other measures were put forth in efforts to enhance the stability of the international financial system, which was losing the confidence of the public and the institutions composing it. For the first time in ninety-five years, the Fed decided to accept equities as collateral for cash loans. It expanded emergency lending programs, while other key central banks, such as the ECB and Bank of England (BOE), injected money into their own financial systems.

On September 29, the US House of Representatives rejected a proposed $700 billion rescue package for banks, unleashing international panic.[24] As a result, the Standard & Poor's 500 stock index fell almost 9 percent and the DJIA decreased nearly 778 points (almost 7 percent) to 10,365.4. The Nikkei shed about 500 points. Three European banks went bankrupt.[25]

The allied central banks moved to jointly cut rates on that fateful day, October 8, 2008. As part of the coordinated measure, the Fed lowered its target for the federal funds rate by 50 basis points to 1.5 percent.[26] The ECB cut rates by 50 basis points.[27] The BOJ said it "welcomes the policy decisions made by six central banks" and engaged "in decisive actions of liquidity supply, ranging from the uninterrupted provision of ample yen liquidity in the market to the introduction of US dollar liquidity operations."[28] It didn't cut rates yet. They were already too low.

As Shirakawa told the joint annual gathering of the IMF and World Bank in Washington on October 13, 2008, "In response to elevated strains in the global financial market, the Bank of Japan, with other central banks, has taken coordinated action to provide US dollar liquidity, and it has supported interest rate cuts implemented by other major central banks."[29]

Nine days later, the yen hit another high against the dollar on risk aversion capital flows (a thirteen-year record) and the euro (a six-year record).[30] An emerging markets crisis deepened. Many developing countries were in talks with the IMF about financing in case of a liquidity squeeze. Some central banks, such as Brazil's, were forced to intervene to boost liquidity.

On October 27, amid the turmoil, the yen became a target. The G7 chose to express dissatisfaction with the stronger yen, considering it a threat to international stability, because it could have adverse implications for economic stability.[31] It was a ridiculous stance given the fact that the United States had just shown itself to be reckless in managing its financial system, so castigating Japan for being the recipient of speculative capital was misplaced criticism—Japanese money was simply returning to Japan from emerging markets, and speculators were riding the wave. Of all the issues caused by the rashness of the US banks, the G7 body considered yen appreciation to be the culprit harming developed nations' way of managing the international economy. Specifically, the G7 was "concerned about the recent excessive volatility in the exchange rate of the yen" and its "adverse implications for economic and financial stability."[32]

The Fed had its own problems, with a US banking system lacking internal confidence and starved for liquidity. On October 29, the Fed cut rates another 50 basis points—to 1 percent for the federal fund rates and 1.25 percent for the discount rate.[33] It noted, "Coordinated interest rate cuts by central banks, extraordinary liquidity measures, and official steps to strengthen financial systems should help over time to improve credit conditions and promote a return to moderate economic growth."

Then came the kicker. Two days later, for the first time in seven years, the BOJ announced it would cut rates. This was one day after the Japanese government announced a $51 billion stimulus package. The key interest rate (uncollateralized overnight call rate) dipped from 0.5 percent to 0.3 percent. The Nikkei fell 5 percent and the yen appreciated counterintuitively after the announcement.

According to Shirakawa, "A reduction in policy interest rates and a further increase in the flexibility of money market operations were necessary to maintain accommodative financial conditions."[34] He likened the situation to the Great Depression of the 1930s.

He explained, "The turmoil in financial markets that began in the summer of 2007 as well as its impact on economic activity were, at first, limited to the US and European economies, but have since gradually spread to Japan as well as to emerging economies. This global turmoil has now become the largest problem facing the world economy."[35]

The central bank moves so far weren't enough to restore confidence to the markets or to ordinary people watching their pensions dwindle and home prices dive. On December 16, the Fed cut the federal funds rate to 0.25 percent. It was the first time it cut rates below 1 percent.[36] That caused the dollar to fall sharply against the yen to levels last touched in July 1995.

The BOJ was widely expected to swing into even bolder action. And that's exactly what it did. On December 19, it slashed the uncollateralized overnight call rate by 20 basis points to 0.1 percent. The motivation reflected the alarming speed with which the US banking collapse spread to the world economy. "Exports have been decreasing, reflecting a slowdown in overseas economies, and domestic demand has become weaker against the background of the declining corporate profits and the worsening employment and income situation in the household sector."[37] The BOJ increased purchases of government bonds from ¥1.2 trillion to ¥1.4 trillion per year.

Shirakawa denied this was a return to the old QE policy.[38] After the 1990s banking crisis, a 1998 law officially declared the BOJ independent from the government to promote "price stability." Shirakawa was trying to preserve that independence and not yield to government pressure to go full throttle on QE in order to accommodate the Fed.

WORSENING WORLD

What Shirakawa set into motion was enough to reinforce his participation in the Fed's collusive efforts. Developed countries' central banks increased their use of conjured money over the following year as a means to inject liquidity into the markets and help their biggest banks access capital. They did not necessarily hold these private banks to account for neglecting to lend that cheap money to ordinary people or small or midsized businesses. The money went toward subsidizing big banks and companies, not to social or infrastructure development. Even as rates dropped, the availability of cheap money didn't filter into the world economy.

Meanwhile, the BOJ did its part and applied near-zero interest rates and QE in combination. This did not dampen the "safe-haven" attraction of the yen for international speculators, a situation hampering profits of several key Japanese companies.

On January 28, 2009, digital camera maker Canon announced an 81 percent fall in quarterly profit and predicted a fourteen-year annual profit record low for the year.[39] A week later, Panasonic Corporation said it would post an annual loss of $4.2 billion and cut fifteen thousand jobs because of the stronger yen and reduction in global demand.[40]

Conditions fared no better in the United States. On January 30, the DJIA and S&P 500 lost 1.8 percent and 2.3 percent, respectively.[41] US firms announced a hundred thousand jobs cuts that week amid rumors that the Republicans could stop Senate approval of an $819 billion stimulus plan.

Because of the US-caused meltdown, Japan was experiencing a double-digit economic slowdown, the biggest drop since 1974. Corporate bankruptcies had increased for eight months, and banks were limiting their extension of loans. In the middle of the financial crisis, a political crisis in the cabinet led to the resignation of Shoichi Nakagawa, the country's finance minister. This further damaged Prime Minister Tarō Asō's already unpopular government. Japanese politics was caught in a choke hold of US banks and Fed collusion.

Japanese exports fell by half compared to exports in the same period the previous year.[42] Car exports hit a ten-year low. As a consequence, Japan posted a trade deficit record of ¥952 billion (US$9.82 billion), the biggest deficit since 1980. To attempt to stem the drop, on February 19, the BOJ announced it would buy ¥1 trillion (US$10.7 billion) in corporate bonds and increase purchases of commercial paper to pump money into the local system.[43] These actions were extended until September 2009, six months longer than originally planned.

Between February 16 and 18, Hillary Clinton took her first official trip to Asia as US secretary of state. In Tokyo, she met with foreign minister Hirofumi Nakasone.[44] Her official mission was to discuss how to "step up the bilateral alliance" between the United States and Japan.[45] But these were choppy times, and she had an ulterior demand.

With the US financial system staggering, she needed to ensure that diplomacy with Japan translated into a continuation of the BOJ buying US Treasury bonds. The situation was dire. By March 5, 2009, the price of a Citigroup share fell below $1 for the first time in history, after the firm posted $37 billion of losses over fifteen months.[46]

Shortly thereafter, two money-conjuring events happened on opposite sides of the globe. On March 18, 2009, the BOJ announced its bond-buying program would be increased by nearly 30 percent, from ¥1.4 to ¥1.8 trillion.[47] And the Fed announced it would purchase $1.2 trillion worth of debt securities to support movement in the credit markets and the nonexistent economic recovery. It would buy long-term government debt and expand purchases of mortgage-related assets.[48]

More such actions loomed. On April 6, 2009, four central banks—the Swiss National Bank (SNB), ECB, BOE, and BOJ—all agreed to cooperate further by providing $287 billion to the Fed in the form of currency swaps to be used as credit lines to financial institutions.[49] Those arrangements supported Fed operations to provide liquidity of up to SF 40 billion (Swiss francs), €80 billion, £30 billion, and ¥10 trillion. Big US banks remained strained.

And if the US banks were crippled, the Fed would keep doing whatever it had to do to support them. This didn't sit well with the world. Japan, like other countries, began to seek non–US dollar alliances as a hedge against the US system. On July 23, 2009, the BOJ announced the first Tripartite Bank Governor's Meeting of the BOJ, PBOC, and Bank of Korea (BOK) leaders (Masaaki Shirakawa, Zhou Xiaochuan, and Seong-Tae Lee) in Shenzhen, China. The purpose of the group was "to strengthen their mutual cooperation and communication and better safeguard economic and financial stability in the region."[50]

A month later, on August 27, for the first time in sixteen years, it became cheaper to borrow in US dollars than in Japanese yen.[51] This reflected the consequences of loose monetary policy pursued not only by both countries but also by other developed economies, as well as a lack of confidence in the Fed and the US dollar. Japanese exporters grew increasingly worried.

Japan had maintained rates at a considerably low level relative to other countries even before the crisis. However, coordinated measures to deal with this crisis had rendered interest rate differentials between countries less significant than before 2008. The Dollar Index fell to 75.2. It had sunk by 15 percent since March 5, as investors abandoned the dollar for higher returns.

On November 11, 2009, Treasury secretary Geithner confirmed the US government's commitment to a strong-dollar policy before Japanese reporters: "It's very important for the US and the economic health of the US that we maintain a strong dollar [to] sustain confidence not just among American investors and savers but investors around the world."[52]

Geithner knew Japan well. His undergraduate degree from Dartmouth College was in government and Asian studies, and his master's from Johns Hopkins University was in international economics and East Asian studies. He had served as an assistant attaché in Tokyo before becoming a special assistant, and later Treasury undersecretary, for Larry Summers during the Clinton administration.[53]

However, Geithner offered no concrete plan for enforcing a higher dollar. Indeed, a weak dollar benefited the US economy because it boosted exports, which would have meant that US workers engaged in the production of exported goods would benefit, but because the United States ran a deficit with most nations, it was arguably better to have a stronger dollar so consumers and businesses that relied on imports would benefit.

It is possible the US Treasury, Fed, and White House chose not to interfere, letting the dollar decline because they found it suitable to US economic recovery while verbally adopting a counterstance because, in the end, one population group benefited from a lower dollar and one from a higher dollar anyway. Simply, a weaker dollar meant there was less money for people, social programs, universities, and research and more money for bankers and big corporations. Instead of turning more money into the families' economy, this policy turned more money into corporations, which proved unsustainable with the second crisis in 2012.

On November 20, 2009, the Japanese government reported the Japanese economy was "in a mild deflationary phase." The BOJ provided a more optimistic assessment. At a monetary policy meeting press conference that same day, Shirakawa defended his policy, yet he affirmed that monetary policies were not the only solution to the nation's price issues, augmenting tension between the BOJ and government. He said, "The cause of sustained price falls is a lack of demand…when demand itself is weak, prices won't rise just through liquidity provision."[54]

A month later, Japan's government, under newly elected Prime Minister Yukio Hatoyama, launched a 7.2 trillion yen (US$81 billion) economic stimulus program to confront deflation and the stronger yen.[55] He would serve as prime minister from September 16, 2009, through June 8, 2010. The BOJ agreed with the Japanese government on the need to fight deflation and remained committed to keeping the call rate at 0.1 percent.[56] It didn't matter who the prime minister was.

SHIFTING—BUT NOT BACK TO NORMAL

Throughout 2010, G7 central banks expanded easy-money policies. The ECB kept key rates at 1 percent. The Fed kept rates between 0 and 0.25 percent. The BOJ released fifteen statements from its monetary policy board meetings confirming its stance;[57] in all of them, rates remain unchanged. The central bank crafted new asset purchase and money injection programs to "promote growth."

The yen continued to appreciate against the dollar, pressuring the Japanese government to consider doing something about it. Big Japanese banks began switching from local to international lending, especially into the United States, augmenting their outside lending. They sought solutions to the lack of credit demand at home that was putting a damper on their profits.

On January 28, 2010, Bernanke was elected for a second term as Fed chairman. The Senate approved him in a 70–30 vote, the weakest endorsement for that position in ninety-six years.[58] Still the reelection provided Obama's administration a political victory. It also substantiated Bernanke's money-conjuring policy, though US Senator Bernie Sanders from Vermont called Bernanke out for being "asleep at the switch while Wall Street became a gambling casino."[59]

Nonetheless, more liquidity clouds formed. On May 9, Bernanke spoke with several of the G7 central bank leaders: BOE's Mervyn King, BOJ's Shirakawa, and ECB's Trichet. The Fed had to respond to "strains in US dollar short-term funding markets" by reestablishing temporary US dollar liquidity swap facilities. The Swiss National Bank and the Bank of Canada joined the team.[60]

Before announcing the decision, on a conference call of the Federal Open Market Committee Bernanke made it seem as if this idea was not his but had risen from the angst of his cheap-money allies. "Yesterday Jean-Claude Trichet called me and made what I would characterize as a personal appeal to reopen the swaps that we had before," he said. "I have gotten, again, personal calls from Mervyn King, of the Bank of England, and Masaaki Shirakawa, of the Bank of Japan, also asking us to reopen the swaps."[61] Bernanke was such a master of collusion that he made it appear as if the colluders didn't include him but were somehow acting completely independently of the Fed's policies and implicit or explicit directives.

Meanwhile, Japanese banks decided to go shopping with the higher yen. On July 8, 2010, Japan's second-largest bank, Sumitomo Mitsui, said it might buy a stake in a US commercial bank for $5 billion.[62] Since 2009, shares of Sumitomo Mitsui had fallen 26 percent. Two weeks later, Mitsubishi UFJ announced it might spend ¥500 billion (US$5.7 billion) to buy more US banks.[63] Mitsubishi had invested $9 billion in Morgan Stanley in 2009.

In June, the Federal Open Market Committee noted that the pace of recovery in output and employment had slowed in recent months. So, on August 10, the Fed announced it would buy more long-term Treasury bonds and increase the QE program.[64] The federal funds rate would remain "exceptionally low" for an "extended period." Yields on ten-year Treasury bonds fell to 2.74 percent, their lowest level since December 2008.

Although the yen appreciation against the dollar was a thorn in the side of Japan's economic performance, it benefited German companies that competed with Japanese exporters because the euro was depreciating. As a consequence, Japanese companies lost market share to German exporters, especially in the Chinese market, which made matters worse.[65] The euro had fallen 19 percent against the yen in 2009, double its decline against the dollar. In September 2010, the euro stood 36 percent lower against the yen than it had in August 2008. According to the Chinese engineering federation, German companies increased their share of imports in China from 20.6 percent to 22.9 percent, whereas Japanese participation fell from 27 percent to 24.1 percent.

Two weeks later, on August 12, the yen hit a fifteen-year high against the dollar.[66] Although new prime minister Naoto Kan (the former finance minister and "veteran bureaucrat"[67] of Japan's governing Democratic Party[68]) said this appreciation was "undesirable," his comments weren't enough to calm the markets.[69] The Nikkei fell to 9,000. The Japanese Trade Union Confederation urged Kan to request a coordinated central bank action at the next G8 meeting to stabilize the yen. After an emergency meeting on August 30, the BOJ had announced a ¥10 trillion increase in lending to commercial banks, putting the total at ¥30 trillion to boost the lending market. But that wasn't enough either. The BOJ said it "believes that the monetary-easing measure, together with government efforts, will be effective in further ensuring Japan's economic recovery."[70] The government launched its own ¥920 billion stimulus package.[71]

The move was politically motivated—it occurred two weeks before Japanese prime minister Naoto Kan won the election in his party. And it seemed successful—at first. The yen fell 3 percent against the dollar.[72] The fall lifted Japanese exporters' performance, boosting Toyota and Sony share prices by 4 percent. The Nikkei closed 217 points higher.

On October 5, 2010, the BOJ announced a new money-conjuring strategy: instead of keeping its overnight rate at 0.1 percent, as it had since December 2008, it would reintroduce a policy of zero interest rates for the first time since July 2006.[73] The decision accompanied creation of a ¥5 trillion fund to buy Japanese government bonds, commercial paper, and other asset-backed securities—all to combat the strong yen.

Shirakawa justified the measure by saying "the central outlook for the economy and prices have worsened more than had initially been predicted." Prime minister Naoto Kan had been calling for BOJ solutions to the yen's appreciation, succumbing to pressure from Japanese exporters who saw their profits threatened by a strong yen. So he looked good as well.

The *New York Times* chimed in, saying that the difficulties regarding the BOJ's capacity to control yen appreciation and restore economic stability brought up discussion of its independence. According to Article Four of the Bank of Japan Act of 1997,[74] the BOJ's "currency and monetary control and the basic stance of the government's economic policy shall be mutually compatible." Opposition groups and some government officials commented on plans to increase government influence over the Japanese central bank.

A month after the strategy was launched, on November 3, the Fed announced its second round of QE (QE2).[75] With a high level of unemployment, feebler economic activity, and low inflation, the Fed added "a further $600 billion of longer-term Treasury securities by the end of the second quarter of 2011, a pace of about $75 billion per month."

This decision was not unanimous. Thomas M. Hoenig, FOMC member and Kansas City Fed president, voted against the increase in the purchase of Treasury securities, affirming that the benefits of that action might be worth less than its risks, especially regarding future financial imbalances, long-term inflation, and economic destabilization.

Japanese banks were successfully leveraging the strong yen. On November 15, Japan's largest publicly traded bank, Mitsubishi UFJ, declared it had doubled annual profits during the six months ending on September 30. Its rivals, Sumitomo Mitsui Financial Group and Mizuho Financial Group, also exhibited huge profits. Mitsubishi UFJ announced plans to expand overseas by buying European banks.

Toward the end of the year, Japanese stocks rose, following the rise in oil and metal prices and as US shares hit levels not seen since before the Lehman Brothers collapse.[76] Since April, the Tokyo Stock Exchange Price Index (TOPIX) had dropped 9.3 percent as a result of lack of confidence in the global growth recovery, Europe's debt crisis, and US economic concerns. Among thirty-three industry groups, Japanese banks were the main drivers of the TOPIX recovery, followed by the real estate sector.

That meant that financial firms were benefiting from the cheap-money supply, whereas the Japanese people were not. University students were concerned about being able to find jobs; the number of temporary job holders (who receive far fewer, if any, benefits than permanent employees) had been increasing steadily as a percentage of the workforce, and in 2010 temporary jobs made up one-third of all jobs, up from 16 percent in the 1980s. The number of suicides resulting from economic uncertainty was rising.[77] In 2010, China also overtook Japan as the world's second-largest economy.[78]

NATURE TAKES ITS TOLL

On March 11, 2011, nature struck Japan a devastating blow. A massive earthquake off the coast of Honshu, Japan's main island, caused extreme tsunami waves that wreaked havoc on coastal areas and a nuclear power plant at Fukushima.[79] Concerns about the financial consequences of that earthquake, the tsunami, and the Fukushima nuclear disaster, coupled with Portugal's credit rating downgrade and political instability in the Middle East, moved investors toward the yen again. It recorded highs against the dollar of ¥76.54, past the April 1995 level. Expectations were that, as Japan needed money to rebuild after the natural disaster, Japanese companies would repatriate large amounts of capital, raising demand for yen.

The Nikkei 225 dove 1.4 percent on March 17, 2011.[80] The BOJ offered to inject ¥6 trillion into the banking system to calm markets, adding to the ¥28 trillion it had already offered.[81] On March 18, 2011, G7 leaders embarked on a coordinated monetary intervention to help Japan and tame the sharp rise in foreign exchange volatility after the earthquake.[82]

On that day, the Fed bought $1 billion against the yen.[83] The last time the United States had intervened against the yen was in June 1998, when it purchased $833 million worth of yen, and it did so again in 2000, aiming to support the euro after its inception. This latest intervention worked: it lowered the yen by 2.1 percent.[84] The measure was seen as a real act of solidarity with Japan by the United States, underscoring an implicit agreement between the two countries about what is and is not necessary regarding the currencies and the international monetary system. The US intervention was motivated not only by solidarity but also by the need to keep the dollar-yen exchange rate over ¥70.

However, the Dollar Index sunk to its lowest level in two years on April 28, 2011, as first-quarter economic data showed US expansion at a slower rate than expected.[85] The yen rose against its counterparts as a result of repatriation of capital. The biggest loser that day was the Brazilian real, which dropped 1.9 percent against the dollar after the Central Bank of Brazil indicated it had executed much of its plan to contain escalating inflation—and it wasn't guaranteed to change anything.

Six weeks later, on June 14, 2011, the BOJ announced it would expand its credit lines.[86] It created a ¥500 billion credit line for banks that extended asset-based lending. The policy's aim was to target growth industries to foster recovery in the wake of the tsunami.

The August 7 G7 emergency conference call brought tighter collaboration.[87] The Fed kept rates at near-zero levels; the ECB intervened in the bond market, and the BOE announced more stimulus would come if needed. The BOJ expressed concerns about the yen's appreciation, and Switzerland announced an effort to avoid an overvalued franc. More united them than divided them. Worried about a new global recession, the G7 leaders stated they would "take all necessary measures to support financial stability and growth in a spirit of close cooperation and confidence."[88]

In Brussels, where European leaders reunited in late October 2011 to discuss the euro and the sovereign debt crisis, German chancellor Angela Merkel stated that "the world is watching" and "if the euro collapses, then Europe collapses."[89] Brussels was the fourteenth summit in twenty-one months. Merkel said she considered the euro the base for peace in Europe: "Nobody should believe that another half century of peace in Europe is a given—it's not."[90]

The next day, on October 27, the BOJ increased the size of its asset purchase program of Japanese bonds, from ¥50 trillion to ¥55 trillion.[91] Three days later, Japan intervened in the foreign exchange markets to weaken the yen for the third time that year, pushing the yen to its lowest level against the dollar since 2008.[92] The yen fell against its sixteen most-traded counterparts. The last time Japan had intervened in the yen was in August, when ¥4.51 trillion (US$57.8 billion) was sold, the largest amount since March 2004.

A month later, the key developed country central banks, on a roll, announced more coordinated measures to provide liquidity. They agreed to lower the pricing on existing US dollar liquidity swap arrangements by 50 points beginning December 5, 2011.[93] They established bilateral swap arrangements through February 2013.

At Christmas, Japan and China were stirring a new initiative in contrast to these dollar arrangements. On December 26, 2011, in Beijing, Chinese premier Wen Jiabao met with Japanese prime minister Yoshihiko Noda as part of the Japan–People's Republic of China Summit.[94] In an unexpected decision, the governments announced both countries would promote direct trading of the yuan and yen, reducing their dependence on the US dollar.

The landmark currency deal was accompanied by an agreement between Japanese banks (Japan Bank for International Cooperation, JGC Corporation, and Mizuho Corporate Bank) and Chinese banks (including the Export-Import Bank of China) and companies to establish a $154 million fund to invest in environmental technology and business.

For Japan, the year 2011 was marked by strong yen appreciation, which rendered it the best currency for investors' gains during the period.[95] The BOJ had sold ¥14.3 trillion to stop these currency gains, to little avail.

WHAT RECOVERY?

In 2012, tension over the absence of a solid economic recovery gripped developed markets. Patience was wearing thin. Political and economic groups in Japan, Europe, and the United States divided mainly into those that supported easy-money policies and those that criticized them.

Into that cauldron, the Fed embarked on a third round of QE (QE3). Emerging countries considered the move as irresponsible, as fostering financial instability and volatility. The Republican Party in the United States seized on the latest round of QE to criticize Bernanke and the Fed, and by extension Obama, in the elections, but it didn't change their outcome.

None of the core central bankers knew what else to do. They believed or wanted to believe in their own hype and power—that they could save economies through the right combination of QE, intervention, and lending money cheaply to big banks and corporations, and that somehow this would trickle down into the real economy people live in day to day. They could not admit that their economies had been crippled by the US financial crisis and that the collusion of the Fed with allied central banks had perpetuated risk in a grand conjured-money scheme.

In Tokyo, nerves were frayed. Shirakawa was summoned to parliament to explain his reluctance to utilize QE in a greater capacity.[96] One parliament member loudly declared, "We need a new governor."[97] Other officials questioned whether the BOJ should remain independent of the government, given Shirakawa's apparent reluctance to conjure money fast enough. For his part, Shirakawa worried that because rates—and therefore borrowing costs—were already so low, more rate cuts could overstimulate the economy.[98]

On February 14, 2012, Shirakawa relented, and the BOJ announced it would add another ¥10 trillion (US$128 billion) to its asset purchase program of government bonds, raising the total figure to ¥65 trillion. Its aim was to achieve a 1 percent annual rise in the CPI rate.[99] The yen subsequently fell to 78.12 per dollar from 77.60. The Nikkei rose on the added supply of money.

The overvalued yen was again hurting exporters such as Sony, which doubled its annual loss forecast to ¥220 billion. That motivated finance minister Jun Azumi to express support for the BOJ's policies, noting the ministry welcomed measures taken by the BOJ: "I hope the BOJ's bold monetary easing gives a boost to the economy." It was the fourth time in two years Shirakawa and the BOJ had expanded asset purchases to manipulate the yen.

This medicine worked—for corporations. The following week, the yen hit a seven-month low against the dollar, its biggest drop since April 2011. And Shirakawa was under pressure to weaken the yen further.[100] During the prior quarter, the yen fell 10 percent versus nine peers. Meanwhile, the Nikkei index gained more than any other major index, up 19 percent.

However, companies like Toyota wanted even more yen depreciation to help make their exports appear attractive (aiming for 95–100 yen per dollar). Sharp Corporation, Sony Corporation, and Panasonic Corporation forecast a combined $16 billion in losses for the fiscal year ending in March 2012. According to Sharp's president, Takashi Okuda, "A weaker yen is a plus, but the 80-level is still harsh."[101]

The corporations advocated the BOJ increasing its effort to intervene to weaken the yen, warning that otherwise it would place the Japanese economy in more jeopardy. If major multinational Japan-based companies couldn't sell their products, sales and employees would suffer.

Shirakawa's efforts to restore economic growth through a weaker currency were undermined by Bernanke, who was considering more easing—meaning the dollar had the potential to depreciate against the yen. So, on April 27, 2012, the BOJ preemptively increased its asset purchase program by another ¥10 trillion, promising to "pursue powerful monetary easing."[102]

The BOJ appeared to be responding to government pressure—politicians were seeking stronger efforts against deflation, low consumption, and investment rates for two reasons: politically to keep domestic voter support, and because low deflation and consumption is bad for any economy, but especially Japan's, whose neighbors China, South Korea, and even Russia were booming in consumption and investment attraction.

That did the trick. By August 3, 2012, Toyota said that its profits during the April–June period jumped to ¥290.3 billion from ¥1.1 billion the year before.[103] Quarterly sales increased 60 percent to ¥5.5 trillion compared to sales in 2011, when the earthquake and tsunami affected Japanese carmakers. Toyota's sales rose in North America, Europe, and the rest of Asia.

Finance minister Jun Azumi said the Japanese government would extend its dollar credit facility to help companies invest overseas as part of its efforts to cope with a strong yen.[104] This program, which began in 2011, was supposed to end in March 2013. Azumi believed the "strong yen gives a headwind to Japanese manufacturers....I want the private sector to make the most of this fund for spending on M&As [mergers and acquisitions] if there are good deals overseas."

By then, Japan had spent a record ¥8 trillion in unilateral intervention in the currency market. On October 14, 2012, facing concerns from emerging countries that the Fed's expansionary policy was affecting their economies, Bernanke told a Tokyo audience at a High-Level Seminar sponsored by the BOJ and IMF that there was no evidence confirming such claims.[105] He warned that foreign exchange intervention could destabilize capital flows. "The perceived advantages of undervaluation and the problem of unwanted capital inflows must be understood as a package—you can't have one without the other."[106]

This speech marked a turning point in multinational antagonism toward Fed policy. At the same October annual IMF and World Bank meetings in Tokyo, Brazilian minister Guido Mantega remarked, before the IMF's 118 member countries, that QE3 was a "selfish" effort by the Fed that harmed emerging countries by stealing their share of exports and provoking volatility in currency markets. According to Mantega, "Advanced countries cannot count on exporting their way out of the crisis at the expense of emerging market economies."[107]

Criticism came from China and Russia, too. PBOC governor Zhou Xiaochuan said of accommodative monetary policies, "This could...lead to (economic) overheating, asset price bubbles and the buildup of financial imbalances." Russian finance minister Anton Siluanov told reporters, "Everything is getting done...without regard to the consequences it could have."[108]

Although IMF chief Christine Lagarde said the steps of the Fed, ECB, and BOJ were "big policy actions in the right direction," she added, "Accommodative monetary policies in many advanced economies are likely to entail large and volatile capital flows to emerging economies."[109]

Two weeks after the IMF meetings in Tokyo ended, Japanese companies took matters into their own hands, weakening the yen through a series of corporate take-overs. They considered Shirakawa's actions against the yen's rise insufficient. Japan's public debt, the highest among the major developed nations, was approaching double the size of its economy and that finally took a toll on the currency.[110] During 2012, the yen depreciated 5.5 percent.[111]

But that drop only had a minimal impact on companies that relied on exports for the bulk of their profits. In general, the economic and social situation in Japan was critical. Sony and Sharp Corporations fired workers and cut expenses by out-sourcing production to places like Taiwan, India, Bangladesh, Vietnam, and even South Korea because the yen's relatively high value still made their products more expensive overseas, which inhibited sales. Nissan Motor Corporation announced a cut of 20 percent in its full-year profit forecast, blaming the exchange rate. Exports fell 10.3 percent in September compared with the same period in 2011.

ELECTIONS AND MORE STIMULUS

A week after Obama won his reelection bid for the US presidency in November 2012, the Liberal Democratic Party won the general election in Japan, making Shinzo Abe the next prime minister on December 26, 2012.[112] Known as a nationalist, he had already served as prime minister in 2007 before resigning for health reasons.

The economic strategy, or phenomenon, "Abenomics" is named after its creator. It entailed a three-point plan to jump-start the domestic economy and consisted of monetary expansion, flexible fiscal policy, and structural reforms. To Abe, his strategy offered a recipe to Japan to become a bigger economic and geopolitical su-perpower. Monetary expansion was the easiest of the pillars to execute, as long as the right man was running the BOJ. That man would be Haruhiko Kuroda. He would expand the BOJ's book of assets faster than any other money conjurer in the world.

Abe used his victory pulpit to criticize the BOJ's policies, saying he would set an inflation target as high as 3 percent. He called for the BOJ to embrace "unlimited easing" so as to "strengthen pressure to lend."[113] Abe didn't think monetary policy change could wait until the end of Shirakawa's term.

Abe's stance affected the market, raising expectations and dampening the yen. On November 20, Shirakawa explained why there would be no change in policy. He said that buying government bonds to finance public works would end up in "reckless money printing" and "that fostering negative interest rates would be risky to financial markets."[114] It seemed like he was done with conjuring money. Japanese government bonds had performed worse than any other developed markets' bonds that year. The prior month, Shirakawa said he was "sad" the Fed was seen as doing more than the BOJ, when it was the BOJ that had pioneered quantitative easing.[115]

On December 13, 2012, the Fed, ECB, SNB, BOE, and Bank of Canada announced the extension to February 2014 of the US dollar liquidity swap arrangements set to expire in February 2013.[116] These arrangements had already been extended in November 2011 to provide liquidity to European banks as the Eurozone sovereign debt crisis came to a boiling point. The peak of the program, which had begun in 2007, was in 2008, when the use of swap lines reached $583 billion. Nevertheless, rumors flew that the BOJ would ease and consider a higher 2 percent inflation target in 2013 in response to Abe's demands. On December 18, 2012, Abe said he had talked to Shirakawa during the general election campaign in 2012. "I called for setting a policy accord with the BOJ," he said. "The governor just listened."[117]

On December 26, 2012, after seven prime ministers in six years, Shinzo Abe assumed his former post.[118] The yen had fallen to a twenty-seven-month low against the US dollar as investors expected stronger measures from the government to weaken the currency.[119] The yen hit 85.84 per dollar, its lowest level since September 2010, and 113.60 per euro, the lowest level since July 2011. Abe's election raised expectations about its value.

Abe's second term as prime minister was marked by his decision to make the economy a priority, using, among other things, easy central bank policy as a means to that end. His ambition to elevate Abenomics led to disagreements with BOJ governor Masaaki Shirakawa, who, though he had engaged in conjured-money policies, was a less aggressive conjurer than Abe wanted.[120] As a consequence, Shirakawa resigned three weeks ahead of the end of his five-year term.[121]

Abe's disappointment with Shirakawa's lack of easy-money policy aggression showed how much the world had changed, particularly because Japan had invented key elements of money conjuring. And yet, now the very instigator of such strategies wasn't perceived to be using them liberally enough by a government ostensibly conducting economic policy independently of its central bank's monetary policy. Years later, on March, 25, 2015, Shirakawa offered the following two points about the post–financial crisis period in an interview with finance education website Money and Banking: "The most impressive new policy measure in the global financial crisis was the arrangement of swap lines between the Federal Reserve and other central banks. This measure was quite effective. I am struck by the fact that these swap lines were opened in only a few days and without any press leakage in advance."

He noted that the unprecedented monetary policies might not necessarily have been as effective as the Fed and other G7 central bankers would have the world believe they were. "As for unconventional monetary policy measures aimed at

macroeconomic stability, I believe that their effect is modest. This tentative conclusion is based on facts rather than on theory. If we look at the path of real GDP in the
post-bubble period relative to the peak of the bubble up to now, there is no difference
between Japan's bubble in the late-1980s and the US bubble in the mid-2000s."[122]

Nonetheless, the stock market was delighted by the news of Shirakawa's early
departure, in anticipation of more artificial money to be lavished upon it. The Nikkei
225 soared 3.77 percentage points on the news, its best performance since September
29, 2008.[123] Shirakawa was accused of being too hawkish on policy, which was said
to have contributed to deflation and keeping the yen too strong—despite its having
fallen recently. Abe appointed Asian Development Bank president Haruhiko Kuroda as the new BOJ head. Kuroda assumed office on March 20, 2013.

The BOJ under Shirakawa—a responsible and eager participant in the G7 plans
to "solve" the crisis and related economic slowdowns, credit crunches, and other
problems—had followed the Fed's directives. Yet, Shirakawa's version of QE was too
tame for Abe.

Kuroda, the thirty-first governor of the BOJ, became a critical player in executing Abe's economic policy; he would be responsible for taking Japan into the
negative interest rates zone. He was also a fan of global coordination. His February
2013 nomination by the incoming government of prime minister Shinzo Abe was
expected. Also nominated at the same time as Kuroda's two deputies were Kikuo
Iwata—"a harsh critic of past BOJ policies"—and Hiroshi Nakaso, a senior BOJ official in charge of international affairs.

Japan, snuggled in between the United States and China, also stood at the
center of the West-to-East power shift that occurred after the crisis. Japan, the
third-largest economy in the world, also had the highest government debt-to-GDP
ratio—at nearly 250 percent of GDP compared to the United States' 105 percent—
which was exacerbated by Kuroda's policies. By 2014, the BOJ held the largest percentage of government bonds (or public debt) versus GDP compared with any other
central bank. The amount of government bonds on its books was equivalent to 87
percent of GDP compared with 26 percent for the United States and 21 percent for
the Eurozone.[124]

Expectations were high that pro-business Abe would revert years of industrial
decline and combat a rising China. Abe adhered to the Fed's cheap-money regi-
men from a fiscal perspective. He promised faster growth by offering ¥10 trillion
(US$120 billion) to public works and emergency stimulus programs. He committed
himself to aggressive monetary policy to confront deflation and weaken the yen,
measures considered essential to stimulating Japanese industry.

Kuroda did not disappoint. He launched the biggest monetary stimulus ever,
twice as fast as the Fed's quantitative easing program. He became the world's

conjurer-in-chief through the design of his new twist on QE: quantitative and qualitative easing (or QQE).

STABILITY RETURNS?

On February 12, 2013, the G7 leaders convened to discuss the yen's movement and
its impact on global trade relations. They released a statement that seemed to accept
a weaker yen, as long as Japan did not actively pursue devaluation as an official strategy.[125] Further discussions about the matter occurred during the G20 Finance Ministers and Central Bank Governors' Meeting held on February 15–16 in Moscow.

In their associated statement, the G7 leaders insisted that they remained
committed to exchange rates driven by the market—not by government policy—and
that they would consult closely when it came to any sharp movements in foreign currency markets.[126]

Even though the G20 leaders agreed not to target exchange rates as a tool for
fostering competitive positions, tensions regarding a "currency war" flourished. In a
similar statement to the G7's issued a week earlier, the G20 vowed, "We will refrain
from competitive devaluation. We will not target our exchange rates for competitive
purposes."[127]

That confirming statement followed a turbulent period in which expectations
were raised that the G20 would reprehend Japan. Though that didn't happen, speculators launched a sell-off in the yen on the grounds that the G20 was tacitly giving its
support to Abe's and Kuroda's plans for aggressive monetary easing, even if that had
the effect of beating up the yen.

IMF managing director Christine Lagarde went so far as to state that this pronouncement signaled the end of currency wars: "The good news is that the G20
responded with co-operation rather than conflict today."

But it wasn't the level of the yen that most concerned the BOJ under its new
leader but the flow of money into the Japanese financial system. On April 4, 2013,
as one of his first measures as BOJ governor, Kuroda vowed to print ¥136 (US$1.4
trillion) within two years to inject into the markets.[128] That would render his money-
conjuring program twice as large as the Fed's. Kuroda agreed it was "an unprecedented degree of monetary easing."[129]

The stock market was thrilled. The Nikkei stock index soared 2.2 percent to hit
a four-and-a-half-year high; Toyota Motor US-traded shares rose 4.6 percent. The
yen fell more than 3 percent against the dollar and 4 percent against the euro, while
the Japanese ten-year government bond yield hit a record low.

In the United States, the news attracted another kind of concern. Atlanta Fed
president Dennis Lockhart, seemingly oblivious to what was going on in his own
country, said watching Japan struggle to confront deflation and revive a sick economy

"is not a healthy element of the global scene." Charles Evans, president of the Chicago Fed, said the move was rather aggressive but added he did "certainly hope that every foreign central bank around the world is able to adopt policies that ultimately lead to the most vibrant economies that those economies can have because we need it around the world."[130]

Around the same time, Japan and the United States began negotiating the Trans-Pacific Partnership (TPP). The Obama administration announced in its April 12, 2013, semiannual report on currency practices that it would monitor Japan to ensure it was not devaluing the yen to increase competitiveness.[131] The report noted Japanese officials wanted to "correct the excessively strong yen" along with its bond-purchasing program as evidence that Japan was targeting a weaker yen.

The US government pressed Japan to refrain from using devaluation as a way of improving trade competitiveness, as agreed in the G7 and G20 meetings.[132] It also noted that China's currency remained undervalued, but this could not be characterized as an act of currency manipulation according to the legal frame. This represented a softening in the relationship between China and the United States concerning currency issues. The yuan's appreciation of 16.2 percent against the dollar since June 2010 demonstrated that perhaps there was no need for name calling over currency manipulation.

Yet, the US Treasury remained vigilant on China, more so than on Japan, noting that "evidence suggests the renminbi remains significantly undervalued, intervention appears to have resumed, and further appreciation of the renminbi against the dollar is warranted."[133] The US Business and Industry Council condemned the statement and urged Obama to use tariffs to punish the yuan's manipulation: "The Treasury Department's latest refusal to label China a currency manipulator once again demonstrates President Obama's deep-seated indifference to a major, ongoing threat to American manufacturing's competitiveness," the council stated.[134]

On August 19, 2013, Japanese exports grew at their fastest annual pace in three years as a weaker yen lifted certain sectors of the real economy, boosting car and electronics sales in the United States, Asia, and Europe.[135] The yen had depreciated 20 percent since November 2012. The new government and its economic policy altered the situation by easing monetary policy to raise the competitiveness of the export-driven Japanese economy. Although an increase of 12.2 percent in exports came in less than the Ministry of Finance had estimated, it was the biggest gain since the end of 2010.

On August 21–23, 2013, the Federal Reserve Bank of Kansas City hosted its annual economic policy symposium conference in the exclusive resort area of Jackson Hole, Wyoming. Central bankers, policymakers, economists and academics from all corners of the world attended.[136]

The event took place without the participation of Ben Bernanke, who had given the introductory speech every year since becoming Fed chairman in 2006, and who was said to have a personal scheduling conflict.[137] It was the first time since 1998 that a Fed president wasn't in attendance at the Fed-hosted shindig.[138] Two other major central bank leaders, who notably had both worked as senior executives for US powerhouse investment bank Goldman Sachs did not attend either: Mario Draghi and Bank of England governor Mark Carney. They were represented by Frank R. Smits, director general, Directorate General Research, European Central Bank, and Charles R. Bean, deputy governor, Bank of England.

But governor Haruhiko Kuroda, Fed vice chairwoman Janet Yellen, IMF director Christine Lagarde, and Bank of Mexico governor Agustín Carstens were all there. Although Bernanke was not present, his easing policies and the global economy were the main topics of conversation.

Kuroda gave a speech titled "Japan's Unconventional Monetary Policy and Initiatives Toward Ensuring Stability of the Global Financial System," noting in his opening remarks that the global economy had not yet recovered completely from what he referred to as the Lehman shock.[139] He went on to outline the quantitative and qualitative monetary easing (QQE) that the BOJ had launched in April and ended with comments about "the relationships between unconventional monetary policy and the global financial markets."

He pinpointed the extent to which the Bank of Japan, "in coordination with other central banks, has endeavored to maintain the stability of the global financial system through instruments such as making currency swap arrangements, improving the frameworks of cross-border collaboration and enhancing regional financial infrastructure, including fostering Asian bond markets." He closed by emphasizing that "it is increasingly important to have international coordination with regard to the prevention and management of a financial crisis."[140]

By that time, Kuroda's zealous adoption of the Fed's policies were actively helping major Japanese banks thrive from a liquidity standpoint. On September 13, 2013, the BIS Quarterly Review revealed that Japanese banks had become the largest suppliers of cross-border credit worldwide, with 13 percent of market share, after having hit a low in 2007. They had even overtaken US banks, which had 12 percent of market share, and German banks, which had 11 percent. This demonstrated a restoration of confidence and the growing economic importance of Japanese banks to levels last seen in the 1980s before the 1990s crisis.

However, while Japan was improving, Europe was flailing, with its citizens keeping a lid on their expenditures because of economic uncertainty. By October 2013, German fears of European inflation had been replaced by a disinflation threat.[141] Since April, the monthly consumer price index data for the Eurozone had fallen short of the ECB's 2 percent inflation target. If the ECB's focus really was inflation, the ECB would opt for loosening monetary policy further. Draghi said the bank would "look to the medium term in order to assess the outlook and...decide about further action on the front of interest rates or...any other instrument that is available."[142]

On October 31, 2013, the Bank of Japan, Bank of Canada, Bank of England, European Central Bank, the Fed, and the Swiss National Bank announced that their existing temporary bilateral liquidity swap arrangements would become standing arrangements until they decided to stop them.[143] They would provide liquidity in any of the five currencies in the agreement and, according to the central banks, would ease lingering strains in financial markets and knock-on negative effects on economic conditions.

Three weeks later, the yen fell as the dollar crossed the mark of 100 yen (100.04) for the first time in two months, after a quarterly report indicated that growth had fallen, which brought new expectations about more stimuli.[144] Currency markets were moving more on the basis of expectations about central bank intervention than on economic growth.

During the week, finance minister Tarō Asō reminded markets that Japan could intervene if the yen moves intensified.[145] A weak yen was the cornerstone of "Abenomics" because it meant that Japanese exports would be more attractive to other countries. The yen had depreciated 15 percent against the dollar during 2013, and Japan's main stock index had risen 43 percent.

On December 27, 2013, the euro reached its strongest level versus the dollar in more than two years.[146] Draghi had said the ECB would assess the capital position of the region's banks at the end of 2013. Counterbalancing the path of the Fed and BOJ, the ECB had not been expanding its balance sheet yet, giving additional strength to the euro. The yen hit a five-year low versus the dollar and euro, motivated by risk-taking momentum rather than safe haven seeking. It was its ninth consecutive week falling against the dollar, a period of movement that had not occurred since the 1941 oil crisis had affected Japan intensely.

INDEPENDENT CONJURERS

The year 2014 brought a hint of divergent monetary policies among the G3 central banks (the Fed, the BOJ, and the ECB). The Fed announced it would end its QE program on October 29, 2014.[147] But it still clung to its unconventional zero interest rate policy (ZIRP). To counterbalance the retreat of one of the Fed's money-conjuring processes, the ECB began pumping more money into the euro financial system, Japan pushed "Abenomics," and Kuroda pressed money-conjuring programs even harder.

The dollar gained considerably on the possibility that, with the Fed putting the brakes on one aspect of its strategy, rates would eventually rise to show that strength had sufficiently returned to the US economy and, with that, so would the dollar. Temporarily, the yen depreciated and the euro waffled as a result of the Fed's announcement.

Vice chairwoman of the Federal Reserve System Janet Yellen was nominated by President Obama to replace Bernanke at the helm of the Fed on October 9, 2013. On January 6, 2014, the US Senate confirmed her nomination. She was sworn in on February 3, 2014. Overall, she was accepted among US policymakers, though some Republicans considered her too dovish. She had, after all, always supported Bernanke's money-conjuring programs.

Kuroda's expanded easing policy had the effect of suppressing the yen, which benefited exporters. The flipside was pain for households relying on imports that became more expensive as a result of the weaker yen. Abenomics pegged yen depreciation as a way to confront deflation. The risk was that public opinion could change because of the higher prices of imports.

As mentioned, on January 16, 2014, a few days before leaving the Fed, Bernanke defended his QE program, underscoring its important effects on the economy. He admitted that the only risk he found credible, among the "many" mentioned by critics of QE and ZIRP, was that bond buying could prompt financial instability, although at the moment, in his view, asset prices were in line with historical norms.

By January 26, the yen had shed 20 percent of its value compared to the prior year, indeed spurring the Japanese economy as exporters recovered their profits.[148] But the weaker yen concerned Japanese importers—and, from a currency-wars perspective, other exporters.

Notably, both China and South Korea, two of Japan's main regional trade rivals, expressed concerns about the strong slide of the yen. The United States therefore welcomed Japan's economic rebound, saying that if the yen's fall was the result and not the aim of Abe's policies, Washington supported it. Still, on January 16, 2014, Treasury secretary Jack Lew warned an audience at the Council on Foreign Relations that Japan's "long-term growth can't be rooted in a strategy that ultimately turns in any way towards reliance on an unfair advantage because of the exchange rate."[149]

The next day, Japan reported a record annual trade deficit after the weak yen had driven up the cost of energy imports. The deficit had risen to ¥11.5 trillion (US$112 billion), a 65 percent increase from a year earlier. The year 2014 would be the third consecutive year that Japan, a country traditionally known for its current account surplus, reported an annual trade deficit because it was costing more money to import necessary products relative to profits from exports.[150]

Less than a month later, on February 18, 2014, the BOJ extended its special loan programs to boost economic growth. Kuroda indicated the possibility of additional future stimulus measures.[151] The Nikkei 225 rose 3.1 percent and the yen fell on that decision to double the funds available to banks.[152]

Kuroda affirmed that the QE expansion sent "a strong message of support" to banks to increase lending to help the economy. He said, "If risks materialize, we will not hesitate adjusting policy, but for now Japan's economy is on track and moving in line with our forecasts."[153] Central bank leaders, despite years of conjured-money policy, still had to explicitly ask banks to lend their cheap money to their customers and, ostensibly, the real economy. But asking was very different from requiring.

On April 11, 2014, speaking with Kuroda at a news conference in Washington, finance minister Tarō Asō said that the G20 welcomed Japan's efforts to revive the economy.[154] This followed discussions about the effectiveness of Japan's current growth strategy as captained by Abe.

About a month later, on May 5, Kuroda announced that consumer inflation would reach its goal of 2 percent within the following year.[155] He refused to comment on whether he would increase the money base more than his prior annual amount of between ¥60 trillion and ¥70 trillion (US$683 billion) per year.[156] Even as the BOJ reduced its growth estimate for 2014, he assured the public that consumer spending and employment were improving.

Here lay the crux of central bank priorities. The central banks' concerns and policies were mainly focused on price stability (or inflation), but with rates at zero and global growth slow everywhere, a rise in domestic inflation didn't necessarily imply growth improvement or better levels of employment. Using inflation as a goalpost, then, was an implicit means for central bankers to align with hitting investors' expectations and vice versa. In the absence of true inflation or growth, central bankers, especially in developed nations, could keep conjuring money, which flowed to banks and market speculators who borrowed it cheaply and in large quantities, because real inflation was so difficult to attain in a faltering economy.

The connection of the conjured money to social issues was minimal to nonexistent because it wasn't up to central banks to make sure the money it provided large financial institutions in return for assets would reach the real economy or be used to create jobs. It was a hope perhaps, but not a policy. It was even less likely in developed countries, where market levels relied on speculative activities and the general perception that money flowed sufficiently to keep them rising, than in developing countries, which tended to regulate capital flows more closely.

Meanwhile, the Nikkei 225 performed the worst among major global stocks, reflecting rising doubts about Abe's economic policies. As of May 30, it had fallen for four straight months.[157]

In the wake of the US financial crisis, Japan's position as a potential superpower was overshadowed by the expansion of its long-time adversary, China. But Japan appeared to have a shot at increasing its global footprint as the second-largest economy in Asia if it could elevate its influence, including with the BRICS. All it needed was the right balance of money and diplomacy, on top of Abenomics and conjured money.

On that note, Kuroda moved to increase Japanese influence by endorsing the BRICS bank. He supported its ability to stoke global growth from a different standpoint than that of the established powerhouse development banks, such as the World Bank and IMF, and other Japanese-Western leading entities, such as the Asian Development Bank.[158]

A few weeks later, on August 13, the BOJ registered a drop in its GDP growth forecast.[159] Sure enough, as per the logic of price targeting to keep money conjuring going, Kuroda confirmed his commitment to the inflation target and to keeping up with his QE policy until that target was reached. He also remarked that the Fed was moving toward tightening and thus saw no reason for the yen to appreciate against the dollar, removing the blame for its weak state.

By early October, Tarō Asō had changed his tune. He claimed the yen was not particularly weak even though it had hit a six-year low against the dollar.[160] Prime Minister Abe also showed little concern about the currency, considering its decline both good and bad for the economy. That was because they both wanted to keep conjured-money policy going.

Although some businesses in Japan and some consumers would suffer from an overly depreciated yen, overall it seemed positive for major export companies. This factor influenced the political stability of Abe's government because Japan relied so much on exporters to sustain economic growth, even if its population's consumption was based on imports. As Abe said, "In general, a weak yen hurts some companies by pushing up import costs. On the other hand, it's positive for exporters and companies doing business overseas."[161]

On October 8, 2014, FOMC released meeting minutes of its September 16–17 meeting. The body expressed concern that a rate hike in the United States could have unintended negative consequences on global financial markets.[162] Policymakers worried about the dual threats of a stronger dollar, which might slow the inflation target progress, and a global slowdown, which could be intensified by an increase in US rates.

The next day, at an event at the Peterson Institute for International Economics in Washington, DC, when secretary of the Treasury Jack Lew was asked whether he was comfortable with recent dollar appreciation or with the European claim for euro depreciation, he repeated his oft-made call on China to stop forcing down the value of its currency.[163] "It is wrong to get into exchange rate competition with the purpose of promoting advantage one over the other," he said. "On the other hand, we have called on many countries of the world to take decisive action to get their economies to grow."[164]

Despite some differences dealing with exchange rate policy, the United States, Europe, and Japan routinely collaborated on money-conjuring policies. With China, perhaps because the PBOC was not one of the G3 trio, the United States seemed to have little tolerance, despite the yuan's movement toward appreciation.

Yen depreciation further strained Japanese policymakers. At the start of Abenomics, the yen's drop was supposed to be one of the key elements used to confront inflation and foster growth. But now, having discussed it with Kuroda, Abe finally had to acknowledge that a weak yen had also been negatively affecting import prices and hurting households and small companies.[165]

As the weak yen hurt the average consumer's buying power for imported items, tensions grew over Abe's policies. Abe's need to achieve his inflation goals was so acute that he had summoned Kuroda to the Japanese Diet to assure the body of the economic benefits of a weaker yen. This was an often-repeated Kuroda refrain throughout Abe's tenure, and one that would erode public confidence in him and his policies, mostly because inflation barely budged anyway.

Abe wanted to preserve the public's admiration of him as long as he could. But he was in a tough spot in regard to the yen because the public didn't benefit directly from a weak yen, whereas the BOJ's QE program helped the government by buying substantive amounts of its debt.

THE FED ENDS QE, THE BOJ INCREASES IT

The Fed officially ended the largest financial stimulus program in US history by finishing the third round of QE (QE3) on October 29, 2014.[166] The Fed had bought trillions of dollars of mortgage and US Treasury bonds to keep rates at zero and provide cheap money to slosh around the banking system and financial markets. Between November 2008 and October 2014, the Fed had doubled the size of its balance sheet through QE, from $2.106 trillion to $4.486 trillion, the largest expansion from any stimulus program in history.[167]

In the process, global popular resentment of banks—the big beneficiaries of the Fed stimulus—and central banks escalated. Wall Street profits increased considerably, whereas ordinary Americans and citizens around the world lost out. Yet banks had the nerve to complain that QE was not good for them, even as they took advantage of its cheap liquidity, accessing money without having to pay much interest on it.

Kuroda picked up where Bernanke left off. On October 31, 2014, Japanese policymakers revealed surprise stimulus plans. The BOJ announced it would inject ¥80 trillion each year into the financial system, mainly through the purchase of government bonds. Before that, the BOJ had injected ¥60 trillion to ¥70 trillion per year.[168]

Kuroda was determined to avoid a return to deflation in the Japanese economy. He paraphrased Draghi, saying, "Whatever we can do, we will."[169] By November 22, the yen dropped to 119.98 per dollar, a seven-year low. Abe called early elections to renew his mandate and continue his economic policy. While Kuroda told the press that Japan's fiscal responsibility lay with the government, Japanese finance minister Tarō Asō said the currency had been falling too quickly. The yen had lost 16 percent of its value since May 2014.

In Europe, tensions surrounding the Greek financial crisis and the election of the leftist Syriza party mounted. Although part of the "troika" (from the Russian "group of three"—the European Commission, IMF, and ECB), Mario Draghi demonstrated more caution about Greece's situation than his colleagues, especially German policymakers. He initiated extra QE measures in attempts to revive growth and cut the deposit rate further into negative territory.

Meanwhile, in collusive style, when one central banker takes a break, another picks up the slack, rendering the average global result the same. Draghi had given Kuroda a breather. So Kuroda put the brakes on easing, temporarily, despite international market expectations of another large bout of easing, because of the declining yen. The stronger yen depreciation made imports more expensive for households, which elevated criticism from Japanese citizens.

However, Kuroda, Abe, and Tarō Asō recognized the difficulties in reaching the inflation target set by the BOJ and in reversing deflation. The biggest Japanese exporting companies publicly praised them—but that optimism didn't translate to the main economy. Consumer spending had fallen for six straight months, and deflation was prevalent. It began to harm Kuroda's credibility as the BOJ governor, and Abenomics in general.

CREATIVE MONEY MAKING

On January 25, 2015, while at the World Economic Forum in Davos, Kuroda told Bloomberg TV that the BOJ might need to get creative with the monetary stimulus to maintain the expansion program. "There are many options and I don't think it's constructive to say this or that could be done."[170] His remarks signaled his openness toward more conjuring. Up to that point, the BOJ confined most of its asset purchases to buying Japanese government bonds, but Kuroda was suggesting this could be augmented with different purchases.

He asserted that every next move depended on expectations regarding the inflation rate. The Japanese economy was showing signs of recovery, especially on exports, which rose 12.9 percent in December 2014 compared to in 2013. However, Japanese households and small companies weren't feeling it because of the higher cost of living and stagnant wages.

Asked about the QE program starting in Europe, Kuroda concurred it would be "beneficial to the world economy including the Japanese economy." He added, "We very much welcome this action."[171] He couldn't say anything different about the ECB's policies because they echoed his own and that of the Fed in one collusive money-conjuring juggernaut.

On February 10, 2015, at the G20 meeting in Istanbul, Kuroda noted that the body (which increasingly represented an "alternative" opinion to the G7's) had not criticized his monetary policy, indicating that the international community approved of BOJ policies. He stated, "I felt it's well understood internationally that Japan will make positive contributions not only to its own economy but to the global economy if the nation ends deflation and achieves 2 percent price stability through quantitative and qualitative monetary easing."[172]

According to his logic, what was good for Japan was good for the globe. That would have been true to the extent that Japanese companies used their extra cheap money for development projects that helped regional economies as well, but actively producing was different from simply achieving price stability around a particular inflation target. The latter was just a figure; the former was more tangible relative to job and wage growth that in turn spurred consumption and price inflation. But it remained to be seen just how much money Japan would pour into development versus driving up asset prices.

Kuroda's statements converged with Jack Lew's affirmation that Japanese policies that led to a weaker yen did not necessarily qualify as an unfair move. It was both a technical and subjective qualification by the US government in support of Abe's government and Japan.

In a parliament session on February 12, 2015, Abe touted his policies as leading to a fifteen-year high in wage growth,[173] which, in regard to minimum wage, had been trending upward even before he got into office.[174] What he did not say, however, was that job stability was an issue or that the ratio of temporary to permanent jobs was near an all-time high.[175] Abe had promised voters that they would feel the benefits of Abenomics. He had also been using words like *hope* and *urge* to move wages at major Japanese companies since he began his term.

It might have seemed naive to just hope wages would increase, but that was a cornerstone not just of Abenomics but of the entire conjured-money experiment. It was all based on hope and magical interpretation—hope that banks would lend their cheap money for productive economic projects that would spur job creation and wage elevation, and magical interpretation of large composite figures like GDP and inflation to gauge whether or not that was happening. In Japan, however, the period of Abenomics and conjured money did not show any obvious correlation to wage growth, just as it didn't in the United States.[176]

A week later, on February 18, after the BOJ's monetary policy meeting, Kuroda commented that, although the central bank noted public complaints about the yen's depreciation, "There is nothing more to say than it is desirable for exchange rates to move stably in reflection of economic fundamentals."[177]

Abenomics had led to a fall in the yen's value of 50 percent against the dollar since the end of 2012. Although the main aim—promoting Japanese major exporters' sales—was achieved, the increase in major import prices had negatively affected consumers and small companies.

According to the *Wall Street Journal*, Kuroda followed the wishes of the Abe administration, which did not want the BOJ to increase easing. But that didn't make sense from the standpoint of the inner coordination of BOJ policy and Abenomics. Kuroda did not commit to ceasing the BOJ's monetary easing. He announced, "I don't see any need to consider additional action for now."[178]

The decrease in the yen's value, resulting from the BOJ's monetary stimulus and Abenomics, made exports more competitive overseas. Toyota, for instance, achieved a record in sales of nearly $230 billion and a record net profit of $17.9 billion.

At a news conference that took place north of Tokyo, on March 5, 2015, Takahide Kiuchi, a member of the policy board of the BOJ, publicly expressed support for Chinese reform and the opening of the currency system. In a gesture of support and taking credit for its successes, he said, "China is already applying lessons from Japan's experience. Even when growth is slowing, Chinese policymakers aren't taking policy measures that could heighten financial imbalances. That's very wise of them."[179] Privately, he expressed concern about the risk of capital outflows. Japanese officials feared that it could bring consequences to the regional economy.

By mid-April, more than a hundred Japanese regional banks were speculating in foreign debt and equity-like securities markets.[180] The BOJ, by virtue of negative rates, had driven them out of government bonds and into more speculative investments (ironically funded by the BOJ's cheap money). This represented a departure from the existing model. For the past twenty years, regional Japanese banks had invested their excess deposits in Japanese government bonds, earning the difference between the near-zero rates paid to depositors and the 1 percent or 2 percent they could get from bonds.

Two days later, Koichi Hamada, an adviser to Abe, told the press, "I don't think it's a bad thing to send a signal that the selling of the yen is coming closer to its limit bit by bit."[181] Since the start of Abe's government in 2012, the yen had dropped 23 percent. On April 14, as it traded at 119.77 against the dollar, Hamada warned that a 120 level would be too "considerably weak."

On May 15, at the Yomiuri International Economic Society in Tokyo, Kuroda delivered a confident speech. He touted the results of his policy, though he hadn't hit his inflation target. "The mechanism of QQE has been operating as intended. . . . the Bank will continue to steadily pursue QQE to achieve the target of 2 percent at the earliest possible time."[182] Kuroda was buying bonds, but this process offered no direct link to economic stability.

Regionally, certain financial wrinkles evoked concern. By June, Chinese stocks had shed more than 40 percent of their value since the start of the year, which worried the Japanese.[183] To avoid past political, geopolitical, and economic mistakes, Japan suggested Beijing move slower in its financial reforms. The shock devaluation of the yuan in August 2015 served as a reminder of how quickly China could lose control of its markets.[184] As China faced billions of dollars of capital outflows and was using its reserves to avoid dramatic impacts on the monetary system, Japan was concerned about contagion.

But Japan didn't need to worry on one score, the yen. It was perceived as a safe-haven currency in the region, and bolstered by Kuroda, who on June 10, told Japan's lower house financial affairs committee that the yen was unlikely to fall further since it was already "very weak." His declaration provoked the sharpest rally in the yen during 2015.[185] His words took the place of true economic strength with respect to markets.

That, plus global events such as a Greek bailout deal being more likely with creditors lifted Japan's stock market on June 24, 2015, to its highest level in more than eighteen years.[186]

A month later, the Japanese media dubbed Kuroda "Helicopter Haruhiko," reassigning the moniker that had been used to describe Bernanke, because of his policies of seemingly dropping money, or financial stimulus, from the skies, as did his Fed counterpart.

At a parliamentary session on August 24, 2015, Abe, though he publicly recognized that the BOJ's 2 percent inflation target was becoming harder to achieve because of falling oil prices, expressed confidence in Kuroda's methods. "We think it's unavoidable that [the BOJ] hasn't been able to achieve its original objective." He added, "We understand the Bank of Japan's explanation that achieving the target is in fact getting difficult."[187]

The BOJ decided to keep monetary policy unchanged in late October even with reductions in economic forecasts and the expectation that it would not reach its 2 percent inflation target until 2017. The inflation target forecast was revised from 0.7 percent to 0.1 percent for fiscal year 2015.[188] The ¥80 trillion stimulus program of buying government bonds was retained. In response to criticism, Kuroda told the audience at the Japanese National Press Club, "We have delayed the timing for reaching our price target but this is mainly due to falling oil prices."[189] He dismissed the notion that his program was losing credibility.

On November 21, Abe announced that Japan would relax the conditions of its yen loan program for emerging countries in Asia as it relied on infrastructure exports to boost its economy. He pledged ¥1.2 trillion (US$10 billion) in loans for public infrastructure projects in other countries as part of Japan's ¥13 trillion initiative. The loans would be jointly provided by the Japan International Cooperation Agency and the Asian Development Bank.[190] It was a bid to raise a Japanese financial and diplomatic flag. As Abe stated in a visit to Kuala Lumpur for the twenty-seventh Association of Southeast Asian Nations summit, "The pace of growth in Asia is gaining steam with each passing year. [The implementation of] yen loans should not be left behind."[191]

Japan reviewed its loan scheme, making it more suitable to regional countries, partly to balance China's strong presence in infrastructure development projects in Asia, especially projects pursued by the China-led multinational development initiative, the Asian Infrastructure Investment Bank (AIIB), which Japan had not joined. Japanese finance minister Tarō Asō had indicated interest in joining the AIIB, but later reversed his stance. And partly to make a bid for expansion.

On December 16, 2015, after seven years of ZIRP, the Fed announced a rise in the target range for the federal funds rate, from 0–0.25 percent to 0.25–0.5 percent.[192] Fed chairwoman Janet Yellen said she believed that with "the economy performing well and expected to continue to do so, the committee judges that a modest increase in the federal funds rate is appropriate." She claimed it was the beginning of a process "likely to proceed gradually."

GOING NEGATIVE

To maintain an average of zero percent interest among the G3, after the Fed hiked rates, the BOJ countered by dipping into negative rate territory on January 29, 2016. Kuroda chopped the cost of ten-year debt. That meant Japan could finance current and new debt even more cheaply for the next decade. It was part of Japan's insistence that monetary policy combined with Abenomics fiscal policy could jump-start economic growth, no matter how long it took.

By the end of January 2017, this raised the BOJ's total holdings to ¥482 trillion (US$4.3 trillion) in assets, of which ¥415.3 trillion (US$3.7 trillion) were Japanese government securities.[193] The amount tripled after Kuroda took over the helm, to a size slightly smaller than the Fed's book at $4.5 trillion, but with more government bonds and a GDP a quarter of the size. The ECB's book at $3 trillion had grown 55 percent since Draghi became head in November 2011.[194] The top three artisanal central banks held nearly $12 trillion of debt.

The Fed's hike sent the global markets into a downward tailspin. On January 28, 2016, in an unexpected measure and after a tight dispute (5 to 4), the BOJ decided to turn Japan rates negative to encourage borrowing and to drive up inflation.[195] It was a preemptive measure to protect against the effects of recent global economic difficulties on Japanese business confidence and rising deflation. It surprised markets mainly because Kuroda had informed the Japanese parliament in December 2015 that he would not go that way on monetary policy. It was also—intentional or not—a further rift with US policy.

The BOJ's decision was "to apply a negative interest rate of −0.1 percent to current accounts that financial institutions hold at the bank."[196] It was called "qualitative and quantitative monetary easing (QQE) with a negative interest rate" because it left unchanged the record asset program decision to continue to inject ¥80 trillion per year by purchasing government bonds. Denmark, Sweden, and Switzerland already had negative interest rates of −0.3 percent.

Said the BOJ, "The Bank will introduce a multiple-tier system which some central banks in Europe (e.g., the Swiss National Bank) have put in place. The outstanding balance of each financial institution's current account at the Bank will be divided into three tiers, to each of which a positive interest rate, a zero interest rate, or a negative interest rate will be applied, respectively."[197]

The negative rate took effect on February 16, 2016. The Nikkei ended the day up by 2.8 percent, and the Shanghai market had a 3.1 percent rise, after months of losses. The yen fell against the dollar. But effects over the yen's value (−1.4 percent) after the BOJ's decision to pursue negative rates were less significant than when the BOJ had started quantitative and qualitative easing in April 2013, when it dropped 3.4 percent; or when the program had expanded in October 2014, prompting a 2.8 percent decrease.[198] It was as if the Japanese money-creation machine was losing its potency.

Negative rates offered the elite a respite from thinking that the markets were going to crumble. They extended that thought into their assessment of the economy as a whole. On April 14, 2016, at the G20 meeting in Washington, financial leaders were heartened by what they considered the "global recovery" and recovery in the financial markets since their February meeting in Shanghai. However, they observed growth remained "modest and uneven" amid "continued financial volatility, challenges faced by commodity exporters and low inflation."[199]

Jack Lew said that China and Japan should pursue structural reforms to help the process. He said China should reduce excess industrial capacity and Japan should promote strategic reforms in specific sectors. Japanese finance minister Tarō Asō criticized the agreements on currencies at the G20 but suggested no appropriate action to prevent exchange rate moves.

Concerns over the effects of a "Brexit"—a British vote to leave the EU—traversed the BOJ, Japanese government, and private banking system. A decision of that magnitude could prove incredibly destabilizing; with the uncertainty it could bring along, it had the capacity to rupture the prevailing financial system—in the worst-case scenario. From a coordinated trade and labor agreement perspective, it could also wreak havoc over the currency markets and trade relationships.[200] The BOJ worried such a move could cause the yen to rise against a weaker euro that could result from a tear in the status quo of nations associated with it. That would increase the problems Japan faced concerning currency appreciation, on the yen's status as a safe haven. The dollar had fallen 7.6 percent against the yen for the year and 6.4 percent in the first quarter, the biggest quarterly decline since the third quarter of 2009.

According to the *Financial Times,* on April 25, 2016, the BOJ faced pressures to ease monetary policy owing to the high level of the yen. Although some BOJ members wanted more time to evaluate negative rates, the *FT* said that it depended largely on Kuroda's opinion.[201]

Kuroda spoke to an audience at Columbia University in New York, saying that monetary policy was positively affecting economic growth.[202] Yet the move from 111 to 120 yen per dollar during the year affected business confidence and restored the deflationary process by making imported goods cheaper. The BOJ had three options: move deeper into negative territory, buy assets faster than the current ¥80 trillion per year, or alter the nature of asset purchases.

The April Fed meeting went as expected. The FOMC kept rates unchanged and said it would move forward "with gradual adjustments in the stance of monetary policy."[203] The decision was not unanimous. Esther L. George, president and chief executive officer of the Federal Reserve Bank of Kansas City and a member of the Federal Open Market Committee, voted against, advocating a 25-basis-point hike. That same day, the BOJ decided to keep rates unchanged.[204] After the decision, the Nikkei fell 3.6 percent and the yen, which was at 111.70 per dollar before the announcement, hit 108.15.

When Japanese monetary authorities entered negative territory, the immediate effects over the yen were evident. "There is plenty, plenty of room to push down the negative rate," Kuroda said, reiterating, "We are going to do whatever is necessary." Asked about the effects on Japanese banks' profits, Kuroda claimed, "We never decide monetary policy based on whether financial institutions are for it or against it."[205]

That might have been what he said in a public statement, but Japanese banks were specifically benefiting from QE. It allowed them to sell assets to the BOJ in return for more-liquid forms of capital, like cash, which in turn required them to keep less reserves at the central bank because their books appeared more liquid, but in effect they were simply exchanging less-liquid assets for cash. In theory, they had more money to lend to customers, but they weren't obligated to do so—they could simply buy their own shares or lend big corporations cheap money with which they could buy their own shares (a practice that funneled artificially fabricated money into boosting the Japanese and US stock markets propelled by historically high levels of corporate share buybacks). It was such an easy game to play, too. Banks could lend money easily to their main corporate clients, who, with the confidence of betting on a sure thing—that their stock would rise if they bought it—were a better "bet" for banks than lending to small business owners in the Main Street economy, who didn't have the capacity to self-invest, so to speak, in such dramatic fashion or manifest such quick results. Plus, corporate clients pay for politicians and policies in a far grander and more direct way than Main Street.

Infusions of conjured money could also artificially elevate the prices of the remaining assets because of the demand for the ones that the central bank bought. In addition, the BOJ was the biggest buyer of Japanese stocks in 2016, which meant it manufactured money just to bet on its own market, which artificially lifted the prices of those shares as well.

As the central bank of Japan, the BOJ declared it "carries out currency and monetary control to achieve price stability, thereby contributing to the sound development of the national economy, as stipulated in Articles 1 and 2 of the Bank of Japan Act. To this end, the Bank encourages short- and long-term interest rates to remain at target levels and purchases assets, mainly through open market operations."[206] Nowhere in its official mandate does it say that the BOJ is also supposed to influence fiscal policy—which is the domain of the government.

On May 3, 2016, the yen hit an eighteen-month high against the dollar on speculation over whether the BOJ would intervene to halt a currency appreciation that might harm its inflation target.[207] So far that year, the yen had risen 12 percent against the dollar. Abe was about to travel to Europe, where he would try to set conditions for a possible intervention in the yen, a move some European and US policymakers opposed.

On May 12, Republican candidate Donald Trump said that the financial reforms enacted by the Obama administration had been harming the US economy, and he promised he would dismantle them as soon as he was elected.[208] On the other hand, Trump provided his opinion on the Fed's monetary policy, agreeing with the low interest rates and stating, "I'm not a person that thinks Janet Yellen is doing a bad job."[209]

Japanese finance minister Tarō Asō and BOJ governor Haruhiko Kuroda addressed challenges of low global growth rates at the G7 meeting in Sendai, Japan.[210] Tarō Asō emphasized adding money laundering and tax evasion, as was occurring in Brazil and Argentina, as problem areas.

The mutual efforts of Asō and Kuroda demonstrated the closeness of Japan's Finance Ministry and BOJ at a moment when the G7 faced internal tensions. The group was having difficulties convincing Germany to abandon its pro-austerity position for a more flexible fiscal policy. Also, Japan and the United States were not aligned on the yen's value; Japan feared its growth may be influenced by currency issues. The Japanese leaders had to persuade the group to coordinate actions, from currency issues to fiscal policies.

On May 27, 2016, the G7 warned that Brexit would harm global trade, investment, and job creation. Kuroda concurred, "If Brexit is agreed, it would have a significant and serious impact on the global economy."[211] Japan was concerned about its trade agreements with the United Kingdom, given its financial dealings and companies headquartered there. The United States still complained about competitive currency devaluation and placed Japan and China on a currency watchlist.

Kuroda dismissed those accusations, pointing out that the yen had risen 10 percent in recent months. He emphasized the role of central banks in promoting dynamism in the global economy. For him, the options regarding monetary policy hadn't been exhausted. "I don't think for Japan, or the ECB, at this stage that monetary policy has reached the limit." He defended these practices in the Japanese economy: "I don't say it will take one year or two years, or something like that," he said. "It will have a clear impact on the economy soon."

Promoting growth was also a topic of discussion. The group disagreed on which policies to pursue to confront global stagnation, too. Japan defended the continuity of monetary policy as a tool to promote liquidity and stimulate growth. Germany and the United Kingdom believed that austerity and fiscal discipline were the best ways and criticized the "cheap money."

On June 14, 2016, still far from his inflation target, Kuroda was feeling increasing pressure from Japanese banks unhappy with his strategy. Japan's biggest lender, Bank of Tokyo-Mitsubishi UFJ, considered Kuroda's negative rates a concern and had been against negative rate policy since January, when Kuroda announced it. It threatened to withdraw from the club of twenty-two financial firms that bought government bonds, worried about the low-yield returns.[212] Banks forecast their low-est profit in five years. Sumitomo Mitsui Banking Corporation blamed the difficult year on the negative rate policy.

From the day the ECB and BOJ entered negative territory, banks criticized them. Fine with zero percent interest rates that provided them liquidity and cheap money, they were less happy about negative rates coupled with lower profits when economic results were not forthcoming.

On June 15, 2016, as the referendum date on Brexit approached, the Japanese government and BOJ stayed in constant contact with their European counterparts to prepare markets for a possible Brexit, which could bring a shortage of dollar liquidity. The BOJ said it was ready to offer dollar funds to domestic banks via auctions if Brexit happened.[213] But Tokyo had no clear plan on how to avoid a yen rise if it took place. The yen had always been a safe haven at times of heightened risk, and the G7 wasn't against Japanese intervention to hold the currency value down.

With the future of the EU on the line, the Fed kept rates unchanged, though the decision was not unanimous, with Kansas City Fed president Esther George dis-agreeing.[214] The Fed said that recent economic results, especially in the labor market, influenced the decision. Janet Yellen emphasized the importance of momentum to increase rates, arguing it would happen when real, solid signs of economic strength appeared. However, she was unclear about when this increase would happen: "I'm not comfortable to say it's in the next meeting or two, but it could be." She acknowl-edged that Brexit was a factor that led the Fed to exercise more caution.

Kuroda had decided not to expand monetary stimulus until after the United Kingdom's Brexit vote.[215] Plus, the opposition party in the domestic election wanted to discuss negative rates. However, recent gains of the yen made Kuroda reaffirm his commitment to act whenever necessary. But, he noted, "we don't decide monetary policy based on currency moves."

When he asked why ten-year government bond yields were at −0.2 percent, Ku-roda blamed Brexit: "Our quantitative and qualitative monetary easing has pushed down yields from short-term to long-term. But behind the recent plunge of the 10-year yield is the so-called Brexit vote. That's making international financial mar-kets somewhat unstable."

The following day, on June 24, just after the Brexit results were tallied, the Fed said that it stood ready to provide dollars to other central banks via the swap lines set up during the 2008 financial crisis to reduce financial market turbulence. This was ostensibly to counter the instability the vote results initiated and concerns about shortages of dollar liquidity in many places, especially Japan.[216]

But it also signaled something else: that central banks would use their money-conjuring tools whenever there was a shock to the system—even if that shock appeared to be a political one—to assuage any market or currency moves that might result.

The G7 released a statement saying the central banks were ready to use their "established liquidity instruments" if needed. Abe instructed finance minister Tarō Asō to pay attention to currency markets "even more closely" than usual, to be prepared for actions that might be necessary to temper any volatility provoked by Brexit voting.[217]

Abe announced, "We need to continue to work toward market stability," indicating that the Japanese government would not let the yen appreciate excessively against the dollar because it would appear to be a safe-haven currency after the Brexit vote. Asō told reporters he "was instructed by the prime minister to take various, aggressive responses to ensure stability in financial and currency markets." The Japanese government argued that actions to stop yen appreciation would be in line with the G7 agreement on currency stability.

The next day, the yuan fell to a five-and-a-half-year low against the dollar, and the PBOC dealt with its currency's weakening after the Brexit vote by setting a sharply weaker midpoint and not intervening in trading.[218] A month later, the US dollar fell from a six-week high against the yen after Kuroda said the BOJ saw no need to stimulate the economy with "helicopter money."[219]

This comment flew in the face of speculators who believed an aggressive round of stimulus would result from the next BOJ meeting and had bet accordingly against the yen in the foreign exchange markets. Kuroda denied the measure during a BBC radio interview, which led the yen to a 105.41-per-dollar high. However, when the BBC said the interview was done in mid-June, it cooled the yen gains. That's how sensitive speculators had become.

On July 26, 2016, despite Japanese insistence, Chinese exchange policies were not a topic at the G20 meeting in Chengdu, China. The finance ministers and central bankers were more worried about Brexit.[220] After the BOJ announcement that it would double exchange-traded fund purchases, financial shares rallied and Japanese stocks ended higher.[221]

After the BOJ announced negative interest rates, the TOPIX was the worst performer among twenty-four developed markets. The BOJ raised its target for purchases of exchange-traded funds (ETFs) to ¥6 trillion (US$58 billion), another form of QE, indicating Kuroda's commitment to offer artificial support to all markets.

Kuroda's decision provided cover for Abe, who had launched a ¥28 trillion fiscal stimulus package two days earlier. It had been three years since Kuroda forced Japan into an unprecedented easing program, but results remained insufficient. Prices were falling again, and the economy was faltering.

On August 3, 2016, Tarō Asō and Kuroda appeared together in public to show they were united.[222] They discussed the bond program and assured they would deal jointly with future pressures that could cause market disruptions. The BOJ injected the third of three rounds of fresh aid into the market: ¥1.2 trillion (US$10.5 billion; €7.8 billion).[223] The injection was pure market stimulation. Yet by August 17, 2016, some economists feared this could lead to hyperinflation and uncontrollable currency depreciation, but the BOJ was relaxed about it. They were, after all, the conjurers of money.

Three days later, perhaps facing backlash about the obvious market manipulation maneuver, the BOJ made an odd declaration—there would be no possibility of "helicopter money"[224] (which happens when a central bank directly finances government spending by underwriting its bonds). The declaration referred to the government's plan to issue bonds longer than forty-year bonds, which made it appear as if a monetization of debt was under way. The BOJ said that as long as it was buying Japanese government bonds (JGBs) from the market, it was not directly underwriting (new) bonds to fund government spending. This distinction became blurred as investors bought bonds only to take profits by selling them directly back, in what was called the "BOJ trade."

One such pressure that hit close to home in Japan was the possibility that interest rates weren't high enough to make good on payments to pensioners. At risk was the ¥140 trillion (US$1.27 trillion) state pension funds pot—under the eye of Hiromichi Mizuno, the first chief investment officer of the ultra-conservative Government Pension Investment Fund (GPIF). The interest on Japanese bonds made an historic investment in them negligible. The only game in town was the stock market, which, like anywhere else, was fine when it was rising, but a disaster when it wasn't.[225] Abe advocated an asset allocation shift to stocks instead of bonds, which worked in 2014 when the market rose but was less attractive when it sank in 2015. In 2016, he noted long-term returns mattered, not short-term volatility.

Japan and Brazil faced a similar problem, with different causes. Whereas in Brazil disjointed monetary and fiscal policies caused the collapse of social security and pensions, in Japan the problem was more demographic than fiscal. There, an aging population, restrictions on non-Japanese migration, and a sluggish economy caused pressure on the population.

Because of the obvious close relationship between the Japanese government and minister of finance with its central bank, the question about the overall independence of the BOJ returned. Yet, Kuroda was not concerned about such appearances of co-dependence at all. According to him, "Monetary policy is part of broader economic policy, so it's more than appropriate to communicate closely with the government from the perspective of a policy mix."[226] But, if the Fed were to start raising rates as a sustained policy, rather than as a periodic or one-off decision, Kuroda would have to compensate, as would Draghi at the ECB, by driving their rates down.

This idea of the Fed switching gears and embarking upon a meaningful tightening mode had real legs. On August 26, 2016, at the annual Jackson Hole symposium, Janet Yellen declared the Fed would take a gradual approach toward raising rates.[227] She affirmed rates would be increased as solid growth was confirmed, the labor market strengthened, and the inflation rate approached the target of 2 percent. Kuroda, in attendance as well,[228] promised, "The Bank will...take additional easing measures without hesitation in terms of three dimensions—quantity, quality, and the interest rate—if it is judged necessary for achieving the price stability target."[229]

As a result, the dollar extended its losses, which was counterintuitive because higher rates should have, in theory, been good for the currency and for speculators to see that they could get higher yields on their US investments. Yet the dollar fell against most of its peers and intensified the already 5 percent loss for 2016. The July FOMC minutes showed divergent opinions among committee members over the next course of action on rates. New York Fed president William Dudley and San Francisco Fed president John Williams signaled that an increase might be coming by year-end. Fed Kansas City president Esther George said inflation gains called for a nearer-term rate increase.[230]

Kuroda shifted monetary policy slightly to target lowering rates on longer-dated Japanese government bonds.[231] He still aimed to reach the 2 percent inflation target after years of massive money printing had failed to do so. His new approach was called "quantitative and qualitative monetary easing with yield curve control."[232]

The measure reassured markets that the BOJ would continue to buy large amounts of bonds, but the policy reboot seemed to revert huge asset purchases and repair the damages provoked by negative rates of −0.1 percent. Under the new rule, BOJ would start buying long-term government bonds as necessary to keep ten-year bond yields at 0 percent current levels.

Abe praised the shift and said the government would work together with the BOJ to achieve the aims of Abenomics. "The government and the BOJ share the policy task to end deflationary stagnation and achieve sustainable economic growth," he remarked. "Listen up. Abenomics is for the future. It is for future growth. It is for future generations. And it is for a future Japan that is robust."

During opening remarks at the dialogue with the New York–based business and financial community of Japan on September 21, 2016, he emphasized the need for promoting structural reform in order to have real effects on the market, especially the labor market.[233] Like other major central bank leaders, he was conflating influence over monetary and fiscal policy, overstepping the bounds of his responsibility for the former by commenting on the latter.

According to economic minister Nobuteru Ishihara, Abe was using any means necessary to put the Japanese economy back on track. "Abe has said we need to use all tools available both for fiscal policy and monetary policy and that we need to accelerate our efforts."[234] Tarō Asō added that Japan should not rely only on the BOJ to boost economic growth and fight deflation.[235]

Five days later, the dollar fell against the yen after a BOJ official commented that the central bank was unable to weaken the yen, despite having every possible policy tool at its disposal.[236] The comments confirmed that the BOJ was maintaining a monetary policy that produced effects opposite of one of its (or at least Abenomics') intents, leading the yen to appreciate. Indeed, the yen had risen by 17 percent since the BOJ had shocked markets by diving into negative interest rate territory. Meanwhile, political tension was building. The Japanese government voiced concerns about the need to improve wages to foster demand and ensure that Abenomics brought results.[237] But that was a domestic issue; Japan also sought to augment its foreign reach.

Meanwhile, Japan sought to strengthen its ties with non-US counterparts. Japan was Brazil's second-largest trading partner in Asia, just behind China, particularly in industry and innovation.[238] On October 4–5, 2016, at the nineteenth Joint Meeting of the Brazil-Japan Economic Cooperation Committees held at Keidanren, Tokyo, negotiations to create a working group for a Patent Prosecution Highway (PPH) pilot project between Brazil and Japan pushed that alliance even further.[239] Brazil's finance minister, Henrique Meirelles, participated in the elaboration of a memorandum on economic cooperation in priority areas in the Brazilian economy with Japanese financing. It was signed by the Japanese ambassador to Brazil.[240]

Such moves, including similar ones in Africa, were harbingers of Japan's commitment to expand its role in the region and the world and effectively compete with China in that regard.[241] Conjured money indirectly funded these initiatives because it was conjured money that purchased the Japanese government bonds (the public debt taken on by the Japanese government) that enabled the government to borrow more to fund international expansion.

Meanwhile, key Asian nations rattling their political sabers prompted each central bank to seek greater global influence—which meant depending on artisanal policies to elevate geopolitical influence. If the BOJ enhanced the size of its balance sheet to fund Japanese debt creation, then Japan could use those funds to finance military or trade agreements or domestic economic pursuits. As the People's Bank of China (PBOC) faced a falling yuan and the United States' ongoing accusations of currency manipulation, the BOJ faced a crisis of confidence. It couldn't elevate inflation, and its massive easing program wasn't doing the trick either. Both central banks' actions had domestic and global implications.

On October 21, 2016, Kuroda said he saw no immediate need to reduce the BOJ's asset purchases as he shifted focus from expanding the monetary base to targeting rates.[242] He told the Japanese parliament that the BOJ might not continue to buy government bonds at the pace of 80 trillion yen annually. Yet, a month later, the BOJ announced its first operation to buy an unlimited amount of securities to maintain its yield-curve target.[243]

China continued to forge a path independent of the United States. Having achieved inclusion of the renminbi in the IMF's special drawing rights basket of major reserve currencies on October 1, 2016, China established stronger side agreements with Russia, the rest of the BRICS nations, the Eurozone, and Britain after the Brexit vote. That was no accident but part of a comprehensive strategy to distance itself from the risk the United States and its central and private banking system posed.

This power shift away from the United States accelerated as China increased its economic, military, and diplomatic presence. Into that shift, Japan would soon have to reconsider its alliances—at least from an economic perspective. The PBOC began selling US Treasuries to *bolster* its currency—depleted by capital outflows, not manipulation. China sold $22 billion worth of US Treasuries in July 2016. (By 2017, its US government debt holdings dropped to their lowest level in six years.) In October 2016, the two largest holders of US Treasuries switched positions: the BOJ overtook the PBOC. By December 2016, the BOJ held $1.098 trillion and the PBOC held $1.058 trillion worth.[244]

Nine days after Trump's election victory, on November 17, prime minister Shinzo Abe met with President-elect Trump at Trump Tower in New York City.[245] Just before Abe flew to the United States, China's president, Xi Jinping, reached out to Trump for a meeting on November 14. He was not given an appointment, though he told Trump during their call that "facts have shown that cooperation is the only correct choice" for the United States and China.[246] Trump chose to speak first with Abe, who had contacted him on November 9, the day after the election.

A week before meeting Trump, Abe had signed a civil nuclear cooperation agreement with India on November 11, six years in the making. India's prime minister Narendra Modi called it an "historic step in our engagement to build a clean energy partnership." The two countries, both wary of China's presence in the East and South China Seas and the Indian Ocean, were also exploring enhanced military and naval partnerships.[247]

To continue to hedge its US alliance, Japan forged tighter relationships with Russia, a strategy that culminated in a meeting between Abe and Russian president Vladimir Putin in mid-December 2016.[248] Greater synergy between the two countries could solve three issues for Japan: temper any threat from China, fortify Japan's position regarding South and North Korean geopolitics, and diversify economic problems. That said, the issue of the Kuril Islands weighed heavily on that possibility.

THE MONEY-CREATION ALLIANCE SHIFT

What the Fed, BOJ, ECB, and other money conjurers had succeeded in doing in the wake of the financial crisis was alter the availability and magnitude of money to the financial system and its elites. But there was no such aid or direction of this money to the foundational economy. Their policies thus hadn't meaningfully altered economic stability, only certain parameters that were considered positive reflection of it, such as the level of the stock market.

The BOJ's insistence on buying ten-year Japanese government bonds to bring its yields or interest rates down was a tripling down on the ineffectiveness of its massive quantitative and qualitative easing policies. As the bullish trend of the dollar extended after the Fed raised rates by 25 basis points in December 2016, the BOJ and other central banks kept "printing" money for reasons that had shifting goals. This, while citizens routinely voted against sitting governments and, in the case of Europe, against allegiances with their neighbors. If the Fed raised rates further, the BOJ would be forced to reconsider its negative rate policy.

From Japan's standpoint, if a second financial crisis was to emanate from the United States, it would be safer if it were allied with China, with the BOJ allied with the PBOC. China fashioned regional free trade agreements with South Korea and other neighbors in the late 1990s, but not with Japan. Those were the years of Japan's own big bank crisis, and its government body, the Financial Services Agency,[249] wanted Japan to focus on regaining stability in its own backyard.

Japan aimed to uphold the free trade rules of the WTO, which China joined in 2001. The WTO wanted a broader role in dictating how China's trade and financial liberalization would evolve, but China wanted to do things at its own pace. According to Kumiko Okazaki of the Canon Institute of Global Studies in Tokyo and a former BOJ official (September 2007 and February 2016[250]), the first "symbolic" regional free trade agreement was between Japan and Singapore in 2002.[251]

When the prevailing currency swap agreement between the PBOC and BOJ expired in March 2002, the program was not renewed because of territorial island disputes. An underground agreement was prepared, but the respective governments were publicly opposed to it.

Starting in December 2008, the PBOC signed more than thirty bilateral currency swap agreements. As of May 15, 2015, its total value of effective currency swap agreements was RMB 2.9 trillion (US$468 billion). In 2014, an equivalent of RMB 1.13 trillion (US$182 billion) of swaps was conducted under these agreements.[252] They did not cover Japan or the United States, even though many US and Japanese companies did business in China.[253]

However, Japan had other avenues of connection with the PBOC that the Fed did not. The BOJ, PBOC, and Bank of Korea[254] heads had established a tripartite group in December 2008.[255] The group held regular meetings ever since, despite any geopolitical rumblings to the contrary.[256] However, the results of those meetings were not publicly disclosed. The BOJ did, however, have a currency swap agreement with the Bank of Korea, as did the PBOC, so technically there was coverage through the South Korean won (currency) in the event of a regional crisis.

TRUMP'S PROMISE OF FRIENDSHIP TO JAPAN

On January 20, 2017, Donald J. Trump became the forty-fifth president of the United States. Three days later, he signed the executive order to officially remove the United States from the Trans-Pacific Partnership, an agreement to "promote economic growth; support the creation and retention of jobs; enhance innovation, productivity and competitiveness; raise living standards; reduce poverty in the signatories' countries; and promote transparency, good governance, and enhanced labor and environmental protections."

The TPP contained measures to lower both nontariff and tariff barriers to trade and to establish an investor-state dispute settlement (ISDS) mechanism. Before Trump opted out, it was to cover twelve countries, including the United States and Japan, but not China. To Japan, it had represented an excellent competitive opportunity relative to China. But if the United States wasn't involved, Japan would have to expand with other TPP members, as well as with China through other means.

The Trump White House geared up to make its mark on the US and global economy with policy directives that included financial deregulation and bilateral trade agreements. America doesn't exist in a vacuum, not politically, militarily, or financially. The mistakes made in handling the financial crisis and the Fed's artisanal money activities shifted the perception of the United States regarding nationalism and Wall Street's role in maiming the economy.

President Xi Jinping reacted by strengthening China's trade ties throughout Asia, championing China's own version of the Trans-Pacific Partnership. Indeed, by the time Obama and then Trump said no to the TPP, China had established free trade agreements (FTAs) with nine of the twelve countries of the TPP and was pursuing more.[257] Japan, on the other hand, took the route of forging a tighter

US connection, continuing its monetary policy collaboration, but it needed China economically.

The two Asian giants had already collaborated on a unified Sino-Japanese equivalent of the TPP, called the Regional Comprehensive Economic Partnership (RCEP), which predated the TPP. On November 20, 2012, at the East Asia Summit in Cambodia, leaders from the Association of Southeast Asian Nations and its free trade agreement partners launched the negotiations.

The RCEP was an Association of Southeast Asian Nations (ASEAN)–centered proposal that initially included the ten ASEAN member states and countries with existing FTAs with ASEAN—Australia, China, India, Japan, New Zealand, and the Republic of Korea. It complemented Australia's participation in bilateral FTAs with individual countries and its plans for the Trans-Pacific Partnership agreement (TPP).[258] The RCEP included sixteen countries, representing half the world's population and 30 percent of global GDP.[259]

Abe believed he could convince Trump to reembrace the TPP. He figured that the TPP (which lacked China's participation) would be "meaningless" without US involvement.[260] The Brookings Institution estimated that had the United States joined the twelve-country agreement, which represented 40 percent of global GDP and 20 percent of global trade, it stood to gain $77 billion annually and Japan even more, $105 billion annually.[261] But Trump wouldn't budge.

Japan had much to consider: Would the nation work with Trump on a separate bilateral trade agreement that would render the US and Japanese economies (both growing more slowly than China's) more codependent? Would it strengthen existing arrangements with China and other countries? Or would it try to do both?

Without the old TPP, China emerged a clear victor in terms of trade. It could strengthen its regional and global role with no competition from a broad Asian coalition in which the United States and Japan were involved. China could subsequently collaborate with Japan on finding other ways to modernize their frosty relationship, economically speaking anyway.

A number of uncertainties plagued Japan. The primary one was the Fed and how possible US rate hikes might strengthen the dollar, though a weaker yen would be good for the export sector. There remained the threat of banking system instability and a possible "Lehman moment."

Then there was the matter of what Trump would do relative to Japan and China in regard to economic, military, and trade policy. In Europe, Brexit provided negotiation opportunities for Japanese corporations with UK-based headquarters. The insertion of China's yuan in the IMF's special drawing rights basket signaled the financial order was shifting from the West to the East, which would elevate tension in the FED, ECB, and BOJ's monetary policy alliance.

IMF influence as a counter-voice to Fed policy rose, as did the importance of the SDR and gold as counterweights to the dollar and related policies. The SDR represented not just a currency but a geopolitical shift. Gold remained a turbulent hedge and its possible future inclusion a way to rebalance power away from the dollar. Japan could decide to hedge its US monetary and currency relationships through accumulating more gold.

Central bank intervention had supported and distorted markets, subsidizing a flawed banking system. Artificial stimulus inflated real estate, debt, and asset bubbles and had the indirect effect of hurting the real economy by deflecting funds away from it. Conjured money propelled stock markets to stratospheric heights; they were literally high off cheap money, hitting dizzying heights pumped up by speculative capital that had no cost and no accountability.

Japan was in a new phase of repositioning itself in the changing financial and geopolitical order. With the onset of the Trump presidency and its tendency toward bilateral rather than multilateral trade agreements, Japan faced new opportunities to establish better ties with the United States as well as to continue to explore them with the United Kingdom, the rest of Europe, Latin America, Asia, and Russia separately. China was an economic necessity, but the military situation between the two countries required more careful diplomacy. Either way, Abe would have to balance his relationship with the United States and Trump while enhancing relationships with Europe and China.[262]

Kuroda would find ways to conjure money for whatever the situation. He was optimistic about the possibility of fiscal stimulus for infrastructure building that Trump promised during his campaign and first months in office, which could benefit from partnerships with Japan. But he considered that Trump's "advocacy of protectionist policies—could be a matter of concern."[263]

At a news conference at the Tokyo headquarters of the BOJ, on April 27, 2017, he announced the latest expansion of the Chinese-led Asian Infrastructure Investment Bank (AIIB), established in 2015 and boasting seventy members, more than the regional development bank, the Asian Development Bank (ADB), which he had run from February 2005 to March 2013.

Kuroda endorsed this "healthy competition" from Chinese, Indian, and Japanese initiatives in terms of building infrastructure and boosting regional economic growth. His most solid support for the AIIB was especially important because he had headed the rival regional development bank, the ADB, jointly led by the United States and Japan. The United States, having initially opposed the AIIB's establishment, was not a member, nor was there a chance it would become one under the protectionist Trump administration. Kuroda's enthusiasm was a sign the winds of

West-to-East change would continue to sweep Japan's focus from the United States to other international allies.[264]

The next key sign arrived during the summer of 2017. Just before the G20 meeting in Hamburg, Germany, Japan and the EU announced a new free trade alliance in Brussels, Belgium. The agreement would span about 30 percent of the global economy, 10 percent of its population, and 40 percent of trade. Now, two of the G3 nations—whose central banks' policies had altered the world through their post-crisis monetary policies—had forged an economic relationship independent of the United States and, as a result, of the Fed and the dollar.

That was a game-changer. One of many.

In October 2017, Abe won a landslide political victory in his self-called-for snap elections. With that, he fortified his position of domestic and international power. The by-product of that vote was the implicit approval of Kuroda's monetary policy. And thus, Japan's rise in the world's hierarchy stood secured.

5

EUROPE PART I: The Trichet Files

It is important to recall that, as the turmoil went on, central banks strengthened their cooperation, first through enhanced information exchange and collective monitoring of market developments and later on by coordinated steps to provide liquidity.

—Jean-Claude Trichet, president of the European Central Bank,
   June 3, 2008

The foundation of the European Union (EU) was, by its construct, a shaky entanglement of diverse nationalities, economies, and historical legacies. The entire premise required member states to open borders, trade as one, and share a common currency, the euro, regardless of economic disparities between them.

One central bank, the European Central Bank (ECB), was set up to coincide with the launch of the euro, a new supracurrency, on January 1, 1999. The ECB would dictate monetary policy for all the EU members—in theory, weighing all their diverse needs.

The euro promised growth and currency stability to the periphery countries of Europe. For a time, these nations did enjoy higher consumption levels, greater investment (especially in real estate), and economic growth. From 1999 to 2008, Ireland grew by more than 5 percent per year and Greece by 3.5 percent in comparison to the Eurozone average of 2.1 percent. European integration proved the Eurozone's greatest strength and most vicious weakness.

During the financial crisis, however, that union of twenty-eight economies, cultures, and backgrounds morphed into a bastion of inequality in power and prosperity. It was no surprise that the main monetary policy kingpins who presided over the ECB had different ideas about how to conjure money. Jean-Claude Trichet (who was referred to as "Monsieur Euro" or "Guardian of the Euro"[1]), a French national, served as head of the ECB from November 1, 2003, to October 31, 2011, and an Italian national, Mario Draghi (or, "Super Mario"), assumed the post on November 1, 2011. His term runs through October 2019.

The French hawk and the Italian dove controlled money according to their monikers and on the basis of their individual relationships with the US elite. And though Trichet was slightly reluctant to follow the Fed's easy-money lead at first, Draghi would adopt the Fed's policies, hook, line, and manufactured-money sinker.

Running the ECB, or indeed most central banks, is lucrative. The president of the ECB makes over $400,000 per year, a little less than the governors of the central banks of Belgium, Italy, and Germany, and somewhat more than the Fed's chair at $199,700.[2] That salary doesn't include all the exclusive travel perks to meet with other bankers (Bank of England governor Mark Carney makes $599,000 per year). Although the income of a central banker pales in comparison to private bank CEO compensation, power and influence over business, government, and the world has its comparative benefits; ones that we populations finance.

TRICHET'S TRAJECTORY INTO THE FINANCIAL CRISIS

Four years before Jean-Claude Trichet would be thrown headfirst into one of Europe's most calamitous financial crises, partly ignited by one of its most prominent French banks, his European pedigree was already firmly established.[3]

By the time Trichet assumed the stewardship of the ECB on November 1, 2003, he had rotated through the world's most prestigious central banks in the previous decades. Noted for his stellar taste in fashion and aristocratic elegance,[4] he went on to place number five on *Newsweek*'s global elite list in 2008. During his illustrious career, he played an array of senior roles at important central banks and as government adviser on economic, energy, and industrial matters. But he stayed away from the private sector.

After he graduated France's École nationale d'administration in 1971, Trichet entered the Ministry of Finance initially as a Socialist before waxing more centrist, and he rose to become director of the Treasury of France in 1987.[5] That year, he was appointed alternate governor of the IMF and the World Bank. He also became a member of the elite Washington-based Group of Thirty, which convenes twice a year in a major global city to discuss international finance away from the fray of ordinary people.

Trichet was governor of the Banque de France from 1993 until 2003 and a member of the board at the BIS. An engineer by training, he adopted a hawkish approach to monetary policy early on, preferring to keep a lid on inflation and a watchful eye on rising oil and food prices, and support the euro without manifesting buckets of money. When he left the ECB, he said that he planned on retiring to Brittany, where he could devote himself to poetry.[6]

Midway through Trichet's tenure, the financial world fell apart at the seams. Even before the financial Armageddon of the fall of 2008, signs were prevalent in

Europe. On August 9, 2007, French mega-bank BNP Paribas suspended redemptions for several funds because its portfolio managers couldn't evaluate the securities in them amid the US subprime crisis.[7] That precipitated a crisis at Northern Rock bank in the United Kingdom, requiring the ECB to pump a record €94.8 billion into Europe's money markets.[8] On September 14, the Bank of England (BOE) stepped in to support Northern Rock as its shares cratered, though the next day, customers, in shades of the Great Depression, executed a run on their money.[9] The banks were all connected, and on January 11, 2008, Northern Rock sold a £2.2 billion portfolio of mortgages to US bank JPMorgan to help repay loans it received from the Bank of England. The international merry-go-round of crisis aid between central banks and the private bank arena had begun.

THE WARM-UP FED AND ECB DANCE

In early 2008, as the United States buckled under a budding housing and banking crisis, Europe faced the milder problem of rising inflation. During the first half of the year, the euro appreciated to record levels against the dollar as investors feared dollar-denominated assets would exacerbate the issue. On February 27, 2008, the euro hit a record high ($1.50) against the dollar since its creation.[10]

Containing inflation as a policy prescriptive, common beforehand, in the post-crisis years would be superseded by global requirements for bank liquidity. These were not normal times. They were times of panic, reminiscent of others in the United States a century earlier. In fact, the Fed was spawned in 1913 largely because the early 1900s mega-banker J. P. Morgan needed a central bank to back him in case another panic like the one of 1907 occurred.

Now, about a century later, the Fed's chief worry was keeping the US banking system functional. Low inflation provided license to fabricate or "print" money. But inflation was low because organic growth was slow—conjured money couldn't fix growth in the real economy because it wasn't specifically directed into the real economy.

On March 11, 2008, increasingly concerned about the squeeze in the credit market, the Fed announced a $200 billion funding package. It would lend Treasury bonds to primary dealers against their federal agency debt and residential mortgage-backed securities (MBSs). The action underscored two truths: first, the Fed's power over other central banks, and, second, their fear of what could happen if they didn't play ball with the Fed's mandates.

As Bear Stearns swooned toward bankruptcy, the international press speculated that the United States might temporarily lose its place as the "world's biggest economy" to the Eurozone. In February 2008, a Gallup poll revealed that "Americans see China crowding out US as economic leader."[11] There was fear of losing the top slot in the economic hierarchy—not just from within the Washington elite but among the American middle class.

On March 17, the Fed effectively became an investment bank, acting as merger adviser, creditor, and backer of risk for JPMorgan Chase's $240 million purchase of Bear Stearns. The next day, the Dollar Index plunged to its lowest level ever, at 69.2802 in a vote of no confidence.[12] Big US banks were in big trouble.

In solidarity with the Fed, Trichet announced a $15 billion auction on March 25, 2008.[13] It was a small trickle of what would become a massive flow of money infusion into private banks. Because private international banks had comingled risk, like playing dominoes, central banks had to consider those codependencies and provide aid and liquidity to cover them.

Monetary policy collusion began quietly—and several months earlier. In mid-2007, banks noticed faulty assets based on defaulting subprime mortgage loans—a much bigger problem than the loans themselves by virtue of their size and complexity. Banks began to lose confidence in each other, and that meant a credit crunch was not far behind. Central banks had to jump to the rescue and ensure there was enough credit or liquidity flowing within the banking system. This is how swap lines between the Fed and ECB first came into being, on December 12, 2007. It was an early sign the Fed knew more than it was telling the public.

The Fed increased existing temporary currency arrangements (swap lines) with its European partners by 50 percent on March 11, 2008. It provided up to $30 billion to the ECB and $6 billion to the Swiss National Bank.

There was no mistaking the importance of this financial aid package in the private international banking community, which was its first beneficiary and needed the money soonest. "The G-10 central banks have continued to work together closely and to consult regularly."[14] This collusion wasn't to create jobs. It was to provide welfare to banks.

The world became a financial battlefield where central bankers fought to preserve their independence while being coerced through circumstance and external demands to fall into line behind the commander-in-monetary-policy, the Federal Reserve.

The G7 central banks united to provide global banks and markets the constant infusion of capital required. Restricting one bank or market in one country could restrict them all. But, equally, each central bank had to consider its own area of official focus because the standard monetary policy didn't always fit their nation. In practice, the central banks of more developed countries colluded, and as the crisis escalated, the Fed had to save its private bank members, its own influence base, and the dollar as the most prevalent and powerful reserve currency.

On April 28, 2008, a group of European journalists interviewed Trichet on the matter. He had been the "it" central banker of 2007—named Central Banker of the

Year by *The Banker* and Person of the Year by the *Financial Times* for steering "a confident path through the choppy waters of 2007's credit crisis."[15] Waters were about to get a lot choppier.

Trichet noted that people increasingly believed that gains were being privatized and losses socialized. But he wanted to correct this assumption and uphold the mantle of central banker as general savior. "It is all about protecting those who behaved properly against the harm that has been done to the market as a whole by those who have taken bad decisions."[16]

Asked if he listened to politicians like Italian prime minister Silvio Berlusconi or French president Nicolas Sarkozy when they criticized the ECB and its unilateral actions, on April 30, Trichet retorted, "The Maastricht Treaty has given us full independence."[17]

Yet, as in Latin America, the crisis shed light on the struggle between governments and central banks as they wrestled over the course of action to best benefit national economies versus multinational banks. Central banks were compelled to follow the Fed and its remedy for the US banking and financial systems—conjured money—in contrast to the best interests of their own countries.

From his post atop the ECB, headquartered in Eurotower, a sleek twenty-five-story glass skyscraper located in the heart of Frankfurt's financial district, Trichet watched inflation—like the hawk he was. Briefly, he struck an independent path from his Fed brethren. On July 3, in contrast to the Fed's money-loosening strategy, the ECB *raised* rates by 0.25 percent to 4.25 percent. Trichet cited the reason as the rise in energy and food prices, the weakening of European GDP in Q2 2008, and high credit and monetary expansion in Europe.

But he was wary. He said, "Starting from here, I have no bias." He claimed that the ECB was "called upon" to do everything it did on behalf of the European people: "We are doing what the Treaty calls upon us to do. It is also what the people of Europe are asking us to do today."[18] Trichet took care to assert the political independence of the ECB by depicting it as a vehicle of the people, not of the banks that it directly supported through making liquidity available to them.

A week and a half later, on July 15, Spain's leading real estate agency, Martinsa-Fadesa, with an estimated debt of €7 billion, filed for bankruptcy. It was the biggest bankruptcy in the history of Spain. This bursting of Spain's speculative, foreign-induced property bubble left the country in a weaker economic position to face the effects of the US subprime crisis and the eventual outbreak of the European sovereign debt crisis. Spain's plight might not have been the catalyst for the crisis in Europe, but it signaled that the entire system was in trouble.

On September 29, the US House of Representatives rejected a $700 billion rescue plan for banks, causing mass panic across international financial markets. If the big US banks weren't given emergency capital to cover their risk-driven bets, the United States could crash the entire global system. The S&P 500 stock index fell almost 9 percent and the DJIA by 778 points (almost 7 percent), its worst decline since the crash of 1987.

Swap lines with Fed allies grew to accommodate the banking system's thirst for liquidity and inability to fashion its own. The largest lines were provided to central banks on September 29 and extended to April 30, 2009. The ECB's line grew to $240 billion, the SNB's to $60 billion, Bank of Canada's to $30 billion, BOE's to $80 billion, BOJ's to $120 billion, the Danmarks Nationalbank's to $15 billion, the Norges Bank's to $15 billion, the Reserve Bank of Australia's to $30 billion, and the Sveriges Riksbank's to $30 billion.[19] It was a dollar party thrown by the Fed.

A frazzled US Treasury secretary Hank Paulson spoke in front of the White House that day. He admitted to reporters, "We've experienced significant turmoil in our financial markets in the last few days including the collapse of Washington Mutual and Wachovia here and the failure of two major financial institutions in Europe...markets around the world are under stress and that reduces the availability of credit." When pressed on whether enough was being done to alleviate the problem, he replied, "We have significant tools in our toolkit but they are not sufficient...so we are going to continue to work...until we get what we need."[20]

At the October 2, 2008, meeting of the ECB in Frankfurt, Trichet expressed fear that the US crisis, having struck Europe, would not be contained by central bank measures. Reinforcements were needed. He said, "And all governments—but not only governments—have to be up to their responsibilities. Of course we are not the United States of America as far as the institutional framework is concerned."

Though he spoke of central banks not being a part of government but still having responsibility, Trichet implied that the United States was less prepared to deal with the problem. He saw economic slowdown in the euro area due to domestic demand contraction and credit restriction.[21] Because of that, the ECB kept rates unchanged. The unanimous decision was the pivot toward expansionary monetary policy.

The next day, the ECB went a step further, though. It allowed more private banks to participate in unscheduled cash auctions through their governments.[22] While Trichet was in the United States, he told Europe 1 Radio that US Treasury "Secretary Paulson's plan [the bailout] obviously must be passed. It must be. It is necessary."[23] President Bush signed the $700 billion bank rescue package that day, October 3, 2008.[24]

That wouldn't be all. According to an October 8 Fed statement released at seven in the morning, several central banks (Bank of England, Fed, European Central Bank, Sveriges Riksbank, Swiss National Bank, Bank of Canada, and Bank of Japan) announced they had "cooperated in unprecedented joint actions such as the provision of liquidity to reduce strains in financial markets."[25] They would collude to cut rates together. It was planned and executed that way. The Fed opened the moves and cut rates by 50 basis points to 1.5 percent.[26]

Trichet realized that he would have to succumb to collusive forces. The ECB cut rates the same day, by half a percentage point to 3.75 percent. The minimum rate on main refinancing operations of the euro system fell to 3.75 percent, on the marginal lending facility to 4.75 percent, and on its deposit facility to 2.75 percent.[27] Drastic times called for drastic measures. The euro depreciated in tandem. G7 central bank collusion was the new black.

The delay in the ECB's decision to follow the Fed was a result of Trichet's consideration of regional economic conditions in contrast to the possibility of crisis contagion slamming Europe. He believed that inflation was too high to warrant a rate cut. That was old school central banking thinking.

Trichet's ECB opted for another 50-basis-point benchmark rate cut to 3.25 percent on November 6.[28] The same day, the BOE slashed its rate in one fell swoop by 1.5 percentage points, or 150 basis points, to reach 3 percent, the lowest level since 1954. On November 14, the *Economist* reported, "The European economy officially fell into its first recession in the ten years since the euro was introduced."[29] Consider the ramifications: it had taken only a few months of global awareness of the extent of the US financial system's rot to take down a major collection of economies that had been collectively chugging along for a decade.

At the fifth ECB Central Banking Conference on November 13, 2008, Trichet touted the joint efforts of the world's dominant central banks like they were war allies: "I would like to mention the fact that the ECB has been providing with euro-denominated collateral US dollar liquidity to the European counterparties through swap arrangements with the Federal Reserve that have no precedent. This action reflects, as much as all the other common actions, the intimate level of trust and cooperation within the community of central banks and, in particular with the Federal Reserve, whose value has been priceless."[30]

On December 4, Trichet told a press conference gathering at the ECB that the central bank had cut rates for the third time in two months, by 75 basis points to 2 percent. It was the biggest reduction since the euro became a supranational currency in 1999.[31] He was petrified that intensification of international financial turmoil would harm euro area demand. According to Trichet, "The level of uncertainty remains exceptionally high."[32] That day, the BOE also cut rates again—to 2 percent, the lowest level in fifty-seven years.

The Eurozone was about to hit an even harder wall. Central banks would not slam on the brakes but stamp the accelerator. Years later, regarding the events of that fall, Nobel Prize–winning economist Joseph Stiglitz remarked, "The structure of the Eurozone built in certain ideas about what was required for economic success—for instance, that the central bank should focus on inflation, as opposed to the mandate of the Federal Reserve in the US, which incorporates unemployment, growth and stability."[33]

On December 15, speaking in Frankfurt, Trichet made his next move. Addressing an exclusive crowd of journalist members of the Internationaler Club Frankfurter Wirtschaftsjournalisten, he defended not his policies, per se, but his ego, in the form of asserting central bank independence: "Today an overwhelming majority of central banks across the globe is independent. The political and functional independence of central banks has been an important milestone in the way towards separating the authority to tax and spend from the power to control credit conditions."[34]

DON'T CALL IT QE, SAYS THE ECB

If the end of 2008 was an entanglement of central banks flexing their muscles to curtail a financial emergency while expressing their independence, 2009 brought even more radical moves. The G7 central banks delved deeper into accommodative territory. But with rates hitting historic lows and the Fed having already adopted zero percent rates, there remained only one way to keep functionally easing. Terrified bankers conjured new money-creation mechanisms.

The world saw no real recovery. But there was a prevailing concern—whether elite central bankers had the power to do anything about it, and if so, how much, and for how long. That anxiety provoked skepticism of the entire international monetary system. In Europe, it began to pit old monetary powers against the young, decade-old ECB.

The ECB didn't just cut rates, it increased bond purchases to provide liquidity under the auspices of promoting growth. German chancellor Angela Merkel opposed this dovish monetary policy as too expansionary for her inflation-obsessed country.[35] On January 13, 2009, Germany passed a €50 billion stimulus plan—the biggest since World War II.[36]

The ideological chasm between the ECB policymakers and Germany splintered the EU and brought up questions about the entire EU paradigm. The Fed remained in denial about US banks' role catalyzing the global crisis, and by extension its own failure as a bank regulator, and about US banking regulatory policy in general.

On January 13, at the London School of Economics, Fed chairman Ben Bernanke gave a lecture titled "The Crisis and the Policy Response."[37] According to him, though rates were already at such low levels, the Fed could still employ many policy tools during the financial crisis. He cited three major tools, like lines of a financial sonnet:

> *lending to financial institutions,*
> *providing liquidity directly to key credit markets,*
> *and buying longer-term securities—*

It was important to Bernanke that his strategies weren't mistaken for Japan's "quantitative easing" policies pursued from 2001 to 2006. He referred to the Fed's moves as "credit easing," which resembled quantitative easing as "an expansion of the central bank's balance sheet." But he contrasted the BOJ's policy, which targeted holding a certain amount of bank reserves, with the Fed's approach, which sought to hold a "mix of loans and securities."

He attributed this difference to wider credit spreads and "more dysfunctional" credit markets in the United States than existed during the "Japanese experiment with quantitative easing."[38] Debt and credit flows were conveniently moving targets.

Not only Bernanke emphasized his policies weren't the same as Japan's. Trichet similarly deflected when the ECB began its quantitative easing programs in May 2009. As the London-based *Telegraph* reported, "The European Central Bank has cut interest rates a quarter point to a record low of 1pc and embraced quantitative easing (QE) for the first time, catching markets off guard with plans to buy €60bn (£53.5bn) of covered bonds."[39]

Both men wanted to affirm their individual ingenuity in the money-creation process. They were both men of power. Both were featured in *Newsweek*'s 2008 fifty most powerful global elite list (Bernanke beat Trichet by one place, coming in fifth).[40]

In practice, the distinction was irrelevant. Whatever they called it, both central banks fabricated money to inject into the markets or private banks in return for some sort of debt, bonds, or loans. The effects of their strategies, regardless of language, were equivalent: benefits accrued to banks and capital markets, not economies. By alluding to their monetary prowess, the central bankers were not only waging monetary warfare but also staging PR stunts. If they could sell the idea of their support to the general public while helping the bankers, the game was on.

On January 15, 2009, the ECB cut rates again, bringing total cuts since October 8 to 225 basis points, including a record-breaking 75 basis points in December. Two weeks later, in an interview with the German weekly *Die Zeit*, IMF head Dominique Strauss-Kahn called for *more* coordination among European governments to follow the Fed's lead.

Concerning the Eurozone, he prophesized, "Differences between states will become too big and stability of the currency zone is in danger."[41] He warned that the fund's cash could run out and be severely affected by the current situation, having its resources consumed in six to eight months. "That's why I'm already asking member states for additional funds."

Two weeks later, and feeling the heat at the Davos World Economic Forum, Trichet fielded questions about the viability of the Eurozone. Replying to criticism from Strauss-Kahn, Trichet said, "There is no risk that the euro will break apart."[42]

His declaration coincided with mounting questions as to whether countries such as Greece and Italy would stay in the European Monetary Union. Yield spreads on Greek, Irish, and Italian bonds had jumped to record levels versus German ones, an indication of the perceived economic risk of those countries relative to the core of Western Europe.

On April 2, 2009, in London, the G20 organized its second meeting (of three) that year to discuss the international crisis. With markets in dire straits around the world and economies no better off, they attempted to devise more coordinated solutions.

In the group's "Leaders' Statement," they unearthed another white knight. They chose to boost the IMF's capacity to provide international liquidity and to cooperate in refraining from currency wars. To help their European-leaning ally, they agreed to triple the resources available to the IMF to $750 billion. All told, this constituted a $1.1 trillion program to "restore credit, growth and jobs in the world economy." Combined with existing measures, this was a "global plan for recovery on an unprecedented scale."[43] Big US banks that hadn't yet died were resuscitated by the Fed, and the rest of the world picked up the conjured-money tab.

The sheer unfairness of this exercise did not go unnoticed. Massive protests beset the G20 event. Demonstrators closed in on the Bank of England and stormed a Royal Bank of Scotland branch. The European population's economic frustration and discontent escalated.[44]

Four days later, four other central banks—Swiss, European Union, England, and Japan—agreed to help the mother ship, to provide $287 billion to the Fed as currency swaps that could be used as credit lines to banks that needed quick cash.[45] They would provide liquidity of up to £30 billion, €80 billion, ¥10 trillion, and SF 40 billion (Swiss francs). They fabricated such sizable funds in the hope of stabilizing an ailing and flailing banking system at the risk of losing credibility for impotence.

A month later, in May 2009, at a press conference at ECB headquarters, Trichet and ECB vice president Lucas Papademos announced another 50-basis-point rate cut on the main refinancing operations and the marginal lending facility, to 1.00 percent and 1.75 percent, respectively. The rate on the deposit facility remained at 0.25 percent.

This was the seventh time the ECB had cut the key rate since October 2008, when it was 4.25 percent. Trichet—his inner hawk shed completely—implied more to come: "We have not decided today that the new level of our policy rates was the lowest level."[46]

The ECB was caught in a land of make-believe—a place where money was crafted to buy up hoards of bonds. The ECB's latest unconventional policy entailed purchasing €60 billion worth of covered bonds[47] and providing *unlimited* money to banks for twelve months. In a news conference that month of May, Trichet emphatically denied this measure could be called "quantitative easing."[48] But it was just that.

These actions, lacking any historical precedent, stirred the pot in Germany. About a month later, in Berlin, at a conference of the Initiative New Social Market Economy, a think tank for Germany's metal and electronics sectors, chancellor Angela Merkel delivered her most public criticism of the central banks' post-crisis actions.

She strongly admonished US political and loose banking policy: "Among the causes [of the crisis]," she said, "is ultimately behavioral patterns that were also politically supported, so for example through monetary policy in the United States and through refusals in the world's biggest [financial] markets to accept any rules."[49] She didn't want the ECB on the same policy path.

Merkel, pressing her commanding role in the EU and ascension in the global political arena, was incensed. "I view with great skepticism the powers of the Fed, for example, and also how, within Europe, the Bank of England has carved out its own small line. The European Central Bank has also bowed somewhat to international pressure with the purchase of covered bonds. We must return together to an independent central-bank policy and to a policy of reason, otherwise we will be in exactly the same situation in 10 years' time."[50] Her words were prescient; that's precisely what has happened. This was a major political statement. The fact that the leader of Germany was critiquing the US Fed was a monumental shift in PC-politics, one that would reverberate for years to come. And it was not just the Fed that Merkel was castigating but also the ECB and the BOE.

Economic conditions had declined, though. The May unemployment real rate for the sixteen Eurozone member nations rose to 9.3 percent, its worst level since the euro's establishment. Conditions in Southern European countries were abysmal. (The rate would rise and eventually fall to that 2009 low in 2017, indicating the sheer lack of usefulness job-wise of the ECB's monetary policy.)

European banks, fighting for their own survival, weren't lending their cheap funds any more than US banks were. On July 2, 2009, Trichet showed his cards. He gave banks a pass for their hoarding behavior, saying, "The flow of bank loans to non-financial corporations and households has remained subdued, reflecting in part the weakening in economic activity and the continued low levels of business and consumer confidence."[51]

About a month later, on August 6, when they warned of a corporate credit crunch at the Associated Press conference, Trichet and Papademos took more heat, this time from companies. To distance himself from corporate wrath and blame,

Trichet said, "We do not intend to set ourselves up as a substitute for the banks."[52] But that's the very thing the ECB had become, one step removed, by financing banks that wouldn't finance companies in return.

The next day, August 7, with a muted recovery the best-case scenario, the BOE and ECB kept their benchmark rates unchanged at record lows—0.5 percent for the BOE and 1 percent for the ECB. The BOE decided to print another $85 billion toward asset purchases, supposedly to boost the availability of bank credit. "In the United Kingdom, the recession appears to have been deeper than previously thought," the Bank of England said in a statement. "Though there are signs that credit conditions may have started to ease," the statement continued, "lending to business has fallen and spreads on bank loans remain elevated. Financial conditions remain fragile."

The adverse economic situation between the United States and Europe had elevated the euro. And with increasing confidence in the wake of dedicated central bank moves to keep money pumping, Germany and France (and Japan) finally returned to positive GDP growth during the second quarter of 2009 relative to a 1 percent GDP growth drop in the United States.[53]

This concerned Trichet, who tried to make it seem as if a strong dollar was the plan all along. On October 8, 2009, at a press conference in Venice, Italy, attended by Mario Draghi in his capacity as governor of the Italian Central Bank, Trichet repeated assurances that the United States wanted a strong dollar: "When the Secretary of the Treasury and our friend Ben Bernanke say that a strong dollar is in the interests of the US economy and that they are pursuing a strong-dollar policy, this is a judgment that is obviously very important for us and for the global economy."[54]

When Trichet and Draghi were asked what message they would pass on from recent summits (the G20 meeting in Pittsburgh in September and the IMF annual meeting in Istanbul in October), Trichet emphasized cooperation. For his part, Draghi wanted a financial system "such that the banks will ultimately be able to finish repairing their balance sheets and which will ensure that the cycle starts up again."[55]

So, although Draghi touted the notion of there being a clear line drawn between the hierarchy of power and the subsequent autonomy of public policies in nations throughout Europe, he remained more concerned with the banks' stability than with that of the various local populations. But that didn't happen in practice. Crises amplified the split of the Eurozone economy into a more or less prosperous north and a debt-driven periphery in the south. With such contrasts, a fair and unified EU was impossible to attain.

When asked about the possibility of joint intervention of the United States and the ECB in the euro-dollar exchange rate, Trichet replied that both regions were cooperating. He said he was not campaigning for the euro's international use.

Another more personnel-oriented question arose: whether Draghi had any interest in occupying Trichet's post. Draghi replied with the perfect stoic composure of a political banker, "We have a President and he could not be better."[56] Draghi was hitting the big time: he was there with Trichet and Lucas Papademos, which boosted his platform and showed that he was not only part of the conversation but an equal in it.

Regarding the low level of current rates on October 9, Trichet remarked that anyone who considered the situation a return to business as normal was "absolutely plain wrong."[57]

By late October 2009, the decline of the US dollar benefited the American economic recovery, making US exports cheaper. This was the type of currency war tactic the United States would complain about other nations using later. The move drew criticism from Europe, Japan, and the Persian Gulf countries. The weaker dollar made American industry more competitive and improved the US trade deficit, but in Europe and Japan the weaker dollar brought reductions in exports and a swerve off the trajectory toward economic recovery.

Trichet later told the *Financial Times* that in late 2009 Bernanke effectively handed over his money-conjuring playbook, saying, "Now, Jean-Claude, it's your turn!" Trichet observed, "We—the central banks of the advanced economies—had to embark on very bold, non-standard measures and the governments had to step in massively....A dramatic great depression was avoided."[58] He might have been skeptical at the onset of the money-conjuring policy, but like his monetary mentor, Bernanke, he believed in his own hype.

"NO-LIMIT" QE

Throughout 2010, central banks of developed countries advocated cheap-money policy despite no discernible evidence of a return to financial normalcy as a result. The ECB left rates at 1 percent the entire year, the Fed kept rates near zero, and the BOJ left rates unchanged—and a slew of newly crafted policy measures littered the markets.

Within continental Europe, new problems were rising; heightened risks of sovereign debt defaults, greater political differences, and a growing economic divide among countries.

In particular, the Greek economy suffered from a prolonged recession that brought it to the verge of bankruptcy. The most elite politicians and central bankers wanted to secure debt repayments through the use of broad reforms and austerity measures.

Greece may have been the first out of the Southern European countries to take on such burdens, but it would not be the last. Western Europe would decide the financial destiny of Southern Europe, but even that provoked dissent. Germany and France were at odds on how to do it. Germany (and the ECB) played hardball. It wanted Greece to undergo a strict austerity program policed by the ECB, European Commission, and the IMF. France wanted a more reasonable approach. Both used the solidity of the EU as a reason for their preference.

Across the Atlantic, on January 28, 2010, Federal Reserve chair Bernanke was confirmed by the US Senate to a second term. The 70–30 vote was the weakest endorsement in the Fed's ninety-six years of existence. While Republicans pushed fiscal conservatism, many Democrats perpetuated the belief that the Fed's cheap money would filter through to the population. Senator Bernie Sanders, who would later run for US president, noted something about the vote relevant to the US and European populations: the tepid vote sent a "clear message to the Fed and to Chairman Bernanke: Start representing the needs of the middle class and working families, not just Wall Street CEOs. Stop credit card ripoffs. Free up credit for small businesses. Break up big banks, and stop the secrecy surrounding trillions of dollars in blind loans."[59] The Fed would begin its second round of QE (or QE2) on November 3, 2010.

As concern spread from Greece to the heavily indebted PIIGS countries (Portugal, Italy, Ireland, Greece, and Spain), on January 14, 2010, Greece announced an ambitious "Stability and Growth Program" designed to cut its budget deficit from 12.7 percent (in 2009) to 2.8 percent by 2012.[60] It would ostensibly bring the deficit into alignment with the convergence criteria of the Maastricht Treaty.[61]

By late March, Eurozone leaders and the IMF reached an agreement on how to rescue Greece.[62] Trichet, who had initially opposed the joint measure, said he was "extraordinarily happy that the governments of the euro area found out a workable solution."[63] French president Nicolas Sarkozy did not want the IMF involved in the agreement, but German chancellor Angela Merkel insisted on it to avoid Germany having to take on a bigger individual burden.

The IMF has always had a unique connection to the French government. Europeans have always steered the IMF, and France has supplied more leaders than any other country. At that time, Dominique Strauss-Kahn, the former French minister of economy and finance, was managing director of the IMF. If Sarkozy was to be all-in on the IMF taking action, it would be as much an IMF move as it would be a French one.

In the central banking arena, if Greece—and, many believed, the Eurozone—was to be saved, it rested on the willingness of France and Germany to come to an agreement. If the IMF was to go it alone without the approval of the Germans, the French would hold the bill for Greece. But if they were to go in with the Germans, it would be a "European" move.

On April 27, rating agency Standard & Poor's cut Greece's credit rating to junk status. It would also downgrade Portugal.[64] The risk of a general European sovereign debt crisis caused the French CAC 40 to fall 3.83 percent and the German DAX 2.73 percent. Gold prices jumped as investors sought safe havens disconnected from central banks and the global monetary system.

The head of Greece's central bank, George Provopoulos, tried to calm markets by reassuring the world of his commitment to spending cuts and austerity measures. But the truth of the matter was that central banks concocted trillions of euros for banks to restore bankers' confidence. The only checks handed out to the average person were in the form of social welfare checks, the same ones they were seeking to cut through austerity-based policy.

Ten days later, on May 7, the German parliament approved the bailout plan the IMF and EU put together to provide Greece with €110 billion (US$146 billion) in loans over three years.[65] Germany provided the largest component, about €22 billion, of the EU's €80 billion portion. In exchange, Greek prime minister Andreas Papandreou committed to austerity measures, including €30 billion in spending cuts and tax increases.[66]

The Fed remained anxious about a European spillover back into the United States. On May 9, the Fed responded to the Greek bailout by reestablishing temporary US dollar liquidity swaps.[67] Bernanke took pride in his role as global policy executor, noting that for the ECB, "There will be no limit to the amount that they are going to be prepared to buy."

Recall that Bernanke said, "I just want to emphasize what an extraordinary step this is, particularly for the ECB....I would also characterize Trichet's call to me as being a personal appeal....I got very much some of the same tone from Mervyn King, and, to a lesser extent, even from Shirakawa, who says that Japan is also facing pressure, and they are very concerned about contagion." Though these bankers hailed from different countries, they were by no means foreign to one another, given their periodic encounters during the year at their regular meetings at the BIS, in Basel, Switzerland.

Also on May 9, 2010, the Eurozone nations created the European Financial Stability Facility (EFSF) with €440 billion in capital. The European financial stabilization mechanism pledged loans up to €60 billion. The IMF pledged €250 billion,[68] concluding that "to buy securities helped to ease some of the more severe euro area bond market pressures. After the announcement of the securities purchase program in early May, spreads over German sovereign bonds on Greek, Portuguese, and Irish debt had narrowed." It would not last. Market liquidity in Europe remained strained. By July 2010, the ECB had purchased €59 billion in government debt from the secondary market to provide liquidity.[69]

Although the euro might have brought the participating members together, it did not mean they shared an equal part in the economy. Germany, a traditional power in Europe, was positioned to guide the major Western states while leaving the southern ones to either follow or be left behind. In many ways, that's what happened. Easy-money policies simply exacerbated the trend.

Less than a week later in May, Spanish prime minister José Luis Rodríguez Zapatero (of the Socialist Workers' Party) announced austerity measures, an "extraordinary effort" to save Spain €50 billion. He cut government spending and employees' pay by 5 percent. In the third quarter of 2008, the Spanish economy had officially entered recession. By February 2010, it had supposedly "exited the recession," but once Greece faltered, the so-called exit was imperiled.

In an attempt to allay the fears of unions and his constituency, Zapatero stressed that, despite new austerity measures, "the pillars of the welfare state will remain untouched."[70] The response brought about the first general strike since 2002, where ten million workers marched in solidarity.[71]

Austerity was a misguided response to a financial crisis caused by banks fortified by monetary policy crafted by the Fed and exported to its G7 allies. But it wasn't seen in that context. On May 25, 2010, Italy agreed to a €25 billion austerity package to cut its deficit from 5.3 percent to 2.7 percent by 2012.[72]

Two months later, on July 8, the IMF highlighted its unease about the ECB's commitment to increase bond purchases if necessary. Seemingly unconcerned about the artificial nature of its money crafting, it called upon the ECB to make its €500 billion rescue fund fully available—especially to European banks—in stress periods. The IMF was worried about the "too-big-to-fail" bank problem and the willingness of governments to save any bank in trouble.[73]

It was right to be. Two and a half weeks later, results of the bank stress tests were disclosed.[74] Six of the seven banks that failed the tests were the Agricultural Bank of Greece SA and five Spanish savings banks. The seventh bank was a German real estate bank. The biggest banks all passed; they had been fortified by ECB subsidies and conjured money.

Over the next few months, the euro staged a recovery. The successful performance of European banks in the stress tests reduced the fear of sovereign debt defaults.[75] In addition, the euro was lifted on positive negotiations regarding Greece's bailout and moderate growth rates in the Eurozone. In comparison, a US unemployment rate stuck at 9.5 percent didn't reflect well on the dollar.

On August 7, 2010, the ECB bought Italian and Spanish bonds on the secondary market for the first time. That kick-started their bond markets, showing speculators they could ride the ECB's plays. But such purchases of indebted countries' government securities, which the ECB portrayed as an endeavor to monetize national debt in the Eurozone, were prohibited by the European Monetary Union founding treaties.[76]

The ECB was creating money to finance countries' public debt. Critics worried it would increase inflation. But the real item that the ECB had to sell the public—or at least public markets—was confidence. If it could get speculators and investors to buy in to its robust plans, it could spur outsiders to purchase the bonds of struggling countries. The monetary battle was as much about perception and psyche as reality.

Across the Atlantic, a cadre of central banking policymakers gathered in August 2010 at Jackson Hole. There, Bernanke proclaimed no intention of slowing down on easing: "The committee is prepared to provide additional monetary accommodation through unconventional measures if it proves necessary."

Trichet concurred. But he wanted to ensure that governments and central banks could safely transition from very high debt levels "incurred in response to the global financial crisis…without compromising economic growth." For Trichet, the "primary macroeconomic challenge for the next 10 years is to ensure that they do not turn into another 'lost decade.'"[77] The hawk was back.

An August 2010 report from the OECD noted: "Banks tend to be heavily exposed to the sovereign debt of their own country. The exposure of Greek banks to Greek sovereign debt represents 226 percent of their Tier 1 capital. In Italy, Hungary, Spain, Portugal, and Ireland these numbers are 157 percent, 133 percent, 113 percent, 69 percent and 26 percent, respectively." It went on to say, "The EU wide loss from the haircut is around €26.4bn. The contribution of the 5 countries where most of the market focus has been (Greece, Portugal, Ireland, Italy and Spain) is only €14.4bn."[78]

That fall, on November 3, the Fed announced its second round of QE measures.[79] With high unemployment, dull economic activity, and low inflation, the Fed offered to "purchase a further $600 billion of longer-term Treasury securities by the end of the second quarter of 2011, a pace of about $75 billion per month."[80] As a result, the dollar fell against its peers and the euro jumped to a nine-month high.[81]

The next day, at a press conference in Frankfurt, Trichet was asked if he would continue to affirm the United States was pursuing a strong-dollar policy, even though extra QE should have weakened it by keeping rates low. He answered, "I have no indication that would change my trust in the fact that the Federal Reserve Chairman and the Secretary of the Treasury, not to mention the President of the United States, are not playing the strategy or tactics of a weak dollar."[82]

He added, "I was also impressed by a recent speech of my colleague and friend, Chairman Ben Bernanke….The world's two largest central banks in the advanced economies could hardly be more closely aligned with regard to the inflation rates they aim to establish in their respective economies over the medium term."[83] The two men were like-minded magicians waving the same wand. Coordination was all part of the act and required an honor code to keep it going.

On December 16, following more financial strife—including a €22.5 billion bailout for Ireland and a €26 billion bailout to Portugal as part of a larger package—the European Council set up a permanent bailout fund called the European Stability Mechanism (ESM) to be managed by the European Commission. It was worth about €500 billion, augmenting the ECB programs.[84]

In the age of central bank excess, money shifted from one crisis to another. Leadership never publicly offered a true diagnosis of the problem or a cure. Prescriptions often leave a patient better in the short term but in desperate need for sustainable treatment for the future.

The ECB, for its part, stood determined to intervene, interject, and craft monetary policy. However, it was like fighting monetary fires with gasoline—especially when political forces were at play. The central bank's actions were not designed to *solve* deep-rooted problems unearthed by the global financial crisis and the mega private banks at its epicenter.

By December 2010, three million people in Spain were unemployed, making Spain Europe's greatest job destroyer.[85] The Spanish youth unemployment rate, which was 24.5 percent in 2008, hit 41.50 percent in 2010. In France and Italy, one-quarter of the youth were unemployed.[86] The ECB's single mandate is to achieve price stability. Using that as the caveat for its monetary policy provided cover for the big banks but left millions of people unemployed.

CHANGING OF THE ECB GUARD

On March 3, 2011, at a press conference in Frankfurt, Trichet announced that the ECB would likely raise interest rates in April. His decision was based on the need to keep the inflation rate, which had touched 2.4 percent in February, just above 2 percent.[87] As a result, the euro rose to $1.3976, its strongest level since November 8, 2010, resurrecting discussions about the psychologically important $1.40 level.

A shadow dogged the ECB's decision, cast over countries with the greatest sovereign debt risk, including Ireland, Portugal, and Greece. A rise in rates and a consequent stronger currency would increase the cost of their debts. Germany, however, wanted higher rates because the German banking system competed for deposits with them.

Trichet had to deny his moves signaled the start of rate hikes. The market didn't want to have to pay for liquidity. This time, Mother Nature intervened. On March 11, 2011, the Pacific coast of Tōhoku off the coast of Japan was ravaged by a magnitude 9.0–9.1 undersea megathrust earthquake. The impact was devastating. It jolted the markets.

In response to the subsequent run on the yen, on March 18, the G7 leaders embarked on a round of joint intervention in the foreign exchange markets. The United States, United Kingdom, Canada, and ECB joined Japan "in concerted intervention in exchange markets."[88]

The collaboration of this group could have simply been a new-normal reaction to currency or market seizures in an emergency, but it was more than that. It was one of a series of interventions the G7 financial leaders believed they could make because they knew they could manufacture all the money that was needed. A sort of natural opportunity had presented itself to some of the most unnatural institutions.

Trichet lifted interest rates from 1 percent to 1.25 percent, on April 7, 2011, even as Europe considered a bailout for Portugal, the latest European country to be mired in a debt crisis. He characterized the move as "in the interests of all members and partners of the single [European] market and single currency." He believed that it would boost economic confidence in Europe. In contrast, the Fed and the Bank of England remained in easy-money mode.[89]

The southern countries were most hurt by the rising cost of servicing debt. When asked about that impact on peripheral economies, Trichet generalized that the ECB was "responsible for ensuring price stability for 331 million people" and that "the hike is unwelcome for peripheral countries, but arguably the core member states were in need of this move already some time ago."[90] He was executing a continent-wide balancing act. The general ECB doctrine was one-size-fits-all—up and down.

Yet, when questioned about possible German bias in the ECB's decision, Trichet became indignant. Comparing the euro area to the United States, as he often did, he said, "I wonder how Ben Bernanke would respond if he was asked whether he did this or that because of California or because of another big state? Germany is a large economy, the largest economy in the constellation of economies that we have in the euro area.... We had an episode of a return to competitiveness, of hard work, and now we see the result of this hard work. It is good for Germany and good for the euro area as a whole."[91]

He wasn't the only conjurer who defied the Fed's easing directive. When asked about the companion Chinese rate hike, Trichet commented on his relationship with the People's Bank of China and its governor, Zhou Xiaochuan. "I personally have a very close relationship with Governor Zhou, and we meet very often.... as I have said in the past, central banks do not take the same decisions, as they are not in the same situation. But what really characterizes all central bankers is that they have a unity of purpose... solidly anchoring inflation expectations."[92] Central bankers used inflation as a crutch to either lower or raise rates. At that moment, Trichet and Governor Zhou were united in combating price increases in their own domains.

The Fed marched on while mega-banks remained the walking wounded in need of resuscitation. Thomas Hoenig, Kansas City Fed president, one of the most outspoken Fed officials regarding the need to enforce better behavior in the US banking system, came upon a sensible trade. He believed that big banks such as Bank of America and Citigroup should have their activity restricted by the US government because they were effectively wards of the government anyway. A critic of the Fed's policy to rescue the banks, he said they were not prepared for the next financial crisis.[93] They had paid billions of dollars in fines, and would pay billions more, but remained too big to fail. American banks would send shockwaves to Europe.

By mid-April 2011, the dollar had dropped to its lowest level against the euro in fifteen months. Even with the Eurozone sovereign debt crisis looming, the Fukushima disaster in Japan, and the ballooning political crisis in the Middle East, the dollar had lost its safe-haven shine. Suddenly, the magic of conjured money was suspect.[94] Central banks from Europe, Asia, and Latin America sensed trouble in the notion of cheap money's omnipotence.

Could more cracks in the greenback come? The answer was yes. A month later, the World Bank released a report on the international monetary system and role of the dollar. It expected the US dollar to lose its dominance by 2025, with the euro and the renminbi establishing a "multi-currency" monetary system of three currencies.[95]

The World Bank also believed "a larger role for the renminbi would help resolve the disparity between China's great economic strength on the global stage and its heavy reliance on foreign currencies."[96] It wasn't the only post–World War II supranational organization to throw support to China—the IMF was on that same track.

At a press conference in Frankfurt on June 9, 2011, Trichet remained in tightening mode. He called for another likely rate rise in July due to rising commodity and energy prices, saying, "We remain strongly determined to secure a firm anchoring of inflation expectations in the euro area. This is a prerequisite for monetary policy to make an ongoing contribution towards supporting growth and job creation in the euro area."[97]

Trichet emphasized the three paths of attack Europe had—monetary policy, fiscal policy, and structural reforms. He stepped out of the confines of monetary policymaker to defend political austerity measures that he believed would restore European growth in a "responsible" way.[98] This was momentous. By treading beyond his official role as major central banker, concerned only with setting rates, he advocated restricting government programs for citizens.

It was not only Trichet but also the euro elite who demanded austerity in return for bailout money. In practice, that meant crippling the population, making the likelihood of Greece repaying a bailout or its debt slim. After the June 2011 Euro Area Summit in Brussels, the heads of state of the euro area and EU institutions welcomed "the measures undertaken by the Greek government…as well as the new package of measures including privatization recently adopted by the Greek parliament. These are unprecedented, but necessary, efforts to bring the Greek economy back on a sustainable growth path."[99] It didn't matter to them what they gave up in the process.

The ECB was split on whether to buy Italian and Spanish debt to help lower its cost.[100] It had bought Irish and Portuguese bonds before, but not Spanish and Italian ones. After Italian prime minister Berlusconi pledged to hasten reforms in return for financial help, his opposition said he was "surrendering sovereignty to the European Central Bank."[101]

The IMF was undergoing its own transformation. On July 5, 2011, former French minister Christine Lagarde was elected to become its managing director.[102] Two days later, the ECB announced another rate hike of 0.25 percent on its main refinancing operations.[103] Trichet considered inflation of 2.7 percent as "clearly" revealing a tendency toward high price levels in the next few months.[104] He was seeing the efficacy of his long-held policies.

The IMF overstepped the Italian government by calling on Italy to do more to reduce public debt—one of the highest in the Eurozone—and push spending cuts.[105] Yields on ten-year Italian bonds had jumped 200 basis points, from 5 percent to above 7 percent, by November. Italy's borrowing costs shot to record highs as parliament rushed through radical budget cuts to stave off debt crisis contagion.[106]

More central bankers overstepped the borders of monetary stewardship. On August 5, 2011, Trichet sent a confidential letter to Zapatero regarding the Spanish public debt market and suggesting reforms.[107] According to the Spanish newspaper *El País*, the letter "makes evident the loss of control of the democratically elected governments of the periphery of the single-currency bloc over their own economic affairs, even those that were not in receipt of full-blown bailouts."[108]

The move didn't come without sharp trepidation. According to the London-based *Independent*, which called Trichet "the Guardian of the Euro" on August 5, 2011, "As governor of the ECB, Mr. Trichet was also accused of being 'more German than the Germans' and being obsessed with inflation rather than growth."[109]

The line between the influence of central bank conjurers and governments was increasingly blurred. In response to market hysteria, the ECB finally announced on August 7 that it would purchase Italian bonds in an attempt to reduce the nation's borrowing costs. This lowered yields to the 5 percent range.

On August 10, the Bank of England promised more stimulus would be provided if needed. The BOJ expressed concern about yen appreciation, and the SNB announced efforts to avoid an overvalued franc. Troubled about global recession, the banks vowed to "take all necessary measures to support financial stability and growth in a spirit of close cooperation and confidence."[110]

About a month later, on September 15, the ECB announced it would lend dollars to Eurozone banks that had limited access to dollars. It would coordinate with the Fed and other central banks on various dollar liquidity operations to ensure enough dollars were available through year-end.[111] After three years of ZIRP, there weren't enough dollars in the system to go around. This announcement was a tacit admission that fabricated money was, in essence, causing the *evaporation* of money.

As previously noted but critical, Christine Lagarde proclaimed the IMF's emergency bailout fund might not be enough to cover problems in the event of an actual emergency. She confessed, "Our lending capacity of almost $400bn looks comfortable today, but pales in comparison with the potential financing needs of vulnerable countries and crisis bystanders."[112] It was a dire prognosis, pointing to not only the IMF's but the entire central banking system's failure to stabilize confidence.

Her warning followed the announcement of a plan to replenish the European Financial Stability Facility bailout fund eightfold from €440 billion to €3 trillion. The German and French Eurozone leaders were in panic mode, fearing a sovereign debt crisis.

Emerging market countries demanded solutions to the Eurozone crisis. Brazil's finance minister Guido Mantega said that Europeans had a responsibility "to ensure that their actions stop contagion beyond the euro periphery."[113] PBOC governor Zhou Xiaochuan said, "The sovereign debt crisis in the euro area needs to be resolved promptly to stabilize market confidence."[114] The tide turned as China stormed the international stage.

In the United States, inflation wasn't a concern, but the unemployment rate had barely budged, holding stubbornly at 8.6 percent. Banks hoarded the money the Fed provided them instead of lending at comparable levels to small businesses that could hire people. In September 2011, their cash holdings rose to 14.2 percent of their financial assets, the highest ratio since 1977.[115]

Also in September, the Italian senate approved a €54 billion (£47 billion; US$74 billion) three-year austerity package. S&P cut Italy's debt rating to A from A+ anyway, an action influenced by "political considerations."[116] On October 14, Prime Minister Berlusconi barely won a confidence vote over his handling of the economy.[117] His victory was short-lived. On November 13, doubts over Italy's debt burden escalated, and Berlusconi resigned after his government failed to achieve a full majority during a budget vote. Former European Union commissioner and hardliner economist Mario Monti took his place. On December 22, Italy's senate approved Monti's $40 billion austerity package.

European leaders reunited in Brussels on October 26, 2011, to discuss the euro and the sovereign debt crisis. German chancellor Angela Merkel warned, "The world is watching" and "if the euro collapses, then Europe collapses."[118] It was the fourteenth summit in twenty-one months. According to Merkel, "Nobody should believe that another half century of peace in Europe is a given—it's not." Although German politicians were united in support of an increased European bailout fund, Germany was unwilling to allow the ECB to lend money directly to countries in the Eurozone. The functioning of the Eurozone took a backseat to Germany's self-interest.

In Southern Europe, things went from bad to worse. On October 31, Greek prime minister Papandreou called for a national referendum on the second bailout agreement. He called it off after the center-right opposition agreed to back a re-vamped EU-IMF deal. He was forced to step down by Western European leadership, in particular, the heads of state of France and Germany. Merkel said: "We would rather achieve a stabilization of the euro with Greece than without Greece, but this goal of stabilizing the euro is more important." Sarkozy hammered home the same message, saying in a joint news conference with Merkel, "Our Greek friends must decide whether they want to continue the journey with us."[119]

Even the IMF's Lagarde levied significant pressure. Without the IMF, Germany, or France, the Greek economy would never survive in such a state on its own, unless its debts could be forgiven, which core European elites were unwilling to contemplate.

"At the IMF's annual meeting in Washington the first thing Lagarde emphasized in talks with Venizelos was the need for consensus," confided a top aide to the minister. "She asked him bluntly, 'What Greece am I talking to, the one who endorses reforms, who accepts austerity or the one who doesn't?' She was very concerned by the stance of the political opposition, especially the [main opposition] conservative party which has repeatedly refused to endorse the [EU-IMF] fiscal adjustment programmes."[120] She was seemingly concerned about whether what was occurring with Greece could be repeated throughout the weaker economies of Europe, which would threaten the strength of the EU more generally as a result.

For instance, in Italy, two days before the IMF meeting, Silvio Berlusconi proclaimed that he alone could save Italy and "there is no chance for me to step aside."[121] It was fortuitous timing—but not for Berlusconi. He knew the economy and financial system were shaky.

Draghi wasn't going down with that ship. He had been announced as the replacement for Trichet on June 24, 2011. Before taking office, he had favored the German policy of inflation fighting with higher rates and a stronger euro over the Fed's cheap-money policy. But power and a higher seat at the table of central banker elites were a potent elixir. Draghi would be exposed to wide skepticism regardless of his actions if the Italian economy truly tanked. He knew he had to act as a part of the establishment, while also setting himself apart enough to show strength.[122]

On November 1, 2011, Draghi assumed Trichet's role as head of the ECB.[123] Draghi, with a fondness for expensive, well-tailored black suits, was sixty-three when he was appointed.[124] Once at the helm of the ECB, he followed the Fed's prescription of cheap money without hesitation. His opening gambit was to reverse Trichet's policies. Draghi cut rates twice before year-end, including by 0.25 percent within two days of his arrival.[125] He also expanded the existing covered bond purchase program.[126]

Draghi, in contrast to Trichet, was brief when questioned about anything. With a PhD in economics from the Massachusetts Institute of Technology, the ascending central banker believed he understood what banks needed: access to cheap capital. He had been a former managing director and vice chairman at Goldman Sachs, where he worked from 2002 to 2005. That post combined with his political experience truly established him in the elite networks of international and European finance. And he would deliver cheap money to big finance in return.

Early in his career, Super Mario, as he was known in Italy, helped draft legislation to govern the Italian financial markets (the so-called Draghi Law). He went on to become governor of the Bank of Italy, where he served from 2006 to 2011 before becoming the ECB president.[127]

On November 10, 2011, Lucas Papademos, former ECB vice president and governor of Greece's central bank, was named interim prime minister of Greece to work on guaranteeing the country's permanence in the Eurozone. Papademos had never held an elected office.[128] The desperate measures confirmed the strong relationship between power and money in turbulent times.

Since the beginning of 2011, foreign bank deposits at the Fed had doubled from $350 billion to $715 billion, ensuring the dollar's status as the world's reserve currency.[129] Even after Standard & Poor's had cut the United States' AAA credit rating on August 5, the dollar went on to appreciate 7.2 percent and was the second-best-performing currency after the yen during the period. This move was counterintuitive, considering the US budget deficit had reached more than $1 trillion and unemployment hovered around 9 percent.

This behavior struck at the core of the problem of international currencies. The market, investors, and most economists couldn't conceive of a change in the international monetary system structure. Instead, they clung to the same unreliable system.

On November 30, the key central banks (of Canada, England, Japan, the European Union, the United States, and Switzerland) searched for proof that their methods were effective. But they still didn't think there was enough liquidity to keep the international financial system humming. Leaders collectively agreed to lower the pricing on existing US dollar liquidity swap arrangements by 50 points.[130] They established temporary bilateral liquidity swap arrangements so they could inject funds into each other's central banks if necessary for use by their respective banking systems.

With that sorted, at the European parliament in Brussels, Draghi moved beyond the scope of a central banker, like his predecessor had, and called for more fiscal policy: "What I believe our economic and monetary union needs is a new fiscal compact—a fundamental restatement of the fiscal rules together with the mutual fiscal commitments that euro area governments have made."[131] What he meant was—more austerity.

By the end of November 2011, Tim Geithner, after five trips alone to Europe to meet with bankers and various figureheads, said that European leaders were "moving ahead, but we just need them to move ahead more quickly and with more force behind it."[132] During the first week of December, Geithner arrived in Germany on the first leg of another trip to meet with European leaders, including a one-and-a-half-hour meeting with Draghi.[133]

Geithner declined to comment on the visit, but his goal was to urge European officials to do something to prevent a full-blown debt crisis.[134] He and Obama worried that a European crisis could affect the fragile US economic recovery. It was important that Europe find a collaborative solution. US officials saw Europe as a critical part of the economic-political system. Geithner went to Europe to "emphasize how important it is to the US and global economy to succeed in building a stronger Europe."[135] The move had a political motive as well—upcoming elections. However, the United States was unwilling to augment the IMF's resources to provide liquidity to Europe.[136]

That meant more money conjuring was on the docket.

Two days after Draghi met with Geithner, the ECB announced it would cut rates by 0.25 percent. The rate on main refinancing operations was reduced to 1 percent, the rate on marginal lending facility to 1.75 percent, and the rate on the deposit facility to 0.25 percent.[137]

On December 16, 2011, at a House Oversight and Government Reform subcommittee hearing in Washington, New York Fed president William Dudley classified the European sovereign debt crisis as "their problem to solve," affirming that the United States would not continue buying European debt. He noted, "The bar to doing that would be extraordinarily high."[138]

Nevertheless, he defended currency swap agreements to provide access to US dollar funding, which for him was "in the US national interest," by ensuring credit flow to US households and business.[139] To him, Europe had the "fiscal capacity needed" to deal with the sovereign debt crisis, it just needed the political will.

Steven Kamin, the Fed's director of international finance, declared, "It is incumbent upon European authorities to address all these issues." The Fed and other regulatory agencies were "very alert" to the risks of short-term European bank debt held by US money market funds, which have "been substantially reducing their exposure" to the most vulnerable European economies. The Fed swap lines could work as a safeguard against market liquidity problems, helping European financial institutions get the dollar funding they needed, he said.

Super Mario leapt to the rescue. He steered the ECB to inject €1 trillion into the European financial system in three installments from December 2011 to January 2012 to maintain liquidity and reduce borrowing costs in Spain and Italy.[140] It worked for a short time, as most temporary Band-Aids do. By May 2012, borrowing costs were rising again.[141]

Another problem was plaguing Europe: the south's swing toward austerity-touting political parties was on the rise, even though austerity seemed to go against their populations' best interests. On December 21, 2011, Mariano Rajoy of Spain's conservative People's Party was elected prime minister. It was the Right's biggest win in Spain since the end of the Franco dictatorship in 1975.[142] Rajoy's first austerity measures were public spending cuts set to start in July 2012.[143]

By year's end, the euro had fallen to its lowest level since June 2001 versus the yen.[144] It also sat at a fifty-two-week low against the dollar.[145] Even after two years of summits to discuss the depressed situation, and the bailouts of Greece, Ireland, and Portugal, the European debt crisis was not contained. The opposite. Contagion now threatened Italy and Spain.

WHAT RECOVERY?

Tensions mounted globally over the absence of a solid economic recovery anywhere, especially in the developed markets. In Europe, concern about the sovereign debt crisis and Italy and Spain rose. Draghi showed his commitment to expansionary policy. Under his guidance, the ECB announced it would cut the deposit rate to zero for the first time on July 5, 2012, and flirted with the idea of expanding its asset purchase program.[146]

Although most of the governments in Europe approved of Draghi's expansionary policy, criticism was in no short supply, especially from conservative parties in Germany, which elevated tensions. Most of the mainstream media accused the ECB of hijacking authority over economic policies in Europe rather than monetary ones.[147]

On January 13, 2012, S&P downgraded France, Italy, Spain, Portugal, and five other Eurozone countries, blaming Eurozone leaders for failing to deal with the debt crisis. Three days later, it downgraded the EU bailout fund and the European Financial Stability Facility. German federal minister of finance Wolfgang Schäuble downplayed the news, saying, "In the past months, we've come to agree that the ratings agencies' judgments should not be overvalued."[148]

Whether their judgments were appropriate or not, Southern European countries had been held hostage to the agencies' ratings since the onset of government bond purchase programs that favored Germany (only investment-grade bonds could be purchased).

On January 24, a new IMF report concluded the world economy, particularly emerging markets, faced risks due to the situation in the Eurozone.[149] Yet to confront deteriorating growth and uncertainty, the IMF embraced the same conjured-money policy that hadn't moved the needle. "There are three requirements for a more resilient recovery: sustained but gradual adjustment, ample liquidity and easy monetary policy, mainly in advanced economies, and restored confidence in policymakers' ability to act."

About a week later, Bernanke explained to the US House Committee on the Budget that the US economic recovery remained "frustratingly slow" and that the European debt crisis represented an extra challenge on the path to restoring growth.[150] He warned that new difficulties coming from Europe or elsewhere could "worsen economic prospects here at home." It was his habit to draw up the facade of action. He was a fan of DC's hometown baseball team the Washington Nationals and harbored a sense of nationalism merged with his ability to dream up a playbook when he told members of Congress that *we will take every available step* to protect the US financial system and the economy."[151]

On February 21, 2012, the second EU-IMF bailout for Greece of €130 billion (US$172 billion) was passed. It included a 53.5 percent debt write-down—or "haircut"—for private Greek bondholders.[152] In exchange, Greece had to reduce its debt-to-GDP ratio from 160 percent to 120.5 percent by 2020. Greece and its private creditors completed the debt restructuring on March 9, the largest in history.[153]

It was the fourth year since the onset of the financial crisis and the mentality of central bankers hadn't changed—it had metastasized; like frenzied gamblers they played long after the house had won. Only they played with fake money. Central banks had bloated their books, swapped lines with one another, and sent cheap money throughout the waning financial industry.

In the United States, Bernanke faced opposition from Republicans in Congress. Rising Wisconsin Republican chairman of the House Committee on the Budget Paul Ryan feared expansionary monetary policy. "This policy," he said, "runs the great risk of fueling asset bubbles, destabilizing prices and eventually eroding the value of the dollar."[154]

Meanwhile, Draghi contended with Josef Ackermann, chief executive of German mega-bank Deutsche Bank, who declared that bankers now feared a stigma from accepting long-term ECB loans. Draghi depicted these bankers as posturing, saying, "Some of these virility statements, manhood statements, often are not correct.... The very same banks that make these statements access funds of different kinds but [they are] still 'government facilities'—the euro-dollar credit swap facility, for example."[155]

According to the *Financial Times*, in December 2011 more than five hundred banks had borrowed €489 billion in three-year loans from the ECB. Ackermann had praised the ECB for extending the loans, as "a very important and very intelligent move."[156] Then, he flipped to say Deutsche Bank preferred to be seen as independent of government support.

On February 28, 2012, the ECB announced a new easing strategy.[157] Draghi's fresh gambit would provide three-year loans to banks at a 1 percent interest rate, a ploy that one senior European banker likened to "methadone for junkies."[158] Criticism of his policies, considered to represent more interventionism, was solid. The ECB tried to sidestep the notion that this was direct QE because the funds would be borrowed in exchange for collateral, not injected into the market directly in return for bonds. However, in practice, it was the same, letting banks access easy money in return for assets they didn't want, or that were less liquid, or less desirable.

In Germany, many said that liquidity provisions were a risk to financial health and might encourage banks to make bad decisions. Jens Weidmann, president of Germany's Bundesbank, warned that "too generous a provision of liquidity will open up business possibilities for banks that could lead to greater risks for the banks" and thus jeopardize financial and price stability.[159] German leaders were prudent to worry that banks might make bad investment decisions. However, divergence with the ECB was a political issue. Germany was not used to seeing the ECB make decisions that might go against its interests (or willing to acknowledge that possibility).

A month later, the euro hit a three-week peak against the dollar as concerns about the European economic slowdown shrank.[160] Eurozone finance ministers solidified an agreement on a rescue fund of €700 billion, to be discussed at an upcoming meeting in Copenhagen.

In May 2012, the success of left-wing and protest parties in local elections was a measure of public discontent with austerity measures, with the center-right People of Freedom Party and its Lega Nord ally performing badly in Italy.[161] In France's presidential election, François Hollande and his anti-austerity platform won against Sarkozy, making Hollande the first Socialist president in seventeen years (Marine Le Pen also increased her influence, deepening the polarity among voters).

In the general election of Greece, the leftist Syriza party achieved strong growth, capturing 16.8 percent of the votes and fifty-two seats.[162] But the swing to the left would ultimately not prevail as euro economic anemia persisted. It was seen as an inflection point.

Meanwhile, debt was rising everywhere. Italian public debt rose above a record €2.2 trillion.[163] Those figures from Draghi's old stomping ground came at a time when the Greek debt crisis was dominating headlines as was the ballooning public debt within the currency union.

On May 31, Draghi declared that the Eurozone could become unsustainable if policymakers didn't take action.[164] He told the European parliament that EU leaders must "clarify the vision" for the future of the common currency area. Draghi defended ECB actions, saying they were working but that they were not a substitute for decisive action by governments. "Can the ECB fill the vacuum left by the lack of euro area governance?" he asked and then responded, "The answer is no." He was a man in the spotlight.

He envisioned the best way of exiting the crisis was to eliminate uncertainty in the financial markets. Draghi supported a banking union in Europe, which was proposed by the European Commission. It would be integrated along three pillars: a Europe-wide deposit guarantee mechanism, resolution fund, and centralized banking supervision and continuous adjustment. It would also increase the power base of the ECB.

Up to that point, the Eurozone had integrated monetary policy, but not fiscal policy. This created economic and power imbalances. The idea Draghi supported was a step toward a fiscal consolidation, but it could only occur if a real political union existed. Difficulties stemming from a lack of unity in the Eurozone would blossom.

In early June, Draghi announced the ECB would keep rates unchanged.[165] This decision wasn't unanimous; some members wanted a cut. Draghi reemphasized the need for Eurozone leaders to collaborate. When asked about a fiscal union, Draghi said this was not under his purview: "These processes have their own independent legislative roots and they cannot be subject to the monetary policy-makers."[166] He nonetheless provided opinions on fiscal matters, rendering the idea that the ECB operated independently of policy ludicrous.

Historically, the Bundesbank was an important tool Germany used to maintain its conservative economic position.[167] Germany believed that to combat sweeping issues of debt, countries should take on massive austerity measures while cutting wages. The theory was that such moves would reduce foreign imports and draw down demand for external financing. In 1999, when the euro was launched, the power of setting rates was transferred to the ECB, but Germany still tried to influence ECB decisions.

According to the *Financial Times*, Draghi understood the need to placate the Bundesbank to successfully implement his policies. So, at the end of 2011 he eliminated the government bond purchase program and instead formed a plan of unlimited three-year loan offers, which was basically the same thing in a different form.

Draghi, for as much criticism as the German media leveled upon him, was a man who could be the nation's greatest ally or its most dangerous threat.

Antonis Samaras was appointed Greece's prime minister on June 20, 2012. He pledged to honor bailout commitments. (Two months later, in the fifth year of the Greek recession, two hundred thousand citizens marched in the streets of Athens against austerity.)[168]

On July 5, 2012, the ECB cut rates by 0.25 percent, placing the deposit rate at 0 percent.[169] Draghi was asked why the Eurozone was not pumping more money into the market with some countries still in a credit crunch. He noted impatiently that "there are at least three sets of reasons why banks may not lend. One is risk aversion, another is a lack of capital, and the third is a lack of funding. We have removed only the third, not the other two."[170]

As the ECB cut rates, the BOE and PBOC did, too. Yet, Draghi denied any co-ordination "beyond the normal exchange of views on the state of the business cycle, on the state of the economy and on the state of global demand." He went on, "In a normally functioning euro area when a bank is short of funding, they simply bor-row from other banks. But in a highly fragmented situation, when a bank is short of funding, they only can go to the ECB. And if the bank is solvent, the ECB stands ready to provide all the liquidity they need."[171]

On July 20, Spain declared the recession was expanding and that it would need help from the central government.[172] As a result, the euro hit its lowest value against the yen since November 2000 and a two-year low against the dollar.

Six days later, at the Global Investment Conference in London, Draghi issued one of his most legacy-establishment statements yet: "Within our mandate, the ECB is ready to do whatever it takes to preserve the euro." Spain was nearing full-fledged crisis mode. If the floodgates were to open in Spain, high waters could quickly inun-date the rest of Europe.

Members of the German government were tired of bailout protocol.[173] "It's a bottomless pit," said Free-Democrat spokesman Frank Schäffler. Even twenty-two members of Merkel's own coalition voted against the Spanish package. Whereas electoral shake-ups in Europe were common, Germany was at the controls. Discon-tent among its leadership party mattered.

In its yearly report on the Eurozone, the IMF warned that the deepening crisis raised concerns about the "viability of the monetary union itself."[174] The Olympics started the very next day in London, but European bankers had already won gold and never even stood on a podium. Draghi characterized the summit as a real suc-cess because "for the first time in many years, all the leaders of the 27 countries of Europe, including UK etc., said that the only way out of this present crisis is to have more Europe, not less Europe."[175]

Every move was about money crafting and the illusion of confidence. On September 6, 2012, the ECB announced it would buy Eurozone countries' short-term bonds to curtail "distortions in financial markets."[176] The ECB, under certain conditions, would buy *unlimited* amounts of short-term government bonds in the secondary market to help those countries at risk of experiencing high long-term interest rates. Draghi was implying the ECB could deploy more firepower to save the euro or, really, do whatever it believed it needed to do. It was a statement, not a supposition.[177]

Draghi's bond purchase program sharpened the divide between him and German policymakers. Several German MPs lambasted the decision, claiming that it was a back door to unlimited funding. Alexander Dobrindt, a right-wing Eurosceptic Bavarian MP, labeled Draghi a "counterfeiter."[178] Jens Weidmann, the president of the German Bundesbank, said the measure was "close to state financing via the printing press" and meant that the ECB was assuming a political role.[179] This wasn't about liquidity or monetary policy; it was a tug-of-war over power.

Despite his critics, Draghi received support from other German leaders. On a political talk show, Martin Schulz, German president of the European parliament, declared Draghi was doing the right thing.[180] Even Angela Merkel publicly supported the ECB policy, though she struggled with her own party behind closed doors over the credibility of the ECB's moves and the legality of Draghi's programs.[181]

Draghi's detractors were vehement. Volker Kauder, leader of the Christian Democrats (Merkel's party), called the ECB plan "very close to the edge" regarding its permissibility. But Germany was the wind behind the EU's sails. Although egos might clash, the ECB needed Germany and Germany needed the ECB. For the EU to remain intact, Draghi had to win German support and take his place as the ultimate central bank craftsman.

Markus Soeder, Bavarian finance minister, said the ECB's plans went "well beyond" its mandate and that the bank was becoming a "super-authority." Jens Weidmann considered Draghi's program to be a serious violation of the "No Bailout Clause" of the Maastricht Treaty, which established the European Monetary Union. If the ECB was buying national government securities, that veered close to mixing monetary with fiscal policy.

The real concern of German politicians was that the ECB was behaving independently. But this independence was suspect to begin with. The fact that its headquarters was situated in Frankfurt was no coincidence. When it came to matters of North versus South, the ECB and Germany were more often than not a unified front.

None of that hampered the Fed, itself unencumbered by any laws restricting it from buying US Treasury bonds or mortgage-backed securities. On September 13, the Fed announced the third round of quantitative easing, or QE3. It would purchase $40 billion in mortgage-backed securities per month. Short-term interest rates would remain at "exceptionally low levels" until 2015—a date three years in the future.[182] The prior forecast had set late 2014 as an end date.

The world was worried. Emergent countries saw US policy as irresponsible, fostering financial instability and volatility. The Republican Party seized upon the new round of QE to criticize Bernanke and the Fed's policies that autumn into the US presidential election.

By mid-November 2012, the euro's pressures stemming from Greece's fiscal problems and the slow growth across Europe nabbed the Fed's attention.[183] While speaking at the Economic Club of New York, Bernanke used Europe's woes to excuse his own ineffectiveness: "A prominent risk at present—and a major source of financial headwinds over the past couple of years—is the fiscal and financial situation in Europe. This situation, of course, was not anticipated when the US recovery began in 2009."[184]

A month later, the Fed, ECB, Bank of Canada, Bank of England, and Swiss National Bank announced an extension to February 2014 of the US dollar liquidity swap arrangements, which were due to expire in February 2013.[185] They had already been extended in November 2011 to provide liquidity to European banks as the Eurozone sovereign debt crisis intensified.

In mid-December, the Fed announced it would buy $45 billion in Treasuries and would keep buying $40 billion in mortgage-backed securities each month.[186] At this point, even the BIS was growing exasperated with all the money conjuring. "Central banks cannot solve structural problems in the economy," said Stephen Cecchetti, who ran the BIS monetary department. "We've been saying this for years, and it's getting tiresome."[187]

His frustration stopped nothing. It had ceased to matter whether the central banks could conjure economic stability, let alone prosperity, for general populations. They would still find ways to lavish the private banking system and capital markets with cheap money. These actions would stoke bubbles in the bond market (and thus historic levels of debt) and the stock market (the hottest cheap-money game in town).

6

EUROPE PART II: The Draghi Money Machine

I want to emphasize that basically the ECB will be in the market for a long time.

—Mario Draghi, president of the European Central Bank, London,
     June 8, 2017

Even with deposit rates slashed to zero percent, strong concerns about the Eurozone's ability to restore growth, service debt, and increase levels of employment lingered. Because of that uncertainty, Draghi faced mounting German opposition.

The press dubbed Draghi "Mr. Somewhere Else," given his propensity to seemingly occupy two places at once geographically and politically.[1] He knew a thing or two about big banks' need for easy money. He was also a trustee at the Brookings Institution in Washington, DC.[2] Brookings had hosted a select event on November 2, 2011, to commemorate the ECB's shift from the "Trichet-era" to the "Draghi-era" with "the euro crisis in firm bloom."[3]

Draghi, though thoroughly European, was very familiar with the United States. He had worked as an executive director at the World Bank in Washington for six years in the 1980s and ran the Italian Treasury in the early 1990s. According to the *New York Times,* Draghi earned his moniker "Super Mario" in the 1990s when he convinced foreign investors that the Italian economy, sunk in an abyss, was worthy of their confidence and capital. He pushed major European privatization deals and helped Italy join the European Monetary Union.[4] From there, he moved to the private sector at Goldman Sachs International, where his Italian connections came in handy for getting deals done. He governed the Bank of Italy from 2006 through October 2011 and then beat out a German for the ECB directorship, which in European politics was noteworthy (even though the other candidate, Bundesbank president Axel Weber, did not have a personal Rolodex of international relationships as Draghi did).

Germany, with its comparatively robust economy and trade surplus with the other sixteen countries in the Eurozone,[5] favored a strong euro. Draghi and other core European leaders worried that appreciation of the euro could harm trade in other parts of the Eurozone that could not afford an economic squeeze. Maintaining low rates meant that foreign capital would be less interested in investing in Europe and therefore would theoretically limit the value of the euro. That dovetailed nicely with his easy-money policy.

The very *possibility* of euro volatility incited significant anxiety. On February 5, 2013, French president François Hollande declared that the Eurozone should develop an exchange rate policy to protect the euro from "irrational movements."[6] He was motivated by the euro's fourteen-month high of around 1.35 per dollar, which could harm French exporters and economic growth. In his first speech before the European parliament in Strasbourg, Hollande warned that competitiveness reforms taken by Eurozone governments might be undermined by a strong euro. Yet the entire EU system challenged the notion of unified currency or monetary policy, for it hinged on unequal economies, governments, and power. The needs and economic prospects of the core European countries were different from those of the peripheral states, and at the core, Germany stood supreme.

Though Hollande defended ECB independence, he supported the idea of reforming the international monetary system so that countries could better protect their own economic interests. This position of criticism was legion in French history. Charles de Gaulle and his finance minister had been staunch critics of the dollar's "exorbitant privilege." Like his predecessors, Hollande called attention to surplus countries, such as Germany and the Nordic nations. He went on to say they should stimulate internal demand to rebalance the economic situation in the EU.

This sentiment echoed the major shifts occurring among non-EU developing nations in response to the five-year monetary policy projections the G7 central banks had crafted. They sought alternatives to the dollar, and by extension to the Fed and US government hegemony. On March 27, 2013, during a meeting in Durban, South Africa, BRICS leaders approved a $100 billion fund to collectively fight currency crises, even though they fell short of reaching an agreement on financing a new development bank. Russian finance minister Anton Siluanov said China would likely provide the largest amount of money for the fund.[7]

Discussions about this development bank had begun a year earlier, when India proposed it as an alternative to the World Bank and IMF. If the BRICS could establish such an entity, it would be more committed to the economic needs of developing countries. Though the BRICS leaders did not agree in full then, the issue had moved forward. After all, the IMF and World Bank were Bretton Woods organizations and instruments of the "old world order." If the BRICS were to rise in prominence, the world of central banking could become a battleground whose lines were drawn along distinct regional monetary policies, with winners and losers. The developing economies were learning from the downturn. Fashioning their own development bank would usher in a "fair world order" and eventually a monetary system to match.

While speaking at a banking conference in Dresden on April 25, 2013, before the German Savings Banks Association, Merkel said, "The ECB is in a difficult position. For Germany it would actually have to raise rates slightly at the moment, but for other countries it would have to do even more for more liquidity to be made available. If we want to arrive at tolerable interest rates again, we have to overcome the divisions of the European currency area."[8]

The dichotomous shift in monetary policy that would benefit Germany, however, was to break up the EU, something Merkel was against. This was one of the first times she admitted publicly that Germany operated on a grander scale than its neighbors. France grew increasingly irritated with Merkel's hard line on austerity as well. As Reuters reported the day after Merkel's speech: "France's ruling Socialist Party is pressing President François Hollande to toughen his stance towards a German counterpart it describes as 'self-centered' arguing that chancellor Angela Merkel's pro-austerity policies are hurting Europe."[9]

The *Financial Times* observed, "The German chancellor's highly unusual intervention on Thursday, a week before many economists expect the independent European Central Bank to cut its main interest rate, highlights how the economies of the prosperous north and austerity-hit south remain far apart." The paper added, "Wolfgang Schäuble, the German finance minister, has also broken the taboo, saying in a recent interview that the ECB should 'drain liquidity' from the system."[10]

Yet, the G7 central banks kept doing the only thing they knew how to do, creatively ease monetary policy by any means. On May 2, 2013, at a press conference in Bratislava, Slovakia, Draghi and ECB vice president Vítor Constâncio announced the ECB would cut rates on the main refinancing operations by another 0.25 percent to 0.5 percent and on the marginal lending facility by 0.5 percent to 1 percent.[11] The deposit facility rate remained at 0 percent. It was the first cut in borrowing costs since July 2012. The ECB was still intervening to supposedly spur growth, not least because shares of the big European banks were trading comparatively lower than their US counterparts, at a share-price-to-book-value ratio last seen in the early 1980s.[12] This, despite their heavy dose of ECB support. They could always use more.

The public certainly wasn't feeling any love toward the banks. A May 2013 Gallup poll reported "European Countries Lead World in Distrust of Banks." The disconnect between the population and the financial system and markets was vast. Money was cheap for banks. Debt was escalating for governments. Economic stability for the masses was beyond reach.

In May 2013, a Pew Research Center report stated the obvious: "Most Europeans are profoundly concerned about the state of their economies. Just 1 percent of the Greeks, 3 percent of the Italians, 4 percent of the Spanish and 9 percent of the French think economic conditions are good. Only the Germans (75 percent) are pleased with their economy."[13] More than three-quarters of the pan-European responders believed their economic system favored the wealthy. The Pew report also claimed, "Except in Germany, overwhelming majorities in many countries say unemployment, the public debt, rising prices and the gap between the rich and the poor are very important problems." The results were in. Cheap-money policy had strengthened Germany at the expense of the rest of the EU. Germany was now against it, and yet, cheap money wasn't actively helping the populations of the rest of Europe either. Many were left to wonder what was the point.

Perhaps, deep in the recesses of his psyche, Draghi wondered that as well, or at least realized that conjuring money wasn't the golden ticket to economic prosperity for all. That month, he set his sights on fiscal policy. Draghi urged euro policymakers to gear their actions toward austerity measures and deficit reductions "to bring debt ratios back on a downward path...and where needed, to take legislative action or otherwise promptly implement structural reforms, in such a way as to mutually reinforce fiscal sustainability and economic growth potential."[14]

During that press conference in Bratislava, one reporter had asked Draghi, "Chancellor Angela Merkel recently said that if you speak about Germany, you would have to raise interest rates. What do you make out of these comments and is she correct?"

His response indicated he was not moved by Merkel's thinly veiled swipe at his money-conjuring ways: "ECB independence is dear to all, and especially, I would say, to German citizens," he said. "We have 17 countries and the business cycles of these 17 countries are not exactly the same...the monetary policy measures which can benefit some countries may not benefit others. Given the weakness that also extends to the core economies, we think it does benefit everybody."

THE GREEK CONDITION

Greece continued to be the major problem in Europe. On June 5, 2013, Lagarde said the country should be in a position to pay off its debts while admitting that the IMF had failed to foresee the damage austerity imposed upon Greece.[15]

The IMF had released an internal report that documented how it had underestimated the damage of austerity. It confirmed what Greek officials had long said: that the first bailout of 110 billion euro in emergency funds in May 2010 in exchange for major budget cuts was the wrong prescription for a country battling a "monumental debt load," "rampant tax evasion," and a "flourishing black economy."[16]

The IMF did not advocate reducing austerity measures, however. By 2013, Greece's debt-to-GDP ratio had risen to 149 percent. All of its debt burden was incurred after the financial crisis, and yet the euro elite blamed Greece and not the speculators who had ransacked the country and headed for the hills during the crisis.

By now, Germany's fear of European inflation had been replaced by the reality of deflation. Since April, the monthly consumer price index data for the Eurozone had failed to reach the ECB inflation target of 2 percent.[17] The results gave Draghi incentive to opt for loosening monetary policy even more. He recognized the governing council was divided on the issue, but he remained undaunted. He would "decide about further action on the front of interest rates or, as I said before, on any other instrument that is available."

An IMF report released in June 2013 noted that the growth assumptions for Greece had been too high and that the handling of the first international bailout had been a mistake. This left the Germans disgruntled yet feeling vindicated for having criticized the bailout structure.[18]

European instability notwithstanding, on June 19, Bernanke proclaimed the US economy was responding positively to *his* policies. He promised, "If the subsequent data remain broadly aligned with our current expectations for the economy...we will continue to reduce the pace of purchases in measured steps through the first half of next year, ending purchases around mid-year."[19] He was potentially putting the brakes on buying, not holding, assets.

Bernanke explained that removing stimulus was out of the question for the moment, though, and that even eventual rate hikes would be gradual. Kansas City Fed president Esther George expressed concern about the consequences expansionary policy would have on financial stability. St. Louis Fed chief James Bullard also dissented, arguing that the Fed should have made more clear its willingness to keep the stimulus to reach the 2 percent goal for inflation.

Minneapolis Fed president Narayana Kocherlakota said that the Fed did not provide clear guidelines regarding rates. He wanted the Fed to target a 5.5 percent unemployment rate and stop easing when it got there. The Fed wasn't operating under an old paradigm of guidelines, though.

If the Fed, in a single unified country had problems, the EU, organizing various cultures and economic environments, was skating on far thinner ice. On July 17, Greece's parliament approved another set of unpopular austerity measures, including a plan to put twenty-five thousand public employees on notice for possible dismissal as a condition of the latest EU-IMF bailout. That opened the way for a fresh tranche of funds worth nearly €7 billion (US$9 billion), pushing Greece's bailout total to €240 billion (US$314 billion).[20] Labor unions had called a general strike in protest the day before.[21] Though Greece was the epicenter of crisis, economic contagion was spreading. By August 2013, Italy's GDP had dropped eight quarters running.[22]

Non-US central banks began solidifying outside alliances. On October 10, 2013, the ECB and the PBOC established a bilateral currency swap agreement to buy and sell yuan and euro from each other.[23] Valid for three years, it would reach RMB 350 billion for the ECB and €45 billion for the PBOC. The ECB announced this step, one of several in the growing number of bilateral trade and investment alliances between the Eurozone and China. This action had two goals: stabilizing financial markets and diversifying against the United States dollar and Fed.

The EU was China's biggest export market: Europe and China traded roughly €480 billion in goods and services each year. Even if the move was not an earthquake, it was a significant tremor. And it was directed at the Fed. In June 2013, China had signed a similar agreement with the Bank of England, worth up to RMB 200 billion in swaps.[24] These moves were signs the Fed had burned both central banks and that they sought relief from further risks by augmenting their associations with each other.

Draghi declared banks viable but in need of state aid to expand their capital base. As he highlighted on October 2, "The ECB wants to have full responsibility for the assessment, but nothing to do with what has to be done following the assessment, namely the task of the resolution authority."[25] Those were just words. The ECB was still heavily involved in keeping banks liquid, as would be obvious by the end of that month.

On October 31, the Bank of Canada, BOE, BOJ, ECB, Fed, and the Swiss National Bank announced that their temporary bilateral liquidity swap arrangements would become permanent—indefinitely.[26] It was the era of conjured money.

For regular people, there was no such relief. The average member of the working class wouldn't be able to readily identify a liquidity swap arrangement because that type of complexity was reserved for the financial elite, and even if they did know, they couldn't access the same privileges central banks afforded to private banks.

A report from the International Federation of Red Cross and Red Crescent Societies warned, "The long-term consequences of this crisis have yet to surface. The problems caused will be felt for decades even if the economy turns for the better in the near future....We wonder if we as a continent really understand what has hit us." The report went on to say, "As the economic crisis has planted its roots, millions of Europeans live with insecurity, uncertain about what the future holds....We see quiet desperation spreading among Europeans, resulting in depression, resignation and loss of hope."[27]

At that point in time, there were twenty-six million people unemployed in the EU, with eleven million of them out of work for more than a year. The figure was more than double what it had been in 2008.[28] According to a Red Cross Survey on Europe, "The amount of people depending on Red Cross food distributions in 22 of the surveyed countries has increased by 75% between 2009 and 2012." The survey concluded, "More people are getting poor, the poor are getting poorer."[29]

The first week in November, at a press conference at ECB headquarters, Draghi announced a 25-basis-point cut of the main refinancing operations rate to 0.25 percent and the marginal lending facility rate to 0.75 percent. The deposit facility remained at 0 percent.[30] Eurozone inflation had fallen to 0.7 percent in October, since the May cut, after falling to 1.2 percent in April. A quarter of the council members, led by Bundesbank chief Jens Weidmann, were against the cuts.[31] Dissention was building at the ECB as it was at the Fed, but that fracturing would meet the same roadblocks. Even if fabricated money wasn't achieving its stated purpose of real economic growth, taking it away would invoke chaos on the financial system. That was a possibility that central bank leaders did not want to risk, not on their watch.

By early December 2013, the yuan had overtaken the euro as the second-most-used currency in international trade and finance after the dollar.[32] It represented an 8.66 percent share of letters of credit and collections, compared to 6.64 percent for the euro. The dollar dropped to an 81.08 percent share versus 84.96 percent in 2012. Previously, in January 2012, the yuan had been the fourth-most-used currency, with 1.89 percent of the share; the euro had been second, with 7.87 percent. This shift was a major step toward balancing out the dollar's power.

By the end of December, the euro reached its strongest level against the dollar in more than two years.[33] Not only was the Chinese yuan charging ahead but the euro was making equal strides. The dollar, seen as a risky currency following the financial crisis, stabilized only because of its prevalence as the world's dominant reserve currency. Diversification away from the dollar meant greater security for the future.

DIVERGENT CHEAP-MONEY POLICIES

On January 9, 2014, Draghi said the Eurozone might need further support to prevent a period of stagnation as Japan had experienced decades ago.[34] He noted that high unemployment, the fall of inflation, and difficult lending conditions pressured the ECB to use all tools available to maintain confidence and growth. He vowed, "The governing council strongly emphasizes that it will maintain an accommodative stance of monetary policy for as long as necessary."[35]

However, he also claimed confidence was gradually returning to the Eurozone and that his monetary policy was affecting the real economy, though not fully. "It's fragile," he said, "there are several risks, from financial to economic to geopolitical to political risks, that could undermine easily this recovery."[36]

Draghi took his cues from the Bernanke school of taking credit for economic success even if it was tenuous at best. The two went way back together in education and ideology. Bernanke received his PhD in economics from MIT in 1979, just two years after Draghi earned his at the same institution. Both had the former vice chair of the Fed, Stanley Fischer, as their adviser. Bernanke later called Fischer one of the most influential figures in his life and economic outlook. CNBC referred to him as the "man who taught the biggest central bankers."

Fischer also taught Larry Summers, Christina Romer, and Greg Mankiw and was an economic adviser to George W. Bush. MIT often houses professors who believe in the Keynesian economic teachings and subscribe to the belief that government intervention can aid economies. Fischer was number two at the IMF during the 1997–1998 crisis that stretched across the emerging markets financial system (Asia, Latin America, Russia). But conjuring money was different from Keynesian theories on government spending aiding the real economy. Big banks had no reason or requirements to care about how the real economy might operate. Speculative activities were faster, often more lucrative, and involved less effort to execute.

On June 2, 2014, Janet Yellen reinforced the status quo in the United States: "I do not presently see a need for monetary policy to deviate from a primary focus on attaining price stability and maximum employment." She brushed aside bubble formations: "Because a resilient financial system can withstand unexpected developments, identification of bubbles is less critical."[37]

Three days later, the ECB became the first G7 central bank to let rates go negative, as it slashed its deposit rate to −0.10 percent.[38] As the ECB said: "In June 2014, following in the footsteps of the Danish National Bank, the European Central Bank (ECB) became the first major central bank to lower one of its key policy rates to negative territory."[39]

In tandem, Draghi announced another package of easing measures too, confirming, "If required, we will act swiftly with further monetary policy easing. The Governing Council is unanimous in its commitment to using also unconventional instruments within its mandate should it become necessary to further address risks of too prolonged a period of low inflation."[40] Inflation, and whether it was low or high, was a convenient devil to be banished at all costs, even if you couldn't see it.

Unlike prior measures, this one did not invoke the same adrenalin-shot response from the markets. Perhaps there was a limit to central bank stimulation effectiveness—on the markets, anyway. But that didn't stop Draghi. He had a choice between dogmatic allegiance to conjured-money policy or the possibility of impacting society with that money. He chose the former.[41]

Draghi's latest policy tool would provide more than €700 billion of cheap funding to banks. The ECB had identified loans to companies and households as key areas of weakness on the books of banks. Because of that, its long-term refinancing operation (LTRO) offered up to four years of low-cost funding tied to this kind of bank lending. According to Draghi, the measure "should ease their financing costs, allowing banks to pass on such attractive conditions to their customers."[42] The idea of trickle-down monetary policy, though not evident in practice, remained prominent in rhetoric.

On June 11, the ECB set its deposit facility interest rate below zero percent, meaning it would cost banks a fraction of a point to keep their money with the ECB. The idea was this would cause banks to loosen their purse strings and lend rather than sit on the massive amounts of cheap money available to them. In practice, banks preferred paying that negligible interest amount to the ECB so as to keep doing what they wanted with their money.

As a result, Draghi's disputes with Germany intensified. Critics doubted the efficacy of QE. The euro's rapid rise affected the ECB's plans to influence the economy. In theory, the euro should have been contained by low rates and bond purchase programs. Draghi was still focused on what he referred to as "the danger zone" and on addressing inflation in the region.[43] His bigger fear was that prices would fall into a deflationary spiral. He reasoned that negative rates would be a way to keep that from happening. He believed conjured money could inspire growth—a strange notion given that years of zero interest rate policy had produced minimal results.[44]

Even the BIS worried that Draghi's blank-check-writing style was causing debt bubbles galore. As public debt blossomed, a chunk of it was subsumed by the ECB in its various QE programs, leaving room for more to be created. On June 29, Jaime Caruana, general manager of the BIS, said, "Rising public debt cannot shore up confidence. Nor can a prolonged extension of ultra-low interest rates. Low rates can certainly increase risk-taking, but it is not evident that this will turn into productive investment."

He added, "If they persist too long, ultra-low rates could validate and entrench a highly undesirable type of equilibrium—one of high debt, low interest rates and anemic growth." The BIS board of directors at the time included Janet Yellen and Mario Draghi.[45] Neither of those conjurers appeared as worried as the central bank of central banks did.

The IMF reaffirmed its concern that the Eurozone faced "a risk of stagnation, which could result from persistently depressed domestic demand due to deleveraging, insufficient policy action, and stalled structural reforms." Yet it prescribed more QE to soak up the government debt: "If inflation remains too low, consideration could be given to a large-scale asset purchase program, primarily of sovereign assets."[46] This raised the question of why it was necessary for central banks to purchase government debt. Rather than providing artificial demand for debt, they could have explored methods to divert that debt to real, tangible growth projects. That simply wasn't a question that the central bank leaders, who were buying trillions of dollars in debt, asked.

On September 4, the ECB dropped its refinancing and lending facility rates by another 10 basis points and dropped the deposit facility rate to −0.2 percent. Yet another wrinkle in the QE plot appeared: the purchase of nonfinancial private-sector assets. Draghi noted these decisions were not unanimous, as they once had been, but "on the scale of the dissent, I could say that there was a comfortable majority in favor of doing the program."[47] He was a man with unlimited power to create money and was not afraid to use it.

The strategy still didn't provide enough money for the financial system. So, as European stagnation remained critical, the G20 agreed to add an extra $2 trillion to the global economy to create millions of new jobs.[48] Finance ministers and central bank chiefs had convened in Cairns, Australia, where they claimed to be making progress on protecting the world's financial system—yet still needed to dump more money into it.

There, US Treasury secretary Jack Lew stressed philosophical differences and concern with some of his counterparts in Europe regarding stimulus: "If the efforts to boost demand are deferred for too long, there's a risk that the headwinds get stronger and what Europe needs is some more tailwinds in the economy."[49] At the time, Lew had been at his post for barely a year. Previously, he had occupied an executive role in Citigroup's alternative investments division, which had contributed to Citigroup's implosion in 2007, and had been a member of the management committee there.[50]

His opinion, steeped in Fed policy, contrasted vastly with that of Wolfgang Schäuble and of Jens Weidmann, the Bundesbank chief, who emphasized the importance of strict budget controls and criticized the ECB and its policies of cuts in borrowing costs. "In my view," Weidmann said, "the recent decisions by the ECB council [are] a fundamental change of course and a drastic change for the ECB's monetary policy." Further, "No matter how you think about the content of the decisions, the majority of the ECB council members are signaling with it that monetary policy is ready to go very far and to enter new territory."[51]

However, Draghi maintained that his asset purchase plans could revive the Eurozone—if only they could grow in scale.[52] "We stand ready to use additional unconventional instruments within our mandate, and alter the size and/or the composition of our unconventional interventions should it become necessary."[53]

Draghi struggled to convince European banks to take more ECB cash to finance their lending. In contrast to other major central banks, the ECB had seen its assets shrink by a third since 2012. That's why Draghi put the option of increasing QE purchases back on the table. There were two main explanations for banks not wanting more ECB money. First, they simply didn't want to lend, one of their primary jobs relative to the public. Second, they had enough cash, and so denying their need for more allowed them to project confidence and strength. The latter reason translates to higher share prices and executive bonuses predicated on those shares.

On October 1, 2014, US Treasury yields versus their German counterparts leapt to their highest spreads since 1999, meaning global speculators were buying the notion that the Fed would tighten, which pushed bond prices down and yields up relative to the easy-money train of the ECB in the EU.[54] Five days later, the minutes of the FOMC meeting expressed concerns that a rate hike in the United States could negatively affect global markets.[55] One moment, it seemed monetary policy collusion could be nearing its end. The next, the conjurers realized that to truly do so would be to wreak global havoc and admit that it all had been a facade.

Policymakers worried about the dual threats of a stronger dollar, which might decelerate inflation target progress, and a global slowdown triggered by an increase in US rates. By conjuring money, the Fed had begun something it couldn't stop. Certain Fed members appeared more worried about looming hikes, with the dollar already strengthening relative to the euro and other currencies. Others didn't seem to care.

In Washington, at another rarified gathering of central bankers at the IMF on October 10, Draghi denied any deliberate ECB action to manipulate the euro. It was not his job to undertake "policies directly targeted to the exchange rate."[56] He explained the euro's fall by divergences in international monetary policy. He could have equally blamed it on the weather. Currencies were becoming impossible to control, as they were battered about by speculators keen on interpreting the head- and tailwinds of every central bank action.[57] But that didn't stop him from trying.

German opposition to the ECB's methods remained strong.[58] When Draghi met with German federal minister of finance Wolfgang Schäuble at the IMF annual meeting in Washington, he was not optimistic about the chances for finding common ground.

On October 20, the ECB started buying more covered bonds (backed by loans, such as residential mortgages). Draghi said the program would return the ECB's total assets to 2012 levels, pushing its balance sheet from €2 trillion to €3 trillion.[59] The hope swirling around the central bank universe was that banks would sell bonds to the ECB and use the money they got in return to lend to businesses. But banks didn't want to lend, not when they could speculate with such cheaply acquired money instead.

Six days later, twenty-five (or about one in five) European banks failed the ECB stress tests that checked their health should another financial crisis emerge.[60] Nine of them were in Italy, three in Greece, and three in Cyprus.

On October 29, the Fed ended the largest monetary stimulus program in US history by finishing its third round of QE.[61] Yet the global policy of quantitative easing remained very much intact. The American population continued to resent the fact that banks were the biggest beneficiaries of Fed generosity.

For bank profits and CEO bonuses had ballooned, whereas ordinary Americans' wages had not. Two weeks later, on November 13, at a Macroeconomics and Finance conference hosted by the Fed, Yellen said the Fed should watch developments overseas and their impact on the US economy to evaluate the moment to raise rates.[62]

A week before another G20 meeting, this one in Brisbane, Lew accused "national authorities and European bodies" of failing to restore growth. He claimed the lack of a plan risked a huge period of stagnation. As if Europe was acting out of simple defiance, he chastised, "The world cannot afford a European lost decade."[63]

Lew stressed the role of the US economy in leading a global recovery but remarked this restoration could not be successful by relying on the United States as the importer of first and last resort. He went further, saying others should not count on the United States to compensate for the low growth in the major economies of the world.

If the United States would not save Europe, Draghi would use the opportunity to raise his voice and offer reassurance. He was not about to sit and watch passively from the sidelines. He vowed, "We must raise inflation and inflation expectations as fast as possible."[64] Ironically, as long as inflation remained low, his power remained high because it provided him a reason to continue to levy his money-conjuring strategies.

Later that month, Draghi promised an audience of bankers at the Frankfurt European Banking Congress that if raising inflation "didn't work...we would step up the pressure and broaden even more the channels through which we intervene, by altering accordingly the size, pace and composition of our purchases."[65] On December 4, he said the ECB could follow its path without German support: "We don't need to have unanimity."[66] That dispute carried on.

Yet, politically, Draghi did need Germany's support before the January 22, 2015, ECB governing council meeting. His challenge was to outflank the German central bank without promoting a national impasse inside Germany regarding support for the euro. Nowhere in any of this did the plight of ordinary citizens meaningfully feature in the discussion.

RISING TENSIONS IN EUROPE

On January 5, 2015, Draghi told the German newspaper *Handelsblatt* that the ECB would likely start buying government bonds following the US and UK central banks' policies: "We are making technical preparations to alter the size, pace and composition of our measures in early 2015."[67] As a response, the euro hit its lowest level since March 2006 against the dollar.

According to Albert Einstein, the definition of insanity is to keep repeating the same action and expecting different results. Draghi initiated another round of QE on January 22, to reach his so far unattainable inflation target of 2 percent. The deposit rate was cut deeper into negative territory.

Also on January 22, Draghi announced another twist of euro QE. The ECB executive board proposed spending €50 billion a month on asset purchases through September 2016. As Draghi commented, "We would believe that the measures taken today will be effective, will raise inflation, medium-term inflation expectations, and basically will address the economic situation in the euro area."[68]

But he expressed fresh caution about the impact of monetary policy absent appropriate fiscal policies. Central bankers were beginning to cover themselves, shifting blame onto governments for their inability to attain its promised goals. The problem was that publicly identifying blame was dangerous, and countries that took on the highest debt burdens were often cast in a very negative light because of politics rather than economics.

Greek political turmoil also influenced the euro's fall. Just ahead of the Greek general elections on January 25, speculators feared a Syriza victory would end austerity policies in the country and perhaps even induce an exit from the Eurozone. Elite euro policymakers wanted to hold tight to their power base, which meant pulling ranks against any perceived threat.

Angela Merkel claimed there was no change in German policy toward Greece. She pressed for Greece to adapt to troika bailout obligations. On the other hand, French president François Hollande said the decision was "up to the Greeks" and warned that "Europe cannot continue to be identified by austerity."[69]

In his op-ed in the *Guardian* on February 5, 2015, historian Jochen Hung attempted to ward off any public castigation of Germany for not doing its part to help its weaker brethren countries in the EU. "Blaming an evil German empire can be a convenient excuse for democratically elected southern European governments who don't want to take the flak for unpopular decisions at home."[70]

The reality was that QE hadn't helped any of the periphery countries, where growth remained slow and wages low. Like Bernanke and Yellen, Draghi ignored the risk of asset bubbles and their popping into future crises: "So far we don't see bubbles. There may be some local episodes of certain specific markets where prices are going up fast. But to have a bubble, besides having that, one should also identify, detect an increase, dramatic increase in leverage or in bank credit, and we don't see that now."[71]

His QE decision provoked more diverging opinions in Europe. Jean-Claude Trichet, former ECB president, declared support for Draghi's initiative on CNBC while arguing on behalf of his successor's' predicament: "To think the ECB has a magic wand and will change all the situation in Europe by its magic wand, in my opinion is not the appropriate reasoning."[72]

In contrast, Bundesbank president Jens Weidmann and executive board member Sabine Lautenschläger said that QE was unnecessary and could negatively affect the incentive of governments to promote structural reforms. It was a damned if you do, damned if you don't euro stalemate. QE had been ineffective at hitting the goals the ECB wanted. And the German contingent wanted more reform. This meant a push for more austerity, which translated to more pain for a wider swath of Southern and increasingly other parts of Europe. Citizens were caught in a vortex between two unpopular and ineffective policies. Governments seemed to forget they existed, while central bankers did not even pretend to be concerned.

The ECB exhibited political favoritism through its QE program by picking and choosing which countries' bonds it would buy, and thus giving those countries higher prices for their debt by virtue of that extra demand. In January 2015, Greek bonds had been determined not eligible for purchase by the ECB's QE program.[73] When the left-wing, anti-austerity Syriza party won, breaking more than forty years of two-party rule, incoming Greek prime minister Alexis Tsipras promised a renegotiation of bailout terms, debt cancelation, and public sector spending.[74]

Germany insisted Greece should stay in the Eurozone, despite news reports claiming Berlin was ready to see Athens leave if Syriza won the snap election and reneged on the country's reform program.[75] Greece did indeed remain in the EU.

On March 9, 2015, Draghi introduced yet another QE program, the Expanded Asset Purchase Programme (EAPP). This one would buy public sector securities, too. The program consisted of a third covered bond purchase program (CBPP3), an asset-backed securities purchase program (ABSPP), and a public sector purchase program (PSPP). It could have equally decided to buy scones and jam or croissants and butter—that would have spread money more directly into the real economy, at least as far as backers and dairy and fruit farms were concerned. These purchases of public- and private-sector securities would run €60 billion per month. They were supposed to continue through March 2017 or until Draghi's governing council deemed inflation was hitting close to 2 percent, or, as it was with conjured money, until they felt like stopping it.[76]

Five weeks later, during an IMF conference in Washington, DC, in mid-April, Draghi dismissed speculation that Greece would be forced to leave the Eurozone and reassured the crowd of central bankers that the single currency "cannot be reversed."[77] He was a Europhile through and through, even down to believing one size QE fits all.

Yet concerns about a "Grexit," or Greece leaving the EU, rose as a result of fears the new leftist Syriza government would shun austerity and force the issue, which could create a domino effect through the rest of Southern Europe that could irrevocably fracture the EU. Asked how the ECB would react to a Greek default, Draghi replied, "I don't want even to contemplate it." He added, "The answer is in the hands of the Greek government."[78]

Other finance authorities were less optimistic. At the same IMF meeting, Jack Lew warned of the unpredictable effects of a larger Greek crisis: "I do not think that anyone can predict how markets will respond to dramatic changes in circumstances."[79] Christine Lagarde said recent talks with new Greek finance minister Yanis Varoufakis were less productive than expected and that she had urged him to present a detailed bailout proposal. "The job of the finance minister…is to go deep in the analysis, pull out the numbers, assessing the efforts undertaken, making a few hypotheticals about what it will deliver in terms of growth, in terms of fiscal revenues, or spending, and then move on," she said.[80]

Varoufakis was not of the banking elites. He hailed from academia, which meant he couldn't leverage decades of establishment connections to get across that the bailout was bogus. As he wrote in his book *And the Weak Suffer What They Must?*, "Terrible earthquakes drive snakes out in the open, causing them to slither in a daze until the tectonic plates have settled again."[81]

During the ECB press conference on June 3, Draghi was asked about movements in the prices of German bonds, which were suddenly at the front lines of a global bond market sell-off. He declared that Europe "should get used to periods of higher volatility" because of the "very low levels of interest rates" but that it would not lead to an alteration in ECB policies.[82] He touted his power even as he warned it might not bear fruit.

The Greek government missed its €1.6 billion (US$1.7 billion) payment to the IMF on June 30, 2015, the first developed country to effectively default to the fund.[83] Negotiations between the government and its official creditors had fallen apart days earlier when Tsipras proposed a referendum on the EU proposals. To stem capital flight, he announced emergency capital controls, limiting bank withdrawals to €60 per day, and calling a bank holiday after the ECB capped its support. The war between the south and elite north raged on, and the ECB was in the thick of it. And now, a war on cash was brewing.

Still, the ECB governing council refused Greece's central bank the right to increase its Emergency Liquidity Assistance (ELA) facility, effectively closing down Greece's commercial banks at enormous cost to Greek businesses, citizens, and the nation's image. It was a clear (financial) attack against the newly elected Greek government, designed to pressure the negotiations and the people of Greece before the referendum. The closed banks were a strong reminder of the ECB's power, a force greater than that of any new Greek government. It was the equivalent to harnessing fear, and a body that could bring a population to its knees with a lack of funds, money, and confidence in the monetary system and its geopolitics.

However, Tsipras soon bent to European creditors and the troika. He pressed his parliament to approve more austerity, despite a July 5 referendum in which Greeks overwhelmingly voted against it.[84] His agreement followed a weekend of talks in which a Greek Eurozone exit was barely averted and that opened the way to a possible third bailout of up to €86 billion (US$94 billion).

The ECB resumed some support for Greek banks, but not without harsh words for the nation, from Draghi, who said, on July 16, 2015, "We have today accommodated the Bank of Greece request, though scaled to one week. We want to see how the situation will evolve." The compromise split the ruling Syriza party and set the stage for new elections.

Varoufakis refused to accept the third bailout deal, eight days after the population voted to reject it in a referendum. In disgust and defiance, Varoufakis quit his post as Greek finance minister on July 6, 2015. In an August 2, 2015, interview with Spanish newspaper *El País,* he chastised the troika in general and, in particular, German finance minister Wolfgang Schäuble's political attitude regarding the European credit crisis. He said, "Schäuble's plan is to put the troika everywhere, in Madrid too, but especially in…Paris.…Paris is the larger prize. It's the final destination of the troika. 'Grexit' is used to create the fear necessary to force Paris, Rome and Madrid to acquiesce."[85]

Conditions were rough everywhere. Italy's youth unemployment hit a record high of 44.2 percent. As for Spain, even with the economy stirring (in a minor way), loan volumes were stagnant or falling, and youth unemployment was at 47.8 percent that October.[86] Greece's was 53.2 percent.[87]

In the midst of that chaos, Lagarde cautioned the Fed against raising rates until the world economy was more secure. Her warning was cast against a summer of global market turmoil triggered by jitters over China's deteriorating economy and prospects of higher borrowing costs in the United States.[88]

Nothing the central bankers could concoct was working. Their policies were hurting rather than helping economic stability and increasing inequality within and between countries. Second-quarter European GDP rose by just 0.3 percent compared to 1.6 percent during the same quarter the prior year.[89] Even Germany saw its sharpest decline in exports in six years, as carmaker Volkswagen was embroiled in a scandal concerning diesel emission tests.

On October 22, speaking at the Governing Council Policy meeting in Malta, Draghi blamed this slowdown on weak emerging markets and slower growth in China. He looked at it as a reason to extend his monetary policy—and reason enough not to blame his own efforts for the current economic malaise. But, at this point, there was major dissention in the EU ranks.

Two weeks later, speaking at the Federation of German Industries (BDI) lobby in Berlin, British chancellor George Osborne said Britain would only support a treaty to save the euro from collapse if its own renegotiation demands were accepted. The project to strengthen the Eurozone through a fresh fiscal arrangement was aimed at avoiding a repeat of crises. It was supported by Germany, France, and European Commission president Jean-Claude Juncker. The idea was to prevent debt crises from attacking the common currency.[90]

The chancellor said the price to be paid for Britain's support would be the guarantee that it would never have to participate in Eurozone bailouts and that a new voting mechanism would prevent coalitions against the United Kingdom's interests. It was the beginning of a potentially irrevocable fracture between the United Kingdom and the European Union. A similar project of Eurozone strengthening had already been vetoed by prime minister David Cameron in 2011, but this one seemed to have more legs.

"There is a deal to be done and we can work together," Osborne said. "You get a Eurozone that works better. We get a guarantee that the Eurozone's decisions and costs are not imposed on us." And further, "You get a stronger Euro. We make sure the voice of the pound is heard where it should be."[91]

Merkel agreed the United Kingdom should remain a member of the EU. "But," she said in Berlin before the Osborne speech, "the decision isn't up to us. It is up to the British." She did allow that "where there are justified concerns—whether competitiveness or better functioning of the EU, the British concerns are our concerns."[92]

Another EU central bank leader was on edge: Mark Carney. Carney had been governor of the Bank of England since July 2013 after having served in the same role at the Bank of Canada from 2008 to 2013. A Canadian economist who attended Harvard and later earned his PhD from Oxford, he also understood the needs of the international banking community elite. He had worked for thirteen years at Goldman Sachs in its London, Tokyo, New York, and Toronto offices. London's *Evening Standard* called the hockey-playing Canadian "the biggest babe in banking" and went on to describe him as having "George Clooney good looks."[93]

Regardless of this star power, Carney was nervous about the sinking euro and its impact on sterling, which had slid on the notion that the BOE might keep interest rates low. The BOE hadn't cut rates since March 2009 (when it cut them from 1 percent to 0.5 percent). As far as conjuring went, his colluding role had been tempered in comparison to Draghi's, but it remained in ready mode. On November 5, 2015, Carney said he had "no regrets" about the Bank of England voting 8–1 to keep rates where they were rather than raise them, as the Fed might do.[94] He had made it clear for months that he wasn't about to advocate raising them anytime soon, and that would remain his position for years.

In a November 11, 2015, speech at the Bank of England Open Forum in London, Carney observed, "It is hardly surprising that only a third of people believe markets work in the interests of society. The more people see, the less they like. People trust markets less with age. And yet, most people think markets will become ever more important. And they're right. As I wrote this week to G20 Leaders, the structure of financial system has changed significantly since the crisis. Virtually all of the net credit since the crisis has been from the bond markets and the size of assets under management has increased by 60 percent to $74 trillion."[95]

Three days later, the ECB announced it would cut the deposit facility rate further to −0.3 percent.[96] The euro rose because of rapid repurchase by traders who had shorted it on expectations of a bolder ECB move. For Draghi, this reopened the possibility of more stimulus.

On December 15, Greek prime minister Alexis Tsipras agreed to a set of reforms that included allowing Greek banks to sell bad business loans to foreign buyers. This would free up capital for the banks and release the next €1 billion (£727 billion; US$1.08 billion) of the bailout.[97] The next day, the Fed hiked rates 25 basis points, the first increase in nearly a decade.

By late December, the euro was on the rise.[98] It marked its best results since April against the dollar, even with the massive QE program in Europe and the first US rate hike since 2006.

The move was short-lived. On December 23, 2015, expectations that US and European monetary policy would continue to diverge drove the dollar up 0.4 percent against the euro.[99] Yellen's actions and rhetoric contrasted with Draghi's enthusiastic pursuit of monetary easing, which led to a stronger US dollar. The markets had just taken a moment to fully process the Fed's hike.

YET MORE EASING IN EUROPE

Even though the other two G3 central banks took up the conjured-money slack where the Fed left off, on January 7, 2016, the DAX, the German stock market index, fell more than its other euro neighbor exchanges, by 7 percent. Draghi and Bank of Japan governor Kuroda expanded their bond purchase programs with a vengeance to compensate for the frenetic sell-offs in their respective areas.

Meanwhile, emergent countries faced graver economic problems due to low commodity prices and a reduction of China's demand. Brazil confronted its most chaotic period in years resulting from currency depreciation, corporate scandal, and political upheaval.

Russia was plagued by low oil prices but eventually staged a recovery in the ruble and stock markets while caught in the crosshairs of public opinion during US elections. Europe tried to hold itself together amid growing dissent within and between countries.

On January 6, 2016, after nearly eight years of the Fed's money-conjuring policy, the BIS released a research paper that indicated the strategy of global central banks was based on a false premise: it relied too much on using inflation as a barometer, and if inflation was low, central banks could keep the cost of money low, which had the effect of spurring more debt creation. It was a self-perpetuating cycle.

A report for which BIS chief economist Claudio Borio was the lead author observed, "If loose monetary policy contributes to credit booms and these booms have long-lasting, if not permanent, effects on output and productivity, including through factor reallocations, once the bust occurs, then it is not reasonable to think of money as neutral over long-term policy horizons. This is at least the case if a financial crisis erupts."[100]

The research indicated it was not "surprising if monetary policy may not be particularly effective in addressing financial busts. This is not just because its force is dampened by debt overhangs and a broken banking system—the usual 'pushing-on-a-string' argument. It may also be because loose monetary policy is a blunt tool to correct the resource misallocations that developed during the previous expansion, as it was a factor contributing to them in the first place." Global debt had grown by $57 trillion since 2007.[101] It stood at three times the level of global GDP.

On January 19, the IMF stated that emerging markets had downside risks that could be deepened by China's slowdown, lower commodities and oil prices, and the Fed's exit from its accommodative monetary policy.[102] The sheer magnitude of this pronouncement and its questioning of the Fed was another indication of a shifting mentality among the rest of the G7 regarding the central bank policies of its core collusion organizer. It also implied that the central bank community still did not know what it was doing. The world's most powerful financial institutions remained conflicted, which masked their fear of a return to the fall of 2008.

Still, the Fed's monetary policy allies weren't ready to throw in the towel. Overall, as the IMF wrote in its World Economic Outlook (WEO) update in January 2016, "Financial conditions within advanced economies remain very accommodative." Despite a deluge of easy money from the main developed economies, and not enough to show for it, there was no real stopping it; all G7 central bank money-conjuring systems remained a "go."

The IMF report warned, "Prospects of a gradual increase in policy interest rates in the United States as well as bouts of financial volatility amid concerns about emerging market growth prospects have contributed to tighter external financial conditions, declining capital flows, and further currency depreciations in many emerging market economies."[103]

More turbulence in Europe was on the docket. The Italian banking index dropped 18 percent. Italy's third-largest and most historically troubled bank, Banca Monte dei Paschi di Siena, lost 50 percent of its value over 2015 resulting from a familiar theme—a pile of bad loans.[104] The Italian economy was mired in its deepest and longest recession. The slow economy meant businesses couldn't repay their loans, which left banks short of cash to finance new business ventures, which held back the economy even more as banks heaped up bad loans. It was a similar vicious cycle throughout the Eurozone.

With no other card to play, on January 21, at ECB headquarters, Draghi and ECB vice president Vítor Constâncio announced the continuation of bond purchases.[105] Only the reasons for continuing those purchased had altered—from being needed to help developed countries to being necessary to help developing ones. The decision to pursue more bond buying resulted from increased risks and uncertainty over emerging economies' growth, volatility of financial and commodities markets, and geopolitical issues. One commonly shared idea was that emerging market countries were the places to fear, when in fact the EU nations themselves were the destabilizers. The first step to tackling a problem is acknowledging its existence. That wasn't the case for many of these central bankers.

The projected end goals had changed, just as they had for the Fed. The ambiguous employment levels, low inflation readings, and various tailwinds had all dampened growth in the Eurozone. Draghi took the opportunity to imply that the March ECB meeting could bring more easing. Past the point of no return, he declared, "There are no limits to how far we're willing to deploy our instruments."[106]

A few days later, the Fed put on the hiking brakes. It would keep rates unchanged. It would make gradual adjustments in monetary policy, but divulged nothing specific.[107] The Fed had forecast four hikes for 2016.[108] Seeing the market chaos one hike had caused, it was suddenly not so sure about that projection. As it turned out, it would hike rates only once in 2016, rendering its own forecast somewhat meaningless.

Any divergence among main central banks ceased a month into 2016. At first, signs of a monetary policy shift by the Fed appeared. But Japan and Europe continued to pursue easing (Europe was facing a 10 percent unemployment rate). The global economy remained weak, so wide-scale tightening never materialized. Both Draghi and Bank of Japan governor Kuroda declared easing would increase in their jurisdictions.

The Fed's stall helped the markets that would have been most affected by a rate rise on their dollar-denominated debts. As a result, emerging markets did exhibit some signs of recuperation: emerging market stocks rose to a two-week high and some currencies gained against the dollar. Others, more entwined with the US economy directly, remained wary.[109] The Russian ruble rose 2.3 percent to 76.3; but the Mexican peso fell 0.1 percent after the Mexican Central Bank announced it would not increase the size of its daily dollar auctions to sell dollars. The Brazilian real dropped 1.4 percent, the worst performer among emerging markets.

At their two-day conference in Shanghai that began on February 26, 2016, the G20 finally recognized the world should look beyond monetary policy—interest rates and printing money—to restore growth, noting, "The global recovery continues, but it remains uneven and falls short of our ambition for strong, sustainable and balanced growth."[110]

Old habits die hard, so the organization tempered its stance: "Monetary policies will continue to support economic activity and ensure price stability…but monetary policy alone cannot lead to balanced growth." The leaders expressed concerns over geopolitical issues such as the European refugee crisis and the possibility of Brexit, which were also causing significant tremors in the Eurozone and for the euro. China used the meeting to calm the international community about the strength of its own economy, despite recent weakness. It was an economy upon which so much of the world, including the United States, relied.

On March 6, the BIS warned of uncertainty over the potential for deeper cuts into negative territory.[111] Undaunted, four days later, Draghi's ECB announced the decision to cut rates. The rate on the deposit facility was lowered by 10 basis points to −0.40 percent.[112] In addition, the ECB expanded its monthly asset purchases (QE) program from €60 billion to €80 billion and announced it would begin buying assets of nonfinancial companies with investment-grade ratings. There was more. Starting in June, the ECB would hold new targeted longer-term refinancing operations (TLTRO) to encourage regional banks to give loans to investors and consumers.[113] That still wasn't happening after all the years of cheap-money aid.

During the related news conference, Draghi blamed the ECB's lower inflation forecast on temporarily lower oil prices and the BIS having expressed concerns that policy tools were becoming less effective and central banks were running out of tactics.

He spoke defiantly of his strategy's ability to reach its goals: "The best answer to this is being given by our decisions today. It's a fairly long list of measures, and each one of them is very significant and devised to have the maximum impact in boosting the economy, and the return to price stability. So we have shown that we are not short of ammunition."[114] He was daring every naysayer by tripling down. There was no central bank checks-and-balances system to stop him.

Regarding worries about general worldwide money expansion and whether there were fresh signs of "currency wars," Draghi was more sanguine. He replied, "The ECB has never started anything like that. Even our measures today are entirely addressed to our economy, domestic economy....Also, let's not forget that in the G20 in Shanghai all countries took a solemn agreement that basically they would avoid such war."[115]

Six days later, on March 19, Jens Weidmann, president of Germany's Bundesbank, criticized the ECB's latest package. He warned against "reckless" moves and unintended fallout. "I have always drawn attention to the fact that the longer the effect of an 'ultra-relaxed' monetary policy lasts the weaker (that effect) becomes.... Financial market bubbles can come about which, if they burst can complicate the work of central banks."

He further suggested, "Rather than reckless experiments on monetary policy it would be more sensible to take a break."[116] Weidmann warned against "helicopter money" whereby the ECB would seek to inject money directly into households to boost spending to avert deflation.

Draghi didn't listen. The next day, at a private meeting in Brussels, Draghi told EU leaders that the ECB had "no alternative" to its recent rate cuts and monetary policy decisions. To the press, Draghi said the ECB cannot do much about the euro area's largest issues, but he reassured them of his commitment to use "all the appropriate instruments" to support European recovery. This time, he hedged the effectiveness of his own prowess and promises, noting, "even though monetary policy has been really the only policy driving the recovery in the last few years; it cannot address some basic structural weaknesses of the euro-zone economy."[117]

Janet Yellen encountered opposition, too. According to CNBC, on March 23, four of the seventeen members of the FOMC disagreed with her dovish backtrack. St. Louis Fed president James Bullard, Chicago Fed president Charles Evans, Philadelphia Fed president Patrick Harker, and Kansas City Fed president Esther George said that at the Fed meeting in April they should consider raising interest rates.[118]

At the end of March 2016, during the G20 meeting held in Paris, called the Paris Forum, PBOC governor Zhou Xiaochuan put the idea of an alternative to conjured money in perspective. He reemphasized his opinion against relying too much on one international currency, the dollar. He called for reform that the IMF could conduct and promoted the use of special drawing rights.[119] For China to call on a Western institution to step away from the dollar so publicly was a groundbreaking move, for the IMF was truly in the United States' backyard—its headquarters only blocks away from the White House, Treasury Department, and Fed. The SDR was made up of UK, EU, US (three Western states), and Japanese currencies, so this was

Zhou sending a shot across the bow in terms of confidence in the prevailing monetary system.

Because China held the rotating presidency of the G20 that year, it had requested the meeting and set the tone. The selection of Paris as a locale had historic significance: since Charles de Gaulle, France had criticized the role of the dollar and favored international monetary reform. Europe would be pivotal in prying the world away from the dominance of the US dollar—if and when the opportunity was to surface.

Emboldened, German political leaders increased criticism of the ECB's monetary policy,[120] criticism that took a far more political than monetary or economic stance. According to German finance minister Wolfgang Schäuble, Draghi's policies were unintentionally supporting the rise of the extreme right wing in Germany and in other parts of Europe: the Alternative for Germany (AfD) party in recent regional elections had scooped up 25 percent of votes away from conservatives. Schäuble said, "I said to Mario Draghi...be very proud: you can attribute 50 per cent of the results of a party that seems to be new and successful in Germany to the design of this policy."[121]

The main criticism German politicians levied at Draghi was that easing was not bringing growth, but it was harming German savers with low rates. Sigmar Gabriel, German vice chancellor and leader of the Social Democratic Party, part of Merkel's coalition, shared Schäuble's opinion. Meanwhile, Merkel was holding a cautious position. Having spoken out against the ECB in years past, she was letting her ministers do the talking.

Gabriel's view was more moderate but still critical of Draghi's programs. "What the European Central Bank is doing now is for many savers, for little people, for workers, for pensioners, an expropriation, but it is not the ECB's fault," he said. "The blame lies with Europe's inability to put together a joint growth program."[122] The bigger issue of the shaky concept of a European Union and how it could manage national and supranational interests simultaneously manifested in Gabriel's defense of a specific class of German citizens.

Across the Atlantic, less attention was paid to the nuances of European policies. US election season was in full swing. On April 15, 2016, in a G20 meeting in Washington, financial leaders were feeling reassured—mostly from the markets, not the real economy, being resuscitated. They noted in their final communiqué statement, "The global recovery continues and the financial markets have recovered most of the ground lost earlier in the year since our February meeting in Shanghai. However, growth remains modest and uneven, and downside risks and uncertainties to the global outlook persist against the backdrop of continued financial volatility, challenges faced by commodity exporters and low inflation."[123] The markets had been elevated by the joint policy of Draghi and Kuroda that kept the average global cost of money at zero.

On some level, G20 leaders might have known about—but did not admit to—collusion. Instead, they chose to reemphasize their commitment to use monetary, fiscal, and structural measures to keep the economy moving toward growth and price stability. Schäuble reaffirmed his concern regarding the ECB going into negative territory and its effects on bank profits and German savers.

A week later, on April 21, the ECB made good on its March 10 announcement to expand the QE program from €60 billion to €80 billion. Draghi defended ECB independence against his German critics: "We have a mandate to pursue price stability for the whole of the Eurozone, not only for Germany. This mandate is established by the Treaty, by European law. We obey the law, not the politicians, because we are independent, as stated by the law. And by the way, all this applies to all countries, to all politicians in the Eurozone."[124]

In an interview with the German newspaper *Bild*, Draghi aggressively touted the legitimacy of his mandate in the ongoing feud between him and Schäuble.[125] He said German criticism was not a good way of strengthening the Eurozone and could damage the whole region. According to Draghi, "The ECB obeys the law, not the politicians."[126]

He flaunted his policies while noting that, given the severity of the crisis, any monetary measures would take time to have an impact. "For two years, the economy in the euro area has been growing month by month, banks are lending and unemployment is steadily falling. Meanwhile, euro area countries are now able to buy more German exports again, which, for German companies, is partly making up for the decline in trade with China. But it is a slow process because the crisis was more severe than anything we'd had since the Second World War."[127]

The problem with his historical argument, however, was that it implied that his policies were fine, that they just needed a longer horizon to achieve the desire effect, whereas his policies' ability to attain real economic growth should have been questioned to begin with.

On May 2, in a panel speech at the annual meeting of the Asian Development Bank in Frankfurt, Draghi further drew battle lines against his German critics by saying that the German current account surplus—not low interest rates—was one of the greatest obstacles to the Eurozone's low growth. He said, "Our largest economy, Germany, has had a [current account] surplus above 5 percent of GDP for almost a decade....Those advocating a lesser role for monetary policy or a shorter period of monetary expansion necessarily imply a larger role for fiscal policy."[128]

Draghi had a point. Germany was a more reluctant participant in the consolidation of the Eurozone than was Greece, for example, which was blamed for the area's problems. Low rates combined with Germany's surplus harmed the rest of the European economy. By the end of 2016, Germany's account surplus hit a record of $297 billion, topping China's as the world's largest.[129] During the economic crisis, Germany's push for austerity contradicted ECB monetary policy—which was actually quite generous, just not to citizens.

Germany feared losing its biggest prize: maximization of the current account surplus, which was boosted by a monetary union that reduced transaction costs. Germany's posture reflected its political position and political aims in sustaining the European Union, which contrasted with the idea of an independent central bank.

On May 25, in an interview with *El País*, ECB governing council member François Villeroy defended Draghi from criticism he characterized as "personal," "excessive and dangerous." According to Villeroy, "It seems to me to be excessive to talk of politicization of the ECB, that it is under the control of this country or another, or that it has been the reason for the growth of a certain party in Germany. It's false."[130]

With a referendum vote scheduled on the matter for June 23, Villeroy also emphasized the risks of Brexit. He said British banks would face strong financial turbulence and the monetary union in Europe would be affected. "It can't expect to leave Europe and at the same time think it can participate in the financial market union or that the role of the City will be the same."[131] Worries about Brexit and the chaos it could cause moved to center stage.

Two days later, the final statement of the G7 meeting in Japan warned that Brexit would harm global trade, investment, and job creation. BOJ governor Haruhiko Kuroda said, "It would have a significant and serious impact on the global economy."[132] He emphasized the role of central banks in promoting dynamism in the global economy and their lack of boundaries for doing so. He said, "I don't think for Japan, or the ECB, at this stage that monetary policy has reached the limit. We still have enough room to further these monetary conditions."[133]

Promoting growth was also a topic of animated discussion. The G7 participants diverged on which policies to pursue to do it. Japan defended the continuity of monetary policy as a tool to promote liquidity and stimulate growth. In contrast, Germany and the United Kingdom believed austerity and fiscal discipline were better ways and strongly criticized "cheap money."

Domestic banks' losses and their complaints had become a cornerstone of ECB-Germany strife. In Germany, the banks and insurers were negatively affected by low interest rates. Nominal yields on ten-year German bonds had fallen from 4 percent in 2008 to less than 0.2 percent in 2016. One bank said low rates had deprived German households of €200 billion since 2010.[134] As that situation intensified, Schäuble's attacks on the ECB widened to blaming it for the overall social collapse in Germany that resulted in the rise of the right wing.

On June 8, the ECB announced that it would enter the corporate bond market to buy the debt of some of Europe's biggest companies.[135] It was an unexpected and risky decision, because the ECB could be buying bonds with lower ratings.

The Eurozone had grown only 1.6 percent in 2015. That didn't bode well for securing citizens' confidence. But Draghi held firm. As he told the Brussels Economic Forum, "Given the harm that has already occurred to potential growth during the crisis, it also means [a need for] acting decisively to raise potential."[136]

The looming fear was that a Brexit vote could alter the currency and trading relationship of the United Kingdom with the EU. Among central bankers, worries about disruption to monetary policy collusion grew. By June 15, 2016, the BOJ was in constant contact with its European counterparts to prepare for a possible Brexit. It stood ready to offer dollar funds to domestic banks to avoid a Lehman-type credit freeze.[137]

For her part, Yellen kept rates unchanged,[138] though the decision to do so was not unanimous; Kansas City Fed president Esther George disagreed. Yellen argued that a rate hike would happen when solid signs of economic strength appeared. She was unclear on when that would be: "I'm not comfortable to say it's in the next meeting or two, but it could be." She acknowledged the Brexit issue was one factor leading the Fed to be more cautious, noting that the referendum may bring "consequences for economic and financial conditions in global financial markets."[139]

BREXIT: A RESULT OF CONJURED-MONEY POLICY

Then it happened. The Brexit vote for the United Kingdom to leave the EU was won by 51.9 percent versus 48.1 percent on June 23, 2016. Voter turnout was 71.8 percent, with more than thirty million people casting a ballot. British working-class citizens embraced the result; the business community did not expect it. The pound shed 10 percent in response, dropping to its weakest level in thirty-one years.[140]

London's *Daily Mail*'s front page blared in all caps "Take a Bow, Britain!," noting that the vote was in part a rise against an "arrogant, out-of-touch political class and a contemptuous Brussels elite."[141] Whereas the anger might have missed targeting the institutions those elites represented, such as the big private banks and central banks, it symbolized gross disenchantment with a status quo. The prevailing sentiment was that politicians and elite bureaucrats put the needs of core Europe over those of the United Kingdom. Refugee, immigrant, and associated security fears over anything from job loss to terrorism also came into play. Economic instability would leave the voting population seeking an outlet for their frustrations—a group to blame.

A few hours after the Brexit results, the Fed said that it stood ready to provide dollars to other central banks via swap lines set up during the 2008 financial crisis. The Fed worried about "pressures in global funding markets, which could have adverse implications for the US economy." It was time for more "co-operation with other central banks."[142] Or more collusion.

In a separate statement, Jack Lew said, "The UK and other policymakers have the tools necessary to support financial stability, which is key to economic growth."[143] The G7 confirmed that central banks were ready to use their "established liquidity instruments" if needed.[144]

On June 28, at a EU summit, Draghi warned EU leaders that Brexit could reduce Eurozone growth over the next three years by a cumulative 0.3–0.5 percent.[145] Before the vote, the ECB had estimated that the Eurozone would show annual growth of 1.6 percent in 2016 and 1.7 percent in 2017 and 2018. Draghi urged national governments to address those complications with joint efforts and to deal with vulnerabilities in their banking sectors in response. Brexit could ruin his already ineffective policy results.

An uncharacteristically shaken Schäuble demanded quick responses from European governments to restore trust in the EU. He told the newspaper *Welt am Sonntag*, "If the [European] Commission does not act jointly, then we'll take the matter into our hands and just solve the problems between governments." He added, "What we can't do ourselves must be done at European level," even if facing "growing demagogy and deeper Euroscepticism."[146]

In an interview with the *Financial Times*, Christine Lagarde called attention to another issue budding from establishment skepticism. Politicians, such as US presidential candidate Donald Trump, increasingly advocated antitrade policies embraced by voters. According to Lagarde, these policies could spark protectionism movements that could harm the global economy. She said Brexit was already stoking concerns about growth. In regard to antitrade policies, she said, "I think it would be quite disastrous, actually…it would certainly have a negative impact on global growth."[147] Indeed, renegade politics could render the IMF, its special drawing rights basket, and the significant influence of central banking power impotent.

The spread between the return on assets and liabilities in domestic business hovered near all-time lows. It signaled that the cheap-money policy that was supposed to raise inflation or help growth or induce bank generosity in lending had failed on every single account.

None of that mattered. The ECB announced that the 80 billion euro asset purchases would continue until March 2017—or "beyond if necessary."[148] Draghi highlighted his "readiness, willingness and ability" to add more stimulus. He believed that the reduced impact of monetary stimulus left the euro more vulnerable to trade flows and geopolitics.

On July 8, the IMF's Independent Evaluation Office (IEO) released a report admitting its top staff made many misjudgments in dealing with the entire European debt crisis, especially Greece's economic situation. The staff's "culture of compla-cency" and a tendency toward "superficial and mechanistic" analysis brought up questions about who was ultimately in charge of the IMF. The report also admitted that internal investigators were unable to obtain key records or delve further into the activities of secretive "ad-hoc task forces."

It was a largely ignored bombshell. Christine Lagarde was not accused of ob-struction. The report cited the approach to the Eurozone as characterized by "group-think" and intellectual capture. There were no alternative plans on how to deal with a systemic crisis in the Eurozone or a multinational currency union.[149]

On August 4, in the aftermath of the Brexit vote, the Bank of England an-nounced a cut in rates (the first since March 2009) to 0.25 percent. That was a record low in the BOE's 322-year history. It also announced a QE program of £60 billion to buy government bonds (which would drive down yields and force investors into risk-ier assets, like it had everywhere else). Measures included a £100 billion scheme to encourage lending from UK banks to UK companies and a pledge to buy £10 billion of corporate debt issued by UK companies that contributed to the UK economy.[150]

BOE governor Mark Carney chastised the banks. He said they had no excuse for not passing on lower official borrowing costs to customers. He presented a range of measures to limit job losses and support growth in the UK economy as it went through "regime change" following the decision to leave the EU. He strongly op-posed negative interest rates, but meeting minutes revealed that a majority of BOE members supported lowering rates if necessary. The minutes also indicated that poli-cymakers did not agree unanimously on the stimulus package.[151]

Three weeks later, at the Jackson Hole symposium, Yellen shifted again and said the Fed would take a gradual approach in raising rates.[152] Minutes from the FOMC's July meeting showed that New York Fed president William Dudley and San Fran-cisco Fed president John Williams indicated a rate increase could come by the end of the year.[153]

Not only were they telling Wall Street to prepare but also they were ensuring their central bank allies knew what was ahead. These money crafters had to sell their policies in tiny soundbites before anything could really be digested with confidence.

According to the *Guardian*, on August 26: "The Federal Open Market Commit-tee (FOMC), the policy-setting branch of the Fed, has met five times this year; each time, its members voted to hold off on raising interest rates."[154] That made Europe anxious. Would its collusive partner in the Fed still keep playing by the same rules in the central banking game?

On September 1, Draghi finally admitted, "Monetary policy has inevita-bly created destabilizing spillovers" and "large exchange rate fluctuations between major currencies...are testament to that." It was the furthest he had gone toward

suggesting these unprecedented policies could have negative impacts. He said competitive devaluations of this kind, or currency wars, were a "lose-lose for the global
economy" that "lead to greater market volatility, to which other central banks are
then forced to react."[155] His position cast central banks as reluctant heroes.

That didn't change his actions. A week later, on September 8, the ECB continued its monthly €80 billion bond purchases but advised this could come to an end in
six months.

Reuters cited, "Facing anemic growth and inflation, the ECB is buying 1.74 trillion euros worth of bonds, holding rates deep in negative territory and giving banks
free loans, hoping to end the bloc's nearly decade-long economic malaise with an
infusion of cheap credit."[156]

Draghi urged governments to assume responsibility in restoring the economy
and conveniently characterized uncertainty concerning Europe markets anxious
from Brexit's immediate impact. He reaffirmed the ECB's readiness to pump more
stimulus if needed to reach the 2 percent inflation target. He called his QE program
"effective" and dismissed any expectations about "helicopter money" or other alternative easing schemes.[157]

In the wake of Brexit turmoil, British prime minister David Cameron stepped
down from his leadership post immediately and, on September 12, 2016, also va-
cated his MP seat.[158] "The country made a decision," he later said, "a decision I
advised against, but nonetheless the decision has been made and I want the government to successfully pursue that decision and get it right. As a result, not being a
backbencher but leaving parliament is the right thing to do."

Theresa May, the fifty-nine-year-old home secretary and member of the Conservative Party and seventeen-year veteran of Parliament, became the second female
prime minister, taking his place. May was not about to invite lack of continuity in
the central banking arena while on a mission to prove her mettle navigating the best
Brexit. In a statement following the vote, Bank of England governor Mark Carney
proclaimed, "We have taken all the necessary steps to prepare for today's events. In
the future we will not hesitate to take any additional measures required to meet our
responsibilities as the United Kingdom moves forward."[159]

Six days later, on September 18, Claudio Borio, head of the Monetary and Economic Department of the BIS, empathized with the central bank money conjurers,
to an extent, at a media briefing: "It is becoming increasingly evident that central
banks have been overburdened for far too long." According to the *Financial Times*,
the BIS had "warned about the risk that central banks' asset purchases boost asset
prices without necessarily boosting economic activity."[160] This was the entire crux of
conjured-money policy: it stoked asset bubbles, with no way to manage how or when
they would inevitably pop.

This coddling of the oppressors depicted the illogic of a situation that hurt all those involved to some degree—except the central bankers themselves. It was the central banking establishment that had no real allegiance to voters and that remained virtually untouchable.

Borio made it clear that "the prospect of lower rates for longer has had a dual effect…has fueled a familiar shift into equities and a broader search for yield, leading to the usual signs of exuberance [and] it has raised serious concerns about banks' profitability, as ultra-low rates and flat yield curves tend to erode their net interest margins and to reduce the cost of carrying non-performing loans, in turn delaying the necessary clean-up of banks' balance sheets."[161]

That jargon meant that artificially stimulated markets, fueled by fabricated funds, hid the true condition of banks. It was a chilling and implicit condemnation of conjured-money policy. The BIS, for all of its discretion, and despite being a composite of elite memberships from within the central bank community itself, could see the writing on the wall.

DRAGHI VS. THE GERMANS: FALL 2016

Four years after he last addressed German lower house members, Draghi returned to a closed session at the German parliament on September 26, 2016. The tussle lasted nearly two hours as Draghi played defense and asked for help beyond his mandate and policies. According to Draghi, "For the euro area to thrive, actions by national governments are needed to unleash growth, reduce unemployment and empower individuals, while offering essential protections for the most vulnerable."[162] He faced opposition from surplus countries such as Germany and the Netherlands about the effects of the ECB's negative rates on bank and pension fund profits.

Draghi had to acknowledge that "the locality of these concerns is definitely higher in Germany," while trying to assure the body that "we are also aware that it is only in reaching our objective of price stability that these concerns can be addressed forever."[163]

Corralled by Schäuble, other politicians accused ECB policies of triggering right-wing populism and damaging the whole EU project.[164] Some blamed Draghi for major problems with German banks, especially Deutsche Bank, whose shares by the end of September 2016 had fallen more than 65 percent from their July 2015 peak, erasing more than half the firm's market value.

Draghi retorted that Germans were net beneficiaries of easing policies and that German banks were in trouble not because of the monetary policy but because of poor efficiency. Of Deutsche Bank he said at a closed-door session, "If a bank represents a systemic threat to the euro zone, it can't be because of low interest rates. It has to do with other reasons."[165]

By late September, the inflation rate in the Eurozone showed a sliver of an increase. That was enough to give Draghi confidence that his stimulus program was working. Consumer prices rose 0.4 percent, twice as much as in August.[166] The increase was associated with recent stabilization of oil prices; the increases, if they continued, could support the ECB's inflation targets.

At the October 8, 2016, G20 meeting, Treasury secretary Lew stated the obvious, that Europe should do more to ensure stability of its financial markets.[167] Schäuble reiterated that financial disruption risks were due to "ultra-loose" monetary policy. He warned, "The danger of a new crisis has not completely vanished."[168] Draghi saw no evidence that his monetary easing led to asset price bubbles.[169]

At an ECB press conference two weeks later, on October 20, Draghi said his "set of measures…exploit[ed] the synergies between the different instruments and [have] been calibrated to further ease financing conditions, stimulate new credit provision and thereby reinforce the momentum of the euro area's economic recovery and accelerate the return of inflation to levels below, but close to, 2 percent."[170] His money-conjuring arsenal had a strategy to deal with everything.

Still, he feared that after years of missing the ECB's inflation target, investors would lose confidence in the ECB's ability to achieve its supposed mandate. Because of that, Draghi added a proclamation of confidence that the Eurozone growth rate appeared to have stabilized in a solid trajectory.

The matter of how the United Kingdom would deal with Brexit still loomed. Mark Carney extended his five-year term as Bank of England governor until the end of June 2019—three months after the United Kingdom was expected to leave the European Union. On October 31, 2016, in a story headlined "The 'Film Star' Bank of England Governor,"[171] the BBC reported that Carney had written to finance minister Philip Hammond accepting the extension of his "term in office beyond the expected period of the Article 50 process [for Britain to leave the EU]," noting "this should help contribute to securing an orderly transition to the UK's new relationship with Europe."[172] The pound was the world's worst-performing currency that month, hitting a six-and-a-half-year low against the euro.[173] If the shock of Brexit was going to subside, Carney would have to continue preaching to the choir. Any pattern disruption to the central banking world could be devastating to confidence and, thus, to the bankers who relied on it.

With the United Kingdom assured consistency on the central banking front, there remained one particularly thorny private banking problem on the European continent: Deutsche Bank. Eight years after the financial crisis struck, the IMF labeled the German behemoth as posing the greatest risk to the global financial system, a risk even more pronounced for the world than just for Germany.[174] The pronouncement didn't even include the implications of the findings of the ongoing investigations.

On December 23, after years of investigations and market speculation about their results, the US Department of Justice ordered Deutsche Bank to pay $7.2 billion in fines for crimes committed during the financial crisis—a sign of all that conjured-money policy had plastered over. The bank's shares dove on concerns about its survival. Global markets fretted about Deutsche Bank's deep connections to other global financial institutions.[175]

All the cheap-money subterfuge had not addressed the prevailing and alarming codependencies among too-big-to-fail banks the world over. That meant systemic risk had not been extinguished, it had only been camouflaged. The fine was just that, a fine, not a shift to prevent any of the looming hazards the financial system could still unleash.

TRUMP ASCENDS, DRAGHI MARCHES ON

At the start of 2017, the United States installed a new president as Europe embarked upon its own set of elections, including major elections in France, Germany, Italy, and more. The threat of political polarization had washed ashore and was now a growing European problem.

Growth remained low, stock prices remained inflated, money manufacturing continued. The geopolitical environment frothed to a peak of nationalism and disdain for elites and central banks, refugees and terrorist attacks.

On January 19, the ECB announced it would continue purchasing under the asset purchase program (APP) €80 billion per month through the end of March 2017. These purchases would be curtailed to €60 billion per month through December 2017, or beyond, if necessary.

"As the recovery will firm up, rates will go up as well," a persistent Draghi said during a Q&A session following the governing council meeting in which he reinforced his plan to continue the ECB's bond-buying program for at least a year. Reporters prompted him about German criticism, and he responded in typical Draghi fashion, saying that "the honest answer would be: Just be patient."[176] When asked later that day for a reaction, German economic point man Schäuble said calmly, "I trust the ECB will always do the right thing."[177]

Theresa May met with Donald Trump at the White House on January 27. This was the day after Mexican president Enrique Peña Nieto canceled his trip to meet with Trump.

May and Trump agreed to maintain the "special relationship" of their two nations through Brexit. There was no discussion about their central banks' influence on their economic relationship, or mutual and resulting career paths.

As Bank of England head Mark Carney said in February 2017, "The Brexit journey is really just beginning. While the direction of travel is clear, there will be twists and turns along the way. Whatever happens, monetary policy will be set to return inflation sustainably to target while supporting the necessary adjustments in the economy."[178]

Carney vowed monetary policy would remain consistent. No lessons were learned through the conjured-money decade—not by the central bankers who crafted it, not by the politicians who did nothing to stop it.

The fragmentation that was baked in to the EU experiment, exacerbated by the financial crisis and the conjured money that elevated markets, came in play. US isolationism in the age of Trump, however, provided Europe an opportunity to strengthen its currency, trade, and diplomatic alliances with other areas.

Sahra Wagenknecht, head of Die Linke (the Left party) in the Bundestag,[179] noted that the deluge of money made available to multinational companies, markets, and the financial system versus extractions from the public in the form of austerity measures showed that Eurozone governments "wanted us to forget the role of de-regulated financial markets and the fact that the increases in public debt after 2008 are mainly due to the enormous costs of bailing out the banks. This wasn't just the case in Europe, but all around the world.[180]

"Together with the Eurozone governments," said Wagenknecht, "the ECB is responsible for the destruction of a million jobs and a dramatic reduction of wages and pensions especially in Southern Europe. This social catastrophe is completely unnecessary given the fact that the ECB is able to finance investment and jobs on a massive scale. However, the ECB prefers to pump billions into financial markets, fueling speculation and asset price inflation."[181]

By the time of the elections in France on May 7 and Germany on September 24, 2017, the anti-euro messaging abated somewhat, but this was all under a relatively stable dose of easy money from the ECB. No matter what changes governments made or how their relationships with each other shifted, there was one constant: the conjured-money policies of their central bankers, which plastered over all the problems of their financial systems.

On June 8, Draghi told reporters in Tallinn, Estonia, "The recovery is pro-ceeding based on consumption and investment, and consumption and investment are growing because of QE also—not only, but also QE. Because interest rates are low, labour income has increased; wealth, households' wealth has also increased. Financing conditions remain extremely favourable, and this is essentially because of QE.... Regarding non-standard monetary policy measures," he assured, "we confirm that our net asset purchases, at the current monthly pace of €60 billion, are intended to run until the end of December 2017, or beyond, if necessary."[182]

Not surprisingly, one of the premier money conjurers was touting his accom-plishments. However, only time and a significant amount of analysis of the period would reveal that his policies, like those of his fellow colluders, fueled another set of asset bubbles, kept flailing and fraudulent big banks solvent, and only randomly coincided with a modicum of support for the global population.

On September 24, 2017, Angela Merkel won her fourth consecutive term as Germany's chancellor. But, in that ongoing reflection of political polarity based upon economic conditions flared by ineffective monetary policy, the far right party, Alternative for Germany, bagged 13 percent of the vote, nearly triple that of 2013.[183]

Three days later, Schäuble announced he was leaving his role as Germany's finance minister. The man whom the *New York Times* called the Architect of Austerity would become president of the Bundestag in October 2017.[184] In that role, he could more directly call out the policies of ECB head Mario Draghi. In the end, though, as the European jobless rate and despair worsened, the two might even come to support the same, ineffective monetary policy. As already noted, this game of central bank thrones and money fabrication with no personal risk to or accountability on the part of the fabricators could make friends of enemies and enemies of friends.

CONCLUSION

The End Is Just the Beginning

If we have this conversation in 10 years' time... we might not be sitting in Washington, DC. We'll do it in our Beijing head office.

—Christine Lagarde, managing director of the IMF, July 24, 2017

The 2007–2008 financial crisis that ravaged the global economy was ignited by a rapacious banking system in the United States. In response, herded by the Fed, the central banks of the G7 nations careened down an endless money-manufacturing trail—in broad daylight.

These central bankers launched a massive, unprecedented, coordinated effort to provide liquidity to their banking systems on a global scale, using terms like *unlimited* and *by all means necessary* along the way. But their maneuvers did not connote a finite exercise with specific goals. Indeed, central bank–mandated goals like inflation or employment targets were constantly in flux. What they said and what they did had little correlation.

The better indicator of what they achieved was market reaction. If the markets faltered, these central bankers reverted to using words that conveyed easing or uncertainty over the exact way that tightening would occur. If statements had adverse effects, they would flip-flop or cart out another member of the central bank with an alternate opinion.

Policies that conjured artificial money to deal with the crisis continued far beyond their originally stated purpose. Measures that were supposed to be temporary lingered, virtually unchecked, unquestioned, and unstoppable by any external authority. The sheer power of central bank complicity remained a dirty little secret, even to central bankers themselves.

On July 31, 2017, vice chairman of the Fed Stanley Fischer attended the sixtieth birthday celebration of Armínio Fraga, former chairman of the Central Bank of Brazil (1999–2003), in Casa das Garças, Rio de Janeiro. The event didn't make the US news cycle, probably subverted by the latest tweet from the Trump White House that day. But, in general, central bankers fly beneath the public radar. They can make pithy pronouncements about the improved state of the global economy without acknowledging their role in providing cheap money to fuel speculation that boosts stock and bond markets with the media barely taking notice.

Yet how central bankers bat about tens of trillions of dollars and dictate the cost of money *is* a big deal. But it takes a fair amount of digging to pull the various strands of their story together in order to grasp the significance. The central banking elite covet reclusiveness, convening at glitzy conferences and using arcane language to keep out of sight and out of mind.

In Rio, when the Fed's number two man emerged to address the phenomenon of globally low interest rates, he offered a glimpse into the alternative reality in which central bankers exist.[1] In his speech, he indicated that factors suppressing rates were many, "some of which could fade over time, including the effects of quantitative easing in the United States and abroad and a heightened demand for safe assets affecting yields on advanced-economy government securities." But rates were purely manufactured. Conjured. Fabricated. Adopted as emergency measures, and then normalized.

He echoed the laments of Bernanke and other major central bank leaders who complained that low rates alone *weren't enough* to stimulate growth…without ever taking responsibility for the policy. Sadly, the Fed vice chair appeared unaware that a low or zero rate policy was incapable of doing what central bankers had promised it would do time and time again—stimulate growth and help people.

"However, as I have said before—and Ben Bernanke before me—'Monetary policy is not a panacea,'" Fischer continued. "Policies to boost productivity growth and the longer-run potential of the economy are more likely to be found in effective fiscal and regulatory measures than in central bank actions."[2]

The financial crisis changed everything, monetarily, geopolitically—even external perception of the elite. Central bankers colluded under the guise of promising real growth. Because they did so in a manner that fluctuated between idle speed and rapid response, it was nearly impossible to qualify or quantify the effectiveness of their actions relative to their stated goals.

During and after the 2008 financial crisis, countries exhibiting the most growth were not those that followed the Fed's lead to zero, or the ECB and BOJ's rush to negative rates. The most resilient were the transitioning economies, like China, that developed local infrastructure and partnered with regional and longer-distance partnerships on long-term growth projects instead of harnessing monetary collusion.

So, what happens now that the policies spawned as "emergency measures" have morphed into opioids for banks and markets? The G3 central banks (the Fed, the ECB, and the BOJ) that drove these policies have no exit plan on the other side. Among the G3 central banks there is occasional talk of "tapering" or reducing the size of their books, but it is always with an open door. There is nothing easy about letting go of the quantitative money addiction. Selling the trillions of dollars in securities banks have hoarded could very well cripple the system—again. Just as garage sale junk values are crushed when there are no buyers for the junk, associated "fire sales" could see multiple asset prices come crashing down.

Existing on a diet of artificial money and demand is anything but normal for an economic or financial system, even if it boosts markets to historic highs. If you take air out of a tire, it collapses; if you take too much QE out of the system too quickly, the system collapses. If the flow, or even the possibility, of conjured money was to stop, markets relying on it would tank.

Since the time of the global financial crisis, the Big Six US banks have benefited tremendously from access to cheap money. They profited from central bank purchases of their securities, which exaggerated the value on their books. Wall Street leveraged central banking largesse to fund buybacks of their own shares. Banks issued new shares and debt into a rising market, artificially boosting their own stock values and those of their major corporate clients. By doing so, Wall Street transformed fabricated market values into stratospheric executive bonuses. This vicious cycle of making money for the elites never ended, it just received a new supplier.

Meanwhile, governments issued record amounts of debt and passed austerity measures regardless of their impact on populations. By mid-2017, the amount of securities that the G3 central banks held on their books, about $14 trillion, was equivalent to a staggering 17 percent of global GDP. In 2017, the ECB, BOJ, and BOE were still buying $200 billion worth of assets per month, injecting artisanal money into world markets atop an ever-changing array of excuses.[3]

Another by-product of the financial crisis and central bank collusion was the rise in economic anxiety that spawned a swing toward nationalism, from Brazil to Great Britain to the United States. The shock of Brexit in the United Kingdom reverberated around the world as voters turned away from the incumbent leadership and its failed economic policies. In the United States, the election victory of Donald Trump, the billionaire "antiestablishment" president, was another manifestation of this trend. These landmark votes were not caused by central banking policy directly but were the effects.

Because central banks operate beyond public scrutiny and government oversight, they are only occasionally called on to explain their actions. They vacillate between taking credit for what they deem are positive results in the world economy and remaining silent in the wake of catastrophic failures that result from their policies. But the mystique around them must dissipate to avoid the general public continually getting whipsawed by their policies.

CHANGE ON THE HORIZON

Because of central bankers' predisposition to collusive meddling, money-conjuring policies are locked in for years to come, regardless of which elites head the banks.

Yet, evolution looms ahead. The addition of the Chinese renminbi to the IMF's special drawing rights basket in October 2016—the first such significant adjustment in the SDR since its inception in 1969—marked real change in the monetary system. Similarly, the establishment of the New Development Bank (formerly known as the BRICS bank) and the Asian Infrastructure Investment Bank in 2014 indicated a significant swing away from the historically Western-Japan-dominated banking system. The IMF, by permitting China to enter its reserve currency basket, allowed a change not seen since the euro replaced the German and French national currencies in 1999. The move signaled a growing trend away from the United States and a dollar-based system.

China's inclusion into the IMF's SDR reserve basket is a game-changer, as much for China as for the IMF. The global financial crisis brought about a shift in power dynamics from West to East, from highly developed to developing countries. In the wake of the Fed's collusive monetary policy, this phenomenon has accelerated and will continue to accelerate given the US national agenda of protectionism and nationalism under the Trump administration.

Non-G7 leaders see themselves as crusaders against the manipulation of money. Policies of sustainability and autonomy are now more important to emerging economies than simply falling into the good graces of the Fed.

Developing nations will continue to seek alternatives to Western-dominated monetary, trade, and financial policy. The Regional Comprehensive Economic Partnership (RCEP), an alliance that includes China and excludes the United States, highlights this intention.

Elite central bankers will attempt to hold onto their immense power even in the face of these shifts. Yet, ongoing cash infusions will eventually provoke major disruptions and volatility if they were to stop or slow down.

That is why noncash instruments, such as crypto currencies and hard assets like gold, will become increasingly attractive. They will continue to be relevant based on the fear that, in another major downturn, central and private banks will collude to freeze cash and retract liquidity from their customers. Protecting themselves will always come first.

The emergence of Bitcoin and alternative money measures is a glimpse into such peer-to-peer substitutes to the prevailing monetary system.[4] So is the resurgence of interest in gold. In response, central and private bankers have sought to curtail or capture the reach of these replacements, eager to maintain their lock on the flow of all "money."[5] But not all of them agree on the evolution of money alternatives. Some see them as the future.

Christine Lagarde expressed as much in one of her many prescient statements at a Bank of England conference on September 30, 2017. There, the managing director of the IMF predicted to the chagrin of the audience:

> For now, virtual currencies such as Bitcoin pose little or no challenge to the existing order of *fiat* currencies and central banks. Why? Because they are too volatile, too risky, too energy intensive, and because the underlying technologies are not yet scalable. Many are too opaque for regulators; and some have been hacked.
>
> But many of these are *technological* challenges that could be addressed over time. Not so long ago, some experts argued that personal computers would never be adopted, and that tablets would only be used as expensive coffee trays. So I think it may not be wise to dismiss virtual currencies.[6]

She concluded,

> Today's central banks typically affect asset prices through primary dealers, or big banks, to which they provide liquidity at fixed prices—so-called open-market operations. But if these banks were to become less relevant in the new financial world, and demand for central bank balances were to diminish, could monetary policy transmission remain as effective?[7]

Meanwhile, in the absence of a benchmark that is outside central bank influence, such as a modern gold standard or more prevalent use of a currency basket like the SDR, currencies will continue to be objects of speculation, which hurts their value as arbiters of fair trading mechanisms that reflect the actual strength and weakness of national economies. Collusion among the bigger players renders the smaller or "outsider" ones perpetually caught in defense mode. That is why they are forging alternative monetary alliances and considering using non-US-dollar currency alternatives like the renminbi for their transactions.

Because G7 conjured-money policy has produced no tangible results, broken confidence in the financial system will continue to steer elections and multinational alliances.

Ambivalence among investors and voters could ultimately have major negative repercussions. Meanwhile, stock indexes continue to soar to new heights, building a false sense of security on a bed of fabricated capital.

With rates already near zero, or negative in some countries, there is little-to-no room to maneuver in the event of a looming crisis. After the decade long money-conjuring policy, one with no real end in sight, one thing has become clear: central bank craftsmanship has been ineffective, at best, and has demonstrated gross negligence for the lasting consequences, at worst. The assumption that these central banking policies will anytime soon evoke real growth is as preposterous as it is wrong.

Markets fall and rise now because of the realpolitik undertow from central banks. Central banks remain powerful, their leaders inculpable. When their terms are up, central bankers cycle through other positions in the upper echelons of the world of big finance, but their legacies transcend time and, often, geography.

WHAT SHOULD BE DONE

As Nobel laureate economist Joseph Stiglitz wrote in an op-ed for the *LA Times* in August 2015, "Quantitative easing was yet another instance of failed trickle-down economics—by giving more to the rich, the Fed hoped that everyone would benefit. But so far, these policies have enriched the few without returning the economy to full employment or broadly shared income growth."[8]

With their massive books, core central banks should have and could have financed investment instead of speculation, could have worked with development banks and public projects rather than funding private ones. That would have been truly unconventional and measurably more effective for the common person. They did not.

Meanwhile, countries amassed historically high debt burdens relative to GDP. As long as central banks kept rates low, the cost of servicing debt remained low as well. That situation enabled governments to issue more debt at a cheaper cost. Yet, if these strategies reversed or rates do rise, so does the cost of servicing this debt, for governments and corporations. That could lead to significant defaults on debts around the world. Even former Fed chairman Alan Greenspan—who stoked the derivatives market and favored bank mergers and deregulation—in August 2017 warned of the dangerous bubble "abnormally low rates" inflate.[9]

With global debt equal to three times global GDP as a result of conjured-money policies, to avoid a devastating crash, we need a debt reset. Without a debt overhaul or relief program, we are headed for another epic credit crisis. If that reoccurs, banks will again turn to governments and central banks to save them at the expense of fortifying broader populations and the foundational economy. Central bankers might not be able to exert the same false market confidence the second time around. That's why they cling to policies they adopted a decade ago.

There are other ways to mitigate a crisis in advance. We could write off all the public debt incurred since 2008 that hasn't been redirected to the real economy— that is, take a deep breath and cancel it out globally. We also need to implement actual oversight of the conjurers and dedicate effective channels through which to question and curtail their authority and actions. Instead of financing speculative bubbles at the hands of the big private banks, central banks should finance large investment and recovery programs. We should break up the banks à la Glass-Steagall so that they can't hold people's deposits hostage during the next crisis. But these are tall orders that require a fundamental power shift, legislative will, and system reboot. If they have any shot of ever happening even in a small dosage, we all need to be better informed about the extent of collusion that has occurred and the ramifications of creating money for no real purpose.

The Fed's crisis and post-crisis monetary policies, adopted by other major central banks, was supposed to "trickle down" to the masses. That didn't happen. The global elites knew this then, and they are more aware of it now.

In January 2017, the World Economic Forum admitted that rising inequality threatens the world economy. These colluders provoke inequality because it benefits them and the preservation of their global power hierarchies to the detriment of everything and everyone else.

The Fed and its allies have created a shaky monetary system that will collapse without their manipulation. It's job security for them, but hazardous for the rest of us. Central bankers, for all their meetings in posh locales the world over, have no plan B to reverse or alter course without causing massive damage and financial pain to billions of people.

They have shown no propensity to do anything different from a decade of impotent policies. As Sir Isaac Newton said, "A body in motion will remain in motion unless acted upon by an external force." That law of motion encapsulates the central bankers' position today. Some will continue advocating conjured-money policy; others will resist inertia and seek an opposing path and relationships—but only if we create an outside force that will change the trajectory of conjured-money policy. If Newton had been a central banker, he would have been better off just eating the apple. There are ostensibly two main types of central bankers: the ones with more legacy power, and the ones with less but rising power, as is the case in China. Thus, there is no objective, truly external force within the prevailing monetary system or around it, except for the continued rise of new players such as China, individually, and the BRICS, collectively, to alter it.

The Fed absolved itself of all responsibility for financial stability in the big bank landscape in June 2017 when it allowed thirty-four of the largest Wall Street banks, including the Big Six, to pass its stress tests. In turn, the banks took this opportunity to buy more of their own shares, elevating their stock prices rather than expanding their loan services for small businesses and Main Street customers.

US banks disclosed plans to buy back $92.8 billion of their own stock as a direct response to the Fed's blessing. The largest US bank, JPMorgan Chase, announced it would buy back $19.4 billion of its own shares, its most ambitious program since the 2008 crisis.[10] Citigroup announced its biggest buyback, at $15.6 billion. "Stock repurchases by financial companies in the S&P 500 rose 10.2 percent in the first quarter [of 2017] and accounted for 22.2 percent of all buybacks."[11] The all-clear was another version of QE for banks courtesy of the Fed, greenlighting legal manipulation of the stock market. The Dow soared.

A decade of money conjuring and collusion helped the same banks take the same risks that spurred that activity and allowed them to reap stock profits to boot. This move was captured by the US Senate Banking Committee in a letter from Thomas Hoenig, vice chairman of the US Federal Deposit Insurance Corporation (FDIC), the government agency in charge of guaranteeing people's deposits.[12] He wrote that US banks in 2017 had used 99 percent of their net earnings for purchases of their own stock and paying dividends to shareholders (including themselves).

The Fed set the precedent of supporting big banks and then dodging criticism as the regulator of those institutions. Similar activities took place around the world, but not to the extent as in the United States where conjured money first took flight. While savers and pensioners are getting close to no interest on their nest eggs and small businesses have to leap through hoops to get loans, grow, and hire workers, big banks game the system repeatedly and central banks abet them.

The threat of a collapse larger than the 2008 financial crisis looms because of the plethora of asset bubbles that central banks have created and fueled—setting the scene for a disastrous fall. That fall could also happen for other reasons given escalating tension in North Korea altering how banks operate in that region, economic sanctions from the United States, a corporate credit meltdown in Latin America, an implosion in the Chinese real estate market, Southern EU countries buckling under the precarious state of their banks and economies, or a big bank bet going wrong.

It only takes one domino to fall to wipe them all out. It will again begin with the banks, cripple the markets, and devastate the global economy.

Yet in the inevitable financial crash—these conjurers will not be blamed. Or monitored. They are simply doing their jobs, even if those jobs have shifting definitions and nebulous goals. They jockey for position among themselves. Their countries jostle for geopolitical hegemony and stronger regional alliances.

The world economy remains imperiled, an opportunistic game to the central banks, a field day for speculators, a hazard for populations.

ACKNOWLEDGMENTS

Collusion has taken me all over the world. And throughout the days, nights, weeks, months, and years I spent in planes, trains, cable cars, buses, cars, towns, villages, cities, hotels, universities, development banks, central banks, and government offices, I have come into contact with the most remarkable people. I have experienced this planet in a manner that has expanded my way of thinking in unimaginable ways.

I am grateful to so many people and places along this journey. To do justice to everyone's contribution is impossible. Even the folks at the twenty-four-hour passport place that secured my visas to Brazil and China under tight deadlines were helpful and necessary to this project.

Foremost, though, I want to thank the most stellar group of economists and researchers I have ever had the fortune to know. My gratitude to Craig Wilson from the United States, who, having worked with me on *All the Presidents' Bankers,* lost many more hours of sleep leading the research effort, with particular focus on the United States, Mexico, and Europe.

Thank you to Roberto Rodolfo Georg Uebel from Brazil, who worked on Latin American–Asian alliances, with particular focus on Japan. Thank you to "the Pedros": Pedro Perfeito and Pedro Marques, who focused on Brazil and global rate and currency movements, respectively. Thank you to Alberto Sanchez and Octavio Olivares for their work on the ground in Mexico. Thank you to Elaine Yu from Hong Kong for her work on the China chapter, after having been fact checker for *All the Presidents' Bankers.* Thank you to Fernando Chafim from Spain for his work on the Europe chapters. They have been outstanding.

Special thanks as always to my awesome agent, Andrew Stuart, without whose coaching and counseling this book wouldn't have happened. My gratitude to the fabulous and dedicated team at Nation Books/PublicAffairs, especially to my dedicated publisher, Alessandra Bastagli, and my amazing publicity director, Jaime Leifer, who helped me every step along the way.

I am grateful for so many interviews and so much information that people and their organizations have provided me from around the world.

Thank you to all my friends and family for their ongoing understanding and support. My gratitude to Danny McGaw for his song "You and Me," and to the town of Ojai for their open arms. Thank you to my dog, Homer, for keeping me company through all of those long writing hours. My love to Nigel for this new chapter.

GLOSSARY

Asset: A resource (physical or financial) that represents economic value over which a government, private company, or individual has control of buying or selling.

Asset bubble: When the price of assets rises above valuations that are justified; asset bubbles usually portend an unexpected drop in price—they are a system ripe for a "pop."

Bailout: The general definition of a bailout is a rescue from financial distress, however in the context of post-financial crisis and elite-power maneuvers, there were often strings attached to bailouts so that countries receiving them weren't able to direct those funds to promote public well-being or real economic growth, but rather had to divert them to banks, creditors, or international speculators.

Benchmark interest rate: The interest rate upon which a security or interest rate swap is based, normally set by central banks.

Bonds: A type of investment that represents a loan in which an investor loans money to a corporation or a government for a certain period of time in exchange for an agreed-on interest rate. Usually, the entity that issues (offers for sale) the bond as a way to borrow money is so large that it must borrow from multiple investors, so a bond is really a piece of a large loan.

Bretton Woods Agreement: The agreement among delegates from forty-four countries that established the prevailing monetary and exchange rate system in 1944 in Bretton Woods, New Hampshire, in which currencies were pegged to the price of gold, and the US dollar was designated the major reserve currency linked to the price of gold.

Capital: Assets or representations of the values of assets that operate in a financial system and that are often used for generating wealth through investment or short-term speculative bets.

Capital markets: Part of a financial system that deals with raising money through equity (stock), bonds, or other types of long-term investment methods, and where buyers and sellers engage in trading those securities.

Central bank: A government-based monetary authority authorized to set monetary policy for, distribute money to, and offer credit to financial institutions. Central banks are responsible for regulating domestic banking and financial institutions.

Credit: An agreement, often made using legal tender, that allows a borrower to receive money or something of value that they will later repay to the lender, typically with interest; sometimes borrowers are required to offer some sort of collateral in exchange for credit.

Credit risk: The risk that a borrower may not meet the repayment obligations of a loan that a lender faces, which would cause the lender to experience loss of principal or interest.

Equity: Stock or any other security representing an ownership interest in a company.

Exchange rates (foreign currency rates): The price of one national currency in comparison to another currency; the exchange rate can be affected by monetary policy, trade, or speculative activity.

G3: For the purposes of this book, the Group of 3 consists of the United States, the European Union, and Japan.

G7: The Group of 7 consists of Canada, France, Germany, Italy, Japan, the United Kingdom, and the United States.

G20: The Group of 20, established in 1999, consists of the governments and central bank governors representing the twenty major economies: Argentina, Australia, Brazil, Canada, China, France, Germany, India, Indonesia, Italy, Japan, Mexico, Russia, Saudi Arabia, South Africa, South Korea, Turkey, United Kingdom, United States, and the European Union.

GDP: The measure of the market value of final goods and services produced by a country during a specified period, usually quarterly or annually.

Interest rate: The amount a borrower is charged by a lender to use an asset (to borrow it), payable at predetermined intervals.

Interest rate swap: An agreement between two counterparties to exchange one stream of interest payments for another, over a certain period of time.

Liquidity: The ability of financial market participants to buy and sell financial securities quickly and with the least amount of cost involved.

Monetary intervention: The influence government agencies or central banks have over the natural monetary cycle, supply and demand, or the cost of money (rates) in a financial system.

Monetary policy: The authority afforded a central bank, currency board, or other regulatory body to set the size and rate of growth of the national money supply by calibrating the level of interest rates, inflation rates, and other targets.

Monetary system: A system of finance that combines central bank policy, private financial institutions, and government-based regulatory systems that influence the way money flows.

NIRP: Negative interest rate policy; a policy tool used by central banks whereby private institutions pay central banks to hold their money, or, in other words, central banks charge depositors interest to keep the deposited money in holding. The opposite of paying interest.

Options: In their most basic form, options are a form of derivative security, because their price depends on or is linked to the price of something else. Basic options trade on exchanges; ones that are composites of others and more complex can trade just between two counterparties.

Private corporate debt: Debt that nonfinancial companies incur; nonfinancial companies are in business making market goods or providing services that are not related to finance.

Private equity: Equity capital not bought or sold on a public exchange mechanism.

Public debt: The amount of money that a country's government owes its lenders or other nations or investors that buy its bonds. It is also called national debt.

Quantitative easing: An unconventional monetary policy in which a central bank purchases government bonds or other securities from the market to lower rates and increase money supply.

Reserve currency: Currency maintained by a central bank or financial institution that is used for paying off debt obligations or influencing domestic exchange rates.

SDR basket: The special drawing rights basket; an international reserve asset created by the International Monetary Fund (IMF) within the Bretton Woods fixed exchange rate system that is composed of weighted currency units from the United States, United Kingdom, European Union, Japan, and China.

Securities: Financial means (or instruments) that represent ownership of shares in stocks, bonds, or other forms of rights (options).

Speculation: Betting on the future value of a market, asset, item, or event.

ZIRP: Zero interest rate policy; a policy undertaken by central banks to keep the base rate at zero percent, theoretically in the hopes of stimulating an economy, but in practice with great benefits to private financial institutions.

NOTES

AUTHOR'S NOTE

1. The London Interbank Offered Rate.
2. "About: Carter Glass," US Department of the Treasury, www.treasury.gov/about/history/pages/cglass.aspx.

INTRODUCTION

1. Dion Rabouin, "Total Global Debt Tops 325 pct of GDP as Government Debt Jumps: IIF," Reuters, January 4, 2017, www.reuters.com/article/us-global-debt-iif-idUSKBN14O1PQ.
2. Edward Yardeni and Mali Quintana, *Global Economic Briefing: Central Bank Balance Sheets* (Yardeni Research, Inc., August 25, 2017), www.yardeni.com/pub/peacockfedecbassets.pdf.
3. *Liquidity* in finance refers to the instant availability of capital, whether in the form of cash, securities, or reserves to be used for buying or selling in the market.
4. "About the Fed," Board of Governors of the Federal Reserve System, www.federalreserve.gov/aboutthefed/mission.htm.
5. "Historical Debt Outstanding—Annual 2000–2015," TreasuryDirect, www.treasurydirect.gov/govt/reports/pd/histdebt/histdebt_histo5.htm.
6. Angela Monaghan, "Income Inequality Still at Record Levels, Says OECD," *Guardian* (Manchester), November 24, 2016, www.theguardian.com/business/2016/nov/24/income-inequality-oecd-financial-crisis.
7. Jaime Caruana, "Stepping Out of the Shadow of the Crisis: Three Transitions for the World Economy" (speech, Bank for International Settlements Annual General Meeting, Basel, Switzerland, June 29, 2014), www.bis.org/speeches/sp140629.pdf.
8. Robert N. McCauley, Patrick McGuire, and Vladyslav Sushko, "Global Dollar Credit: Links to US Monetary Policy and Leverage" (BIS Working Papers No. 483, Bank for International Settlements, Basel, Switzerland, January 2015), www.bis.org/publ/work483.pdf.
9. Binyamin Appelbaum, "I.M.F. Urges Fed to Delay Raising Interest Rates," *New York Times,* June 4, 2015, www.nytimes.com/2015/06/05/business/economy/imf-recommends-fed-delay-raising-interest-rates.html?mcubz=2.
10. At first a Goldman Sachs–conceived term connoting fast-growing developing countries Brazil, Russia, India, China, and South Africa; in the wake of the artisanal money era, the BRICS nations would form long-lasting economic, infrastructure-development, and diplomatic ties as well.

11. Oliver Stuenkel, "Why Brazil Shouldn't Turn Its Back on the BRICS," *Americas Quarterly,* June 28, 2016, www.americasquarterly.org/content/why-brazil-shouldnt-turn-its-back-brics.

12. Renminbi is the official name of the Chinese currency, or "the people's currency," as translated from Mandarin. Yuan are units of renminbi.

13. Alessandro Speciale, "ECB Post-Summer Boost to Bond Purchases Slows Near Month End," Bloomberg, October 5, 2015, www.bloomberg.com/news/articles/2015-10-05/ecb-bought-63-billion-euros-of-debt-under-qe-in-september.

14. The European Commission (EC), the European Central Bank (ECB), and the International Monetary Fund (IMF).

15. "Fed's Yellen Expects No New Financial Crisis in 'Our Lifetimes,'" Reuters, June 27, 2017, www.reuters.com/article/us-usa-fed-yellen-idUSKBN19I2I5.

16. Ben S. Bernanke, "The Subprime Mortgage Market" (speech, Federal Reserve Bank of Chicago's 43rd Annual Conference on Bank Structure and Competition, Chicago, IL, May 17, 2007), www.federalreserve.gov/newsevents/speech/bernanke20070517a.htm.

17. Richard Dobbs, Susan Lund, Jonathan Woetzel, and Mina Mutafchieva, "Debt and (Not Much) Deleveraging," (report, McKinsey Global Institute, February 2015), www.mckinsey.com/global-themes/employment-and-growth/debt-and-not-much-deleveraging.

CHAPTER 1: MEXICO: THERE'S NO WALL AGAINST US FINANCIAL CRISES

1. "Mexico: GDP (Current US$): 2002–2009," World Bank, accessed September 6, 2017, http://data.worldbank.org/indicator/NY.GDP.MKTP.CD?end=2009&locations=MX&start=2002.

2. Anthony DePalma, "Dogged Doctor for Mexico's Morass," *New York Times,* December 31, 1994, www.nytimes.com/1994/12/31/business/dogged-doctor-for-mexico-s-morass.html.

3. "Current Member Biography, 'Guillermo Ortiz,'" Group of Thirty, accessed September 6, 2017, http://group30.org/members/bio_current/ortiz.

4. "Personalidades: Guillermo Ortiz Martínez, gobernador de Banxico," Es Mas, accessed September 6, 2017, http://web.archive.org/web/20120716192333/www.esmas.com/noticierostelevisa/biografias/406198.html.

5. The Bank of Mexico is the Central Bank of Mexico, also referred to as "BANXICO."

6. World Economic Forum, www3.weforum.org/docs/WEF_AM08_Report.pdf. (This section of the website is unavailable.)

7. Thomas Atkins and Mike Dolan, "Bank Rules under Fire After Losses and Scandal," Reuters, January 26, 2008, www.reuters.com/article/us-davos-baselii-idUSL2668610220080126.

8. Nomi Prins, *It Takes a Pillage* (Hoboken, NJ: Wiley, 2009).

9. Then at CNBC.

10. "Mexico's Ortiz Sees Risk in Overregulating," Davos Live (blog), *Wall Street Journal,* January 26, 2008, http://blogs.wsj.com/davos/2008/01/26/mexicos-ortiz-sees-risk-in-overregulating/.

11. Ibid.

12. Lisa J. Adams, "Seeing US Slowdown, Mexico Cuts Growth," *USA Today,* January 30, 2008, http://usatoday30.usatoday.com/money/economy/2008-01-30-1083465555_x.htm.

13. "Banco de México Governor Ortiz Joins Dallas Fed's Globalization Institute Advisory Board" (press release), Federal Reserve Bank of Dallas, February 14, 2008, https://www.dallasfed.org/news/releases/2008/nr080214.aspx.

14. Brian Naylor, "Bush's Final Budget Proposal: $3.1 Trillion," NPR, February 4, 2008, www.npr.org/templates/story/story.php?storyId=18672648.

15. "Bush Says US Spending Plans Will Help Mexico," Reuters, February 5, 2008, www.reuters.com/article/bush-mexico-idUSN0521809020080205.

16. In 2008 dollars.

17. Mary Swire, "Mexican Government Unveils USD5.6bn Stimulus Package," Tax-News, March 5, 2008, https://www.tax-news.com/news/Mexican_Government_Unveils_USD56bn_Stimulus_Package_____30193.html.

18. "FOMC Statement" (press release), Board of Governors of the Federal Reserve System, March 18, 2008, www.federalreserve.gov/newsevents/press/monetary/20080318a.htm.

19. Frank Newport, "Bush Job Approval at 28%, Lowest of His Administration," Gallup, April 11, 2008, www.gallup.com/poll/106426/bush-job-approval-28-lowest-administration.aspx.

20. George W. Bush, "The President's News Conference with President Felipe de Jesus Calderon Hinojosa of Mexico and Prime Minister Stephen Harper of Canada in New Orleans," American Presidency Project, April 22, 2008, www.presidency.ucsb.edu/ws/?pid=77159.

21. "Bush Praises Nafta Treaty," CNBC Times Video, April 22, 2008, www.nytimes.com/video/business/1194817111807/bush-praises-nafta-treaty.html.

22. Bush, "The President's News Conference with President Felipe de Jesus Calderon Hinojosa of Mexico and Prime Minister Stephen Harper of Canada in New Orleans."

23. According to the World Economic Forum (WEF) as of May 2015.

24. Marla Dickerson, "Rising Costs Push Mexico to Hike Rates," *Los Angeles Times*, June 21, 2008, http://articles.latimes.com/2008/jun/21/business/fi-mexinflation21.

25. *Annual Report Summary: 2007* (Mexico City: Banco de Mexico, April 2008), www.banxico.org.mx/publicaciones-y-discursos/publicaciones/informes-periodicos/anual/%7B7E9262F3-949C-D1DC-FFA3-88CEAC8794FC%7D.pdf.

26. Noel Randewic, "Mexico's Ortiz, Anti-Inflation Warrior, to Leave Cenbank," Reuters, December 9, 2008, www.reuters.com/article/mexico-ortiz-idUSN0916903420091209.

27. "Exhibit 1: Recent Developments" (supplement to Mexico's annual report on Form 18-K for the fiscal year ended December 31, 2007), www.sec.gov/Archives/edgar/data/101368/000090342308001047/ums-18ka1ex1_1218.htm.

28. "Peso Power: Mexican Currency Nears Six-Year High vs. Dollar," Money & Company (blog), *Los Angeles Times*, July 23, 2008, http://latimesblogs.latimes.com/money_co/2008/07/its-good-to-be.html.

29. "Federal Funds Data," Federal Reserve Bank of New York, accessed October 8, 2017, https://apps.newyorkfed.org/markets/autorates/fed funds/.

30. Calderón (a member of the Partido Acción Nacional, or PAN) was elected president of Mexico in December 2006 (and served until November 2012). He enjoyed a close alliance with Bush, who cemented his appreciation for the Mexican president after exiting the Oval Office in a portrait featured in his Texas exhibit.

31. Jo Tuckman, "Mexico Freezes Food Prices in Response to Global Crisis," *Guardian* (Manchester), June 19, 2008, www.theguardian.com/world/2008/jun/20/mexico.food.

32. Santiago García-Verdú and Miguel Zerecero, "On Central Bank Interventions in the Mexican Peso/Dollar Foreign Exchange Market" (Banco de México Working Papers No. 2014-19, Banco de México, Mexico City, August 2014), www.banxico.org .mx/publicaciones-y-discursos/publicaciones/documentos-de-investigacion/banxico/ %7BE6A86055-2BD4-E061-EAF9-6B5A162B0BC1%7D.pdf.

33. Heidi N. Moore, "Bank of America–Merrill Lynch: A $50 Billion Deal from Hell," *Deal Journal* (blog), *Wall Street Journal*, January 22, 2009, http://blogs.wsj.com/ deals/2009/01/22/bank-of-america-merrill-lynch-a-50-billion-deal-from-hell/.

34. Ben S. Bernanke, "Current Economic and Financial Conditions" (speech, National Association for Business Economics 50th Annual Meeting, Washington, DC, October 7, 2008), www.federalreserve.gov/newsevents/speech/bernanke20081007a.htm.

35. David Luhnow, "Mexican Crisis Holds Lessons for US," *Wall Street Journal*, October 13, 2008, www.wsj.com/articles/SB122385649246427253.

36. Erwan Quintin and Edward Skelton, "How Much Will the Global Financial Storm Hurt Mexico?" *Southwest Economy* (Federal Reserve Bank of Dallas), November–December 2008, 10–13, www.dallasfed.org/assets/documents/research/swe/2008/swe0806c.pdf.

37. "Bad Bets," *Economist*, October 16, 2008, www.economist.com/node/12432297.

38. Marla Dickerson, "Sell-Off Drives Mexican Peso Above 13-per-Dollar Mark," Money & Company (blog), *Los Angeles Times*, October 9, 2008, http://latimesblogs.latimes.com/ money_co/2008/10/so-much-for-the.html.

39. "World Markets Return to Selloff," CNN, October 8, 2008, http://money.cnn.com/ 2008/10/08/news/international/world_crisis/index.htm?postversion=2008100814.

40. Composed of Mexico's Ministry of Finance and Banco de México members.

41. Agustín G. Carstens and Alejandro M. Werner, "Mexico's Monetary Policy Framework under a Floating Exchange Rate Regime" (Documento de Investigación No. 9905, Banco de México, Mexico City, May 1999), 40, www.imf.org/external/pubs/ft/seminar/ 2000/targets/carstens.pdf.

42. *Report to Congress on International Economic and Exchange Rate Policies* (Washington, DC: US Department of the Treasury, December 10, 2008), www.treasury.gov/resource -center/international/exchange-rate-policies/Documents/FX%20REPORT%20--%20 Final%20December%202008.pdf.

43. Chris Isidore, "Fed: Emergency Cut," CNN, October 8, 2008, http://money.cnn.com/ 2008/10/08/news/economy/fed_move/index.htm?postversion=2008100811.

44. Robert Kuttner, "Alan Greenspan and the Temple of Boom," review of *Maestro: Greenspan's Fed and the American Boom*, by Bob Woodward, and *Greenspan: The Man Behind Money*, by Justin Martin, New York Times on the Web, www.nytimes.com/ books/00/12/17/reviews/001217.17kuttnet.html.

45. Banxico uses the term *minister of finance* on its English-language site, but the direct translation is *secretary*. "Agustín Guillermo Carstens Carstens," Banco de México, www.banxico.org.mx/acerca-del-banco-de-mexico/junta-de-gobierno/%7BD51F01E6 -E0AE-681D-233A-C369CAD3103E%7D.pdf.

46. "Governor of the Central Bank of Mexico" (photo), Getty Images, www.gettyimages .com/detail/news-photo/governor-of-the-central-bank-of-mexico-guillermo-ortiz-and -news-photo/83180485.

47. "October 2008—Extraordinary Auctions of US Dollars," Banco de México, www
.banxico.org.mx/sistema-financiero/estadisticas/mercado-cambiario/operaciones-vigentes
-del-banco-de-mexico-en-el-mer/mecanismos/october-2008---extraordinary-.html.

48. José Sidaoui, Manuel Ramos-Francia, and Gabriel Cuadra, "The Global Financial Crisis
and Policy Response in Mexico" (BIS Papers No. 54, Bank for International Settlements,
Basel, Switzerland, n.d.), 279–298, www.bis.org/publ/bppdf/bispap54q.pdf.

49. Rubén Aguilar Valenzuela, "Los afectados, 22.3 millones en el 2009," El Economista, March
5, 2010, http://eleconomista.com.mx/sociedad/2010/03/05/pobreza-extrema-mexico.

50. "Mexico's Response to the Crisis" (paper in the G20 Country Briefs series, International
Labour Office, for the G20 Meeting of Labour and Employment Ministers, Washing-
ton, DC, April 20–21, 2010), www.dol.gov/ilab/diplomacy/G20_ministersmeeting/G20
-Mexico-brief.pdf.

51. Robert Campbell, "Mexico Spends Tenth of Foreign Reserves to Aid Peso," Reuters, October 10, 2008, www.reuters.com/article/markets-mexico-idUSN1036858020081010.

52. Sidaoui, Ramos-Francia, and Cuadra, "The Global Financial Crisis and Policy Response
in Mexico," www.bis.org/publ/bppdf/bispap54q.pdf.

53. Chairman Ben Bernanke's schedule, January 2008, Fraser, https://fraser.stlouisfed
.org/scribd/?item_id=529144&filepath=/docs/historical/bernanke/bernanke_calendar
_2008.pdf.

54. Luhnow, "Mexican Crisis Holds Lessons for US."

55. Ben S. Bernanke, The Courage to Act: A Memoir of a Crisis and Its Aftermath (New York:
W. W. Norton Books, 2017), 118.

56. "Mexico Unveils Emergency Spending," BBC News, October 9, 2008, http://news.bbc
.co.uk/2/hi/7660582.stm.

57. "Mexico Spends Tenth of Foreign Reserves to Aid Peso," Reuters, October 10, 2009,
www.reuters.com/article/markets-mexico-idUSN1036858020081010.

58. "2008 International Council Meeting" recap, Bretton Woods Committee, October 10, 2008,
www.brettonwoods.org/event/2008-10-10-0000/2008-international-council-meeting.

59. Ibid.

60. Alexandra Twin, "Wall Street's 8 Brutal Days," CNN, October 12, 2008, http://money
.cnn.com/2008/10/12/markets/markets_sunday/index.htm?postversion=2008101209.

61. Ian Swanson and Manu Raju, "Bush: World Coming Together," The Hill, October 11,
2008, http://thehill.com/homenews/news/16687-bush-world-coming-together.

62. "Diary: G7, IMF and World Bank Meetings in Washington," Reuters, October 11,
2008, www.reuters.com/article/us-imf-diary-idUSTRE49B08220081012.

63. Krishna Guha, "World Races to Limit Harm Before Recession Hits," Financial Times,
October 14, 2008, www.ft.com/intl/cms/s/0/b2560842-9989-11dd-9d48-000077b07658
.html#axzz3tnb439uX.

64. Luhnow, "Mexican Crisis Holds Lessons for US."

65. "Crisis Management in Mexico," Economist, November 12, 2008, www.economist.com/
node/12587590.

66. John Lipsky, "Finance and Economic Growth, Remarks by First Deputy Managing Director John Lipsky," International Monetary Fund, October 19, 2009, www.imf.org/en/
News/Articles/2015/09/28/04/53/sp101909.

67. Ben S. Bernanke, "Economic Outlook and Financial Markets" (testimony before the Committee on the Budget, US House of Representatives), Board of Governors of the Federal Reserve System, October 20, 2008, www.federalreserve.gov/newsevents/ testimony/bernanke20081020a.htm.

68. Alexandra Twin, "Dow's 2nd Best Day Ever," CNN, October 28, 2008, http://money .cnn.com/2008/10/28/markets/markets_newyork/index.htm.

69. "October 2008—Extraordinary Auctions of US Dollars," Banco de México, October 8, 2008, www.banxico.org.mx/sistema-financiero/estadisticas/mercado-cambiario /operaciones-vigentes-del-banco-de-mexico-en-el-mer/mecanismos/october-2008 ---extraordinary-.html.

70. "Timothy F. Geithner Confirmed as Assistant Secretary for International Affairs" (press release), US Department of the Treasury, September 19, 1997, www.treasury.gov/press -center/press-releases/Pages/rr1940.aspx.

71. "Meeting of the Federal Open Market Committee on October 28–29, 2008" (transcript), www.federalreserve.gov/monetarypolicy/files/FOMC20081029meeting.pdf.

72. Ibid., 30–33.

73. *Citi Annual Report* (New York: Citigroup, 2009), www.citigroup.com/citi/investor/ quarterly/2009/ar08c_en.pdf.

74. Neil Irwin, "Federal Reserve to Lend Cash to Emerging Nations," *Washington Post*, October 29, 2008, www.washingtonpost.com/wp-dyn/content/article/2008/10/29/ AR2008102902606.html.

75. "Federal Reserve, Banco Central do Brasil, Banco de Mexico, Bank of Korea, and Monetary Authority of Singapore Announce the Establishment of Temporary Reciprocal Currency Arrangements" (press release), Board of Governors of the Federal Reserve System, October 29, 2008, www.federalreserve.gov/newsevents/press/monetary/20081029b.htm.

76. Sidaoui, Ramos-Francia, and Cuadra, "The Global Financial Crisis and Policy Response in Mexico."

77. "Federal Reserve, Banco Central do Brasil, Banco de Mexico, Bank of Korea, and Monetary Authority of Singapore Announce the Establishment of Temporary Reciprocal Currency Arrangements" (press release).

78. "IMF Creates Short-Term Liquidity Facility for Market-Access Countries" (press release), International Monetary Fund, October 29, 2008, www.imf.org/external/np/sec/ pr/2008/pr08262.htm.

79. Ban Ki-moon, "Secretary-General's Address to the General Assembly," United Nations Secretary-General, September 23, 2008, www.un.org/sg/en/content/sg/statement/ 2008-09-23/secretary-generals-address-general-assembly-englishfrench-version.

80. "Exhibit 1: Recent Developments" (supplement to Mexico's annual report on Form 18-K for the fiscal year ended December 31, 2007), www.sec.gov/Archives/edgar/ data/101368/000090342308001047/ums-18ka1ex1_1218.htm.

81. Ibid.

82. *Annual Report: 2008* (Mexico City: Banco de México, April 2009), www.banxico.org.mx/ publicaciones-y-discursos/publicaciones/informes-periodicos/anual/%7B837CB8F9 -E67C-14BF-1452-FEE2E1A6FD11%7D.pdf.

83. Ibid.

84. James R. Kraus, "Clinton's Executive Order to Back Peso Raises New Worries on Bank Exposure," *American Banker*, February 1, 1995.

85. Juanita Darling and Chris Kraul, "US Banks Anxious to Enter Mexico: Finance: Banking Is among the First Sectors to Be Opened Up by NAFTA. Mexican Companies and Consumers Can Expect Better Services, Lower Rates," *Los Angeles Times*, December 13, 1993, http://articles.latimes.com/1993-12-13/business/fi-1560_1_retail-banking.

86. Bureau of Economic and Business Affairs, "2015 Investment Climate Statement— Mexico," US Department of State, May 2015, www.state.gov/e/eb/rls/othr/ics/2015/241661.htm.

87. *Mexico: Financial Sector Assessment* (Washington, DC: World Bank, December 2006), http://documents.worldbank.org/curated/en/424941468278736155/pdf/38310.pdf.

88. "Citi Board Nominates Ernesto Zedillo to Board of Directors" (press release), Citigroup, Bank Press Room, February 26, 2010, www.citigroup.com/citi/press/2010/100226a.htm.

89. Nomi Prins, "Mexico and the US: Rising Volatility, Economic, Finance, and Bank Risk" (presentation to the Annual Financial Investigation Congress, Mexico City, August 28, 2015), www.slideshare.net/nomiprins/mexico-and-the-us-rising-volatility-economic-finance-and-bank-risk.

90. Dick K. Nanto, *The Global Financial Crisis: Analysis and Policy Implications* (Washington, DC: Congressional Research Service, October 2, 2009), https://fas.org/sgp/crs/misc/RL34742.pdf.

91. "G20 Finance Conclusions on Financial Crises, 1999–2009," G20 Information Centre, August 2009, www.g20.utoronto.ca/analysis/conclusions/financialcrisis.html.

92. "Communiqué" (document from Finance Ministers and Central Bank Governors Meeting, Berlin, Germany, December 15–16, 1999), G20 Information Centre, www.g20.utoronto.ca/1999/1999communique.htm.

93. "G20 Finance Conclusions on Financial Crises, 1999–2009."

94. "G20 Summit: In Quotes," BBC News, November 16, 2008, http://news.bbc.co.uk/2/hi/business/7731735.stm.

95. "ECB Publishes the Proceedings of the Fifth ECB Central Banking Conference" (press release), European Central Bank, February 5, 2010, www.ecb.europa.eu/press/pr/date/2010/html/pr100205.en.html.

96. Bartosz Maćkowiak, Francesco Paolo Mongelli, Gilles Noblet, and Frank Smets, eds., *The Euro at Ten: Lessons and Challenges* (Frankfurt: European Central Bank, 2009), www.ecb.europa.eu/pub/pdf/other/euroattenen2009en.pdf.

97. Elisabeth Malkin, "When the US Sneezes, Mexico Catches Cold," *New York Times*, December 30, 2008, www.nytimes.com/2008/12/30/business/worldbusiness/30iht-30peso.18988868.html?pagewanted=all%20.

98. *Inflation Report: October–December 2008* (Mexico City: Banco de México, 2009), www.banxico.org.mx/dyn/publicaciones-y-discursos/publicaciones/informes-periodicos/trimestral-inflacion/%7B0241C75D-AC03-3656-E79E-8DB376BAE2EE%7D.pdf.

99. "Exhibit 1: Recent Developments" (supplement to Mexico's annual report on Form 18-K for the fiscal year ended December 31, 2007), www.sec.gov/Archives/edgar/data/101368/000090342308001047/ums-18ka1ex1_1218.htm.

100. Guillermo Ortiz, "QE Exit and the Emerging Market Challenge," in *Think Tank 20: The G-20 and Central Banks in the New World of Unconventional Monetary Policy* (Washington, DC: Brookings Institution, August 2013), 65–72, www.brookings.edu/wp-content/uploads/2016/07/TT20-mexico_ortiz-2.pdf

101. "GDP Growth (Annual %): 2007–2009," World Bank, https://data.worldbank.org/indicator/NY.GDP.MKTP.KD.ZG?end=2009&locations=MX&start=2007.

102. Chris Isidore, "Economy: Sharpest Decline in 26 Years," CNN, January 30, 2009, http://money.cnn.com/2009/01/30/news/economy/gdp/.

103. "Mexico's Ortiz Sees Risk in Overregulating," Davos Live (blog), *Wall Street Journal*, January 26, 2008, http://blogs.wsj.com/davos/2008/01/26/mexicos-ortiz-sees-risk-in-overregulating/.

104. "Securities Market (Interest Rates)," Banco de México, www.banxico.org.mx/portal-mercado-valores/securities-market--interest-r.html.

105. David Jolly, "Global Financial Crisis Has One Beneficiary: The Dollar," *New York Times*, October 22, 2008, www.nytimes.com/2008/10/22/business/worldbusiness/22iht-dollar.4.17174760.html.

106. Dickerson, "Sell-Off Drives Mexican Peso Above 13-per-Dollar Mark."

107. *Inflation Report: October–December 2008* (Banco de México).

108. M. Angeles Villarreal, *The Mexican Economy After the Global Financial Crisis* (Washington, DC: Congressional Research Service, September 2010), www.fas.org/sgp/crs/row/R41402.pdf; Eastern Illinois University, "Mexico Economy: Pseudo Recovery," ViewsWire, December 4, 2009.

109. Associated Press, "Geithner Sworn in As Treasury Secretary," NBC News, January 26, 2009, www.nbcnews.com/id/28862809/ns/politics-white_house/t/geithner-sworn-treasury-secretary/#.WdLzwjOZP0E.

110. "Federal Reserve Will Offer $150 Billion in 84-Day Credit through Its Term Auction Facility Today" (press release), Board of Governors of the Federal Reserve System, January 26, 2009, www.federalreserve.gov/newsevents/press/monetary/20090126a.htm.

111. "Federal Reserve Announces Results of Auction of $150 Billion in 28-Day Credit Held on February 9, 2009" (press release), Board of Governors of the Federal Reserve System, February 10, 2009, www.federalreserve.gov/newsevents/press/monetary/20090210a.htm.

112. "Mexican Central Bank Predicts Economic Contraction This Year," *Los Angeles Times*, January 28, 2009, http://articles.latimes.com/2009/jan/28/business/fi-mexgdp28.

113. *Annual Report: 2009* (Mexico City: Banco de México, April 2010), graph 33, www.banxico.org.mx/publicaciones-y-discursos/publicaciones/informes-periodicos/anual/%7B540EDE66-3E95-C943-C1D8-3C929F1BDDA3%7D.pdf.

114. "BIS Board Elects New Chairman" (press release), Bank for International Settlements, January 12, 2009, www.bis.org/press/p090112.htm.

115. Ibid.

116. Ben S. Bernanke, "Semiannual Monetary Policy Report to the Congress," Board of Governors of the Federal Reserve System, February 24, 2009, www.federalreserve.gov/newsevents/testimony/bernanke20090224a.htm.

117. Sidaoui, Ramos-Francia, and Cuadra, "The Global Financial Crisis and Policy Response in Mexico."

118. Gerardo Reyes Guzmán and Carlos Moslares García, "The Mexican Economic Crisis (2007–2009)," *Annales Universitatis Mariae Curie-Skłodowska*, Lublin–Polonia XVI, no. 2 Section K (2009), http://annales.umcs.lublin.pl/tt_p.php?rok=2009&tom=16&se ctio=K&numer_artykulu=06&zeszyt=2.

119. "US Dollar Sales," Banco de México, www.banxico.org.mx/sistema-financiero/ estadisticas/mercado-cambiario/operaciones-vigentes-del-banco-de-mexico-en-el-mer/ operaciones/us-dollar-sales.html; International Monetary Fund, Monetary and Capital Markets Department, *Annual Report on Exchange Arrangements and Exchange Restrictions 2009* (Washington, DC: International Monetary Fund, November 30, 2009).

120. Guzmán and García, "The Mexican Economic Crisis (2007–2009)."

121. "Dólar mantiene escalada; tipo de cambio, en $15.45," *El Economista,* March 2, 2009, http://eleconomista.com.mx/notas-online/finanzas/2009/03/02/dolar-mantiene -escalada-tipo-cambio-1545.

122. Mary Anastasia O'Grady, "The Financial Storm Hits Mexico," *Wall Street Journal,* March 9, 2009, www.wsj.com/articles/SB123655372162565665.

123. Jason Lange and Alistair Bell, "Global Crisis May Be Past Worst: Mexico," Reuters, May 8, 2009, www.reuters.com/article/us-latam-summit-ortiz-idUSTRE5475SI20090508.

124. Andrew Selee and Katie Putnam, *Mexico's 2009 Midterm Elections: Winners and Losers* (Washington, DC: Mexico Institute, Woodrow Wilson International Center for Scholars, July 2009), www.wilsoncenter.org/sites/default/files/Mexico%2527s%20 Midterm%20Elections%20F2.pdf.

125. Gustavo Flores-Macías, "Mexico's 2012 Elections: The Return of the PRI," *Journal of Democracy* 24, no. 1 (January 2013): 128–141, https://muse.jhu.edu/article/495760.

126. Edward C. Skelton and Erwan Quintin, "Mexico's *Año Horrible*: Global Crisis Stings Economy," *Southwest Economy* (Federal Reserve Bank of Dallas), third quarter 2009, 3–7, http://dallasfed.org/assets/documents/research/swe/2009/swe0903b.pdf.

127. *Committee on IMF Governance: Final Report* (Washington, DC: International Monetary Fund, March 24, 2009), www.imf.org/external/np/omd/2009/govref/032409.pdf.

128. "IMF Executive Board Approves US$47 Billion Arrangement for Mexico Under the Flexible Credit Line" (press release), International Monetary Fund, April 17, 2009, www.imf.org/external/np/sec/pr/2009/pr09130.htm.

129. Angeles Villarreal, *Mexican Economy After the Global Financial Crisis,* https://www.fas .org/sgp/crs/row/R41402.pdf.

130. "Pese a costos, es necesario el plan fiscal: Ortiz," *El Economista,* September 9, 2009, http:// eleconomista.com.mx/finanzas/2009/09/09/pese-costos-necesario-plan-fiscal-ortiz.

131. Skelton and Quintin, "Mexico's *Año Horrible:* Global Crisis Stings Economy."

132. Cynthia Haven, "Innovation Will Deliver US from Recession, Experts Predict at Stanford's 2009 Roundtable," Stanford News, October 24, 2009, http://news.stanford.edu/ news/2009/october26/stanford-2009-roundtable-102409.html.

133. *Inflation Report: July–September 2009* (Mexico City: Banco de México, 2009), www.banxico .org.mx/dyn/publicaciones-y-discursos/publicaciones/informes-periodicos/trimestral -inflacion/%7B896E6AEE-3613-751A-112C-FE1ABB21FA3A%7D.pdf.

134. *Addendum to the Inflation Report: July–September 2009* (Mexico City: Banco de México, 2009), www.banxico.org.mx/dyn/publicaciones-y-discursos/publicaciones/informes

-periodicos/trimestral-inflacion/%7BF6EFBA44-DFD3-E1CF-0F6F-DC1602A4A
913%7D.pdf.

135. Guillermo Ortiz, "The Global Financial Crisis—a Latin American Perspective"
(speech given at Financial Globalization: Culprit, Survivor or Casualty of the Great
Crisis? conference, Yale University, New Haven, CT, November 13, 2009), www.bis
.org/review/r091207a.pdf.

136. Ibid.

137. Elisabeth Malkin, "New Chief Nominated for Mexico's Central Bank," *New York
Times*, December 9, 2009, www.nytimes.com/2009/12/10/business/global/10peso
.html.

138. Tracy Wilkinson, "Calderon Taps New Mexico Central Bank Chief," *Los Angeles Times*, December 10, 2009, http://articles.latimes.com/2009/dec/10/world/
la-fg-mexico-central-bank10-2009dec10.

139. Howard Schneider, "'Groupthink' Blocked IMF's Foresight of Crisis," *Washington Post*,
February 10, 2011, www.washingtonpost.com/wp-dyn/content/article/2011/02/09/
AR2011020906222.html.

140. "Mexico Economic Growth Hits 10-Year High," BBC News, February 22, 2011, www
.bbc.com/news/business-12538168.

141. *OECD Perspectives: Mexico Key Policies for Sustainable Development* (OECD, October
2010), www.oecd.org/mexico/45570125.pdf.

142. "Update 5—Mexico's Economy Stumbles at End of 2011," Reuters, February 16,
2012, www.reuters.com/article/mexico-economy-idUSL4E8DG45020120216;
Adam Thompson, "Mexico: Don't Leave Us Out of the Currency War," Beyond-
Brics (blog), *Financial Times*, October 25, 2010, http://blogs.ft.com/beyond-brics/
2010/10/25/mexico-dont-leave-us-out-of-currency-war/.

143. Thompson, "Mexico: Don't Leave Us Out of the Currency War," BeyondBrics (blog).

144. Jens Erik Gould and Andres R. Martinez, "Currency War Hits Mexico as Carstens
Signals Rate Cuts," Bloomberg, November 10, 2010, www.bloomberg.com/news/
articles/2010-11-10/currency-war-spreading-to-mexico-as-carstens-signals-lower-rates
-next-year.

145. "Mexico's Inflation Report" (image), Getty Images, www.gettyimages.ch/detail/
nachrichtenfoto/governor-of-the-bank-of-mexico-agustin-carstens-nachrichtenfoto/
106193591#governor-of-the-bank-of-mexico-agustin-carstens-presents-the-report
-picture-id106193591.

146. "Update 1—Mexico Central Bank Sees Emerging Mkts Bubble Risk," Reuters, November 17, 2010, http://uk.reuters.com/article/mexico-economy-idUSN1722247520101117.

147. Arnaldo Galvao and Andre Soliani, "Mantega Says US Throwing 'Money from
a Helicopter,'" Bloomberg, November 4, 2010, www.bloomberg.com/news/
articles/2010-11-04/mantega-says-u-s-throwing-money-won-t-force-brazil-to-act-on
-currency.

148. Jens Erik Gould, "Carstens Eyes Fed While Weighing Mexico Rate Cut," Bloomberg, November 11, 2010, www.bloomberg.com/news/articles/2010-11-11/carstens
-monitors-fed-easing-effect-while-considering-mexico-rate-decision.

149. "Agustín Guillermo Carstens Carstens," Banco de México, www.banxico.org.mx/
acerca-del-banco-de-mexico/junta-de-gobierno/agustin-carstens-curriculum-b.html.

150. Pedro Nicolaci da Costa, "Carstens Says Mexico Resilient to US Softness," Reuters, April 16, 2011, www.reuters.com/article/us-mexico-economy-carstens-interview -idUSTRE73F2QC20110416.

151. "Update 5—Mexico's Economy Stumbles at End of 2011," Reuters, February 16, 2012, www.reuters.com/article/mexico-economy-idUSL4E8DG45020120216.

152. Giles Tremlett, "Portugal's PM Calls on EU for Bailout," *Guardian* (Manchester), April 6, 2011, www.theguardian.com/world/2011/apr/07/portugal-eu-bailout.

153. "Timeline: The Unfolding Eurozone Crisis," BBC News, June 13, 2012, www.bbc .com/news/business-13856580.

154. Alicia Gonzalez, "Europa no necesita un europeo en el FMI, necesita soluciones," *El País* (Madrid), May 31, 2011, http://elpaís.com/diario/2011/05/31/economia/ 1306792810_850215.html.

155. Agustín Carstens, "Remarks by Agustín Carstens, Governor of Banco de México at the US-Mexico Chamber of Commerce Good Neighbor Awards, Washington, DC, May 12, 2011," www.banxico.org.mx/publicaciones-y-discursos/discursos-y-presentaciones/ discursos/%7BAA4A2D69-8582-D17B-E62B-608FF1672F14%7D.pdf.

156. "IMF Executive Board to Consider the Nominations of Agustín Carstens and Christine Lagarde for the Position of IMF Managing Director" (press release), International Monetary Fund, June 13, 2011, www.imf.org/external/np/sec/pr/2011/pr11230.htm.

157. "Update 2—Brazil Backs France's Lagarde in IMF Race," Reuters, June 28, 2011, www.reuters.com/article/imf-brazil-idUSN1E75R0HA20110628.

158. David Luhnow, "'San Agustín' Tries to Settle IMF's 65-0 Score," *Wall Street Journal*, June 11, 2011, www.wsj.com/articles/SB10001424052702304259304576377913327 550124.

159. Leon Lazaroff and Jose Enrique Arrioja, "Carstens Expects Mexican Peso to Pare Decline Against Dollar," Bloomberg, September 15, 2011, www.bloomberg.com/news/ articles/2011-09-15/carstens-says-peso-to-pare-decline-against-dollar-on-mexican -fundamentals.

160. Agustín Carstens's daily schedule, Friday, July 1, 2011, www.newyorkfed.org/media library/media/aboutthefed/dailyschedules_120127.pdf.

161. Jonathan J. Levin and Ben Bain, "Banxico Rate-Cut Bets Tossed Out as Peso Plunges: Mexico Credit," Bloomberg, September 23, 2011, www.bloomberg.com/news/articles/ 2011-09-23/banxico-rate-cut-bets-tossed-out-as-peso-plunges-mexico-credit.

162. Mark Weisbrot, "For Mexicans, It Was the Economy, Stupid," *New York Times*, July 2, 2012, www.nytimes.com/2012/07/03/opinion/for-mexicans-it-was-the-economy -stupid.html.

163. Elizabeth A. Duke, "Central Bank Cooperation in Times of Crisis" (speech, Center for Latin American Monetary Studies 60th Anniversary Conference, Mexico City, Mexico, July 20, 2012), www.federalreserve.gov/newsevents/speech/duke20120720a .htm.

164. Agustín Carstens, "Cooperation among Central Banks at the Beginning of the XXI Century" (keynote speech, 60th anniversary of the Center for Latin American Monetary Studies, Mexico City, Mexico, July 19, 2012), www.bis.org/review/r120816d.pdf.

165. Alejandro Toledo Patiño, "The Euro Crisis and the Mexican Economy," *Revista Voices of Mexico* 93 (2015): 24–28, www.revistascisan.unam.mx/Voices/pdfs/9306.pdf.

166. "Federal Reserve Issues FOMC Statement" (press release), Board of Governors of the Federal Reserve System, September 13, 2012, www.federalreserve.gov/newsevents/press/monetary/20120913a.htm.

167. "Mexico's Carstens Says Fed's Move Helps Mexico," Reuters, September 13, 2012, www.reuters.com/article/us-mexico-economy-carstens-idUSBRE88C1FA20120913.

168. Eleazar David Meléndez, "Mexican Stock Exchange Having Record-Breaking Month on Bank Strength, Economic Confidence," International Business Times, December 11, 2012, www.ibtimes.com/mexican-stock-exchange-having-record-breaking-month-bank-strength-economic-confidence-933339.

169. *Inflation Report: April–June 2013* (Mexico City: Banco de México, 2013), www.banxico.org.mx/publicaciones-y-discursos/publicaciones/informes-periodicos/trimestral-inflacion/%7BC3536BCA-AA75-49B3-3803-18E611061E36%7D.pdf.

170. *Quarterly Report: October–December 2013* (Mexico City: Banco de México, February 2014), www.banxico.org.mx/publicaciones-y-discursos/publicaciones/informes-periodicos/trimestral-inflacion/%7B09ABB759-CBE0-E08A-86F3-FCD6609F9300%7D.pdf.

171. Rodrigo A. Rosales, "Termina economía mexicana con debilidad en el 2013," *El Economista,* February 23, 2014, http://eleconomista.com.mx/finanzas-publicas/2014/02/23/termina-economia-mexicana-debilidad-2013.

172. Roberto González Amador, "Llega cartera vencida de créditos bancarios al consumo a la cifra más alta desde 2009," *La Jornada,* March 4, 2013, www.lja.mx/2013/04/llega-cartera-vencida-de-creditos-bancarios-al-consumo-a-la-cifra-mas-alta-desde-2009/.

173. Dave Graham and Jean Arce, "Mexico to Escape Recession After Floods, but Risks to Growth Rise: Reuters Poll," Reuters, September 25, 2013, www.reuters.com/article/us-mexico-economy-idUSBRE98O1A920130925.

174. Lourdes Contreras, "Reforma financiera: ¿más crédito para las Pymes?" *Forbes Mexico,* April 27, 2013, www.forbes.com.mx/pymes-prestar-mas-ganar-mas/#gs.5g0s7Ak.

175. Agustín Carstens, "Monetary Policy Options and Tools" (handout at Federal Reserve Bank of Kansas City symposium, 2013), 135–148, www.kansascityfed.org/publicat/sympos/2013/2013Carstenshandout.pdf.

176. International conference to commemorate the twentieth anniversary of the autonomy of Banco de México: "Central Bank Independence—Progress and Challenges," Banco de México, Mexico City, Mexico, October 14–15, 2013, www.banxico.org.mx/dyn/publicaciones-y-discursos/publicaciones/seminarios/central-bank-independence-_-p.html.

177. Ben S. Bernanke, "Celebrating 20 Years of the Bank of Mexico's Independence" (speech, Central Bank Independence—Progress and Challenges conference, Banco de México, Mexico City, Mexico, October 14–15, 2013), www.federalreserve.gov/newsevents/speech/bernanke20131014a.htm.

178. Manuel Sánchez, "Mexico's Prospects for Economic Growth" (remarks, United States–Mexico Chamber of Commerce, New York City, October 18, 2013), www.bis.org/review/r131024a.htm.

179. "Update 4—Mexico Central Bank Unexpectedly Cuts Rate to Spur Weak Economy," Reuters, June 6, 2014, http://lta.reuters.com/article/idLTAL1N0ON0XW20140606.

180. Peter Vanham, "Top 10 Things to Know About the Mexican Economy," World Economic Forum, May 5, 2014, www.weforum.org/agenda/2015/05/top-10-things-to-know-about-the-mexican-economy/.

181. *Mexico: Economic Update* (Dallas, TX: Federal Reserve Bank of Dallas, May 2, 2014), https://dallasfed.org/assets/documents/research/update/mex/2014/mex1403.pdf.

182. "Citi Banamex Announces $1.5 Billion Investment Program in Mexico" (press release), Citigroup, September 9, 2014, www.citigroup.com/citi/news/2014/141002b.htm.

183. Amy Guthrie, "Citigroup to Bolster Mexican Unit," *Wall Street Journal*, September 9, 2014, www.wsj.com/articles/citigroup-to-bolster-mexican-unit-1410292427.

184. "Citi Banamex Announces $1.5 Billion Investment Program in Mexico" (press release).

185. "Crédito a pymes creció 12% anual en seis años: Banxico," *El Financiero*, April 22, 2015, www.elfinanciero.com.mx/economia/credito-a-pymes-crecio-12-anual-en-seis-anos-banxico.html.

186. Christina Rexrode, "Citigroup Consumer Chief Plans to Leave," *Wall Street Journal*, October 15, 2014, www.wsj.com/articles/citigroup-consumer-chief-plans-to-leave-1413338403?tesla=y.

187. "Mexico Regulators Fine Citi Unit $2 Million over Loan Scandal," Reuters, October 15, 2014, www.reuters.com/article/citigroup-banamex-idUSL2N0S91OF20141016.

188. Anthony Harrup, "Mexican Inflation Ends 2014 Above Central Bank's Target," *Wall Street Journal*, January 8, 2015, www.wsj.com/articles/mexican-inflation-ends-2014-above-central-banks-target-1420727839.

189. "Agustín Guillermo Carstens Carstens," Banco de México, www.banxico.org.mx/acerca-del-banco-de-mexico/junta-de-gobierno/agustin-carstens-curriculum-b.html.

190. "Challenges for Emerging Economies in the Face of Unconventional Monetary Policies in Advanced Economies" (Stavros Niarchos Foundation Lecture, Peterson Institute for International Economics, April 20, 2015), https://piie.com/sites/default/files/publications/papers/carstens20150420.pdf.

191. Anthony Harrup, "Mexico to Sell Dollars to Support Peso," *Wall Street Journal*, March 11, 2015, www.wsj.com/articles/mexico-to-sell-dollars-to-support-peso-1426087391.

192. "Update 4—Mexico Central Bank Moves to Defend Peso, Eyes Weak Economy," Reuters, July 30, 2015, www.reuters.com/article/mexico-economy-idUSL1N10A2SQ20150730.

193. Eric Martin and Isabella Cota, "Bank of Mexico Is Betting $8.6 Billion on Ending Peso's Plunge," Bloomberg, July 31, 2015, www.bloomberg.com/news/articles/2015-07-31/bank-of-mexico-is-betting-8-6-billion-on-ending-peso-s-plunge.

194. Michael O'Boyle, "Mexico Will Protect Peso, Fed Not Only Factor for Rates: Carstens," Reuters, December 7, 2015, www.reuters.com/article/us-mexico-economy-carstens-idUSKBN0TQ2MD20151208.

195. Martin and Cota, "Bank of Mexico Is Betting $8.6 Billion on Ending Peso's Plunge."

196. "Update 1—Mexico Consumer Confidence Plunges in April by Most in 9 Months," Reuters, May 8, 2015, www.reuters.com/article/mexico-economy-idUSL1N0XZ0ZK20150508.

197. "Update 1—Mexico's Carstens Says Could Raise Rates at Any Time to Defend Peso," Reuters, July 31, 2015, www.reuters.com/article/mexico-peso-idUSL1N10B12T20150731.

198. Institute of International Finance report, "Corporate Debt in Emerging Markets: What Should We Be Worried About?" Institute of International Finance, March 31,

2015, www.iif.com/publication/html-publication/corporate-debt-emerging-markets
-what-should-we-be-worried-about.

199. Rosalía Lara and Ana Valle, "Deuda de empresas crece 22% a junio por dólar caro," *El Financiero*, August 5, 2015, www.elfinanciero.com.mx/empresas/deuda-de-empresas
-crece-22-a-junio-por-dolar-caro.html.

200. Mario Villalpando B. "Bank Credit and Productivity: Evidence from Mexican Firms" (Banco de México Working Papers No. 2015-06, Banco de México, Mexico City, March 2015), www.banxico.org.mx/publicaciones-y-discursos/publicaciones/documentos-de-investigacion/banxico/%7BD57584CB-47BF-D55D-99BE-53A3B7 A88AA6%7D.pdf.

201. Heather Long, "The Stock Market Drop…by the Numbers," CNN, August 24, 2015, http://money.cnn.com/2015/08/24/investing/stocks-market-crash-by-the-numbers/.

202. AFP, "Mexico Raises Key Interest Rate After Fed Move," Yahoo!, December 17, 2015, http://news.yahoo.com/mexico-raises-key-interest-rate-fed-move-195530640.html.

203. "Mexico Interest Rate: 2005–2017," Trading Economics, accessed September 7, 2017, www.tradingeconomics.com/mexico/interest-rate.

204. O'Boyle, "Mexico Will Protect Peso, Fed Not Only Factor for Rates: Carstens."

205. "Of Cars and Capital Flows: Mexican Central Bank Leader Discusses Auto Production, Global Challenges," Federal Reserve Bank of Atlanta, December 17, 2015, www
.frbatlanta.org/economy-matters/2015/12/17/mexican-central-bank-leader-discusses
-auto-production-global-challenges.

206. Christine Lagarde, "The Case for a Global Policy Upgrade by Managing Director Christine Lagarde" (speech, Farewell Symposium for Christian Noyer, Banque de France, Paris, January 12, 2016), www.imf.org/external/np/speeches/2016/011216
.htm.

207. Agustín Carstens, "Unconventional Monetary Policies, Spillovers and Policy Options for EMEs" (presentation, Farewell Symposium for Christian Noyer, Banque de France, Paris, January 12, 2016), www.banxico.org.mx/publicaciones-y-discursos/discursos-y-presentaciones/presentaciones/%7BFE4CAF98-C2FD-E352-749B-07C 588024377%7D.pdf.

208. Jude Webber, "Mexico's Markets Stand Out from Turmoil," *Financial Times*, January 25, 2016.

209. "Mexico's Carstens Sees Growth Slightly Above 2.5 pct in 2016," Reuters, February 5, 2016, www.reuters.com/article/mexico-carstens-idUSE1N14R017.

210. Pablo Medina Uribe, "Explainer: Latin America's Minimum Wage Increases," Americas Society/Council of the Americas, January 26, 2016, www.as-coa.org/articles/explainer-latin-americas-minimum-wage-increases.

211. *Investment in Mexico: 2015* (Mexico City: KPMG, 2015), https://assets.kpmg.com/content/dam/kpmg/mx/pdf/2016/09/Investment-in-Mexico-2015.pdf.

212. "Mexico's Carstens Says 'Implicitly' Weighing Risk of Trump Victory," Reuters, March 11, 2016, www.reuters.com/article/us-mexico-economy-trump-idUSMTZSAPEC3B W2MTK2.

213. "Wilson Center Study Finds 5 Million US Jobs Depend on Trade with Mexico," Wilson Center, November 4, 2016, https://www.wilsoncenter.org/article/wilson-center
-study-finds-5-million-us-jobs-depend-trade-mexico.

214. "Banxico vende 400 mdd en subastas ante caída del peso," *El Economista*, February 11, 2016, http://eleconomista.com.mx/sistema-financiero/2016/02/11/banxico-vende-400 -mdd-subastas-ante-desplome-peso.

215. Yolanda Morales, "Banxico inyectó en defensa del peso 24,455 mdd en un año," *El Economista*, December 13, 2015, http://eleconomista.com.mx/finanzas-publicas/2015/ 12/13/banxico-inyecto-defensa-peso-24455-mdd-ano.

216. "Agustín Carstens: el Banco Central de México no será tímido para mover las tasas de interés," Reuters, April 19, 2016, www.americaeconomia.com/economia-mercados/ finanzas/agustin-carstens-el-banco-central-de-mexico-no-sera-timido-para-mover-las.

217. Sam Fleming, "Central Bankers Fear Threat of Low-Growth Rut," *Financial Times*, August 28, 2016, www.ft.com/content/e93cec28-6ce8-11e6-9ac1-1055824ca907.

218. Alejandro Poiré, interview with author via Skype, August 9, 2016.

219. In February 2016, I addressed Tecnológico de Monterrey students and exchanged ideas with faculty at the university's modern Guadalajara campus.

220. "Encuesta sobre las Expectativas de los Especialistas en Economía del Sector Privado: Enero de 2016," Banco de México, February 2, 2016, www.banxico.org.mx/dyn/ informacion-para-la-prensa/comunicados/resultados-de-encuestas/expectativas-de-los -especialistas/%7B4632B968-0FD4-8306-3395-8FD2E01FDFC6%7D.pdf.

221. Gabriel Stargardter, "Mexico Sees Trade Deals in TPP Leftovers, Flags China Opportunity," Reuters, November 22, 2016, www.reuters.com/article/us-usa-trump-mexico -idUSKBN13H1ZV.

222. Christopher Woody, "Mexican Central-Bank Chief: The Donald Trump 'Horror Movie' Is About to Start," Business Insider, December 20, 2016, www.businessinsider .com/mexican-central-bank-chief-trump-horror-movie-2016-12.

223. Jude Webber, "Carstens Quits Mexican Central Bank to Head BIS," *Financial Times*, December 1, 2016, www.ft.com/content/8be6aae6-b7e8-11e6-ba85-95d1533d9a62.

224. Donald J. Trump, Twitter post, January 26, 2017, 5:55 a.m., https://twitter.com/ realdonaldtrump/status/824616644370714627?lang=en.

225. Enrique Peña Nieto, Twitter post, January 26, 2017, 8:48 a.m., https://twitter.com/ EPN/status/824660333964824576.

226. "Visits by Foreign Leaders in 2009," Office of the Historian, Bureau of Public Affairs, US Department of State, https://history.state.gov/departmenthistory/visits/2009.

227. Eric Wuestewald, "Today in Trump Tweets: January 27, 2017," McClatchy DC Bureau, January 27, 2017, www.mcclatchydc.com/news/politics-government/article129156129.html.

228. "Central Banks Should Revert to Conventional Tools, New BIS Head Says," Reuters, January 30, 2017, www.reuters.com/article/us-mexico-economy-carstens-idUSKBN15E26W.

229. Michael O'Boyle and Dave Graham, "Mexico Central Bank Hikes Interest Rate, Hints It's Done," Reuters, June 22, 2017, www.reuters.com/article/us-mexico-economy-rate -idUSKBN19D2E6?il=0.

230. Jeff Mason and David Lawder, "Trump Says Was 'Psyched to Terminate NAFTA' but Reconsidered," Reuters, April 26, 2017, www.reuters.com/article/us-usa-trade -nafta-idUSKBN17S2DG.

231. Julie Pace and Catherine Lucey, "Kushner Emerged as Conduit for Canada on NAFTA Talks," Associated Press, May 9, 2017, https://apnews.com/83a8c5856a5c4f48adcd1e0 7980144d3.

CHAPTER 2: BRAZIL: NATIONAL POLITICS MEETS THE FEDERAL RESERVE MEETS CHINA

1. Bill Vann, "Brazil: Lula's Appointments Point to More Rigorous Austerity," World Socialist Web Site, December 31, 2002, https://translate.google.com.br/translate?sl=pt&tl=en&js=y&prev=_t&hl=pt-BR&ie=UTF-8&u=https%3A%2F%2Fwww.wsws.org%2Fpt%2F2002%2Fdec2002%2Fpor1-d31.shtml&edit-text=&act=url.

2. "Henrique Meirelles," Globe.com, published May 30, 2016, updated July 20, 2017, https://translate.google.com.br/translate?sl=pt&tl=en&js=y&prev=_t&hl=pt-BR&ie=UTF-8&u=http%3A%2F%2Fepoca.globo.com%2Ftudo-sobre%2Fnoticia%2F2016%2F05%2Fhenrique-meirelles.html&edit-text=&act=url.

3. José Roberto Afonsoa, Eliane Cristina Araújo, Bernardo Guelber Fajardo, "The Role of Fiscal and Monetary Policies in the Brazilian Economy: Understanding Recent Institutional Reforms and Economic Changes," *Quarterly Review of Economics and Finance* 62 (November 2016): 41–55, www.sciencedirect.com/science/article/pii/S1062976916300527.

4. Brazil, Russia, India, China, and South Africa.

5. Kristina Cooke, Walter Brandimarte, and Ana da Costa, "Exclusive: Brazil's Meirelles Asked US to Lobby Lula: Cable," Reuters, March 25, 2011, www.reuters.com/article/2011/03/25/us-brazil-meirelles-idUSTRE72O5BG20110325#YpQhOqYsQMLRTJWr.99.

6. "About the Latin America Conservation Council," Latin America Conservation Council, http://laconservationcouncil.org/en/what-is-lacc.

7. Shanny Basar, "Bankers Take the Road to Rio," Financial News, May 5, 2008, www.efinancialnews.com/story/2008-05-05/bankers-take-the-road-to-rio-1.

8. Geri Smith, "Brazil Goes Investment-Grade," Bloomberg, May 1, 2008, www.bloomberg.com/bw/stories/2008-05-01/brazil-goes-investment-gradebusinessweek-business-news-stock-market-and-financial-advice.

9. Esther Bintliff, "Winning Brokers of 2008," *Financial Times,* March 13, 2009, www.ft.com/content/7ca4c1de-0f22-11de-ba10-0000779fd2ac.

10. Ricardo Galhardo, "Lula: Crisis Is Tsunami in the US and, If It Arrives in Brazil, It Will Be 'Marolinha,'" *O Globo* (Rio de Janeiro), October 4, 2008, updated February 1, 2012, https://translate.google.com.br/translate?sl=pt&tl=en&js=y&prev=_t&hl=pt-BR&ie=UTF-8&u=http%3A%2F%2Foglobo.globo.com%2Feconomia%2Flula-crise-tsunami-nos-eua-se-chegar-ao-brasil-sera-marolinha-3827410&edit-text=&act=url.

11. "Palácio da Alvorada," Wikipedia, edited on April 27, 2017, https://en.wikipedia.org/wiki/Pal%C3%A1cio_da_Alvorada.

12. "Meirelles Warned About Raising the High Interest and Lula Supported Him, Says Newspaper," *Zero Hora,* July 25, 2008, http://zh.clicrbs.com.br/rs/noticia/2008/07/meirelles-avisou-sobre-alta-do-juro-e-lula-apoiou-diz-jornal-2069333.html.

13. "Mantega and Meirelles Defend Interest Rates and Say That Inflation Target Will Be Met," *Diario do Grande ABC,* June 9, 2008, https://translate.google.com.br/translate?sl=pt&tl=en&js=y&prev=_t&hl=pt-BR&ie=UTF-8&u=http%3A%2F%2Fwww.dgabc.com.br%2FNoticia%2F874168%2Fmantega-e-meirelles-defendem-alta-de-juros-e-dizem-que-meta-de-inflacao-sera-cumprida&edit-text=&act=url.

14. Kennedy Alencar, "Lula pressiona Banco Central por queda na taxa de juros," *Folha de S.Paulo,* December 4, 2008, www1.folha.uol.com.br/fsp/dinheiro/fi0412200809.htm.

15. "Bovespa Ups and Downs in 2008" (infographic), UOL, December 30, 2008, https://economia.uol.com.br/cotacoes/ultnot/2008/12/30/ult1918u1605.jhtm?action=print.

16. Kennedy Alencar, "Lula Puts Pressure on Central Bank for Falling Interest Rates," *Folha de S.Paulo,* December 4, 2008, www1.folha.uol.com.br/fsp/dinheiro/fi0412200809.htm.

17. Terence Corcoran, "Looks Like ZIRP, the Fed's Seven Years of Low Rates and High Debt Spending, Is Going to Add Up to ZIP," *Financial Post,* November 30, 2015, http://business.financialpost.com/news/economy/looks-like-zirp-the-feds-seven-years-of-low-rates-and-high-debt-is-going-to-add-up-to-zip.

18. Acronym for Metropolitan Industrial Region of São Paulo: Santo André, São Bernardo do Campo, São Caetano do Sul, and Diadema.

19. She was energy minister between January 1, 2003, and June 21, 2005.

20. "Interview with Guido Mantega: Government to Make New Round of Industry Incentives," *Folha de S.Paulo,* September 13, 2009, https://translate.google.com.br/translate?sl=pt&tl=en&js=y&prev=_t&hl=pt-BR&ie=UTF-8&u=http%3A%2F%2Fwww1.folha.uol.com.br%2Ffsp%2Fdinheiro%2Ffi1309200912.htm&edit-text=.

21. "Bank of America Exchanges BankBoston Franchise for Stock in Banco Itaú," Bank of America Corporation, May 2, 2006, http://investor.bankofamerica.com/phoenix.zhtml?c=71595&p=irol-newsArticle&ID=850480#fbid=GH80Lriwcij.

22. "Unibanco compra participação da AIG em negócio conjunto no Brasil," *Opinião e Notícia,* November 27, 2008, http://opiniaoenoticia.com.br/economia/negocios/unibanco-compra-participacao-da-aig-em-negocio-conjunto-no-brasil/.

23. "Our History," BTGPactual, www.btgpactual.com/home_en/WhoWeAre.aspx/OurHistory.

24. "Interview with Henrique Meirelles: Juros ao consumidor devem cair mais rápido," *Folha de S.Paulo,* September 13, 2009, www1.folha.uol.com.br/fsp/dinheiro/fi1309200910.htm.

25. Ibid.

26. "Growth of 7% in GDP Is 'Exaggeration,' Says Mantega," *O Globo* (Rio de Janeiro), April 16, 2010, https://translate.google.com.br/translate?sl=pt&tl=en&js=y&prev=_t&hl=pt-BR&ie=UTF-8&u=http%3A%2F%2Fwww.gazetadopovo.com.br%2Feconomia%2Fcrescimento-de-7-no-pib-e-exagero-diz-mantega-072l65ch93s4m69alq364urm6&edit-text=&act=url.

27. "Minutes of the 150th Meeting of the Monetary Policy Committee (Copom)," Banco Central do Brasil, April 27, 2010, www4.bcb.gov.br/pec/gci/ingl/COPOM/COPOM20090430-150th%20Copom%20Minutes.pdf.

28. Jonathan Wheatley, "Brazil in 'Currency War' Alert," *Financial Times,* September 27, 2010, www.ft.com/content/33ff9624-ca48-11df-a860-00144feab49a.

29. Alexandro Martello, "Trade Balance Has Worst Result in Eight Years," *O Globo* (Rio de Janeiro), March 1, 2011, https://translate.google.com.br/translate?sl=pt&tl=en&js=y&prev=_t&hl=pt-BR&ie=UTF-8&u=http%3A%2F%2Fg1.globo.com%2Feconomia%2Fnoticia%2F2011%2F01%2Fbalanca-comercial-tem-pior-resultado-em-oito-anos.html&edit-text=&act=url.

30. "Stock Market Owes Its Progress to Lula, Says Mantega," *Folha de S.Paulo,* October 23, 2010.

31. Mayer Brown LLP, "Brazilian Government Increases the IOF Rate to 6 Percent on the Foreign Investments in the Financial and Capital Market," Tauil & Chequer

Legal UpdadeLexology, October 26, 2010, www.lexology.com/library/detail
.aspx?g=28f3e22b-e917-49b6-837e-95154c9e4399.

32. "The Buys from Brazil," *Economist,* February 17, 2011, www.economist.com/
node/18178275.

33. Cecília Araújo, "Private Equity: o que é e qual é o perfil do professional," *Na Prática,*
August 29, 2017, https://www.napratica.org.br/o-que-e-private-equity/.

34. Matthew Bristow and Andre Soliani, "Brazil Will Have Room to Cut Interest Rate
in 2011, Mantega Says," Bloomberg, November 14, 2010, www.bloomberg.com/news/
articles/2010-11-14/brazil-will-have-room-to-cut-interest-rate-in-2011-mantega-says.

35. "Dilma Economic Team Promises Fiscal Austerity," *O Globo* (Rio de Janeiro), November
25, 2010, https://translate.google.com.br/translate?sl=pt&tl=en&js=y&prev=_t&hl=pt-B
R&ie=UTF-8&u=http%3A%2F%2Fg1.globo.com%2Feconomia-e-negocios%2Fnoticia
%2F2010%2F11%2Fequipe-economica-de-dilma-promete-austeridade-fiscal.html&edit
-text=&act=url.

36. "Presidenciável em eleição indireta, Meirelles foi artífice da ascensão de Joesley," Carta-
Capital, May 24, 2017, www.cartacapital.com.br/economia/Presidenciavel%20em%20
eleicaoo%20indireta,%20Meirelles%20foi%20artfice%20da%20ascensao%20de%20
Joesley.

37. Joaquim Levy held it from January 1, 2015, to December 18, 2015; Nelson Barbosa, from
December 18, 2015, to May 12, 2016.

38. Robert Plummer, "Brazil's Inflation Hawk Henrique Meirelles Bows Out," BBC News,
November 24, 2010, www.bbc.com/news/business-11819681.

39. Ian Talley and Matthew Cowley, "Brazil Finance Minister: Opposed to Constraints on
Capital Controls," Dispatch (blog), *Wall Street Journal,* April 14, 2011, http://blogs.wsj
.com/dispatch/2011/04/14/brazil-finance-minister-opposed-to-constraints-on-capital
-controls/.

40. Nathalia Silva, "Private Equity: o que é e qual é o perfil do professional," *Na Prática,*
September 8, 2014, www.napratica.org.br/private-equity-o-que-e-e-qual-e-o-perfil-do
-profissional/.

41. Andre Soliani, "Brazil's Unpredictable Central Banker Tombini Confounds Critics," Bloomberg, April 16, 2012, www.bloomberg.com/news/articles/2012-04-17/
brazil-s-unpredictable-central-banker-tombini-confounds-critics.

42. *Brazil of Dialogue, of Production, of Employment* (São Paulo: São Paulo Industry Federation, Unified Central of Workers and Labor Force Union, May 26, 2011), www.smabc
.org.br/Interag/temp_img/%7B810B756E-4C7F-460D-936B-3E53A6382B94%7D
_Brasil%20do%20Dialogo%20HIGH%20QUALITY.pdf.

43. Alexandro Martello, "Banks' Spread Is Still at the Beginning, Says Tombini,"
O Globo (Rio de Janeiro), December 6, 2012, https://translate.google.com.br/translate
?sl=pt&tl=en&js=y&prev=_t&hl=pt-BR&ie=UTF-8&u=http%3A%2F%2Fg1.globo
.com%2Feconomia%2Fseu-dinheiro%2Fnoticia%2F2012%2F06%2Freducao-do-spread
-dos-bancos-ainda-esta-no-inicio-diz-tombini.html&edit-text.

44. Alexandro Martello, "Falling of Banking Spread Is a Dilma Order, Says Tombini,"
O Globo (Rio de Janeiro), February 28, 2012, http://g1.globo.com/economia/seu-dinheiro/
noticia/2012/02/queda-do-spread-bancario-e-determinacao-de-dilma-diz-tombini
.html.

45. Agência Estado, "Spreads Are Absurd and Will Be Reduced, Says Mantega," *O Globo* (Rio de Janeiro), March 13, 2012, http://g1.globo.com/economia/noticia/2012/03/spreads-sao-um-absurdo-e-serao-reduzidos-diz-mantega.html.

46. Matthew Malinowski and Mario Sergio Lima, "Brazil to Crack Down on 476% Annual Credit Card Rates, Again," Bloomberg, December 19, 2016, www.bloomberg.com/news/articles/2016-12-19/brazil-to-crack-down-on-476-annual-credit-card-rates-again.

47. Alexandro Martello, "Private Banks Have Scope to Reduce Interest Rates, Says Mantega," *O Globo* (Rio de Janeiro), April 12, 2012, http://g1.globo.com/economia/seu-dinheiro/noticia/2012/04/bancos-tem-margem-para-reduzir-juros-diz-mantega.html.

48. Agência Estado, "Febraban reconhece que spread no Brasil é elevado," Economia, April 10, 2012, www.gazetadopovo.com.br/economia/febraban-reconhece-que-spread-no-brasil-e-elevado-2enzguzup4fm096o0fswephla.

49. Martello, "Private Banks Have Scope to Reduce Interest Rates, Says Mantega."

50. "Febraban Makes Suggestions to Reduce Default and Spread," Brazil Agency, April 10, 2012, http://oprogressonet.com/geral/febraban-apresenta-sugestoes-para-reduzir-inadimplencia-e-spread/19205.html.

51. Dilma Rousseff speech on Labor Day, April 30, 2012, www2.planalto.gov.br/acompanhe-o-planalto/discursos/discursos-da-presidenta/pronunciamento-a-nacao-da-presidenta-da-republica-dilma-rousseff-por-ocasiao-do-dia-do-trabalho.

52. Toni Sciarretta, "Under Pressure from Dilma, Bank of Brazil Decreases Interest Rates," *Folha de S.Paulo*, April 5, 2012, www1.folha.uol.com.br/fsp/mercado/35397-sob-pressao-de-dilma-bb-diminui-juros.shtml.

53. Banco Data, "Bancos Comerciais," December 2016, https://bancodata.com.br/bancos.

54. Matthew Bristow and Raymond Colitt, "Brazil Signals More Cuts After Reducing Rate to Record Low," Bloomberg, May 31, 2012, www.bloomberg.com/news/articles/2012-05-30/brazil-cuts-rate-to-record-low-8-5-as-euro-crisis-deepens-1-.

55. "Banks Will Reduce Spreads," *Diário do Nordeste*, December 17, 2012, http://diariodonordeste.verdesmares.com.br/mobile/cadernos/negocios/bancos-vao-reduzir-os-spreads-1.47450.

56. "IMF New View on Capital Flows: 'Landmark' but Still Only a 'Baby-Step Forward,'" Bretton Woods Project, December 6, 2012, www.brettonwoodsproject.org/2012/12/art-571589/.

57. Guido Mantega, "The First Year of the New Economic Approach," *Valor Econômico*, December 19, 2012, http://jornalggn.com.br/blog/luisnassif/o-primeiro-ano-da-nova-matriz-economica-por-mantega.

58. Ibid.

59. "Northeast of Brazil Had Worst Drought in the Last 50 Years in 2013, Report Says," *O Globo* (Rio de Janeiro), March 24, 2014, https://translate.google.com.br/translate?sl=pt&tl=en&js=y&prev=_t&hl=pt-BR&ie=UTF-8&u=http%3A%2F%2Fg1.globo.com%2Fnatureza%2Fnoticia%2F2014%2F03%2Fnordeste-do-brasil-teve-pior-seca-dos-ultimos-50-anos-em-2013-diz-relatorio.html&edit-text=&act=url.

60. "Interview—Brazil's Mantega Downplays Inflation, Hints at Rift," Reuters, February 7, 2013, http://articles.chicagotribune.com/2013-02-07/news/sns-rt-brazil-economymantega-urgent-20130207_1_inflation-finance-minister-guido-mantega-rift.

61. Walter Brandimarte, "Special—Tombini: A Hawk Against Inflation, Believe It or Not," *O Globo* (Rio de Janeiro), August 23, 2013, https://translate.google.com.br/translate?sl

=pt&tl=en&js=y&prev=_t&hl=pt-BR&ie=UTF-8&u=http%3A%2F%2Fg1.globo .com%2Fpolitica%2Fnoticia%2F2013%2F08%2Fespecial-tombini-um-falcao-contra- a-inflacao-acredite-ou-nao-2.html&e.

62. Ibid.

63. Walter Brandimarte, "ESPECIAL—Tombini: um falcão contra a inflação, acred- ite ou não," *O Globo* (Rio de Janeiro), August 23, 2013, http://g1.globo.com/politica/ noticia/2013/08/especial-tombini-um-falcao-contra-a-inflacao-acredite-ou-nao-2.html.

64. Mônica Izaguirre, Murilo Rodrigues Alves, José de Castro, and João José Oliveira, "BC Provides Higher Inflation, but Says It Will Act with 'Caution,'" AFABB-DF, March 14, 2013, www.afabbdf.org.br/mais-noticias-2013/10853-bc-preve-inflacao-mais-alta-mas -diz-que-agira-com-cautela.

65. "Ana Maria aparece no Mais Você usando colar de tomate," Globo Play video, 2:00, April 10, 2013, http://globoplay.globo.com/v/2508387/.

66. Cristiano Romero, "BCB Minutes Might Speak in Demand Pressure," *O Globo* (Rio de Janeiro), April 25, 2013, www.valor.com.br/valor-investe/casa-das-caldeiras/3100102/ ata-do-copom-deve-falar-em-pressao-de-demanda.

67. Alexandro Martello, "Government Restores IOF to Foreigners in Fixed Income, An- nounces Mantega," *O Globo* (Rio de Janeiro), April 6, 2013, https://translate.google .com.br/translate?sl=pt&tl=en&js=y&prev=_t&hl=pt-BR&ie=UTF-8&u=http%3A%2 F%2Fg1.globo.com%2Feconomia%2Fnoticia%2F2013%2F06%2Fgoverno-zera-iof-para -estrangeiros-na-renda-fixa-anuncia-mantega.html&edit-text=&act=url.

68. Roberta P. Caneca and Thais Bandeira de Mello Rodrigues, "Brazil: Decree No. 8,023/2013: Reduces to Zero the IOF Tax on Certain Foreign Exchange Transactions," Tauil & Che- quer, June 24, 2013, www.mondaq.com/brazil/x/246624/tax+authorities/Decree+No+8023 2013+Reduces+To+Zero+The+IOF+Tax+On+Certain+Foreign+Exchange+Transactions.

69. Walter Brandimarte, "Special—Tombini: A Hawk Against Inflation, Believe It or Not," Reuters, August 23, 2013, www.reuters.com/article/2013/08/23/us-brazil-economy -tombini-insight-idUSBRE97M05F20130823#fP52rBxAR4qupQS8.99.

70. Jeffrey T. Lewis, "How Brazil's Central Bank Propped Up the Real, and Hardly Spent a Dime," Moneybeat (blog), *Wall Street Journal*, August 21, 2013, http://blogs.wsj.com/ moneybeat/2013/08/21/how-brazils-central-bank-propped-up-the-real-and-hardly -spent-a-dime/.

71. Alonso Soto, "Update 3—Brazil Raises Interest Rate Back to Double Digits," Reu- ters, November 27, 2013, www.reuters.com/article/2013/11/27/brazil-economy-rates -idUSL2N0JC0GR20131127#ItjLSBiyVewKPQY7.99.

72. Kevin P. Gallagher, *Ruling Capital: Emerging Markets and the Reregulation of Cross-Border Finance* (Ithaca, NY: Cornell University Press, 2014).

73. Charles Penty, "Brazil's Rousseff Criticizes Austerity as Solution for Crisis," Bloomberg, November 17, 2012, www.bloomberg.com/news/articles/2012-11-17/ brazil-s-rousseff-criticizes-austerity-as-solution-for-crisis.

74. "Has Brazil Blown It?" *Economist*, September 27, 2013, www.economist.com/news/ leaders/21586833-stagnant-economy-bloated-state-and-mass-protests-mean-dilma -rousseff-must-change-course-has.

75. Henrique Meirelles, "Creationism," Comunicação Millenium, January 12, 2014, www .institutomillenium.org.br/artigos/criacionismo/.

76. Alex Ribeiro and Eduardo Campos, "Brazil Has a Current Account Deficit of $7.907 Billion in September," Valor, October 24, 2014, www.valor.com.br/brasil/3747842/brasil-tem-deficit-em-conta-corrente-de-us-7907-bi-em-setembro.

77. "The 1st Post-election Decision, BC Surprises and Raises the Basic Interest Rate to 11.25% per Year," UOL, October 29, 2014, http://economia.uol.com.br/noticias/redacao/2014/10/29/juros-selic-banco-central-copom.htm.

78. Banco Central do Brasil, *Minutes of the 187th Meeting of the Monetary Policy Committee (Copom)* (Brasília: Banco Central do Brasil, December 2, 2014), www4.bcb.gov.br/pec/gci/ingl/COPOM/COPOM20141217-187th_Copom_Minutes.pdf.

79. André Uzêda, "'New Government, New Team,' Says Dilma on the Future of Mantega," *Folha de S.Paulo*, September 9, 2014, https://translate.google.com.br/translate?sl=pt&tl=en&js=y&prev=_t&hl=pt-BR&ie=UTF-8&u=http%3A%2F%2Fwww1.folha.uol.com.br%2Fpoder%2F2014%2F09%2F1511129-governo-novo-equipe-nova-diz-dilma-sobre-o-futuro-de-mantega.shtml&edit-text=&act=url.

80. Fabiano Rodrigues Bastos, Herman Kamil, and Bennett Sutton, "Corporate Financing Trends and Balance Sheet Risks in Latin America: Taking Stock of 'The Bon(d)anza'" (IMF Working Paper WP/15/10, International Monetary Fund, Washington, DC, January 2015), www.imf.org/external/pubs/ft/wp/2015/wp1510.pdf.

81. Estadão Conteúdo, "Fiscal Austerity Helps Fight against Inflation," *Época*, January 24, 2015, http://epocanegocios.globo.com/Informacao/Visao/noticia/2015/01/tombini-austeridade-fiscal-ajuda-inflacao.html.

82. John Kennedy, "Petrobas Hit with Another NYSE Stockholder Suit over Bribes," Law360, May 18, 2015, www.law360.com/articles/656868/petrobras-hit-with-another-nyse-stockholder-suit-over-bribes.

83. John Ozorio de Melo and Felipe Luchete, "Judge Marks the First Hearing of the Class Action Lawsuit against Petrobras in the US," Consultor Jurídico, February 10, 2015, www.conjur.com.br/2015-fev-10/juiz-marca-audiencia-acao-coletiva-petrobras-eua2. In August 2016, after Rousseff was overthrown, Rakoff suspended the lawsuit, a sign of US support for a non-Rousseff government.

84. David Biller and Paula Sambo, "Brazil Scales Back Currency Support as Real Sinks to 12-Year Low," Bloomberg, March 24, 2015, updated on March 25, 2015, www.bloomberg.com/news/articles/2015-03-24/brazil-s-tombini-says-in-no-hurry-to-reduce-currency-swap-volume.

85. Will Connors and Luciana Magalhaes, "Brazil's Petrobras Obtains $3.5 Billion in Financing from China Development Bank," *Wall Street Journal*, April 1, 2015, www.wsj.com/articles/brazils-petrobras-obtains-3-5-billion-financing-from-china-development-bank-1427892756.

86. Paul Kiernan, "Brazil's Petrobras Signs $10 Billion China Loan Pact," *Wall Street Journal*, February 26, 2016, www.wsj.com/articles/brazils-petrobras-signs-pact-for-10-billion-in-loans-from-china-1456529796.

87. "Levy Adheres to the Serra Plan and Suggests Opening the Pre-Salt," Reuters, October 31, 2015, https://translate.google.com.br/translate?sl=pt&tl=en&js=y&prev=_t&hl=pt-BR&ie=UTF-8&u=https%3A%2F%2Fwww.brasil247.com%2Fpt%2F247%2Feconomia%2F203311%2FLevy-adere-ao-Plano-Serra-e-sugere-abrir-o-pr%25C3%25A9-sal.htm&edit-text=&act=url.

88. Ted Piccone, "The Geopolitics of China's Rise in Latin America" (report, Brookings Institution, November 2016), www.brookings.edu/research/the-geopolitics-of-chinas-rise-in-latin-america/.

89. Lúcia Müzell, "For Dilma, Austerity Is 'Different' in Greece and Brazil," *As Vozes do Mundo*, June 11, 2015, www.brasil.rfi.fr/economia/20150611-para-dilma-austeridade-e-diferente-na-grecia-e-no-brasil.

90. "Interview with Joaquim Levy," *El País* (Madrid), September 7, 2015, https://brasil.elpaís.com/brasil/2015/09/04/politica/1441399950_475629.html.

91. Alejandro Bolaños and Heloísa Mendonça, "FMI reduz previsão de crescimento do Brasil e desemprego chega a 8,1%," *El País* (Madrid), July 9, 2015, https://brasil.elpaís.com/brasil/2015/07/09/economia/1436434891_459136.html.

92. Anay Cury and Cristiane Caoli, "Desemprego tem maior taxa desde 2010, diz IBGE," *O Globo* (Rio de Janeiro), July 23, 2015, http://g1.globo.com/economia/noticia/2015/07/desemprego-fica-em-69-em-junho-diz-ibge.html.

93. Bruno Villas Bôas, "Inflação acumulada em 12 meses chega a 8,89%, maior taxa desde 2003," *Folha de S.Paulo*, August 7, 2015, www1.folha.uol.com.br/mercado/2015/07/1653094-inflacao-acelera-para-079-em-junho-maior-taxa-desde-1996.shtml.

94. "In a Speech, Rousseff Talks About 'Mistakes' of the Government and 'Bitter Medicine' against Crisis," Reuters, September 7, 2015, http://noticias.uol.com.br/ultimas-noticias/reuters/2015/09/07/dilma-admite-erros-e-diz-que-e-preciso-reavaliar-medidas-tomadas-pelo-governo.htm.

95. Fernando Bizerra Jr., "Dilma Government Announces Austerity Measures," *Observador*, September 15, 2015, http://observador.pt/2015/09/15/governo-dilma-anunciou-medidas-austeridade/.

96. Lisa M Schineller, "Research Update: Brazil Foreign Currency Ratings Lowered to 'BB+/B'; Outlook Is Negative," S&P Global Market Intelligence, September 9, 2015, www.globalcreditportal.com/ratingsdirect/renderArticle.do?articleId=1448685&SctArtId=339649&from=CM&nsl_code=LIME&sourceObjectId=9329662&sourceRevId=1&fee_ind=N&exp_date=20250909-04:05:17&sp_mid=58283&sp_rid=1830987.

97. Administered prices were made by government decision or authorization such as on buses, water, and electricity.

98. Rob Dwyer, "LatAm Central Banks: Monetary Policymakers Need Fiscal Friends," *Euromoney*, October 28, 2015, www.euromoney.com/article/b12km88hnpsyt7/latam-central-banks-monetary-policymakers-need-fiscal-friends.

99. Data Team, "Brazilian Waxing and Waning," *Economist*, April 18, 2016, www.economist.com/blogs/graphicdetail/2015/10/economic-backgrounder.

100. Robert Neil McCauley, Patrick McGuire, and Vladyslav Sushko, "Dollar Credit to Emerging Market Economies," *BIS Quarterly Review*, December 6, 2015, www.bis.org/publ/qtrpdf/r_qt1512e.htm.

101. Data Team, "Brazilian Waxing and Waning," www.economist.com/blogs/graphicdetail/2015/12/economic-backgrounder.

102. Henrique Gomes Batista, "Tombini: Fiscal Adjustment Is Slower Than Expected," *O Globo* (Rio de Janeiro), October 8, 2015, http://oglobo.globo.com/economia/tombini-ajuste-fiscal-esta-mais-lento-que-esperado-17731241.

103. Yara Aquino, "At a Meeting of the PT, Lula Defends Government Fiscal Adjustment to Recover Prestige," Brazil Agency, October 29, 2015, http://agenciabrasil.ebc.com.br/politica/noticia/2015-10/em-reuniao-do-diretorio-do-pt-lula-defende-ajuste-fiscal.

104. Marla Dickerson and Luciana Magalhaes, "Head of Brazil's Largest Investment Bank and a Senator Arrested in Petrobras Probe," *Wall Street Journal,* November 25, 2015, www.wsj.com/articles/brazil-police-arrest-ceo-of-brazilian-bank-btg-pactual-in-corruption-probe-1448457954.

105. "A Indústria em Novembro de 2015: mais perdas: Sumário," Institute for Studies about Industrial Development, January 8, 2016, www.iedi.org.br/cartas/carta_iedi_n_713.html.

106. David Biller, "Goldman Warns of Brazil Depression After GDP Plunges Again," Bloomberg, December 1, 2015, www.bloomberg.com/news/articles/2015-12-01/brazil-gdp-falls-more-than-analysts-expected-as-demand-withers.

107. Paulo Trevisani and Rogerio Jelmayer, "Brazil Vice President Sends Letter Criticizing President Dilma Rousseff," *Wall Street Journal,* December 8, 2015, www.wsj.com/articles/brazil-vice-president-sends-letter-criticizing-president-dilma-rousseff-1449576925.

108. "Brazil's Pro-austerity Finance Minister Joaquim Levy Replaced," BBC News, December 18, 2015, www.bbc.co.uk/news/world-latin-america-35138522.

109. Reuters, "Barbosa: 'Não há necessidade de injeção de capital na Petrobras,'" December 22, 2015, www.brasil247.com/pt/247/economia/210663/Barbosa-'N%C3%A3o-h%C3%A1-necessidade-de-inje%C3%A7%C3%A3o-de-capital-na-Petrobras'.htm.

110. *Impactos da redução dos investimentos do setor de óleo e gás no PIB* (Ministério da Fazenda, October 21, 2015), www.fazenda.gov.br/assuntos/destaques/nota-a-imprensa-2015-10-21-impacto-da-reducao-dos-investimentos-do-setor-de-oleo-e-gas-no-pib-1.pdf.

111. Vitor Abdala, "Fitch Ratings Agency Downgrades Petrobras and Eletrobras Notes," *ECB,* May 11, 2016, https://translate.google.com.br/translate?sl=pt&tl=en&js=y&prev=_t&hl=pt-BR&ie=UTF-8&u=http%3A%2F%2Fagenciabrasil.ebc.com.br%2Feconomia%2Fnoticia%2F2016-05%2Fagencia-de-classificacao-de-risco-fitch-rebaixa-notas-da-petrobras-e&edit-text=&act=url.

112. Paul Kiernan, "Brazil's Unemployment Rate Rose Sharply," *Wall Street Journal,* September 29, 2015, www.wsj.com/articles/brazils-unemployment-rate-rose-sharply-1443530134; David Biller and Matthew Malinowski, "Brazil's Inflation Surpasses 10% for First Time in 12 Years," Bloomberg, November 19, 2015, www.bloomberg.com/news/articles/2015-11-19/brazil-consumer-inflation-exceeds-10-for-first-time-in-12-years.

113. Kenneth Rapoza, "Brazil's Lousy Christmas," *Forbes,* December 27, 2015, www.forbes.com/sites/kenrapoza/2015/12/27/brazils-lousy-christmas/.

114. Kelly Oliveira, "IMF Improves Brazil GDP Outlook from −3.8% to −3.3%," EBC, July 19, 2016, http://agenciabrasil.ebc.com.br/en/economia/noticia/2016-07/imf-improves-brazil-gdp-outlook-38-33.

115. Marcelo Ninio, "'Political Crisis Delays Fiscal Adjustment,' Says Central Bank President," *Folha de S.Paulo,* October 8, 2015, www1.folha.uol.com.br/mercado/2015/10/1691744-crise-politica-atrasa-ajuste-fiscal-diz-tombini.shtml.

116. Paula Sambo and Josue Leonel, "Brazil's Central Bank U-Turn Isn't New. It Didn't Work Before," Bloomberg, January 22, 2016, www.bloomberg.com/news/articles/2016-01-22/brazil-s-central-bank-u-turn-isn-t-new-it-didn-t-work-before--ijp1iajh.

117. AFP, "China and Brazil Confirm Trade and Investment Deals Worth Billions," *Guardian* (Manchester), May 19, 2015, www.theguardian.com/world/2015/may/19/china -brazil-trade-deals-billions.

118. Daniel Bland, "China Firms Visit Brazil for US$10bn Transcontinental Railway Talks," BN Americas, February 19, 2016, www.bnamericas.com/en/news/privatization/china -firms-visit-brazil-for-us10bn-transcontinental-railway-talks.

119. "Chineses vão construir e operar o Porto Sul e a Fiol," UOL, March 8, 2016, http://atarde .uol.com.br/economia/noticias/1751003-chineses-vao-construir-e-operar-o-porto-sul -e-a-fiol.

120. "Tríplex, sítio e venda de MP: entenda os casos em que Lula é investigado," UOL, February 11, 2016, http://noticias.uol.com.br/politica/ultimas-noticias/2016/02/11/triplex -sitio-e-venda-de-mp-veja-casos-em-que-lula-e-alvo.htm.

121. Donna Bowater, "Dilma Rousseff makes former president Lula chief of staff to shield him from prosecution," *Telegraph*, March 16, 2016, www.telegraph.co.uk/news/ worldnews/southamerica/brazil/12194162/Brazils-former-president-Lula-da-Silva -offered-cabinet-post.html.

122. Associated Press, "Brazil: Police Claim to Have Evidence President Michel Temer Received Bribes," *Guardian* (Manchester), June 20, 2017, www.theguardian.com/world/2017/ jun/21/brazil-police-claim-to-have-evidence-president-michel-temer-received-bribes.

123. Joao Barroso, meeting with author, Central Bank of Brazil offices, Brasília, April 7, 2016.

124. Joao Barroso, meeting with author, Brasília, April 2016.

125. Luiz Bresser, meeting with author at his home, March 29, 2016.

126. Glenn Greenwald, "Watch: Exclusive Interview by Glenn Greenwald with Former Brazilian President Lula da Silva," Intercept, April 11, 2016, https://theintercept.com/ 2016/04/11/watch-exclusive-interview-with-former-brazilian-president-lula-da-silva/.

127. Joe Leahy and Samantha Pearson, "Brazil Speaker Annuls Impeachment Vote," *Financial Times,* May 9, 2016, www.ft.com/content/1a5a260e-1604-11e6-b8d5-4c1fcdbe169f.

128. Carol Siqueira, "Chamber Clears Dilma Impeachment Process with 367 Votes in Favor and 137 Votes Against," Camara dos Deputados, April 17, 2016, updated April 19, 2016, https://translate.google.com.br/translate?sl=pt&tl=en&js=y&prev=_t&hl= pt-BR&ie=UTF-8&u=http%3A%2F%2Fwww2.camara.leg.br%2Fcamaranoticias% 2Fnoticias%2FPOLITICA%2F507325-CAMARA-AUTORIZA-INSTAURACAO -DE-PROCESSO-DE-IMPEACHMENT-DE-DILMA-COM-367-VOTOS-A -FAVOR-E-137-CONTRA.html&edit-text=&act=url.

129. "New Brazil Gov't to Cut Public Spending, Audit Social Welfare Programs," *Agencia EFE,* May 13, 2016, www.efe.com/efe/english/portada/new-brazil-gov-t-to-cut-public -spending-audit-social-welfare-programs/50000260-2925534.

130. Kelly Oliveira, "Banco Central diz que pretende alcançar meta de inflação em 2017," Agência Brasil (Brazil's state media), June 28, 2016, http://agenciabrasil.ebc.com.br/economia/ noticia/2016-06/banco-central-diz-que-pretende-alcancar-meta-de-inflacao-em-2017.

131. Daniel Lima, "Ilan Goldfajn Appointed as Brazil Central Bank Governor," Agência Brasil, May 17, 2016, http://agenciabrasil.ebc.com.br/en/economia/noticia/2016-05/ ilan-goldfajn-appointed-brazil-central-bank-governor.

132. "Ilan Goldfajn," Banco Central do Brasil, www.bcb.gov.br/pre/quemequem/ingl/ ilanGoldfajn-i.asp?idpai=who.

133. Afonso Benites, "Efeito dominó: cai ministro do Turismo, o terceiro do Governo Temer," *El País* (Madrid), June 16, 2016, http://brasil.elpaís.com/brasil/2016/06/16/politica/1466106529_072116.html.

134. "Temer se prepara para privatizar Petrobrás, Banco do Brasil, Correios, Infraero e mais 4 estatais," Plantão Brasil, May 16, 2016, www.plantaobrasil.net/news.asp?nID=94352.

135. "Brazil's New Government Imposes Rio Water Privatisation to Pay for Olympic Games," Corporate Europe Observatory, July 14, 2016, http://corporateeurope.org/water/2016/07/brazil-new-government-imposes-rio-water-privatisation-pay-olympic-games.

136. "Temer Is Booed During the Opening of the Olympiad in Rio," *O Globo* (Rio de Janeiro), August 8, 2016, https://translate.google.com.br/translate?sl=pt&tl=en&js=y&prev=_t&hl=pt-BR&ie=UTF-8&u=http%3A%2F%2Fg1.globo.com%2Frio-de-janeiro%2Folimpiadas%2Frio2016%2Fnoticia%2F2016%2F08%2Ftemer-e-vaiado-durante-abertura-da-olimpiada-no-rio.html&edit-text=&act=url.

137. Reuters, "Brazil's Unemployment Rate Hits 4-Year High as Recession Bites," *Daily Mail*, July 29, 2016, www.dailymail.co.uk/wires/reuters/article-3714665/Brazils-unemployment-rate-hits-4-year-high-recession-bites.html#ixzz4Fwu0WdRN.

138. David Biller, "Brazil's Meirelles Calls for Tighter Budget to Avoid More Taxes," Bloomberg, July 25, 2016, www.bloomberg.com/news/articles/2016-07-25/brazil-s-meirelles-calls-for-tighter-budget-to-avoid-more-taxes.

139. Alonso Soto and Lisandra Paraguassu, "Brazil's Foreign Minister Warns against Overappreciation of Real," Reuters, July 15, 2016, www.reuters.com/article/us-brazil-serra-real/brazils-foreign-minister-warns-against-overappreciation-of-real-idUSKCN0ZV24V.

140. Carolina Meyer, "The Price of Henrique Meirelles for the JBS," Exame, May 20, 2017, https://translate.google.com.br/translate?sl=pt&tl=en&js=y&prev=_t&hl=pt-BR&ie=UTF-8&u=http%3A%2F%2Fexame.abril.com.br%2Frevista-exame%2Fo-preco-de-henrique-meirelles%2F&edit-text=.

141. Samantha Pearson, "Brazil Taps Veteran Economist as Central Bank Chief," *Financial Times*, May 17, 2016, www.ft.com/content/5ef4dd4a-1c49-11e6-a7bc-ee846770ec15.

142. Arthur Ordones, "Conheça o homem que irá salvar a economia do Brasil," Arena, May 12, 2016, http://arenadodinheiro.com.br/educacao-financeira/conheca-o-homem-que-ira-salvar-a-economia-do-brasil/.

143. Julia Leite and Raymond Colitt, "Brazil Economy Chief Not Worried About Austerity Backlash," Bloomberg, May 13, 2016, https://www.bloomberg.com/news/articles/2016-05-13/brazil-economy-chief-not-worried-about-austerity-backlash.

144. Jonathan Watts and Donna Bowater, "Brazil's Dilma Rousseff Impeached by Senate in Crushing Defeat," *Guardian* (Manchester), September 1, 2016, www.theguardian.com/world/2016/aug/31/dilma-rousseff-impeached-president-brazilian-senate-michel-temer.

145. Gustavo Garcia, Fernanda Calgaro, Filipe Matoso, Laís Lis, and Mateus Rodrigues, "Senate Approves Impeachment, Dilma Loses Term, and Temer Takes Over," *O Globo* (Rio de Janeiro), August 31, 2016, https://translate.google.com.br/translate?sl=pt&tl=en&js=y&prev=_t&hl=pt-BR&ie=UTF-8&u=http%3A%2F%2Fg1.globo.com%2Fpolitica%2Fprocesso-de-impeachment-de-dilma%2Fnoticia%2F2016%2F08%2Fsenado-aprova-impeachment-dilma-perde-mandato-e-temer-assume.html&edit-text=&act=url.

146. Matt Sandy, "Brazilian Politician Who Led Rousseff Impeachment Arrested on Corruption Charges," *Guardian* (Manchester), October 19, 2016, www.theguardian.com/world/2016/oct/19/eduardo-cunha-arrested-corruption-charges-brazil.

147. "Brazil's Temer Announces Labor Reform Proposal," *Global Times,* December 16, 2016, www.globaltimes.cn/content/1025347.shtml.

148. Silvio Cascione and Marcela Ayres, "Interview—Brazil Has No 'Plan B' for Pension Reform—Meirelles," Reuters, February 21, 2017, www.reuters.com/article/brazil-economy-meirelles/interview-brazil-has-no-plan-b-for-pension-reform-meirelles-id UKL1N1G61Y7.

149. Lise Alves, "S&P Maintains Brazil's Junk Status and Negative Outlook," *Rio Times,* February 13, 2017, http://riotimesonline.com/brazil-news/rio-business/sp-maintains-brazils-junk-status-and-negative-outlook/.

150. Kelly Oliveira, "In New York, Meirelles Says That Recession Is Over and It's Time to Invest in Brazil," EBC, September 20, 2017, https://translate.google.com.br/translate?sl=pt&tl=en&js=y&prev=_t&hl=pt-BR&ie=UTF-8&u=http%3A%2F%2Fagenciabrasil.ebc.com.br%2Feconomia%2Fnoticia%2F2017-09%2Fem-nova-york-meirelles-diz-que-recessao-acabou-e-e-hora-de-investir-no&edit-text=&act=url.

151. "'Brazil Is Growing, and the Recession Is Over,' Says Henrique Meirelles," *Brazil Monitor,* February 21, 2017, www.brazilmonitor.com/index.php/2017/02/21/brazil-is-growing-and-the-recession-is-over-says-henrique-meirelles/.

152. Joe Leahy, "Brazil's Central Bank Cuts Benchmark Rate to 12.25%," *Financial Times,* February 22, 2017, www.ft.com/content/49f29774-0f3e-38bd-bbfb-451f4bdb3ca8.

153. Anthony Boadle and Marcela Ayres, "Brazil Senate Passes Spending Cap in Win for Temer," Reuters, December 13, 2016, www.reuters.com/article/us-brazil-politics-idUSKBN142203.

154. Radioculture, "Minimum Wage May Be $979 in 2018," Rádio Online, July 7, 2017, https://translate.google.com.br/translate?sl=pt&tl=en&js=y&prev=_t&hl=pt-BR&ie=UTF-8&u=http%3A%2F%2Fwww.radioculturafoz.com.br%2Fsalario-minimo-podera-ser-de-r-979-em-2018%2F&edit-text=&act=url.

155. Wellton Máximo and Marcelo Brandão, "Labor Reform to Boost Economic Recovery, Says Brazil Finance Minister," Agência Brasil, July 13, 2017, http://agenciabrasil.ebc.com.br/en/politica/noticia/2017-07/labor-reform-boost-economic-recovery-says-brazil-finance-minister.

156. "'Economics Go Well,' Says Henrique Meirelles to Journalists During G20 Summit," *Brasil Economico,* July 7, 2017, https://translate.google.com.br/translate?sl=pt&tl=en&js=y&prev=_t&hl=pt-BR&ie=UTF-8&u=http%3A%2F%2Feconomia.ig.com.br%2F2017-07-07%2Fhenrique-meirelles-g20.html&edit-text=&act=url.

157. "Brazil May Economic Activity Falls Unexpectedly as Recovery Seesaws," Reuters, July 14, 2017, www.reuters.com/article/us-brazil-economy-activity-idUSKBN19Z19W.

158. Mary Sadler, "Political Tensions in Brazil: Former President Lula's Conviction," Market Realist, July 13, 2017, http://marketrealist.com/2017/07/political-tensions-in-brazil-former-president-lulas-conviction/.

159. Idiana Tomazelli, "PSD Invites Meirelles to Run for President in 2018," *Estadão,* September 13, 2017, https://translate.google.com.br/translate?sl=pt&tl=en&js=y&prev=_t&hl=pt-BR&ie=UTF-8&u=http%3A%2F%2Fpolitica.estadao.com

.br%2Fnoticias%2Fgcral%2Cpsdb-convida-meirelles-para-disputar-a-presidencia-em
-2018%2C70001993411&edit-text=&act=url.

CHAPTER 3: CHINA: DRAGON RISING

1. Zhiyuan Cui, "Making Sense of the Chinese 'Socialist Market Economy': A Note," *Modern China* 38, no. 6 (2012): 665–676, www.jstor.org/stable/41702477?seq=1#page _scan_tab_contents.

2. Jiang Zemin, speech by President Jiang Zemin of the People's Republic of China, at luncheon by the America China Society and five other organizations, October 30, 1997, Asia Society, http://asiasociety.org/speech-president-jiang-zemin-peoples-republic-china?page=0,0.

3. "Profile: Jiang Zemin," BBC News, October 23, 2012, www.bbc.com/news/world-asia -china-20038774.

4. Keith Bradsher, "China's Central Bank Cuts Interest Rates," *New York Times*, November 26, 2008, www.nytimes.com/2008/11/27/business/worldbusiness/27yuan.html; "China Interest Rate: 1996–2017" chart, TradingEconomics.com, https://tradingeconomics .com/china/interest-rate.

5. Olivia Oran and Sruthi Shankar, "Morgan Stanley Claims Another Trading Victory over Rival Goldman Sachs," Reuters, July 19, 2017, www.reuters.com/article/us-morgan -stanley-results-idUSKBN1A411F.

6. Reuters and AFP, "China: Yuan Not Key to Curbing Inflation," *China Post*, March 7, 2008, http://webcache.googleusercontent.com/search?q=cache:6dSbYD8SbzoJ:www .chinapost.com.tw/business/2008/03/07/146039/China%253A-Yuan.htm+&cd=1&hl=p t-BR&ct=clnk&gl=br&client=firefox-b-ab.

7. "Chinese Yuan Renminbi (CNY) to US Dollar (USD) 2008 History," FX-Exchange .com, www.fx-exchange.com/currencyimages/2008/cny/the-year-of-2008-cny-usd -exchange-rates-history-graph.png.

8. Gao Ying, "China Should Be Cautious of US Subprime Crisis," Xinhua, March 6, 2008, www.gov.cn/english/2008-03/06/content_911457.htm; "China Central Bank Says Di- rect Impact of US Subprime Crisis Limited," *Nuclear Power Daily*, March 6, 2008, www .nuclearpowerdaily.com/reports/China_Central_Bank_Says_Direct_Impact_Of_US _Subprime_Crisis_Limited_999.html.

9. "China Inflation Hits 11-Year High," BBC News, February 19, 2008, http://news.bbc.co .uk/2/hi/business/7252010.stm.

10. Lu Jianxin, "Yuan Hits High vs Dlr, Worries of Policy Shift Ease," Reuters, March 14, 2008, www.reuters.com/article/markets-china-yuan-midday-idCNTSHA26727720080314.

11. *Renminbi* directly translates to "the people's currency." The yuan is the unit of renminbi, as in what something costs. The two terms are used interchangeably.

12. "Remarks by Secretary Henry M. Paulson, Jr.: Meeting the Challenge: A Partnership on Energy and the Environment" (press center), US Department of the Treasury, April 2, 2008, https://www.treasury.gov/press-center/press-releases/Pages/hp903.aspx.

13. He had been assistant to John Ehrlichman, assistant to the president for domestic affairs under President Richard Nixon.

14. "Paulson Supports Beijing on Yuan Effort," *New York Times*, April 2, 2008, www.nytimes .com/2008/04/02/business/worldbusiness/02iht-paulson.2.11620642.html.

15. Andriy Moraru, "Chinese Yuan at New High vs. Dollar," Forex News, July 10, 2008, www.topforexnews.com/2008/07/10/chinese-yuan-at-new-high-vs-dollar/.

16. Kerry Brown, "Hu Jintao's Legacy," *Foreign Policy*, November 8, 2012, http://foreign policy.com/2012/11/08/hu-jintaos-legacy/.

17. "Premier Wen Jiabao Attends and Addresses the Opening Ceremony of the Second Annual Meeting of Summer Davos," Ministry of Foreign Affairs, the People's Republic of China, September 27, 2008, www.fmprc.gov.cn/mfa_eng/wjdt_665385/zyjh_665391/t516624.shtml.

18. "Premier Wen Jiabao Answered the Questions at the Opening Ceremony of Summer Davos and at the Meeting with Entrepreneurs," Commissioner's Office of China's Foreign Ministry in the Hong Kong SAR, September 28, 2008, www.fmcoprc.gov.hk/eng/zgwjsw/t516628.htm.

19. "Lehman Bros Files for Bankruptcy," BBC News, September 16, 2008, http://news.bbc.co.uk/2/hi/business/7615931.stm.

20. DOW Jones Industrial Average for historical period September 9, 2001, to September 15, 2008, Yahoo! Finance, https://finance.yahoo.com/quote/%5EDJI/history?period1=1000090800&period2=1221534000&interval=1d&filter=history&frequency=1d.

21. John Kicklighter, "EURUSD Sees Biggest Drop Since Its Creation," Daily FX, September 30, 2008, https://www4.dailyfx.com/story/market_alerts/technical_alert/2008/09/30/EURUSD_Sees_Biggest_Drop_Since_1222786916316.html; Vikas Bajaj and Michael M. Grynbaum, "For Stocks, Worst Single-Day Drop in Two Decades," *New York Times*, September 29, 2008, www.nytimes.com/2008/09/30/business/30markets.html?_r=0; "In response to continued strains..." (press release), Board of Governors of the Federal Reserve System, September 29, 2008, www.federalreserve.gov/monetary policy/20080929a.htm.

22. Associated Press, "Chinese Central Bank Trims Its Interest Rates," *New York Times*, October 29, 2008, www.nytimes.com/2008/10/30/business/worldbusiness/30yuan.html?pagewanted=print.

23. Judy Hua and Kevin Yao, "China Cuts Interest Rates for Third Time in Six Months as Economy Sputters," Reuters, May 10, 2015, www.reuters.com/article/us-china-economy-rates-idUSKBN0NV0A320150510.

24. Keith Bradsher, "China's Central Bank Cuts Interest Rates," *New York Times*, November 26, 2008, www.nytimes.com/2008/11/27/business/worldbusiness/27yuan.html?mcubz=1.

25. Kathryn Hopkins, "China Forced into Fourth Interest Rate Cut of the Year," *Guardian* (Manchester), November 26, 2008, www.theguardian.com/business/2008/nov/26/global-recession-china-banking.

26. Kathryn Hopkins, "China Cuts Interest Rates to Protect Jobs," *Guardian* (Manchester), December 22, 2008, www.theguardian.com/business/2008/dec/22/china-interest-rates.

27. *Finance Committee Questions for the Record: United States Senate Committee on Finance Hearing on Confirmation of Mr. Timothy F. Geithner to be Secretary of the US Department of Treasury, January 21, 2009: Answers to Questions from Chairman Baucus,* www.finance.senate.gov/imo/media/doc/012209%20TFG%20Questions1.pdf.

28. *United States Senate Committee on Finance Hearing on Confirmation of Mr. Timothy F. Geithner,* www.finance.senate.gov/imo/media/doc/012209%20TFG%20Questions1.pdf, question 13.

29. Martin Crutsinger and Economics Writer, "US Declines to Cite China for Currency Manipulation," ABC News, n.d., accessed September 11, 2017, http://abcnews.go.com/Business/story?id=7348223.

30. "Major Foreign Holders of Treasury Securities" (table), Department of the Treasury/Federal Reserve Board, August 15, 2017, http://ticdata.treasury.gov/Publish/mfh.txt.

31. "What Did Geithner Do?" *People's Daily*, June 2, 2009, https://translate.google.com.br/translate?sl=zh-CN&tl=en&js=y&prev=_t&hl=pt-BR&ie=UTF-8&u=www.people.com.cn%2FBIG5%2F32306%2F33232%2F9401232.html&edit-text=.

32. Ibid.

33. Arshad Mohammed, "Clinton Says US and China Are in the Same Economic Boat," Reuters, February 22, 2009, www.reuters.com/article/us-china-clinton-economy-idUSPEK28223020090222.

34. Ambrose Evans-Pritchard, "Hillary Clinton Pleads with China to Buy US Treasuries as Japan Looks On," *Telegraph*, February 22, 2009, www.telegraph.co.uk/finance/financialcrisis/4782755/Hillary-Clinton-pleads-with-China-to-buy-US-Treasuries-as-Japan-looks-on.html.

35. "Clinton Says US Deficit Sends Message of Weakness," Reuters, September 8, 2010, www.reuters.com/article/usa-deficit-clinton-idUSN0811406820100908.

36. Tony Capaccio and Daniel Kruger, "China's US Debt Holdings Aren't Threat, Pentagon Says," Bloomberg, September 10, 2012, www.bloomberg.com/news/articles/2012-09-11/china-s-u-s-debt-holdings-aren-t-threat-pentagon-says.

37. Ben S. Bernanke, "Financial Reform to Address Systemic Risk" (speech, Council on Foreign Relations, Washington, DC, March 10, 2009), www.federalreserve.gov/news events/speech/bernanke20090310a.htm, Financial Reform to Address Systemic Risk.

38. Ibid.

39. Bloomberg, "China Concerned for US Investments," *New York Times*, March 13, 2009, www.nytimes.com/2009/03/13/business/worldbusiness/13china.html.

40. "Shenzhen Traders Profit from Currency Uncertainty," *South China Morning Post*, March 31, 2009, www.scmp.com/article/675278/shenzhen-traders-profit-currency-uncertainty.

41. "Premier Wen Jiabao Answered the Questions at the Opening Ceremony of Summer Davos," www.fmcoprc.gov.hk/eng/zgwjsw/t516628.htm; Kevin Yao and Aileen Wang, "China Puts Focus on Consumers to Drive Growth," Reuters, March 4, 2013, http://in.reuters.com/article/china-parliament-economy-gdp-idINDEE92402N20130305.

42. Jason Dean, James T. Areddy, and Serena Ng, "Chinese Premier Blames Recession on US Actions," *Wall Street Journal*, January 29, 2009, www.wsj.com/articles/SB1233189 34318826787.

43. Zhou, "Reform the International Monetary System."

44. "Definition of Triffin Dilemma," *Financial Times*, http://lexicon.ft.com/Term?term =Triffin-dilemma&mhq5j=e1.

45. Zhou, "Reform the International Monetary System."

46. Lesley Wroughton and David Lawder, "Update 3—Obama Dismisses Idea of Single Global Currency," Reuters, March 24, 2009, www.reuters.com/article/forex-usa-geithner -idUSN2434732920090325.

47. Group of Twenty, "London Summit: Leaders' Statement," International Monetary Fund, April 2, 2009, www.imf.org/external/np/sec/pr/2009/pdf/g20_040209.pdf.

48. The BRIC nations consisted of Brazil, Russia, India, and China. Adding in South Africa later made it the BRICS.

49. Natalia Viana, "Brazil to Lend $10 Billion to the IMF," Frontline Club, June 10, 2009, www.frontlineclub.com/brazil_to_lend_10bi_to_the_imf/.

50. Todd Benson and Raymond Colitt, "Exclusive—Brazil Lends IMF Money Ahead of BRIC Summit," Reuters, June 10, 2009, http://in.reuters.com/article/idININdia -40228820090610.

51. "Joint Statement of the BRIC Countries' Leaders," President of Russia Official Web Portal, June 16, 2009, http://tinyurl.com/yasr9w7u.

52. Malcolm Moore, "Top Chinese Banker Guo Shuqing Calls for Wider Use of Yuan," Telegraph, June 8, 2009, www.telegraph.co.uk/finance/financialcrisis/5473491/Top -Chinese-banker-Guo-Shuqing-calls-for-wider-use-of-yuan.html.

53. "TEXT-Japan, China, S. Korea Central Bank Governors Meet," Reuters, July 23, 2009, http://uk.reuters.com/article/china-japan-korea-centralbanks/text-japan-china-s-korea -central-bank-governors-meet-idUKSP52668920090723.

54. "IMF to Make $250 Billion SDR Allocation on August 28," International Monetary Fund, August 13, 2009, www.imf.org/external/np/exr/cs/news/2009/cso79.htm.

55. Glenn Gottselig, "IMF Survey: IMF Injecting $283 Billion in SDRs into Global Economy, Boosting Reserves," International Monetary Fund, August 28, 2009, www.imf.org/ external/pubs/ft/survey/so/2009/POL082809A.htm.

56. Associated Press, "China to Buy $50 Billion of First I.M.F. Bonds," New York Times, September 3, 2009, www.nytimes.com/2009/09/04/business/global/04imf.html.

57. "China in Offshore Renminbi Bond Issue," Financial Times, September 8, 2009, https:// www.ft.com/content/5683a16e-9c3f-11de-ab58-00144feabdc0.

58. Brian Love, "G7 Presses for Stronger Yuan," Reuters, October 4, 2009, www.reuters .com/article/us-g-idUSL342133820091004.

59. Ibid.

60. China Monetary Policy Report: Quarter Three, 2009 (Monetary Policy Analysis Group of the People's Bank of China, December 16, 2009), www.pbc.gov.cn/eportal/fileDir/ image_public/UserFiles/english/upload/File/report_2009_3rdQtr.pdf.

61. David Lawder and Kevin Yao, "Yuan Revaluation 'China's Choice': Geithner," Reuters, April 6, 2010, www.reuters.com/article/us-india-us-geithner-yuan-idUSTRE63524 M20100407.

62. Associated Press, "Wang, Geithner Exchange Views on Economic Relations," China Daily, April 9, 2010, www.chinadaily.com.cn/china/2010-04/09/content_9705057.htm.

63. Simon Rabinovitch and Paul Eckert, "China to Make Its Own Call on Yuan—Hu," Reuters, April 12, 2010, www.reuters.com/article/uk-usa-china-yuan-idUKTRE63C04 Y20100413.

64. Philip Aldrick, "Yuan Jumps After China Loses Peg," Telegraph, June 22, 2010, www .telegraph.co.uk/finance/currency/7844619/Yuan-jumps-after-China-loses-peg.html; Kevin Voigt, "Q&A: China's Currency Moves," CNN, June 22, 2010, http://edition.cnn .com/2010/BUSINESS/06/21/china.yuan.explainer/.

65. "J.P. Morgan Provides Rmb Cross-Border Trade Settlement Services from Mainland China" (press release), JPMorgan Chase & Co., May 11, 2010, https://investor .shareholder.com/jpmorganchase/releasedetail.cfm?releaseid=468669.

66. "Statement by the Honorable Zhou Xiaochuan, Governor of the People's Bank of China and Governor of the IMF for China" (statement, Twenty-Second Meeting of the International and Monetary Financial Committee, Washington, DC, October 9, 2010), www.imf.org/External/AM/2010/imfc/statement/eng/chn.pdf.

67. "Brazil Warns Currency War Could Threaten G20," *O Globo* (Rio de Janeiro), October 8, 2010, https://translate.google.com.br/translate?sl=pt&tl=en&js=y&prev=_t&hl=pt-BR&ie=UTF-8&u=http%3A%2F%2Fg1.globo.com%2Fmundo%2Fnoticia%2F2010%2F10%2Fbrasil-adverte-que-guerra-de-divisas-pode-ameacar-g20.html&edit-text=&act=url.

68. Interview with German Finance Minister Schäuble: "The US Has Lived on Borrowed Money for Too Long," *Der Spiegel* (Hamburg), November 8, 2010, www.spiegel.de/international/world/interview-with-german-finance-minister-schaeuble-the-us-has-lived-on-borrowed-money-for-too-long-a-727801.html.

69. Graeme Wearden, "Obama Defends QE2 Ahead of G20," *Guardian* (Manchester), November 8, 2010, www.theguardian.com/business/2010/nov/08/obama-defends-qe2-g20-summit.

70. Chris Isidore, "China Hikes Interest Rates," CNN, October 19, 2010, http://money.cnn.com/2010/10/19/news/international/china_rates/.

71. "China Increases Rates to Counter Highest Inflation in Two Years," Bloomberg, December 25, 2010, www.bloomberg.com/news/articles/2010-12-25/china-raises-interest-rates-by-25-basis-points-in-bid-to-curb-inflation.

72. "China's Hu Jintao: Currency System Is 'Product of Past,'" BBC News, January 17, 2011, www.bbc.co.uk/news/world-asia-pacific-12203391.

73. Chris Hogg, "China Banks Lend More Than World Bank—Report," BBC News, January 18, 2011, www.bbc.com/news/world-asia-pacific-12212936.

74. Bob Davis and Aaron Back, "Inflation Worries Spread," *Wall Street Journal,* February 9, 2011, www.wsj.com/articles/SB10001424052748704364004576131670845358208.

75. Ibid.

76. "China's Premier Wen Jiabao Targets 'Social Stability,'" BBC News, March 5, 2011, www.bbc.com/news/world-asia-pacific-12654931.

77. "Chinese Inflation Hits Three-Year High," BBC News, July 9, 2011, www.bbc.com/news/world-asia-pacific-14090908; Keith Bradsher, "Rising Chinese Inflation to Show Up in US Imports," *New York Times,* January 11, 2011, www.nytimes.com/2011/01/12/business/global/12inflate.html.

78. Katie Allen, "Acronym Acrimony: The Problem with Pigs," *Guardian* (Manchester), February 12, 2010, www.theguardian.com/business/2010/feb/12/pigs-piigs-debted-eu-countries.

79. William Lee Adams, "Anti-Cuts 'March for the Alternative' Draws 500,000 Protesters in London," *Time,* March 26, 2011, http://newsfeed.time.com/2011/03/26/anti-cuts-march-for-the-alternative-draws-500000-protestors-in-london/.

80. AFP, "Lagarde 'Very Positive' with Talks in China," Emirates 24/7 News, June 9, 2011, www.emirates247.com/news/lagarde-very-positive-with-talks-in-china-2011-06-09-1.401839.

81. "Lagarde Begins 1st Day as Head of IMF," CNN, July 5, 2011, http://edition.cnn.com/2011/BUSINESS/07/05/imf.lagarde/.

82. Kevin Gallagher, "Why Agustín Carstens Should Not Be Next Head of the IMF," *Guardian* (Manchester), June 3, 2011, www.theguardian.com/commentisfree/cifamerica/2011/jun/03/imf-economics.

83. Fion Li, "Yuan Strengthens Beyond 6.4 per Dollar for First Time Since 1993," Bloomberg, August 22, 2011, www.bloomberg.com/news/articles/2011-08-11/china-s-yuan-strengthens-beyond-6-40-per-dollar-for-first-time-since-1993.

84. "G7 to Hold Emergency Debt Crisis Talks," Raidió Teilifís Éireann (Ireland), August 5, 2011, www.rte.ie/news/2011/0805/304613-economy/.

85. Alex Hawkes, "ECB Intervention Brings Short-Term Relief in Volatile Day for Markets," *Guardian* (Manchester), August 8, 2011, www.theguardian.com/business/2011/aug/08/ecb-intervention-european-stock-markets.

86. Jana Randow, Jeannine Aversa, and Scott Lanman, "Central Bankers Race to Protect Growth in 72 Hours of Crisis," Bloomberg, August 11, 2011, www.bloomberg.com/news/articles/2011-08-10/central-bankers-become-tower-of-strength-amid-debt-turmoil.

87. Louise Armitstead and Jonathan Russell, "Christine Lagarde: IMF May Need Billions in Extra Funding," *Telegraph* (London), September 25, 2011, www.telegraph.co.uk/finance/financialcrisis/8788223/Christine-Lagarde-IMF-may-need-billions-in-extra-funding.html

88. Alessandra Corrêa, "Mantega cobra ação rápida da União Europeia contra a crise," BBC Brasil, September 23, 2011, www.bbc.com/portuguese/noticias/2011/09/110923_mantega_washington_ac.shtml.

89. "Global Leaders Call for Euro Debt Action," BBC News, September 24, 2011, www.bbc.com/news/business-15048705.

90. "Zhou Xiaochuan: Monetary Policy Has Not Changed the Timing of Aid to Europe," CRNTT, September 26, 2011, https://translate.google.com.br/translate?sl=zh-CN&tl=en&js=y&prev=_t&hl=pt-BR&ie=UTF-8&u=http%3A%2F%2Fhk.crntt.com%2Fcrn-webapp%2Fdoc%2FdocDetailCreate.jsp%3Fcoluid%3D7%26kindid%3D0%26docid%3D101847361&edit-text=&act=url.

91. Ibid.

92. Michael Bristow, "China and Vietnam Sign Deal on South China Sea Dispute," BBC News, October 12, 2011, www.bbc.co.uk/news/world-asia-pacific-15273007; Jane Perlez, "China Gives Pakistan 50 Fighter Jets," *New York Times*, May 19, 2011, www.nytimes.com/2011/05/20/world/asia/20pakistan.html; "Russia-China Oil Pipeline Opens," BBC News, January 2, 2011, www.bbc.com/news/world-asia-pacific-12103865.

93. Toru Fujioka, "Yen-Yuan Trade Plan to Cut Dollar Dependence of China, Japan," Bloomberg, December 26, 2011, www.bloomberg.com/news/articles/2011-12-25/china-japan-to-promote-direct-trading-of-currencies-to-cut-company-costs.

94. "China Central Bank Chief Vows Prudent 2012 Monetary Policy," Bloomberg, December 31, 2011, www.bloomberg.com/news/articles/2011-12-31/china-s-central-bank-to-keep-monetary-policy-prudent-in-2012-zhou-says.

95. Dexter Roberts, "Understanding the China Slowdown," Bloomberg, May 31, 2012, www.bloomberg.com/news/articles/2012-05-31/understanding-the-china-slowdown.

96. "China Foreign-Exchange Reserves Drop First Time Since 1998," Bloomberg, January 13, 2012, www.bloomberg.com/news/articles/2012-01-13/china-foreign-exchange-reserves-drop-for-first-quarter-in-more-than-decade.

97. Nick Edwards and Zhou Xin, "China Central Bank Eyes Freer Yuan, Policy Flexibility," Reuters, March 12, 2012, www.reuters.com/article/us-china-economy-idUSBRE82B0F220120312.

98. "Timeline—China's Interest Rate Reforms," Reuters, July 19, 2013, www.reuters.com/article/uk-china-economy-rates-timeline-idUKBRE96I0L120130719?mod=related&channelName=businessNews.

99. "Chairman Bernanke's College Lecture Series," Board of Governors of the Federal Reserve System, www.federalreserve.gov/aboutthefed/educational-tools/chairmans-lecture-series-about.htm.

100. "Chinese Central Bank Widens Yuan Currency Trading Band," Reuters, April 13, 2012, www.reuters.com/article/china-cbank-yuan-band-idUSB9E8D701U20120414; Ye Xie, "PBOC's Yi Says Market Has Bigger Role Deciding Yuan Value," Bloomberg, April 21, 2012, www.bloomberg.com/news/articles/2012-04-21/pboc-s-yi-says-market-should-help-decide-yuan-s-value.

101. Fion Li and Kyoungwha Kim, "Yuan Drops Most in Three Months as China Widens Band," Bloomberg, April 16, 2012, www.bloomberg.com/news/articles/2012-04-16/pboc-weakens-yuan-fixing-by-0-13-after-widening-trading-band.

102. "2012 US-China Strategic and Economic Dialogue," US Department of State, https://2009-2017.state.gov/e/eb/tpp/bta/sed/2012/index.htm.

103. "Geithner Says Yuan Gains Would Aid China Economic Shift," Bloomberg, May 3, 2012, www.bloomberg.com/news/articles/2012-05-03/geithner-sees-need-for-1970s-style-shift-in-china-economy.

104. "Zhou Xiaochuan: Let the Market Verify the RMB Exchange Rate Imbalance or Not," China News Network, April 4, 2012, https://translate.google.com.br/translate?sl=zh-CN&tl=en&js=y&prev=_t&hl=pt-BR&ie=UTF-8&u=http%3A%2F%2Ffinance.people.com.cn%2Fforex%2FGB%2F17805424.html&edit-text=&act=url.

105. "China Reduces Interest Rates for First Time Since 2008," Bloomberg, June 7, 2012, www.bloomberg.com/news/articles/2012-06-07/china-cuts-interest-rates-for-first-time-since-2008.

106. Bob Davis, Aaron Back, and Lingling Wei, "China Cuts Key Interest Rates," Wall Street Journal, July 5, 2012, www.wsj.com/articles/SB10001424052702303962304577507510579917988.

107. "China Economic Growth Dips to 8.1% in the First Quarter," BBC News, April 13, 2012, www.bbc.co.uk/news/business-17686247.

108. "Bank of China Governor Pulls Out of IMF Meeting Amid Islands Row," Financial Post (Toronto), October 10, 2012, http://business.financialpost.com/news/economy/bank-of-china-governor-pulls-out-of-imf-meeting-amid-islands-row/wcm/d5419442-47d7-4620-b722-b7771132b2f4; Kevin Voigt, "China's Top Banker Snubs IMF Meeting," CNN, October 10, 2012, http://edition.cnn.com/2012/10/10/business/japan-china-imf-zhou/.

109. Fion Li, "China's Currency Just Hit a 19-Year High," Business Insider, October 11, 2012, www.businessinsider.com/yuan-strengthens-beyond-628-a-dollar-2012-10.

110. "Inflation China's Key Long-Term Risk: Central Bank Chief," Reuters, November 17, 2012, www.reuters.com/article/us-china-economy-inflation-idUSBRE8AG04P20121117.

111. Ibid.

112. Ibid.

113. *China Monetary Policy Report, Quarter Three* (Beijing: Monetary Policy Analysis Group of the People's Bank of China, November 2, 2012), www.pbc.gov.cn/eportal/fileDir/image_public/UserFiles/english/upload/File/China%20Monetary%20Policy%20Report,%20Quarter%20Three(2).pdf.

114. Kasia Klimasinska and Ian Katz, "US Treasury Declines to Name China Currency Manipulator," Bloomberg, November 27, 2012, www.bloomberg.com/news/articles/2012-11-27/u-s-treasury-declines-to-name-china-currency-manipulator.

115. *Report to Congress on International Economic and Exchange Rate Policies* (Washington, DC: US Department of the Treasury, Office of International Affairs, November 27, 2012), www.treasury.gov/resource-center/international/exchange-rate-policies/Documents/Foreign%20Exchange%20Report%20November%202012.pdf.

116. Cary Huang, "China's Third Plenum: Party's Third Plenum Pledges 'Decisive Role' for Markets in China's Economy," *South China Morning News,* November 12, 2013, updated November 13, 2013, www.scmp.com/news/china/article/1354411/chinas-leadership-approves-key-reform-package-close-third-plenum.

117. "Is the Head of China's Central Bank Going?" Ekina, September 25, 2014, http://ekina.gr/en/news/55-epikairotita/379-central-banker.

118. "China's Zhou Xiaochuan Announced as Euromoney's Central Bank Governor of the Year" (press release), *Euromoney,* September 22, 2011, www.euromoney.com/Article/2904332/Press-release-Chinas-Zhou-Xiaochuan-announced-as-Euromoneys-Central-Bank-Governor-of-the-Year.html.

119. "Current Members," Group of Thirty, http://group30.org/members. Established in 1978, the Group of Thirty is a private, nonprofit, international body composed of elite representatives from the private and public sectors and academia. It explores global economic and financial issues.

120. Ibid.

121. "Romney Hits Obama on China Policies," Reuters, October 13, 2012, www.reuters.com/article/us-usa-campaign-china-idUSBRE89C0HQ20121013.

122. "Questions for the Record: Nomination of Jacob J. Lew to Be Secretary of the Treasury, Hearing Date: February 13, 2013," www.finance.senate.gov/imo/media/doc/2-20-2013%20Lew%20QFRs.pdf.

123. "China Reforms Chip Away at Privileges of State-Owned Companies," *Financial Times,* November 19, 2013, www.ft.com/content/42fc92d4-510a-11e3-b499-00144feabdc0.

124. Franz Wild, Arnaldo Galvao, and Ilya Arkhipov, "BRICS Approve Currency Fund as Bank Start-Up Stalls," Bloomberg, March 27, 2013, www.bloomberg.com/news/articles/2013-03-27/brics-approve-currency-fund-as-bank-start-up-stalls.

125. Mamta Badkar, "China's Yuan Hit a 19-Year High," *Business Insider,* March 31, 2013, www.businessinsider.com/chinas-yuan-hit-a-19-year-high-2013-3.

126. *Report to Congress on International Economic and Exchange Rate Policies* (Washington, DC: US Department of the Treasury, Office of International Affairs, April 12, 2013), www.treasury.gov/resource-center/international/exchange-rate-policies/Documents/Foreign%20Exchange%20Report%20April%202013.pdf.

127. "Treasury Releases Semi-Annual Report to Congress on International Economic and Exchange Rate Policies" (press release), US Department of the Treasury, April 12, 2013, www.treasury.gov/press-center/press-releases/Pages/jl1895.aspx.

128. Kasia Klimasinska and Ian Katz, "US Urges Japan to Refrain from Competitive Yen Devalue," Bloomberg, April 12, 2013, www.bloomberg.com/news/articles/2013-04-12/u-s-to-press-japan-to-refrain-from-competitive-devaluation.

129. Kyoungwha Kim, "Yuan Gains Most in 3 Weeks as Central Bank Sets Record Fixing," Bloomberg, June 17, 2013, www.bloomberg.com/news/articles/2013-06-17/yuan-gains-most-in-3-weeks-as-central-bank-sets-record-fixing.

130. Nathaniel Lubin, "President Obama Nominates Dr. Janet Yellen as Fed Chair," The White House (blog), October 9, 2013, www.whitehouse.gov/blog/2013/10/09/president-obama-nominates-dr-janet-yellen-fed-chair.

131. "ECB and the People's Bank of China Establish a Bilateral Currency Swap Agreement" (press release), European Central Bank, October 10, 2013, www.ecb.europa.eu/press/pr/date/2013/html/pr131010.en.html.

132. Fion Li, "Yuan Passes Euro as 2nd-Most Used Trade-Finance Currency," Bloomberg, December 3, 2013, www.bloomberg.com/news/articles/2013-12-03/yuan-passes-euro-to-be-second-most-used-trade-finance-currency.

133. "PBOC Will 'Basically' End Normal Yuan Intervention: Zhou," Bloomberg, November 19, 2013, www.bloomberg.com/news/articles/2013-11-19/pboc-will-basically-exit-normal-yuan-intervention-zhou-says.

134. Jeff Kearns and Joshua Zumbrun, "Bernanke Says QE Works While Posing No Immediate Bubble Risk," Bloomberg, January 16, 2014, www.bloomberg.com/news/articles/2014-01-16/bernanke-says-qe-effective-while-posing-no-immediate-bubble-risk.

135. Ibid.

136. Keith Bradsher, "With China Awash in Money, Leaders Start to Weigh Raising the Floodgates," New York Times, January 15, 2014, www.nytimes.com/2014/01/16/business/international/china-dwarfs-us-in-monetary-stimulus.html.

137. William Mallard, "After Fall, Japan Yen in Sweet Spot for Economy, but US Watching," Reuters, January 26, 2014, www.reuters.com/article/us-japan-yen-idUSBREA0P0MX20140126.

138. James Glynn, "South Korea Urges Japan Not to Rely on Yen Weakness," Wall Street Journal, February 21, 2014, www.wsj.com/news/articles/SB10001424052702303636404579396303754316122.

139. "Economic Policy After the Omnibus" (transcript of event of the Council on Foreign Relations, January 16, 2014), www.cfr.org/event/economic-policy-after-omnibus-0.

140. Fion Li and Kyoungwha Kim, "Yuan Drops Most on Record Amid Band Widening Speculation," Bloomberg, February 28, 2014, www.bloomberg.com/news/articles/2014-02-28/china-yuan-set-for-worst-month-in-20-years-on-band-widening-bets.

141. Matthew Boesler, "China's Currency Just Saw Its Biggest Weekly Drop Since 2011," Business Insider, February 21, 2014, http://www.businessinsider.com/chinese-yuan-drops-most-since-2011-2014-2.

142. "Zhou Xiaochuan: China's Deposit Rates to Be Freed within 2 Years," China Economic Net, March 11, 2014, http://en.ce.cn/subject/exclusive/201403/11/t20140311_2460792.shtml.

143. "China Sees Expansion Outweighing Yuan, Shadow Bank Risk," Bloomberg, February 23, 2014, www.bloomberg.com/news/articles/2014-02-23/china-downplays-yuan-banking-risk-as-zhou-sees-7-to-8-growth.

144. "Chair Yellen's Press Conference" (transcript), Board of Governors of the Federal Reserve System, March 19, 2014, www.federalreserve.gov/mediacenter/files/FOMC presconf20140319.pdf.

145. Jane Perlez, "Lew Urges China to Ease Exchange Rate Controls," *New York Times*, May 13, 2014, www.nytimes.com/2014/05/14/business/lew-urges-china-to-ease-controls-on-exchange-rate.html.

146. "Press Statements Following Russian-Chinese Talks" (transcript), President of Russia, May 8, 2015, http://en.kremlin.ru/events/president/transcripts/49433; "Xi Jinping Holds Talks with President Vladimir Putin of Russia, Stressing to Expand and Deepen Practical Cooperation, Promoting China-Russia Comprehensive Strategic Partnership of Coordination to Higher Level," Ministry of Foreign Affairs of the People's Republic of China, May 20, 2014, www.fmprc.gov.cn/mfa_eng/topics_665678/yzxhxzyxrcshydscfh/t1158516.shtml.

147. "Sanctions Will Make Russia Stronger—Medvedev," RT News, April 22, 2014, www.rt.com/business/154012-sanctions-russia-stronger-medvedev/.

148. Nicole Hong and Lingling Wei, "US Companies Step Up Business Conducted in Yuan," *Wall Street Journal*, July 9, 2014, www.wsj.com/articles/u-s-companies-step-up-business-conducted-in-yuan-1404947781.

149. Ben Yue, "Cross-Border Trade in Yunnan Shows the Road Ahead," *China Daily*, July 5, 2013, www.chinadailyasia.com/business/2013-07/05/content_15077137.html.

150. Kevin Yao and Lesley Wroughton, "China Agrees to Reduce FX Intervention 'as Conditions Permit,'" Reuters, July 10, 2014, www.reuters.com/article/us-china-usa-cenbank-idUSKBN0FF0BQ20140710.

151. Ibid.

152. *China Monetary Policy Report Quarter Two, 2014, August 01, 2014* (Beijing: Monetary Policy Analysis Group of the People's Bank of China, August 1, 2014), www.pbc.gov.cn/eportal/fileDir/image_public/UserFiles/english/upload/File/2014MPRQ2%28after%20Nancy%29%281%29.pdf.

153. *China Monetary Policy Report Quarter One, 2014* (Beijing: Monetary Policy Analysis Group of the People's Bank of China, May 6, 2014), 30, www.pbc.gov.cn/eportal/fileDir/image_public/UserFiles/english/upload/File/2014Q1_MPR_Nancy_(1).pdf.

154. Reuters, "China Says Has No Intention of Using Currency Devaluation to Its Advantage," CNBC, February 24, 2017, www.cnbc.com/2017/02/24/china-says-has-no-intention-of-using-currency-devaluation-to-its-advantage.html.

155. Kasia Klimasinska and Simon Kennedy, "Lew Warns Against Competitive Devaluation as Dollar Gains," Bloomberg, October 10, 2014, www.bloomberg.com/news/articles/2014-10-10/lew-warns-against-competitive-devaluation-as-dollar-gains.

156. *Foreign Exchange Policies of Major Trading Partners of the United States* (Washington, DC: US Department of the Treasury, Office of International Affairs, April 29, 2016), www.treasury.gov/resource-center/international/exchange-rate-policies/Documents/2016-4-29%20(FX%20Pol%20of%20Major%20Trade%20Partner)_final.pdf.

157. Ibid.

158. "Statement by the Honorable Yi Gang, Alternate Governor of the International Monetary Fund for the People's Republic of China" (Governor's Statement No. 35, 2014 Annual meetings, International Monetary Fund World Bank Group, Washington, DC, October 10, 2014), www.imf.org/external/am/2014/speeches/pr35e.pdf.

159. Stefan Riecher and Jeff Black, "ECB Said to Consider Step to Add Yuan for Foreign Reserves," Live Mint, October 11, 2014, www.livemint.com/Politics/nIjUHnmg0J6tMzt9ScBVTM/ECB-said-to-consider-step-to-add-yuan-for-foreign-reserves.html.

160. Belinda Cao, "China's Zhou Says Some Countries Using Yuan in Reserves," Bloomberg, October 11, 2014, www.bloomberg.com/news/articles/2014-10-11/china-s-zhou-says-some-countries-using-yuan-in-reserves.

161. SR, "Say It Ain't So, Zhou," Economist, September 25, 2014, www.economist.com/blogs/freeexchange/2014/09/new-central-banker-china.

162. "G20 Worried About the 'Stumbling Block' of Europe's Slow Growth," Guardian (Manchester), September 21, 2014, www.theguardian.com/world/2014/sep/21/g20-concerns-europe-slow-growth-stumbling-block-ecb.

163. "PBOC Confirms New Liquidity Tool as It Holds Off Easing," Bloomberg, November 6, 2014, www.bloomberg.com/news/articles/2014-11-06/china-central-bank-confirms-126-billion-in-liquidity-injections.

164. "China Cuts Interest Rates to Lower Financing Costs," China Daily, November 22, 2014, www.chinadaily.com.cn/business/2014-11/22/content_18958698.htm.

165. Kevin Yao and Pete Sweeney, "China's 2014 Economic Growth Misses Target, Hits 24-Year Low," Reuters, January 19, 2015, www.reuters.com/article/us-china-economy-idUSKBN0KT04920150120.

166. Liyan Chen, Ryan Mac, and Brian Solomon, "Alibaba Claims Title For Largest Global IPO Ever With Extra Share Sales," Forbes, September 22, 2014, www.forbes.com/sites/ryanmac/2014/09/22/alibaba-claims-title-for-largest-global-ipo-ever-with-extra-share-sales/#6055386c8dcc.

167. Fion Li, "Yuan Drops to Lowest Since July on Trade Data, Swap-Rate Surge," Bloomberg, December 8, 2014, www.bloomberg.com/news/articles/2014-12-09/yuan-drops-to-lowest-since-july-on-trade-data-swap-rate-surge.

168. Operation Twist: the Fed's program of selling short-term bonds in order to buy long-term ones; an older form of QE that reduces rates for longer-term bonds; named after the 1960s dance the Twist.

169. Jianguang Shen, China's New Monetary Policy Framework (Hong Kong: Mizuho Securities Asia, November 2014), 5, http://research.mizuho-sc.com/mizuhoapp/newDownloadAuth.do?T=EQ&TM=mail&R=ys4YXyeYFAvsw2U8TOJJog%3D%3D&RND=141653822295.

170. An Lu, "Xi Attends Russia's V-Day Parade, Marking Shared Victory with Putin," Xinhuanet, May 9, 2015, http://news.xinhuanet.com/english/2015-05/09/c_134224722.htm.

171. "New Development Bank Appoints 4 New Vice Presidents, Allocates Roles," Economic Times, November 26, 2015, http://articles.economictimes.indiatimes.com/2015-11-26/news/68582359_1_world-bank-new-development-bank-human-resources.

172. Katie Allen, "Why Is China's Stock Market in Crisis?" *Guardian* (Manchester), July 8, 2015, www.theguardian.com/business/2015/jul/08/china-stock-market-crisis -explained.

173. "What Does China's Stock Market Crash Tell Us?" BBC News, July 22, 2015, www .bbc.com/news/business-33540763.

174. "IMF's Executive Board Completes Review of SDR Basket, Includes Chinese Renminbi" (press release), International Monetary Fund, November 30, 2015, www.imf .org/external/np/sec/pr/2015/pr15540.htm.

175. "The People's Bank of China and the Central Bank of the Russian Federation Signed the Memorandum of Understanding on Cooperation" (press release), People's Bank of China, December 17, 2015, www.pbc.gov.cn/english/130721/2990563/index.html.

176. Keith Bradsher, "China's Renminbi Declines After Being Named a Global Currency, Posing Challenges," *New York Times*, December 18, 2015, www.nytimes.com/ 2015/12/19/business/dealbook/chinas-renminbi-declines-after-being-named-a-global -currency-posing-challenges.html.

177. Keith Bradsher and Amie Tsang, "Stock Markets Shudder After Chinese Stock Plunge Forces a Trading Halt," *New York Times*, January 6, 2016, www.nytimes .com/2016/01/08/business/dealbook/china-shanghai-stocks-fall.html?_r=0; "China's Stockmarket Crashes—Again," *Economist*, January 4, 2016, www.economist.com/ news/business-and-finance/21685146-chinas-stocks-and-currency-start-2016-big -tumbles-chinas-stockmarket.

178. "Yuan Drops Most Since August, Losses Mount in Extended Trading," Bloomberg, January 3, 2016, www.bloomberg.com/news/articles/2016-01-04/offshore-yuan-falls -most-since-august-as-pboc-seen-allowing-drop.

179. "Commentary: RMB Devaluation Warrants No Currency War," *Xinhua News*, August 12, 2015, http://news.xinhuanet.com/english/2015-08/12/c_134508481.htm.

180. "The Central Parity of RMB against US Dollar Became More Market-based in 2015," People's Bank of China, January 7, 2016, www.pbc.gov.cn/english/130721/3002189/ index.html.

181. Sophia Yan, "China Slowdown Not as Bad as Feared," CNN Money, July 15, 2016, http://money.cnn.com/2016/07/14/news/economy/china-gdp/.

182. Patrick McGee, "PBoC Holds Fix Steady," *Financial Times*, January 11, 2016, www.ft .com/fastft/2016/01/12/pboc-holds-fix-steady/.

183. Ma Jun, "RMB Exchange Rate Formation Mechanism Will Be More Reference to a Basket of Currencies," the People's Bank of China, November 1, 2016, http://www.pbc .gov.cn/goutongjiaoliu/113456/113469/3003537/index.html.

184. "Subdued Demand, Diminished Prospects," *World Economic Outlook Update*, January 19, 2016, www.imf.org/external/pubs/ft/weo/2016/update/01/pdf/0116.pdf.

185. Ben Chu, "Davos: Chinese Regulator Denies Devaluation of the RMB Is Being Used to Boost Exports," *Independent* (London), January 21, 2016, www.independent.co.uk/ news/business/news/davos-chinese-regulator-denies-devaluation-of-the-rmb-is-being -used-to-boost-exports-a6825021.html.

186. Agence France-Presse, "China Accuses George Soros of 'Declaring War' on Yuan," *Guardian* (Manchester), January 27, 2016, www.theguardian.com/business/2016/jan/ 27/china-accuses-george-soros-of-declaring-war-on-yuan.

187. Chuck Mikolajczak, "Wall St. Declines on Tech Selloff, North Korea Concern," Reuters, September 25, 2017, https://www.reuters.com/article/us-usa-stocks/wall-st-falls -on-north-korea-warnings-tech-selloff-idUSKCN1C01FI.

188. "Li Keqiang Holds Telephone Talks with IMF Managing Director Christine Lagarde at Request," Ministry of Foreign Affairs of the People's Republic of China, January 28, 2016, www.fmprc.gov.cn/mfa_eng/zxxx_662805/t1336812.shtml.

189. Samuel Shen and Pete Sweeney, "China Shares Rally, but Biggest Monthly Drop in Seven Years," Reuters, January 26, 2016, http://uk.reuters.com/article/us-china -markets-idUKKCN0V40J2.

190. Sam Forgione, "Dollar Tumbles as Dudley Comments, US Data Suggest Dovish Fed," Reuters, February 2, 2016, www.reuters.com/article/us-global-forex -idUSKCN0VC003.

191. "China Central Bank to Inject $91 Billion to Ease Liquidity Strains," Reuters, January 19, 2016, www.reuters.com/article/us-china-economy-liquidity-idUSKCN0UX1AT.

192. "China Eyes PBOC's Zhang as Next IMF Deputy, Caixin Reports," Bloomberg, May 19, 2016, www.bloomberg.com/news/articles/2016-05-20/china-eyes-pboc-veteran -zhang-as-next-imf-deputy-caixin-reports.

193. "China's Yuan Hits Five-Year Low as Brexit Fears Roil Global Currency Markets," Reuters, June 14, 2016, http://uk.reuters.com/article/us-china-yuan-idUSKCN0Z1065.

194. Larry Luxner, "China Overtakes West in Development Funding to Latin America," *Tico Times* (San José), February 25, 2016, www.ticotimes.net/2016/02/25/china -overtakes-west-development-funding-latin-america.

195. "Chineses vão construir e operar o Porto Sul e a Fiol," UOL, March 8, 2016, updated March 9, 2016, http://atarde.uol.com.br/economia/noticias/1751003-chineses-vao -construir-e-operar-o-porto-sul-e-a-fiol.

196. Author's note: I traveled between Beijing and Shanghai on the impressive, fast, and green railway.

197. "India Signs First Loan Agreement with New Development Bank for US$ 350 Million for Development and Upgradation of Major District Roads Project in Madhya Pradesh" (press release), Press Information Bureau, Government of India, Ministry of Finance, March 30, 2017, http://pib.nic.in/newsite/PrintRelease.aspx?relid=160253.

198. Dhwani Mehta, "BRICS Bank to Issue First Debt Instrument in Q2 2016," FX Street, March 28, 2016, www.fxstreet.com/news/forex-news/article.aspx?storyid=f47bbbd2 -f0bc-4720-adc9-2d4c3837e109.

199. Zhou Xiaochuan, "Statement by the Governor for China" (AB-3078, CII/AB-1449, Annual Meeting of the Board of Governors, Nassau, Bahamas, April 9, 2016), http:// idbdocs.iadb.org/wsdocs/getdocument.aspx?docnum=40231373.

200. "Refile—China to Implement Appropriate Monetary Policy, More Forceful Fiscal Policies," Reuters, April 17, 2016, www.reuters.com/article/china-economy-zhou -idUSL3N17K04M.

201. *IMF World Economic and Financial Surveys, Regional Economic Outlook: Asia and Pacific: Building on Asia's Strengths during Turbulent Times* (Washington, DC: International Monetary Fund, April 2016), 31, Box 1.3, www.imf.org/en/Publications/REO/APAC/ Issues/2017/03/06/Building-on-Asia-s-Strengths-during-Turbulent-Times.

202. Ibid., Executive Summary, 13–14.

203. "China Must Be 'More Adept' at Policy Communication, Lew Says," Bloomberg, June 5, 2016, updated June 6, 2016, www.bloomberg.com/news/articles/2016-06-05/china -must-become-more-adept-at-policy-communication-lew-says-ip32o96x.

204. *Brexit* is the term for the referendum presented to UK voters to withdraw from the EU.

205. Zhou Xiaochuan, Michel Camdessus Central Banking Lecture, International Monetary Fund, Washington, DC, June 24, 2016, www.imf.org/external/np/seminars/ eng/2016/camdessus/.

206. Ibid.

207. Ibid.

208. Salam, "Zhou Xiaochuan Lagarde Dialogue Transcript Talking About Supervision of Alibaba," East Buzz, June 25, 2016, www.eastbuzz.com/2016/06/25/zhou-xiaochuan -lagarde-dialogue-transcript-talking-about-supervision-of-alibaba/.

209. David Lawder and Howard Schneider, "China Central Bank Chief Sees 'Dynamic' Monetary Policy Adjustments," Reuters, June 24, 2016, www.reuters.com/article/ us-china-economy-zhou/china-central-bank-chief-sees-dynamic-monetary-policy -adjustments-idUSKCN0ZA2WD?il=0

210. José Viñals, Christine Lagarde, and Zhou Xiaochuan, 2016 Michel Camdessus Central Banking Lecture, International Monetary Fund, Washington, DC, June 24, 2016, www.imf.org/external/mmedia/view.aspx?vid=4984593154001.

211. "Zhou Xiaochuan: China's Central Bank Objective Function Will Eventually Be Simplified," New Financial Network, July 24, 2016, https://translate.google.com.br/translate? sl=zh-CN&tl=en&js=y&prev=_t&hl=pt-BR&ie=UTF-8&u=http%3A%2F%2Ffinance .caixin.com%2F2016-06-24%2F100958543.html&edit-text=&act=url.

212. Wang Yanfei and Xin Zhiming, "Growth Stable, Meets Expectations, Xi Says," *China Daily*, July 9, 2016.

213. Liu Xin, "Li Calls for Cross-Eurasia Cooperation at Summit, Warns on S. China Sea Issue," *Global Times Weekend*, July 16–17, 2016.

214. Peter Cobus, "Conflict and Diplomacy on the High Seas," Voice of America, accessed September 13, 2017, https://projects.voanews.com/south-china-sea/.

215. Martin Farrer, "Beijing Warns US to Stay Out of South China Sea Dispute," *Guardian* (Manchester), September 8, 2016, www.theguardian.com/world/2016/ sep/08/beijing-warns-us-to-stay-out-of-south-china-sea-dispute.

216. Ibid.

217. Liu Tian, "China's First Half GDP Up 6.7%," *Global Times Weekend*, July 16–17, 2016.

218. Richard Hall, "World Growth at a Glance," Bevblog.net, January 5, 2016, https:// www.bevblog.net/?p=3545.

219. "To Promote the Vision and Action of the Silk Road Economic Zone and the 21st Century Maritime Silk Road," Ministry of Commerce of the People's Republic of China, January 26, 2016, https://translate.google.com.br/translate?sl=zh-CN&tl=en&js=y&pr ev=_t&hl=pt-BR&ie=UTF-8&u=www.mofcom.gov.cn%2Farticle%2Fi%2Fdxfw%2Fjl yd%2F201601%2F20160101243342.shtml&edit-text=&act=url.

220. "China's New Silk Road: The One Belt One Road Explained," *Sydney Morning Herald*, June 1, 2017, www.smh.com.au/world/chinas-new-silk-road-the-one-belt-one-road -explained-20170512-gw3ntx.html; *Vision and Actions on Jointly Building Silk Road Economic Belt and 21st-Century Maritime Silk Road* (Beijing: National Development and

Reform Commission, Ministry of Foreign Affairs, and Ministry of Commerce of the People's Republic of China, with State Council authorization, March 2015), http://en.ndrc.gov.cn/newsrelease/201503/t20150330_669367.html.

221. *IMF World Economic and Financial Surveys, Regional Economic Outlook: Asia and Pacific: Building on Asia's Strengths during Turbulent Times*, 17, www.imf.org/en/Publications/REO/APAC/Issues/2017/03/06/Building-on-Asia-s-Strengths-during-Turbulent-Times.

222. Ibid., 104.

223. Michael Pettis (author and economist), interview with author, Beijing, July 11, 2016.

224. "Communiqué" (G20 Finance Ministers and Central Bank Governors Meeting, Chengdu, China, July 24, 2016), www.g20.utoronto.ca/2016/160724-finance.html.

225. "G20's Deference for China's Economic Policies Irks Japan," Reuters, July 25, 2016, www.reuters.com/article/us-g20-china-diplomacy-idUSKCN1051DQ.

226. Justina Lee, "Offshore Yuan Falls Most in Two Weeks as Fed Outlook Reassessed," Bloomberg, August 1, 2016, www.bloomberg.com/news/articles/2016-08-01/yuan-drops-most-in-two-months-against-basket-amid-growth-concern.

227. "China's Top Economic Researchers Call for More Monetary Easing," Bloomberg, August 2, 2016, www.bloomberg.com/news/articles/2016-08-03/china-should-cut-interest-rates-and-rrr-ndrc-researchers-say.

228. "In 2016 the People's Bank of China Branch Line President of the Forum Held...," the People's Bank of China, August 3, 2016, www.pbc.gov.cn/goutongjiaoliu/113456/113469/3112811/index.html.

229. "China's Opaque Central Bank Tries Something New: Communication," Bloomberg, August 16, 2016, www.bloomberg.com/news/articles/2016-08-16/china-s-opaque-central-bank-finds-new-policy-tool-communication.

230. "PBOC Boosts Weekly Injections as Yuan Climbs Amid Stability Bets," Bloomberg, September 13, 2016, www.bloomberg.com/news/articles/2016-09-14/pboc-boosts-weekly-injections-yuan-climbs-amid-stability-bets.

231. "PBOC Appoints Bank of China as First Yuan Clearing Bank in US," Bloomberg, September 20, 2016, www.bloomberg.com/news/articles/2016-09-21/pboc-appoints-bank-of-china-as-first-yuan-clearing-bank-in-u-s.

232. "IMF Launches New SDR Basket Including Chinese Renminbi, Determines New Currency Amounts" (press release no. 16/440), International Monetary Fund, September 30, 2016, www.imf.org/en/News/Articles/2016/09/30/AM16-PR16440-IMF-Launches-New-SDR-Basket-Including-Chinese-Renminbi.

233. "Chinese Renminbi Officially Included in the SDR" (press release), People's Bank of China, October 1, 2016, www.pbc.gov.cn/english/130721/3154437/index.html.

234. *Statement by the Hon. Zhou Xiaochuan, Governor of the Fund for the People's Republic of China* (Governor's Statement No. 30, 2016 Annual Meetings, International Monetary Fund World Bank Group, Washington, DC, October 7, 2016), www.imf.org/external/am/2016/speeches/pr30e.pdf.

235. Jane Cai and Wendy Wu, "Don't Blame Globalisation for World's Ills, Xi Jinping Tells Davos," *South China Morning Post*, January 17, 2017, updated January 18, 2017, www.scmp.com/news/china/economy/article/2062840/watch-xi-jinping-live-davos.

236. Ibid.

237. "Presidential Memorandum Regarding Withdrawal of the United States from the Trans-Pacific Partnership Negotiations and Agreement," The White House, Office of the Press Secretary, January 23, 2017, www.whitehouse.gov/the-press-office/ 2017/01/23/presidential-memorandum-regarding-withdrawal-united-states-trans -pacific.

238. "Trans-Pacific Partnership Agreement," Australian Government, Department of Foreign Affairs and Trade, accessed September 13, 2017, http://dfat.gov.au/trade/ agreements/tpp/pages/trans-pacific-partnership-agreement-tpp.aspx.

239. Emiko Jozuka, "TPP vs RCEP? Trade Deals Explained," CNN, January 26, 2017, http://edition.cnn.com/2017/01/24/asia/tpp-rcep-nafta-explained/index.html.

240. Reuters, "China Raises Short-Term Interest Rates in Fresh Tightening Signal," CNBC, February 3, 2017, www.cnbc.com/2017/02/03/china-economy-news-pboc-raises-short -term-interest-rates-in-fresh-tightening-signal.html.

241. Fran Wang, "China Export, Import Growth Rebounds to Multiyear Highs in January," *Caixin,* February 10, 2017, www.caixinglobal.com/2017-02-10/101054049.html.

242. Hu Shuli, "Editorial: Why China Is Shifting to a 'Neutral' Monetary Policy Stance," *Caixin,* February 13, 2017, www.caixinglobal.com/2017-02-14/101054914.html.

243. "Rising Anti-Globalisation Pose Challenges to Global Growth: Zhou Xiaochuan," *Economic Times,* April 22, 2017, http://economictimes.indiatimes.com/articleshow/58314943 .cms?utm_source=contentofinterest&utm_medium=text&utm_campaign=cppst.

244. Jozuka, "TPP vs RCEP? Trade Deals Explained."

245. "China's Growth Target 'Within Reach': Central Bank Governor," *China Daily,* April 22, 2017, http://europe.chinadaily.com.cn/business/2017-04/22/content_29041635 .htm.

246. Elena Holodny, "REPORT: China Tells Its Banks to Stop Doing Business with North Korea," Business Insider, September 21, 2017, www.businessinsider.com/china-tells -banks-to-stop-business-with-north-korea-2017-9.

247. Jane Cai, "Calls for a Freer Yuan from Inner Circle of China's Central Bank," *South China Morning Post,* September 25, 2017, www.scmp.com/news/china/economy/ article/2112759/calls-freer-yuan-inner-circle-chinas-central-bank.

248. Sophia Yan, "China's About to Get Its First New Central Bank Head in 15 Years," CNBC, September 21, 2017, www.cnbc.com/2017/09/21/china-to-get-first-new -central-bank-pboc-head-in-15-years.html.

CHAPTER 4: JAPAN: CONJURED-MONEY INCUBATOR

1. "The Bank of Japan's Policy Measures during the Financial Crisis," Bank of Japan, www .boj.or.jp/en/mopo/outline/cfc.htm/.

2. Masaaki Shirakawa, "Global Players," Thomas White International, November 2010, www .thomaswhite.com/global-perspectives/masaaki-shirakawa-governor-bank-of-japan/.

3. Mitsuhiro Fukao, *Japanese Financial Crisis and Crisis Management* (Japan Center for Economic Research, September 21, 2009), www.oecd.org/eco/43762939.pdf.

4. Mayumi Otsuma, "Masaru Hayami; His Tactics Widely Used to Stir Economy," Bloomberg, May 19, 2009, http://archive.boston.com/bostonglobe/obituaries/articles/ 2009/05/19/masaru_hayami_his_tactics_widely_used_to_stir_economy/.

5. Masaru Hayami, "Towards a Sustainable Growth Path," Bank of Japan, February 25, 2003, www.boj.or.jp/en/announcements/press/koen_2003/ko0302a.htm/.

6. "Federal Reserve Announces It Will Initiate a Program to Purchase the Direct Obligations of Housing-Related Government-Sponsored Enterprises and Mortgage-Backed Securities Backed by Fannie Mae, Freddie Mac, and Ginnie Mae" (press release), Board of Governors of the Federal Reserve System, November 25, 2008, www.federalreserve .gov/newsevents/press/monetary/20081125b.htm.

7. "Structure of the Federal Reserve System," Board of Governors of the Federal Reserve System, www.federalreserve.gov/aboutthefed/structure-federal-reserve-system.htm.

8. David Andolfatto and Li Li, "Quantitative Easing in Japan: Past and Present," Economic Research of the Federal Reserve Bank of St. Louis, January 10, 2014, https:// research.stlouisfed.org/publications/economic-synopses/2014/01/10/quantitative-easing -in-japan-past-and-present/.

9. Ben S. Bernanke, "Semiannual Monetary Policy Report to the Congress" (testimony before the Committee on Financial Services, US House of Representatives, Washington, DC, February 27, 2008), www.federalreserve.gov/newsevents/testimony/bernanke 20080227a.htm.

10. "Bernanke Signals Another Rate Cut," CBN News, February 27, 2008, www.cbn.com/ cbnnews/politics/2008/february/bernanke-signals-another-rate-cut-/?mobile=false.

11. *Monetary Policy Report to the Congress* (Washington, DC: Board of Governors of the Federal Reserve System, February 27, 2008), www.federalreserve.gov/monetarypolicy/files/ 20080227_mprfullreport.pdf.

12. "Paulson Defends Bear Stearns Bailout," *New York Times,* March 16, 2008, www.nytimes .com/2008/03/16/business/worldbusiness/16iht-paulson.4.11139473.html.

13. Rika Otsuka, "The Dollar in Japan: Investment Risk or Opportunity?" Reuters, March 18, 2008, www.reuters.com/article/markets-forex-japan-idUST29700420080318.

14. Kenji Hall, "Bank of Japan: Who's at the Wheel?" Bloomberg, March 19, 2008, www.bloomberg.com/bw/stories/2008-03-18/bank-of-japan-whos-at-the-wheel -businessweek-business-news-stock-market-and-financial-advice.

15. "Stalemate Ends as Shirakawa Is Approved," Central Banking, April 9, 2008, www .centralbanking.com/central-banking/news/1423574/stalemate-shirakawa-approved.

16. Sherman Hollar, "Shirakawa Masaaki: Japanese Banker and Economist," *Encyclopaedia Britannica,* www.britannica.com/biography/Shirakawa-Masaaki.

17. Ibid.

18. Biography of Masaaki Shirakawa, Federal Reserve Bank of San Francisco, www.frbsf .org/banking/files/Masaaki_Shirakawa.pdf.

19. Leika Kihara, "Special Report: After a Bashing, BOJ Weighs 'Big Bang' War on Deflation," Reuters, November 29, 2012, www.reuters.com/article/us-japan-boj -idUSBRE8AT00420121130.

20. Masaaki Shirakawa, "Revisiting the Philosophy behind Central Bank Policy" (speech, Economic Club of New York, New York, April 22, 2010), *BIS Review* 55 (2010), www .bis.org/review/r100427b.pdf.

21. "Recent Economic and Financial Developments and the Conduct of Monetary Policy," Bank of Japan, May 23, 2008, www.boj.or.jp/en/announcements/press/koen_2008/ ko0805b.htm/.

22. *Minutes of the Monetary Policy Meeting on July 14 and 15, 2008* (Tokyo: Bank of Japan, August 22, 2008), www.boj.or.jp/en/mopo/mpmsche_minu/minu_2008/g080715.pdf.

23. "Lehman Bros Files for Bankruptcy," BBC News, September 16, 2008, http://news.bbc .co.uk/2/hi/business/7615931.stm.

24. Vikas Bajaj and Michael M. Grynbaum, "For Stocks, Worst Single-Day Drop in Two Decades," *New York Times*, September 29, 2008, www.nytimes.com/2008/09/30/ business/30markets.html?_r=0.

25. David Teather, "Wall Street Crisis Spreads through Europe's Banks," *Guardian* (Manchester), September 29, 2008, www.theguardian.com/business/2008/sep/30/banking .europeanbanks.

26. "FOMC Statement: Federal Reserve and Other Central Banks Announce Reductions in Policy Interest Rates" (press release), Board of Governors of the Federal Reserve System, October 8, 2008, www.federalreserve.gov/newsevents/press/monetary/20081008a .htm.

27. "Monetary Policy Decision," European Central Bank, October 8, 2008, www.ecb .europa.eu/press/pr/date/2008/html/pr081008.en.html.

28. "On the Policy Actions by Major Central Banks," Bank of Japan, October 8, 2008, www .boj.or.jp/en/announcements/release_2008/un0810a.pdf.

29. "Statement by the Hon. Masaaki Shirakawa, Alternate Governor of the Fund and the Bank for Japan, at the Joint Annual Discussion" (press release no. 33), Board of Governors of the International Monetary Fund, October 13, 2008, www.imf.org/external/am/ 2008/speeches/pr33e.pdf.

30. "Forex—Yen Strikes 13-Year High vs Dollar on Global Gloom," FX Street, October 24, 2008, www.fxstreet.com/news/forex-news/article.aspx?storyid=c68851fd-1f52-4120 -926d-d9421b845b12.

31. Ministry of Finance of Japan, "Statement of G7 Finance Ministers and Central Bank Governors," G7 Information Centre, October 27, 2008, www.g8.utoronto.ca/finance/ fm081027.htm.

32. "Wrapup 2—G7 Warns on Yen, Markets Shrug Off Intervention Risk," Reuters, October 27, 2008, www.reuters.com/article/financial-g-idUSSP9649220081027.

33. "FOMC Statement" (press release), Board of Governors of the Federal Reserve System, October 29, 2008, www.federalreserve.gov/newsevents/press/monetary/20081029a .htm.

34. "On Monetary Policy Decisions," Bank of Japan, October 31, 2008, www.boj.or.jp/en/ announcements/release_2008/k081031.pdf.

35. Masaaki Shirakawa, "The Turmoil in Global Financial Markets and Economic and Financial Developments in Japan" (speech at the Kisaragi-kai Meeting, Bank of Japan, Tokyo, November 5, 2008), www.boj.or.jp/en/announcements/press/koen_2008/data/ ko0811a.pdf.

36. "FOMC Statement" (press release), Board of Governors of the Federal Reserve System, December 16, 2008, www.federalreserve.gov/newsevents/press/monetary/ 20081216b.htm.

37. "On Monetary Policy Decisions," Bank of Japan, December 19, 2008, www.boj.or.jp/en/ announcements/release_2008/k081219.pdf.

38. Lindsay Whipp and Mure Dickie, "Bank of Japan slashes rates to 0.1%," *Financial Times*, December 19, 2008, https://www.ft.com/content/6acbcbbc-cd8a-11dd-8b30 -000077b07658.

39. Kiyoshi Takenaka, "Canon Profit Tumbles, Predicts Further Slide," Reuters, January 28, 2009, www.reuters.com/article/us-canon-idUSTRE50R12Y20090128.

40. Kiyoshi Takenaka and Nathan Layne, "Panasonic to Cut 15,000 Jobs," Reuters, February 4, 2009, www.reuters.com/article/us-panasonic-results-idUSTRE51316S20090204.

41. Alexandra Twin, "Worst January ever for Dow, S&P 500," CNN Money, January 30, 2009, http://money.cnn.com/2009/01/30/markets/markets_newyork/?postversion= 2009013018.

42. Yuzo Saeki, "Japan Exports Nearly Halve in Deepening Recession," Reuters, February 25, 2009, http://uk.reuters.com/article/businesspro-us-japan-economy -idUKTRE51O2HJ20090225.

43. Oko Tabuchi, "Bank of Japan to Raise Bond Buys," *New York Times*, March 18, 2009, www.nytimes.com/2009/03/19/business/19japan.html.

44. Hillary Rodham Clinton travel abroad schedule, Office of the Historian, https://history .state.gov/departmenthistory/travels/secretary/clinton-hillary-rodham.

45. "Clinton, Nakasone Agree to Step Up Japan-U.S. Alliance," Sina, February 17, 2009, http://english.sina.com/world/2009/0216/219039.html.

46. Jonathan Stempel, "Citigroup Stock Falls below $1 for First Time," Reuters, March 5, 2009, www.reuters.com/article/us-citigroup-idUSN0532847720090305.

47. Tabuchi, "Bank of Japan to Raise Bond Buys."

48. "FOMC Statement" (press release), Board of Governors of the Federal Reserve System, March 18, 2009, www.federalreserve.gov/newsevents/press/monetary/20090318a.htm.

49. "Federal Reserve, Bank of England, European Central Bank, Bank of Japan, and Swiss National Bank Announce Swap Arrangements" (press release), Board of Governors of the Federal Reserve System, April 6, 2009, www.federalreserve.gov/newsevents/press/ monetary/20090406a.htm.

50. Bank of Japan, Announcements, www.boj.or.jp/en/announcements/release_2009/index .htm/. The announcement of the Tripartite Bank Governor's Meeting was removed from the server.

51. "Dollar Hits Multi-Week Low vs. Yen, Euro," CNN Money, August 27, 2009, http:// money.cnn.com/2009/08/27/markets/dollar.reut/.

52. Takashi Nakamichi, "Geithner Affirms Strong Dollar Policy," *Wall Street Journal*, November 11, 2009, www.wsj.com/articles/SB125792362908743307.

53. "Timothy F. Geithner, Secretary of the Treasury," Konrad Adenauer Stiftung, www.kas .de/wf/en/71.6753/.

54. *Minutes of the Monetary Policy Meeting on November 19 and 20, 2009* (Tokyo: Bank of Japan, December 24, 2009), www.boj.or.jp/en/mopo/mpmsche_minu/minu_2009/ g091120.pdf.

55. "Highlights—Japan Govt Unveils $81 Bln Economic Stimulus," Reuters, December 8, 2009, www.reuters.com/article/japan-economy-stimulus-idUST211173200912O8.

56. *Minutes of the Monetary Policy Meeting on December 17 and 18, 2009* (Tokyo: Bank of Japan, January 29, 2010), www.boj.or.jp/en/mopo/mpmsche_minu/minu_2009/g091218.pdf.

57. "Statements on Monetary Policy," Bank of Japan, www.boj.or.jp/en/mopo/mpmdeci/state_2011/index.htm/.

58. Sewell Chan, "Senate, Weakly, Backs New Term for Bernanke," *New York Times*, January 28, 2010, www.nytimes.com/2010/01/29/business/economy/29fed.html.

59. Bernie Sanders, "'Bernanke Was Asleep at the Switch,'" Bernie Sanders, US Senator for Vermont, January 27, 2010, www.sanders.senate.gov/newsroom/recent-business/bernanke-was-asleep-at-the-switch.

60. "FOMC Statement: Federal Reserve, European Central Bank, Bank of Canada, Bank of England, and Swiss National Bank Announce Reestablishment of Temporary US Dollar Liquidity Swap Facilities" (press release), Board of Governors of the Federal Reserve System, May 9, 2010, www.federalreserve.gov/newsevents/press/monetary/20100509a.htm.

61. "Conference Call of the Federal Open Market Committee," Board of Governors of the Federal Reserve System, May 9, 2010, www.federalreserve.gov/monetarypolicy/files/FOMC20100509confcall.pdf.

62. Finbarr Flynn and Takako Taniguchi, "SMFG May Spend Up to $5 Billion on Stake in US Bank," Bloomberg, July 8, 2010, www.bloomberg.com/news/articles/2010-07-08/sumitomo-mitsui-may-invest-as-much-as-5-billion-in-u-s-commercial-bank.

63. Finbarr Flynn and Takako Taniguchi, "Mitsubishi UFJ May Buy Additional U.S. Banking Assets," Bloomberg, July 21, 2010, www.bloomberg.com/news/articles/2010-07-20/mitsubishi-ufj-s-tatsuo-tanaka-says-it-may-buy-more-u-s-banking-assets.

64. Chris Isidore, "Fed Decision: Recovery Losing Steam," CNN Money, August 10, 2010, http://money.cnn.com/2010/08/10/news/economy/fed_decision/index.htm.

65. Jack Ewing, "Strong Yen Helps to Fuel Germany's Export Boom," *New York Times*, September 2, 2010, www.nytimes.com/2010/09/03/business/global/03yen.html.

66. Jill Treanor, "Japan Plays Down Yen's 15-Year High against the US Dollar," *Guardian* (Manchester), August 12, 2010, www.theguardian.com/business/2010/aug/12/currencies-japan.

67. Martin Fackler, "Change in Japan a Tough Task for Finance Minister," *New York Times*, January 8, 2010, www.nytimes.com/2010/01/09/world/asia/09japan.html.

68. Martin Fackler, "Finance Chief Chosen as Next Japanese Leader," *New York Times*, June 3, 2010, www.nytimes.com/2010/06/04/world/asia/04japan.html.

69. Michiyo Nakamoto and Lindsay Whipp, "Tokyo under Pressure to Tackle Rising Yen," *Financial Times*, August 24, 2010, https://www.ft.com/content/970fed02-afa1-11df-b45b-00144feabdc0.

70. "The Fixed-Rate Funds-Supplying Operation against Pooled Collateral," Bank of Japan, August 30, 2010, www.boj.or.jp/en/announcements/release_2010/un1008d.pdf.

71. "Land of the Rising Sun Worries About the Rising Yen," Wise Money, August 31, 2010, www.wisemoney.com/2010/08.

72. Matthew Brown and Bo Nielsen, "Yen Tumbles from 15-Year High After Japan Intervenes in Market," Bloomberg, September 15, 2010, www.bloomberg.com/news/articles/2010-09-15/yen-falls-on-speculation-of-intervention-noda-to-meet-press.

73. Hiroko Tabuchi, "Bank of Japan Moves to Buy More Assets," *New York Times*, October 5, 2010, www.nytimes.com/2010/10/06/business/global/06yen.html?_r=0.

74. Bank of Japan Act, Act No. 89 of June 18, 1997, Japanese Law Translation, www.japaneselawtranslation.go.jp/law/detail/?id=92&vm=02&re=01.

75. "FOMC Statement" (press release), Board of Governors of the Federal Reserve System, November 3, 2010, www.federalreserve.gov/newsevents/press/monetary/20101103a .htm.

76. Norie Kuboyama, "Japanese Stocks Gain for Second Day on Commodity, S&P Recovery," Bloomberg, December 21, 2010, www.bloomberg.com/news/articles/2010-12-22/ most-japanese-stocks-gain-on-higher-commodity-prices-mitsubishi-advances.

77. Malcolm Foster, "For Japan, 2010 Was a Year to Forget on Many Fronts," NBC News, December 29, 2010, www.nbcnews.com/id/40821587/ns/business-world_business/t/ japan-was-year-forget-many-fronts/#.WYd82NMrL0E.

78. David Teather, "China Overtakes Japan as World's Second-Largest Economy," *Guardian* (Manchester), August 16, 2010, www.theguardian.com/business/2010/ aug/16/china-overtakes-japan-second-largest-economy1.

79. John P. Rafferty and Kenneth Pletcher, "Japan Earthquake and Tsunami of 2011," *Encyclopaedia Britannica,* https://global.britannica.com/event/Japan-earthquake-and-tsunami -of-2011.

80. Alex Hawkes, "Japan Crisis Sees Yen Hit Record High against Dollar," *Guardian* (Manchester), March 17, 2011, www.theguardian.com/business/2011/mar/17/japan-crisis -yen-surges-nikkei-falls.

81. Ibid.

82. "Statement of G7 Finance Ministers and Central Bank Governors" (press release), European Central Bank, March 18, 2011, www.ecb.europa.eu/press/pr/date/2011/html/ pr110318.en.html.

83. Brian Sack and Kevin McNeil, "Treasury and Federal Reserve Foreign Exchange Operations: January–March 2011," Federal Reserve Bank of New York, www.newyorkfed.org/ medialibrary/media/newsevents/news/markets/2011/fxq111.pdf.

84. Catarina Saraiva and Charles Mead, "Yen Decline After G-7's Post-Earthquake Intervention Pares Gain," Bloomberg, March 19, 2011, www.bloomberg.com/news/ articles/2011-03-19/yen-decline-after-g-7-s-post-earthquake-intervention-pares-gain.

85. Allison Bennett, "Dollar Index Declines to Lowest Since 2008 on Economy; Yen Gains," Bloomberg, April 28, 2011, www.bloomberg.com/news/articles/2011-04-28/ dollar-hits-16-month-low-versus-euro-after-bernanke-comment-kiwi-declines.

86. "Statement on Monetary Policy," Bank of Japan, June 14, 2011, www.boj.or.jp/en/ announcements/release_2011/k110614a.pdf.

87. "Emergency Talks Held to Calm Global Markets Turmoil," BBC News, August 7, 2011, www.bbc.com/news/world-europe-14434831.

88. Jana Randow, Jeannine Aversa, and Scott Lanman, "Central Bankers Race to Protect Growth in 72 Hours of Crisis," Bloomberg, August 11, 2011, www.bloomberg.com/news/ articles/2011-08-10/central-bankers-become-tower-of-strength-amid-debt-turmoil.

89. Robert Winnett, "Collapse of Euro Could Pose Threat to Peace, Says Angela Merkel," *Telegraph* (London), October 26, 2011, www.telegraph.co.uk/news/worldnews/europe/ germany/8851912/Merkel-wins-rescue-fund-vote-after-raising-spectre-of-war.html.

90. "Euro Summit Statement," European Council, Council of the European Union, October 26, 2011, www.consilium.europa.eu/uedocs/cms_data/docs/pressdata/en/ec/125644.pdf.

91. "Enhancement of Monetary Easing," Bank of Japan, October 27, 2011, www.boj.or.jp/ en/announcements/release_2011/k111027a.pdf.

92. Catarina Saraiva, "Yen Slides Most in Three Years After Intervention; Dollar Rises," Bloomberg, October 31, 2011, www.bloomberg.com/news/articles/2011-10-31/yen -tumbles-4-as-japan-intervenes-to-sell-currency-third-time-this-year.

93. "Coordinated Central Bank Action to Address Pressures in Global Money Markets" (press release), Board of Governors of the Federal Reserve System, November 30, 2011, www.federalreserve.gov/newsevents/press/monetary/20111130a.htm.

94. Toru Fujioka, "Yen-Yuan Trade Plan to Cut Dollar Dependence of China, Japan," Bloomberg, December 26, 2011, www.bloomberg.com/news/articles/2011-12-25/china -japan-to-promote-direct-trading-of-currencies-to-cut-company-costs.

95. Masaki Kondo, "Yen Intervention Failing as Best Currency Poised to Advance," Bloomberg, December 27, 2011, www.bloomberg.com/news/articles/2011-12-26/yen -intervention-failing-means-world-s-best-currency-poised-to-strengthen.

96. Leika Kihara, "Special Report: After a Bashing, BOJ Weighs 'Big Bang' War on Deflation," Reuters, November 29, 2012, www.reuters.com/article/us-japan-boj -idUSBRE8AT00420121130.

97. Ibid.

98. Justin McCurry, "Japan Set to End Resistance to Interest Rate Cuts," *Guardian* (Manchester), October 30, 2008, www.theguardian.com/business/2008/ oct/30/economy-japan-interest-rates.

99. "Enhancement of Monetary Easing," Bank of Japan, February 14, 2012, www.boj.or.jp/ en/announcements/release_2012/k120214a.pdf.

100. Monami Yui and Allison Bennett, "Yen Losing Most Since '95 Not Enough for Toyota," Bloomberg, April 2, 2012, www.bloomberg.com/news/articles/2012 -04-01/yen-losing-most-since-95-not-enough-for-toyota-in-boj-crusade.

101. Monami Yui and Allison Bennett, "Yen Losing Most Since '95 Not Enough for Toyota," *Korea Herald,* April 2, 2012, www.koreaherald.com/view.php?ud= 20120402000640&mod=skb.

102. Leika Kihara and Rie Ishiguro, "Bank of Japan Boosts Stimulus Again, but Fails to Impress Markets," Reuters, April 27, 2012, www.reuters.com/article/us-japan-economy -boj-idUSBRE83Q06V20120427.

103. "Toyota Raises 2012 Sales Target as Profits Bounce Back," *Telegraph* (London), August 3, 2012, www.telegraph.co.uk/finance/newsbysector/transport/9448759/Toyota-raises -2012-sales-target-as-profits-bounce-back.html.

104. Tetsushi Kajimoto, "Japan Extends Dollar Loan Scheme to Deal with Strong Yen," Reuters, August 6, 2012, http://uk.reuters.com/article/uk-japan-economy-azumi -idUKBRE87602W20120807.

105. Timothy Ahmann, "Bernanke Defends Fed Stimulus as China, Brazil Raise Concerns," Reuters, October 14, 2012, www.reuters.com/article/us-usa-fed-bernanke -idUSBRE89D01C20121014.

106. Ben S. Bernanke, "US Monetary Policy and International Implications" (speech given at Challenges of the Global Financial System: Risks and Governance under Evolving Globalization seminar, Bank of Japan–International Monetary Fund, Tokyo, Japan, October 14, 2012), www.federalreserve.gov/newsevents/speech/bernanke20121014a .htm.

107. Ahmann, "Bernanke Defends Fed Stimulus as China, Brazil Raise Concerns."

108. Ibid.

109. Christine Lagarde, opening remarks at Challenges of the Global Financial System: Risks and Governance under Evolving Globalization seminar, Bank of Japan–International Monetary Fund, Tokyo, Japan, October 14, 2012, www.imf.org/en/News/Articles/2015/09/28/04/53/sp101412.

110. Rodrigo Campos, "World Stocks Tick Up to Record High; Oil Slips," Reuters, August 6, 2017, www.reuters.com/article/us-global-markets-idUSKBN1AN026.

111. Mariko Ishikawa, Masaki Kondo, and Hiroko Komiya, "Softbank Succeeds Where Shirakawa Struggled on M&A Deals," Bloomberg, October 29, 2012, www.bloomberg.com/news/articles/2012-10-29/softbank-succeeds-where-shirakawa-struggled-on-m-a-deals.

112. "Japan Elections: Shares Rise and Yen Weakens on Abe Win," BBC News, December 17, 2012, www.bbc.com/news/business-20752215.

113. Mure Dickie, "Abe Calls for 'Unlimited' Easing from BoJ," *Financial Times*, November 15, 2012, www.ft.com/content/7e64027c-2f04-11e2-b88b-00144feabdc0.

114. Leika Kihara and Stanley White, "Bank of Japan to Mull 2 Percent Inflation Target as Abe Turns Up Heat," Reuters, December 17, 2012, www.reuters.com/article/us-japan-economy-boj-idUSBRE8BG14V20121218.

115. Bloomberg, "Abe Ups Pressure on BOJ for Unlimited Stimulus," *Japan Times* (Tokyo), November 16, 2012, www.japantimes.co.jp/news/2012/11/16/business/abe-ups-pressure-on-boj-for-unlimited-stimulus/#.WKKqGBIrL0E.

116. "Federal Reserve and Other Central Banks Announce an Extension of the Existing Temporary US Dollar Liquidity Swap Arrangements through February 1, 2014" (press release), Board of Governors of the Federal Reserve System, December 13, 2012, www.federalreserve.gov/newsevents/press/monetary/20121213a.htm.

117. Tatsuo Ito and William Mallard, "Global Currency Tensions Rise," *Wall Street Journal*, December 23, 2012, www.wsj.com/articles/SB10001424127887324660404578196892204462394.

118. Martin Fackler, "Ex-Premier Is Chosen to Govern Japan Again," *New York Times*, December 26, 2012, www.nytimes.com/2012/12/27/world/asia/shinzo-abe-selected-as-japans-prime-minister.html?_r=0.

119. "Japanese Yen Hits 27-Month Low against US Dollar," BBC News, December 27, 2012, www.bbc.com/news/business-20849204.

120. Kaori Kaneko, "Bank of Japan Head to Leave Job Early, Could Advance Policy Shift," Reuters, February 5, 2013, www.reuters.com/article/us-japan-economy-shirakawa-resignation-idUSBRE9140C220130205.

121. Marketwired, "Former BOJ Governor Masaaki Shirakawa Appointed Distinguished Visiting Fellow at NUS Business School," Yahoo! Finance, August 21, 2014, https://finance.yahoo.com/news/former-boj-governor-masaaki-shirakawa-060000520.html. He had also served as vice chairman of the BIS during the last two years of that term.

122. "Interview with Masaaki Shirakawa," Money & Banking (blog), March 25, 2015, www.moneyandbanking.com/commentary/2015/3/25/interview-with-masaaki-shirakawa.

123. Ayako Mie, "Stocks Soar on News of Shirakawa's Early Exit," *Japan Times* (Tokyo), February 7, 2013, www.japantimes.co.jp/news/2013/02/07/business/stocks-soar-on-news-of-shirakawas-early-exit/#.WYyhmdMrL0E.

124. "Japan Government Debt to GDP: 1980–2017" (chart), Trading Economics, https://tradingeconomics.com/japan/government-debt-to-gdp.

125. Joseph Ciolli and Taylor Tepper, "Yen Gains as G-7 Officials Offer Conflicting Views on Volatility," Bloomberg, February 12, 2013, www.bloomberg.com/news/articles/2013-02-12/euro-advances-after-g-7-pledge-not-to-devalue-exchange-rates.

126. "G7 Warns About 'Currency Wars,'" CBC News, February 12, 2013, www.cbc.ca/news/business/g7-warns-about-currency-wars-1.1364860.

127. Charles Clover, Robin Harding, and Alice Ross, "G20 Agrees to Avoid Currency Wars," Financial Times, February 17, 2013, www.ft.com/content/789439ae-784f-11e2-8a97-00144feabdc0.

128. "Introduction of the 'Quantitative and Qualitative Monetary Easing,'" Bank of Japan, April 4, 2013, www.boj.or.jp/en/announcements/release_2013/k130404a.pdf.

129. Leika Kihara and Stanley White, "BOJ to Pump $1.4 Trillion into Economy in Unprecedented Stimulus," Reuters, April 4, 2013, www.reuters.com/article/us-japan-economy-boj-idUSBRE93216U20130404.

130. Ibid.

131. Report to Congress on International Economic and Exchange Rate Policies (Washington, DC: US Department of the Treasury, Office of International Affairs, April 12, 2013), www.treasury.gov/resource-center/international/exchange-rate-policies/Documents/Foreign%20Exchange%20Report%20April%202013.pdf.

132. Kasia Klimasinska and Ian Katz, "US Urges Japan to Refrain from Competitive Yen Devalue," Reuters, April 12, 2013, www.bloomberg.com/news/articles/2013-04-12/u-s-to-press-japan-to-refrain-from-competitive-devaluation.

133. Report to Congress on International Economic and Exchange Rate Policies.

134. Anna Yukhananov, "United States Puts Japan on Notice in Currency Report," Reuters, April 12, 2013, www.reuters.com/article/us-usa-treasury-currency-idUSBRE93B12E20130412.

135. Leika Kihara, "Japan Exports Hit Three-Year High on Weak Yen, Trade Deficit Jumps," Reuters, August 18, 2013, www.reuters.com/article/us-japan-economy-trade-idUSBRE97I00G20130819.

136. Global Dimensions of Unconventional Monetary Policy symposium, August 21–23, 2013, Jackson Hole, WY, www.kansascityfed.org/publications/research/escp/symposiums/escp-2013.

137. Alister Bull, "Exclusive: Bernanke to Skip Jackson Hole Due to Scheduling Conflict," Reuters, April 20, 2013, www.reuters.com/article/us-usa-fed-bernanke-idUSBRE93J0JX20130421.

138. Steve Matthews and Joshua Zumbrun, "Jackson Hole Without Bernanke Focuses on Global Policy," Bloomberg, August 22, 2013, www.bloomberg.com/news/articles/2013-08-22/jackson-hole-without-bernanke-to-focus-on-global-monetary-policy.

139. Haruhiko Kuroda, "Japan's Unconventional Monetary Policy and Initiatives Toward Ensuring Stability of the Global Financial System," in Proceedings of the Global Dimensions of Unconventional Monetary Policy Symposium, Federal Reserve Bank of Kansas City, Jackson Hole, WY, August 21–23, 2013, www.kansascityfed.org/publicat/sympos/2013/2013kuroda.pdf.

140. Ibid.

141. Michael Steen, "Mario Draghi Faces Dilemma over Eurozone Inflation Level," *Financial Times*, October 16, 2013, https://next.ft.com/content/466e7956-34f3-11e3 -8148-00144feab7de.

142. Mario Draghi and Vítor Constâncio, introductory statement to the press conference (with Q&A), European Central Bank, October 2, 2013, www.ecb.europa.eu/press/ pressconf/2013/html/is131002.en.html.

143. "ECB Establishes Standing Swap Arrangements with Other Central Banks" (press release), European Central Bank, October 31, 2013, www.ecb.europa.eu/press/pr/ date/2013/html/pr131031.en.html.

144. Neil Dennis, "Yen Weakens on Japan Growth Concerns," *Financial Times,* November 14, 2013, https://www.ft.com/content/461e725a-4d38-11e3-bf32-00144feabdc0.

145. Dan Blystone, "USD/JPY Rallies Above Key 100 Level After Finance Minister Aso Comments," Benzinga, November 15, 2013, www.benzinga.com/news/13/11/4083514/ usdjpy-rallies-above-key-100-level-after-finance-minister-aso-comments.

146. Wanfeng Zhou, "Euro Rises to More Than 2-Year High vs. Dollar; Yen Falls," Reuters, December 26, 2013, www.reuters.com/article/us-markets-forex-idUSBRE9BJ 0EF20131227.

147. Angela Monaghan, "US Federal Reserve to End Quantitative Easing Programme," *Guardian* (Manchester), October 29, 2014, www.theguardian.com/business/2014/ oct/29/us-federal-reserve-end-quantitative-easing-programme.

148. William Mallard, "After Fall, Japan Yen in Sweet Spot for Economy, but US Watching," Reuters, January 26, 2014, www.reuters.com/article/us-japan-yen -idUSBREA0P0MX20140126.

149. Jacob J. Lew and John C. Bussey, transcript of Economic Policy After the Omnibus event, Council on Foreign Relations, January 16, 2014, www.cfr.org/economics/ economic-policy-after-omnibus/p35574.

150. "Japan Reports Record Annual Trade Deficit," BBC News, January 27, 2014, www.bbc .com/news/business-25908413.

151. "Minutes of the Monetary Policy Meeting on February 17 and 18, 2014," Bank of Japan, March 14, 2014, www.boj.or.jp/en/mopo/mpmsche_minu/minu_2014/g140218 .pdf.

152. "Japan Reports Record Annual Trade Deficit."

153. Ibid.

154. *Japan Times,* www.japantimes.co.jp/news/2014/04/12/business/g-20-lauds-abenomics -tax-hike-but-not-reforms-aso/#.V5oi_vkrLIV. The article is no longer available on the *Japan Times* system.

155. Li Anne Wong and Susan Li, "Kuroda: Impact of Japan Tax Hike Will Be Contained," CNBC, May 4, 2014, www.cnbc.com/2014/05/04/kuroda-impact-of-japan-tax-hike -will-be-contained.html.

156. Toru Fujioka and Masahiro Hidaka, "BOJ Refrains from Extra Ease as It Predicts Faster Inflation," Bloomberg, April 30, 2014, www.bloomberg.com/news/articles/2014 -04-30/boj-sticks-with-record-easing-as-kuroda-gauges-sales-tax-effect.

157. Patrick Graham, "Yen Rally Slackens Off, All Eyes on ECB Meeting," Reuters, May 29, 2014, www.reuters.com/article/us-markets-forex-idUSKBN0EA08320140530.

158. Toru Takahashi, "BRICS Bank Can Contribute to Global Growth: BOJ's Kuroda," *Nikkei Asian Review,* July 25, 2014, https://asia.nikkei.com/Politics-Economy/Economy/BRICS-bank-can-contribute-to-global-growth-BOJ-s-Kuroda.

159. "Minutes of the Monetary Policy Meeting on July 14 and 15, 2014," Bank of Japan, August 13, 2014, www.boj.or.jp/en/mopo/mpmsche_minu/minu_2014/g140715.pdf.

160. Leika Kihara and Tetsushi Kajimoto, "Japan PM, Finance Minister Unalarmed by Weak Yen for Now," Reuters, October 6, 2014, www.reuters.com/article/us-japan-economy-abe-idUSKCN0HV0DM20141006.

161. Lew and Bussey, transcript of Economic Policy After the Omnibus event.

162. Michael Flaherty and Jonathan Spicer, "US Fed Frets over Strong Dollar, Global Woes: Minutes," Reuters, October 8, 2014, www.reuters.com/article/us-usa-fed-idUSKCN0HX20M20141008.

163. Jacob J. Lew, "A Conversation with US Treasury Secretary Jacob J. Lew," Peterson Institute for International Economics, Washington, DC, October 7, 2014, https://piie.com/sites/default/files/publications/papers/transcript-20141007.pdf.

164. "US Treasury's Lew Unfazed by Dollar's Recent Appreciation," Reuters, October 7, 2014,www.reuters.com/article/us-usa-economy-currency-idUSKCN0HW1AU20141007.

165. Louise Lucas, "Yen Tensions Emerge between Shinzo Abe and Haruhiko Kuroda," *Financial Times,* October 9, 2014.

166. Heidi Moore, "The Fed Has Quietly Ended Its Stimulus. Now the Hard Work Really Begins," *Guardian* (Manchester), October 29, 2014, www.theguardian.com/business/2014/oct/29/fed-quietly-ends-stimulus-hard-work.

167. Kimberly Amadeo, "What Is Quantitative Easing? Definition and Explanation," Balance, June 15, 2017, www.thebalance.com/what-is-quantitative-easing-definition-and-explanation-3305881.

168. Angela Monaghan and Graeme Wearden, "Bank of Japan to Inject 80 Trillion Yen into Its Economy," *Guardian* (Manchester), October 31, 2014, www.theguardian.com/business/2014/oct/31/bank-of-japan-80-trillion-yen-economy.

169. Toru Fujioka and Masahiro Hidaka, "Kuroda Surprises with Stimulus Boost as Japan Struggles," Bloomberg, October 31, 2014, www.bloomberg.com/news/articles/2014-10-31/boj-unexpectedly-boosts-easing-amid-weak-price-gains.

170. "Kuroda Remarks Open Possibilities for Shift in BOJ Stimulus," *Business Times* (Singapore), January 26, 2015, www.businesstimes.com.sg/government-economy/kuroda-remarks-open-possibilities-for-shift-in-boj-stimulus.

171. "BOJ Governor Kuroda Speaks in Bloomberg Interview (Transcript)," Bloomberg, January 23, 2015, www.bloomberg.com/news/articles/2015-01-23/boj-governor-kuroda-speaks-in-bloomberg-interview-transcript-.

172. Toru Fujioka, "Kuroda Signals Confidence on Easing with No G-20 Backlash on Yen," Bloomberg, February 10, 2015, www.bloomberg.com/news/articles/2015-02-10/kuroda-signals-confidence-on-easing-with-no-g-20-backlash-on-yen.

173. Shinzo Abe, "Policy Speech by Prime Minister Shinzo Abe to the 189th Session of the Diet," Prime Minister of Japan and His Cabinet, Thursday, February 12, 2015, http://japan.kantei.go.jp/97_abe/statement/201502/policy.html.

174. "Japan Minimum Hourly Wagers: 2010–2017" (chart), Trading Economics, https://tradingeconomics.com/japan/minimum-wages.

175. "Japan Part Time Employment: 1990–2017" (chart), Trading Economics, https://tradingeconomics.com/japan/part-time-employment.

176. "Japan Total Cash Earnings Growth: 1972–2017" (chart), Trading Economics, https://tradingeconomics.com/japan/wage-growth.

177. Takashi Nakamichi and Tatsuo Ito, "BOJ's Kuroda Signals Desire for Stable Yen," *Wall Street Journal,* February 18, 2015, www.wsj.com/articles/bank-of-japan-stands-pat-on-policy-1424229828.

178. "Central Bank Governor Rules Out New Stimulus," *Wall Street Journal,* February 18, 2015, www.wsj.com/articles/world-watch-news-digest-1424310082.

179. Kazunori Takada and Leika Kihara, "Exclusive: China Takes Lessons from Japan, Past Master on Slowdown, Deflation," Reuters, March 7, 2015, www.reuters.com/article/us-china-japan-economy-idUSKBN0M401U20150308.

180. "Japan's Regional Banks Feel Impact of BoJ Stimulus," *Financial Times,* April 11, 2015, www.ft.com/content/6c036d62-e0c2-11e4-9f72-00144feab7de.

181. Toru Fujioka, "Yen's Drop Is Approaching Its Limit, Says Abe Adviser Hamada," Bloomberg, April 13, 2015, www.bloomberg.com/news/articles/2015-04-14/yen-s-decline-is-approaching-its-limit-says-abe-adviser-hamada.

182. Haruhiko Kuroda, "Two Years under QQE" (speech, Yomiuri International Economic Society meeting, Bank of Japan, Tokyo, May 15, 2015), www.boj.or.jp/en/announcements/press/koen_2015/data/ko150515a1.pdf.

183. "The Great Fall of China," *Economist,* August 29, 2015, www.economist.com/news/leaders/21662544-fear-about-chinas-economy-can-be-overdone-investors-are-right-be-nervous-great-fall.

184. Phillip Inman, "China Ends Three Days of Yuan Devaluation," *Guardian* (Manchester), August 14, 2015, https://www.theguardian.com/business/2015/aug/14/china-halts-yuan-devaluation-with-slight-official-rise-against-us-dollar.

185. Toru Fujioka and Masahiro Hidaka, "Bank of Japan Meets After Kuroda Moves Yen: Decision-Day Guide," Bloomberg, June 18, 2015, www.bloomberg.com/news/articles/2015-06-18/bank-of-japan-meets-after-kuroda-moves-yen-decision-day-guide.

186. Chao Deng, "Japan's Nikkei Hits Highest Level in More Than 18 Years," *Wall Street Journal,* June 24, 2015, www.wsj.com/articles/japans-nikkei-hits-more-than-18-year-high-1435112079.

187. Keiko Ujikane and Joji Mochida, "Abe Offers Kuroda Understanding as Markets Undercut Price Goal," Bloomberg, August 24, 2015, www.bloomberg.com/news/articles/2015-08-24/abe-offers-understanding-to-boj-in-its-struggle-for-inflation.

188. "BoJ Holds Course Despite Deepening Gloom," *Financial Times,* October 30, 2015, http://www.usagold.com/cpmforum/2015/10/30/boj-holds-course-despite-deepening-gloom/.

189. Haruhiko Kuroda, "Crude Oil Prices and Price Stability" (speech at Japan's National Press Club, Bank of Japan, Tokyo, February 27, 2015), www.boj.or.jp/en/announcements/press/koen_2015/data/ko150227a1.pdf.

190. "Southeast Asia Set to Launch Economic Community," SunStar Network, November 21, 2015, http://www.sunstar.com.ph/network/local-news/2015/11/21/southeast-asia-set-launch-economic-community-442716.

191. Ibid.

192. "Federal Reserve Issues FOMC Statement" (press release), Board of Governors of the Federal Reserve System, December 16, 2015, www.federalreserve.gov/newsevents/press/monetary/20151216a.htm.

193. "Bank of Japan Balance Sheet: 2005–2017," Japan Macro Advisors, accessed September 14, 2017, www.japanmacroadvisors.com/page/category/bank-of-japan/boj-balance-sheet/.

194. "Central Bank Assets for Euro Area (11–19 Countries): 1998–2017," FRED Economic Data, accessed September 14, 2017, https://fred.stlouisfed.org/series/ECBASSETS.

195. "Key Points of Today's Policy Decisions," Bank of Japan, January 29, 2016, www.boj.or.jp/en/announcements/release_2016/k160129b.pdf.

196. Ibid.

197. Ibid.

198. Netty Idayu Ismail and Candice Zachariahs, "Yen's Drop Lags Previous Shocks as Kuroda's Firepower Stutters," Bloomberg, January 29, 2016, www.bloomberg.com/news/articles/2016-01-29/yen-s-drop-lags-previous-shocks-as-kuroda-s-firepower-stutters.

199. David Lawder and Jason Lange, "G20 Worried by 'Modest' Global Growth, Commodities Weakness," Reuters, April 14, 2016, www.reuters.com/article/us-imf-g-idUSKCN0XB2O3.

200. "Communiqué: G20 Finance Ministers and Central Bank Governors Meeting," International Monetary Fund, April 15, 2016, www.imf.org/external/np/cm/2016/041616.htm; Takashi Nakamichi, "BOJ Worried About Possible 'Brexit' Hit to Yen," MarketWatch, April 20, 2016, www.marketwatch.com/story/boj-worried-about-possible-brexit-hit-to-yen-2016-04-20#:gQ1nKcwUL7E43A.

201. "Big Week for BoJ as Surging Yen Piles on Easing Pressure," Financial Times, April 25, 2016.

202. Haruhiko Kuroda, "The Battle against Deflation: The Evolution of Monetary Policy and Japan's Experience" (speech, Columbia University, New York, April 13, 2016), www.boj.or.jp/en/announcements/press/koen_2016/ko160414a.htm/.

203. "Decisions Regarding Monetary Policy Implementation" (press release), Board of Governors of the Federal Reserve System, April 27, 2016, www.federalreserve.gov/monetarypolicy/files/monetary20160427a1.pdf.

204. Takashi Nakamichi and Megumi Fujikawa, "Bank of Japan Keeps Policy Unchanged; Yen Rises," Wall Street Journal, April 28, 2016, www.wsj.com/articles/bank-of-japan-keeps-policy-unchanged-1461813743#:cFLO8Ezc5QaaUA.

205. Ibid.

206. "What Is Monetary Policy and How Is It Carried Out in Japan?" Bank of Japan, accessed September 15, 2017, www.boj.or.jp/en/announcements/education/oshiete/seisaku/b26.htm/.

207. Richard Leong, "Yen Rises to 18-Month High on Intervention Doubts," Reuters, May 2, 2016, www.reuters.com/article/us-global-forex-idUSKCN0XU01B.

208. Emily Flitter and Steve Holland, "Trump Preparing Plan to Dismantle Obama's Wall Street Reform Law," Reuters, May 17, 2016, www.reuters.com/article/us-usa-election-trump-banks-idUSKCN0Y900J.

209. Steve Holland and Emily Flitter, "Exclusive: Trump Would Talk to North Korea's Kim, Wants to Renegotiate Climate Accord," Reuters, May 17, 2016, www.reuters.com/article/us-usa-election-trump-exclusive-idUSKCN0Y82JO.

210. "Japan Hopes to Steer 'Frank' G7 Debate on Economy, Tax Evasion: Aso," Reuters, May 19, 2016, http://www.reuters.com/article/us-g7-japan-aso/japan-hopes-to-steer-frank-g7-debate-on-economy-tax-evasion-aso-idUSKCN0YA0UN.

211. "Brexit 'Serious Risk to Growth' Says G7," BBC News, May 27, 2016, www.bbc.com/news/business-36394905.

212. Toru Fujioka, Masahiro Hidaka, and Shingo Kawamoto, "Kuroda Faces Unhappy Banks as BOJ's Policy Decision Looms," Bloomberg, June 14, 2016, updated June 15, 2016, www.bloomberg.com/news/articles/2016-06-14/add-banks-to-list-of-kuroda-s-headaches-as-boj-decides-policy.

213. Leika Kihara, "BOJ Makes Contingency Plans for Brexit, Sees Dollar Squeeze, Yen Spike as Risks," Reuters, June 15, 2016, www.reuters.com/article/us-britain-eu-boj-idUSKCN0Z11BB.

214. "Federal Reserve Issues FOMC Statement" (press release), Board of Governors of the Federal Reserve System, June 15, 2016, www.federalreserve.gov/newsevents/press/monetary/20160615a.htm.

215. Toru Fujioka, "BOJ Keeps Policy Unchanged Even as Kuroda Warns on Yen," Bloomberg, June 15, 2016, www.bloomberg.com/news/articles/2016-06-16/boj-keeps-policy-unchanged-shifting-stimulus-focus-to-july.

216. "Federal Reserve Is Carefully Monitoring Developments in Global Financial Markets" (press release), Board of Governors of the Federal Reserve System, June 24, 2016, www.federalreserve.gov/newsevents/press/monetary/20160624a.htm.

217. Reuters, "Japan PM Abe Tells FinMin Taro Aso to Take Necessary Steps to Calm Yen," CNBC, June 26, 2016, www.cnbc.com/2016/06/26/japan-pm-abe-says-he-has-told-finmin-taro-aso-to-take-steps-to-calm-yen-if-needed.html.

218. "China's Yuan Weakens to Five-and-Half Year Low as Central Bank Tolerates Depreciation," Reuters, June 27, 2016, www.reuters.com/article/us-china-yuan-idUSKCN0ZD0FM.

219. Dion Rabouin, "Dollar Drops versus Yen as BOJ's Kuroda Plays Down 'Helicopter Money,'" Reuters, July 20, 2016, www.reuters.com/article/us-global-forex-idUSKCN10101T.

220. Pete Sweeney and Tetsushi Kajimoto, "G20's Deference for China's Economic Policies Irks Japan," Reuters, July 26, 2016, www.reuters.com/article/us-g20-china-diplomacy-idUSKCN1051DQ.

221. Nao Sano and Hiroyuki Sekine, "Japan Stocks Rise After BOJ Decision Sends Markets on Wild Ride," Bloomberg, July 28, 2016, www.bloomberg.com/news/articles/2016-07-29/japan-stocks-fluctuate-as-yen-climbs-before-boj-policy-decision.

222. "Japanese Central Banker, Finance Chief Put Up Tenuous Front," *Nikkei Asian Review*, August 3, 2016, http://asia.nikkei.com/Politics-Economy/Policy-Politics/Japanese-central-banker-finance-chief-put-up-tenuous-front.

223. Sean Alfano, "Nikkei Plunges to Lowest Close in a Year," CBS News, August 17, 2007, www.cbsnews.com/news/nikkei-plunges-to-lowest-close-in-a-year/.

224. Leika Kihara, "Japan Sinking Deeper into De-Facto Helicopter Money," Reuters, August 19, 2016, www.reuters.com/article/us-japan-economy-boj-helicopter-analysis -idUSKCN10U0DS.

225. "That Sinking Feeling," *Economist*, May 26, 2016, www.economist.com/news/finance-and -economics/21699469-volatile-stockmarkets-spell-pressure-gpif-and-its-new-leadership.

226. Kihara, "Japan Sinking Deeper into De-Facto Helicopter Money."

227. Angela Monaghan and Katie Allen, "Jackson Hole: Yellen Leaves Door Open to Rate Rise Before Year-End—As It Happened," *Guardian* (Manchester), August 26, 2016, www.theguardian.com/business/live/2016/aug/26/all-eyes-on-yellen-as-jackson-hole -kicks-off-business-live.

228. Haruhiko Kuroda, "Re-anchoring Inflation Expectations via 'Quantitative and Quali- tative Monetary Easing with a Negative Interest Rate'" (remarks at Economic Policy Symposium, Federal Reserve Bank of Kansas City, Jackson Hole, WY, August 27, 2016), www.kansascityfed.org/~/media/files/publicat/sympos/2016/econsymposium -kuroda-remarks.pdf?la=en.

229. Ibid.

230. "Minutes of the Federal Open Market Committee, July 26–27, 2016," Board of Governors of the Federal Reserve System, www.federalreserve.gov/monetarypolicy/ fomcminutes20160727.htm.

231. Leika Kihara and Stanley White, "BOJ Overhauls Policy Focus, Sets Target for Government Bond Yields," Reuters, September 21, 2016, www.reuters.com/article/ us-japan-economy-boj-idUSKCN11R0BU.

232. William Watts, "Here's Why the Bank of Japan Is Putting Its Focus on the Yield Curve," CNBC News, September 21, 2016, www.marketwatch.com/story/heres-why -the-bank-of-japan-is-putting-its-focus-on-the-yield-curve-2016-09-21.

233. Shinzo Abe, opening remarks by Prime Minister Shinzo Abe (at Dialogue with the New York–based Business and Financial Community of Japan, Prime Minister of Japan and His Cabinet, September 21, 2016), http://japan.kantei.go.jp/97_abe/statement/ 201609/1219240_11015.html.

234. Tetsushi Kajimoto and Stanley White, "Japan Must Not Rely Solely on Bank of Japan to Revive Economy: Finance Minister," Reuters, September 22, 2016, www.reuters .com/article/us-japan-economy-aso-idUSKCN11T05R.

235. Ibid.

236. Sam Forgione, "Dollar Falls on Comments from BOJ's Kuroda, US Debate Un- certainty," Reuters, September 25, 2016, www.reuters.com/article/us-global-forex -idUSKCN11W01F.

237. "Corporate Japan Tries to Deflect Pressure on Wage Hikes," *Nikkei Asian Review*, October 6, 2016, http://asia.nikkei.com/Politics-Economy/Policy-Politics/Corporate -Japan-tries-to-deflect-pressure-on-wage-hikes.

238. "Comex Vis: Países Parceiros: Exportações, Importações e Balança Comercial— Parceiro: Japão," Brasil Governo Federal, accessed October 11, 2017, www.mdic.gov.br/ comercio-exterior/estatisticas-de-comercio-exterior/comex-vis/frame-país?país=jpn.

239. Agência Brasil, "Brazil Seeks to Strengthen Trade Agreements in Japan," BrazilGov- News, October 4, 2016, updated October 5, 2016, www.brazilgovnews.gov.br/news/ 2016/10/brazil-seeks-to-strengthen-trade-agreements-in-japan.

240. "Memorando de Cooperação entre a República Federativa do Brasil e o Japão Para a Promoção de Investimentos e Cooperação econômica no setor de Infraestrutura," October 19, 2016, https://aplicacao.itamaraty.gov.br/ApiConcordia/Documento/download/16023.

241. Yun Sun, "Rising Sino-Japanese Competition in Africa," Brookings Institution, August 31, 2016, www.brookings.edu/blog/africa-in-focus/2016/08/31/rising-sino-japanese-competition-in-africa/.

242. Yoshiaki Nohara, "BOJ's Kuroda Says No Immediate Need to Reduce Asset Purchases," Bloomberg, October 21, 2016, www.bloomberg.com/news/articles/2016-10-21/boj-s-kuroda-says-no-immediate-need-to-reduce-asset-purchases.

243. Kevin Buckland and Shigeki Nozawa, "BOJ Fires Warning at Bond Market with Unlimited Buying Plan," Bloomberg, November 16, 2016, updated November 17, 2016, www.bloomberg.com/news/articles/2016-11-16/yields-above-zero-dare-kuroda-to-unleash-unlimited-bond-buying.

244. "Major Foreign Holders of Treasury Securities, 2016–2017" (table), Treasury International Capital (TIC) System, US Department of the Treasury, accessed September 15, 2017, http://ticdata.treasury.gov/Publish/mfh.txt.

245. Shinzo Abe, meeting with the president-elect of the United States, Prime Minister of Japan and His Cabinet, November 17, 2016, http://japan.kantei.go.jp/97_abe/actions/201611/17article2.html.

246. Mo Jingxi, "Xi, Trump Discuss China-US Cooperation," *China Daily*, November 15, 2016, http://usa.chinadaily.com.cn/epaper/2016-11/15/content_27397411.htm.

247. "India Mulls Enhanced Naval Cooperation with Japan," *American Interest*, December 20, 2016, www.the-american-interest.com/2016/12/20/india-mulls-enhanced-naval-cooperation-with-japan/.

248. Kiyoshi Takenaka and Katya Golubkova, "Abe, Putin Agree to Revive Japan-Russia Security Talks, Discuss Syria," Reuters, December 14, 2016, www.reuters.com/article/us-japan-russia-idUSKBN143332.

249. Also called the FSA; the government agency and financial regulator responsible for overseeing banking, securities and exchange, and insurance sectors to ensure the stability of the financial system of Japan.

250. Toru Takahashi, "BRICS Bank Can Contribute to Global Growth: BOJ's Kuroda," *Nikkei Asian Review*, July 25, 2014, https://asia.nikkei.com/Politics-Economy/Economy/BRICS-bank-can-contribute-to-global-growth-BOJ-s-Kuroda.

251. Okazaki had been working unofficially with the People's Bank of China since the State Council determined it would function as a central bank in 1983 ("About PBC," People's Bank of China, www.pbc.gov.cn/english/130712/index.html). Officially, she worked as a senior economist in the International Department and seconded to the People's Bank of China Shanghai Head Office (from October 2011 to August 2014). She effectively worked for two central banks at the same time, not a common situation, even less so between two politically competing countries like Japan and China. Although the two governments were officially at a distance, in 2006 she moved to Shanghai as part of an exchange program with the PBOC. Her stay was extended through 2013 (Kumiko Okazaki profile page, Canon Institute for Global Studies, www.canon-igs.org/en/fellows/kumiko_okazaki.html).

252. Cindy Li, "Banking on China through Currency Swap Agreements," Federal Reserve bank of San Francisco, October 23, 2015, www.frbsf.org/banking/asia-program/pacific-exchange-blog/banking-on-china-renminbi-currency-swap-agreements/.

253. "Cooperation with Other Central Banks," Bank of Japan, accessed September 15, 2017, www.boj.or.jp/en/intl_finance/cooperate/index.htm/.

254. The central bank of the Republic of Korea and issuer of South Korean won.

255. Bank of Japan, Announcements, https://www.boj.or.jp/en/announcements/release_2008/un081. The announcement of the formation of the tripartite group was removed from the server.

256. "Cooperation with Other Central Banks," Bank of Japan, https://www.boj.or.jp/en/intl_finance/cooperate/index.htm/#p.

257. Alvaro Vargas Llosa, "How China Has Created Its Own TPP," *National Interest*, November 8, 2016, http://nationalinterest.org/feature/how-china-has-created-its-own-tpp-18337.

258. "Regional Comprehensive Economic Partnership," Australian Government, Department of Foreign Affairs and Trade, accessed September 15, 2017, http://dfat.gov.au/trade/agreements/rcep/Pages/regional-comprehensive-economic-partnership.aspx.

259. Emiko Jozuka, "TPP vs RCEP? Trade Deals Explained," CNN, January 26, 2017, http://edition.cnn.com/2017/01/24/asia/tpp-rcep-nafta-explained/.

260. Reuters, "Japan PM Says TPP Trade Pact Meaningless Without US," Yahoo!, November 21, 2016, www.yahoo.com/news/tpp-trade-pact-meaningless-without-u-japan-pm-225702119.html.

261. Jeffrey A. Bader and David Dollar, "Why the TPP Is the Linchpin of the Asia Rebalance," Brookings Institution, July 28, 2015, www.brookings.edu/blog/order-from-chaos/2015/07/28/why-the-tpp-is-the-linchpin-of-the-asia-rebalance/.

262. Leika Kihara, "BOJ's Kuroda Welcomes Expansion of China-Led Infrastructure Bank," Reuters, May 1, 2017, www.reuters.com/article/us-japan-economy-boj-adb-idUSKBN17Y09I?il=0.

263. Toru Fujioka, "Kuroda Says Reaching Inflation Target a Little Easier with Trump," Bloomberg, January 18, 2017, www.bloomberg.com/news/articles/2017-01-18/kuroda-says-reaching-inflation-target-a-little-easier-with-trump.

264. Kihara, "BOJ's Kuroda Welcomes Expansion of China-Led Infrastructure Bank."

CHAPTER 5: EUROPE PART I: THE TRICHET FILES

1. John Lichfield, "Jean-Claude Trichet: The Guardian of the Euro," *Independent* (London), August 5, 2011, www.independent.co.uk/news/people/profiles/jean-claude-trichet-the-guardian-of-the-euro-2332716.html.

2. Aaron Eglitis, "When It Comes to Central-Banker Salaries, It Pays to Be Belgian," Bloomberg, November 22, 2016, www.bloomberg.com/news/articles/2016-11-22/when-it-comes-to-central-banker-salaries-it-pays-to-be-belgian.

3. "Looking Back: The Financial Crisis Began 10 Years Ago This Week," Money & Banking (blog), August 7, 2017, www.moneyandbanking.com/commentary/2017/8/6/looking-back-the-financial-crisis-began-10-years-ago-this-week.

4. "Lunch with the FT: Jean-Claude Trichet," *Financial Times*, July 6, 2012.

5. "Trichet Navigates Choppy Waters," *Financial Times*, December 23, 2007.

6. David Gow, "Trichet to Trumpet 'Solidity' of the Euro as He Bows Out of the ECB," *Guardian* (Manchester), October 5, 2011, www.theguardian.com/business/2011/oct/05/trichet-defends-his-time-at-ecb-as-he-bows-out.

7. "Looking Back: The Financial Crisis Began 10 Years Ago This Week," Money & Banking (blog), August 7, 2017, www.moneyandbanking.com/commentary/2017/8/6/looking-back-the-financial-crisis-began-10-years-ago-this-week.

8. "The Rise and Fall of Northern Rock," *Telegraph* (London), August 14, 2014, http://www.telegraph.co.uk/finance/newsbysector/banksandfinance/11032772/The-rise-and-fall-of-Northern-Rock.html.

9. Ibid.

10. "Euro Reaches New High Against Dollar," CBS News, February 27, 2008, www.cbsnews.com/news/euro-reaches-new-high-against-dollar/.

11. Lydia Saad, "Americans See China Crowding Out US as Economic Leader," Gallup, February 21, 2008, www.gallup.com/poll/104479/americans-see-china-crowding-us-economic-leader.aspx.

12. "Foreign Exchange Rates—H.10," Board of Governors of the Federal Reserve System, updated September 11, 2017, www.federalreserve.gov/releases/h10/summary/indexn96_b.htm.

13. "La Fed, el BCE y otros bancos centrales vuelven a inyectar liquidez contra la crisis financier," *El Mundo*, March 11, 2008, www.elmundo.es/mundodinero/2008/03/11/economia/1205240099.html.

14. "FOMC Statement: Federal Reserve and Other Central Banks Announce Specific Measures Designed to Address Liquidity Pressures in Funding Markets" (press release), Board of Governors of the Federal Reserve System, March 11, 2008, www.federalreserve.gov/newsevents/press/monetary/20080311a.htm.

15. "FT: Person of the Year," *Financial Times*, https://ig.ft.com/sites/person-of-the-year/; "Trichet Navigates Choppy Waters," *Financial Times*, December 23, 2007.

16. Jean-Claude Trichet, "Interview with Die Presse, Der Kurier, Der Standard and Salzburger Nachrichten on April 28, 2008," European Central Bank, April 30, 2008, www.ecb.europa.eu/press/inter/date/2008/html/sp080430.en.html.

17. Ibid.

18. Jean-Claude Trichet and Lucas Papademos, "Introductory Statement with Q&A," European Central Bank, July 3, 2008, www.ecb.europa.eu/press/pressconf/2008/html/is080703.en.html.

19. Linda S. Goldberg, Craig Kennedy, and Jason Miu, "Central Bank Dollar Swap Lines and Overseas Dollar Funding Costs," *FRBNY Economic Policy Review*, May 2011, 11, www.newyorkfed.org/medialibrary/media/research/epr/11v17n1/1105gold.pdf.

20. "Secretary Paulson Economic Intervention Vote Reaction," C-SPAN, September 29, 2008, www.c-span.org/video/?281498-1/secretary-paulson-economic-intervention-vote-reaction.

21. Jean-Claude Trichet and Lucas Papademos, "Introductory Statement with Q&A," European Central Bank, October 2, 2008, www.ecb.europa.eu/press/pressconf/2008/html/is081002.en.html.

22. *Financial Stress and Deleveraging: Macrofinancial Implications and Policy,* World Economic and Financial Surveys, Global Financial Stability Report (Washington,

DC: International Monetary Fund, October 2008), www.imf.org/external/pubs/ft/gfsr/2008/02/pdf/text.pdf.

23. Ralph Boulton and Tony Munroe, "European Banking Chief Urges US Bailout Approval," Reuters, October 3, 2008, www.reuters.com/article/idINIndia-35783620081003.

24. David M. Herszenhorn, "Congress Approves $700 Billion Wall Street Bailout," *New York Times*, October 3, 2008, www.nytimes.com/2008/10/03/business/worldbusiness/03iht-bailout.4.16679355.html.

25. "FOMC Statement: Federal Reserve and Other Central Banks Announce Reductions in Policy Interest Rates" (press release), Board of Governors of the Federal Reserve System, October 8, 2008, www.federalreserve.gov/newsevents/press/monetary/20081008a.htm.

26. Ibid.

27. "Monetary Policy Decisions" (press release), European Central Bank, October 8, 2008, www.ecb.europa.eu/press/pr/date/2008/html/pr081008.en.html.

28. "Monetary Policy Decisions" (press release), European Central Bank, November 6, 2008, www.ecb.europa.eu/press/pr/date/2008/html/pr081106.en.html.

29. "The Euro Zone's First Recession," *Economist*, November 14, 2008, www.economist.com/node/12623045.

30. Jean-Claude Trichet, "Undervalued Risk and Uncertainty: Some Thoughts on the Market Turmoil" (speech given at the Fifth ECB Central Banking Conference, Frankfurt am Main, November 13, 2008), www.ecb.europa.eu/press/key/date/2008/html/sp081113_1.en.html.

31. Jean-Claude Trichet and Lucas Papademos, "Introductory Statement with Q&A," European Central Bank, December 4, 2008, www.ecb.europa.eu/press/pressconf/2008/html/is081204.en.html.

32. Ibid.

33. Joseph Stiglitz, "The Problem with Europe Is the Euro," *Guardian* (Manchester), August 10, 2016, www.theguardian.com/business/2016/aug/10/joseph-stiglitz-the-problem-with-europe-is-the-euro.

34. Jean-Claude Trichet, "The Changing Role of Communication" (introductory remarks at a dinner with members of the Internationaler Club Frankfurter Wirtschaftsjournalisten, Frankfurt am Main, December 15, 2008), www.ecb.europa.eu/press/key/date/2008/html/sp081215_2.en.html.

35. "Merkel Hints at Billions for New Stimulus Plan," The Local, December 16, 2008, www.thelocal.de/20081216/16177.

36. "Germany Seals 50 Billion Euro Stimulus Plan," Spiegel Online, January 13, 2009, www.spiegel.de/international/germany/help-for-europe-s-biggest-economy-germany-seals-50-billion-euro-stimulus-plan-a-600977.html.

37. Ben S. Bernanke, "The Crisis and the Policy Response" (speech at the Stamp Lecture, London School of Economics, London, England, January 13, 2009), www.federalreserve.gov/newsevents/speech/bernanke20090113a.htm.

38. Ibid.

39. Ambrose Evans-Pritchard, "European Central Bank Falls into Line and Embraces Quantitative Easing," *Telegraph* (London), May 7, 2009, www.telegraph.co.uk/finance/

financialcrisis/5292781/European-Central-Bank-falls-into-line-and-embraces-quantitative-easing.html.

40. Robert J. Samuelson, "The Newsweek 50: Bernanke, Trichet, Shirakawa," *Newsweek*, December 19, 2008, www.newsweek.com/newsweek-50-bernanke-trichet-shirakawa-83099.

41. "Update 3—IMF Warns on Euro Zone Stability Risk, Cash Reserves," Reuters, January 28, 2009, http://uk.reuters.com/article/imf-strausskahn-eurozone-idUKLS48269020090128.

42. Ambrose Evans-Pritchard, "Trichet Is Bounced into Defence of the Euro," *Telegraph* (London), January 30, 2009, www.telegraph.co.uk/finance/financetopics/davos/4394914/Trichet-is-bounced-into-defence-of-the-euro.html.

43. "London Summit: Leaders' Statement," International Monetary Fund, April 2, 2009, www.imf.org/external/np/sec/pr/2009/pdf/g20_040209.pdf.

44. Sam Jones, Jenny Percival, and Paul Lewis, "G20 Protests: Riot Police Clash with Demonstrators," *Guardian* (Manchester), April 1, 2009, www.theguardian.com/world/2009/apr/01/g20-summit-protests.

45. "Federal Reserve, Bank of England, European Central Bank, Bank of Japan, and Swiss National Bank Announce Swap Arrangements" (press release), Board of Governors of the Federal Reserve System, April 6, 2009, www.federalreserve.gov/newsevents/press/monetary/20090406a.htm.

46. Jean-Claude Trichet and Lucas Papademos, "Introductory Statement with Q&A," European Central Bank, May 7, 2009, www.ecb.europa.eu/press/pressconf/2009/html/is090507.en.html.

47. The program is called the Covered Bond Purchase Programme (CBPP) and €60 billion of covered bonds were purchased from July 2009 to July 2010. They are European debt securities backed by mortgages or public sector loans.

48. Trichet and Papademos, "Introductory Statement with Q&A," European Central Bank, May 7, 2009.

49. Joellen Perry, "Merkel vs. Central Banks: In Her Words," Real Time Economics (blog), *Wall Street Journal*, June 3, 2009, https://blogs.wsj.com/economics/2009/06/03/merkel-vs-central-banks-in-her-words/.

50. Joellen Perry, "Germany Blasts 'Powers of the Fed,'" *Wall Street Journal*, June 3, 2009, www.wsj.com/articles/SB124398546796379239.

51. "Monetary Policy Decisions" (press release), European Central Bank, July 2, 2009, www.ecb.europa.eu/press/pr/date/2009/html/pr090702.en.html.

52. Jean-Claude Trichet and Lucas Papademos, "Introductory Statement with Q&A," European Central Bank, August 6, 2009, www.ecb.europa.eu/press/pressconf/2009/html/is090806.en.html.

53. "Is the World Losing Faith in the US Dollar?" Wharton School of the University of Pennsylvania, September 2, 2009, http://knowledge.wharton.upenn.edu/article/is-the-world-losing-faith-in-the-u-s-dollar/.

54. Jean-Claude Trichet, Lucas Papademos, and Mario Draghi, "Introductory Statement with Q&A," European Central Bank, October 8, 2009, www.ecb.europa.eu/press/pressconf/2009/html/is091008.en.html.

55. Ibid.

56. Ibid.

57. Una McCaffrey, "ECB Holds 1% Rate as Rise Not Expected Until Late Summer," *Irish Times*, October 9, 2009, www.irishtimes.com/business/ecb-holds-1-rate-as-rise -not-expected-until-late-summer-1.753708.

58. Martin Wolf, "Lunch with the FT: Jean-Claude Trichet," *Financial Times*, July 6, 2012, www.ft.com/content/d3508ac0-c687-11e1-943a-00144feabdc0.

59. "Senate Vote Sends Strong Message to the Fed" (press release), Bernie Sanders web-site, January 28, 2010, https://www.sanders.senate.gov/newsroom/press-releases/release -senate-vote-sends-strong-message-to-the-fed.

60. "Timeline: Greece's Economic Crisis," Reuters, February 3, 2010, www.reuters.com/ article/us-greece-economy-events-idUSTRE6124EL20100203.

61. "EU Casts Doubt on Greece Economic Figures," BBC News, January 13, 2010, http:// news.bbc.co.uk/2/hi/europe/8456216.stm.

62. "IMF Survey: Europe and IMF Agree €110 Billion Financing Plan with Greece: IMF Survey Online," International Monetary Fund, May 2, 2010, www.imf.org/external/ pubs/ft/survey/so/2010/car050210a.htm.

63. Ben Levisohn, "Dollar Soars against Euro As EU Dithers on Greece Aid," *Independent* (London), March 29, 2010, http://www.independent.ie/business/world/dollar-soars -against-euro-as-eu-dithers-on-greece-aid-26644916.html.

64. Richard Wachman and Nick Fletcher, "Standard & Poor's Downgrade Greek Credit Rating to Junk Status," *Guardian* (Manchester), April 27, 2010, www.theguardian.com/ business/2010/apr/27/greece-credit-rating-downgraded.

65. Edward Cody, "Greek Bailout Plan Approved by German Parliament," *Washington Post*, May 7, 2010, www.washingtonpost.com/wp-dyn/content/article/2010/05/07/ AR2010050701987.html.

66. Dan Bilefsky and Landon Thomas Jr., "Greece Takes Its Bailout, but Doubts for the Region Persist," *New York Times*, May 2, 2010, www.nytimes.com/2010/05/03/business/ global/03drachma.html?pagewanted=all.

67. "FOMC Statement: Federal Reserve, European Central Bank, Bank of Canada, Bank of England, and Swiss National Bank Announce Reestablishment of Temporary US Dol-lar Liquidity Swap Facilities" (press release), Board of Governors of the Federal Reserve System, May 9, 2010, www.federalreserve.gov/newsevents/press/monetary/20100509a .htm.

68. "Financial Stability Set Back as Sovereign Risks Materialize," *Global Financial Sta-bility Report Market Update*, July 2010, http://www.imf.org/external/pubs/ft/fmu/ eng/2010/02/pdf/0710.pdf.

69. "Global Financial Stability Report: GFSR Market Update," International Monetary Fund, July 7, 2010, Figure 3: Selected Euro Area Sovereign Bank Rollovers, Q3 2010–Q4 2012, www.imf.org/external/pubs/ft/fmu/eng/2010/02/#P15_3140.

70. Anita Brooks, "Spain Faces Unrest as New Austerity Plan Is Announced," *Independent* (London), May 12, 2010, www.independent.co.uk/news/world/europe/spain-faces -unrest-as-new-austerity-plan-is-announced-1972211.html.

71. Fiona Gova, "General Strike in Spain to Protest against Austerity Measures," *Telegraph* (London), September 29, 2010, www.telegraph.co.uk/travel/destinations/europe/spain/ 8032647/General-strike-in-Spain-to-protest-against-austerity-measures.html.

72. "Interview with Jean-Claude Trichet, President of the ECB, and *La Repubblica,* conducted by Elena Polidori on Wednesday 16 June 2010," European Central Bank, June 24, 2010, www.ecb.europa.eu/press/key/date/2010/html/sp100624.en.html.

73. Ambrose Evans-Pritchard, "IMF Tells Europe to Inject More Stimulus," *Telegraph* (London), July 8, 2010, www.telegraph.co.uk/finance/economics/7880333/IMF-tells-Europe-to-inject-more-stimulus.html; "Global Financial Stability Report: GFSR Market Update," July 7, 2010.

74. Jann Bettinga and Charles Penty, "Seven EU Banks Fail Tests with $4.5 Billion Shortfall," Bloomberg, July 23, 2010, www.bloomberg.com/news/articles/2010-07-23/seven-of-91-eu-banks-fail-stress-test-face-4-5-billion-capital-shortfall.

75. Ben Shore, "Euro Strengthens as Dollar Stalls," BBC News, August 9, 2010, www.bbc.com/news/business-10920766.

76. Stefan Gerlach, *Defining and Measuring Systemic Risk* (Brussels: European Parliament Committee on Economic and Monetary Affairs, 2009), www.europarl.europa.eu/document/activities/cont/200911/20091124ATT65154/20091124ATT65154EN.pdf.

77. Mark Felsenthal and Pedro da Costa, "Bernanke Says Fed to Act If Needed," Reuters, August 7, 2010, http://in.reuters.com/article/columns-us-usa-fed-bernanke-idINTRE67O0MF20100828.

78. Adrian Blundell-Wignall and Patrick Slovik, "The EU Stress Test and Sovereign Debt Exposures" (OECD Working Papers on Finance, Insurance and Private Pensions, No. 4, OECD Financial Affairs Division, August 2010), www.oecd.org/finance/financial-markets/45820698.pdf.

79. "FOMC Statement" (press release), Board of Governors of the Federal Reserve System, November 3, 2010, www.federalreserve.gov/newsevents/press/monetary/20101103a.htm.

80. "Fast Facts: $600 Billion Treasury Large-Scale Asset Purchase Program," Federal Reserve Bank of New York, www.newyorkfed.org/markets/fast_facts_lsap.html.

81. Jean-Claude Trichet and Vítor Constâncio, "Introductory Statement with Q&A," European Central Bank, November 4, 2010, www.ecb.europa.eu/press/pressconf/2010/html/is101104.en.html.

82. Ibid.

83. Jean-Claude Trichet, "Reflections on the Nature of Monetary Policy Non-Standard Measures and Finance Theory" (opening address, ECB Central Banking Conference, Frankfurt, November 18, 2010), www.ecb.europa.eu/press/key/date/2010/html/sp101118.en.html.

84. "The European Stability Mechanism," *ECB Monthly Bulletin,* July 2011, 71–84, www.ecb.europa.eu/pub/pdf/other/art2_mb201107en_pp71-84en.pdf.

85. "Unemployment Rates," *Economist,* December 30, 2008, www.economist.com/node/12863599.

86. Stefano Scarpetta, Anne Sonnet, and Thomas Manfredi, "Rising Youth Unemployment During the Crisis: How to Prevent Negative Long-Term Consequences on a Generation?" (OECD Social, Employment and Migration Papers, No. 106, Organisation for Economic Co-operation and Development, Paris, April 14, 2010), www.oecd.org/officialdocuments/publicdisplaydocumentpdf/?cote=DELSA/ELSA/WD/SEM(2010)6&doclanguage=en.

87. Jean-Claude Trichet and Vítor Constâncio, "Introductory Statement with Q&A," European Central Bank, March 3, 2011, www.ecb.europa.eu/press/pressconf/2011/html/is110303.en.html.

88. "Statement of G7 Finance Ministers and Central Bank Governors" (press release), European Central Bank, March 18, 2011, www.ecb.europa.eu/press/pr/date/2011/html/pr110318.en.html.

89. Hannah Smith, "Trichet Defends ECB Rate Increase Ahead of Portugal Talks," *Investment Week,* April 8, 2011, https://www.investmentweek.co.uk/investment-week/news/2041981/trichet-defends-ecb-rate-increase-ahead-portugal-talks.

90. "Eurozone Interest Rates Raised to 1.25% by ECB," BBC News, April 7, 2011, www.bbc.com/news/business-12997333.

91. Jean-Claude Trichet and Vítor Constâncio, "Introductory Statement with Q&A," European Central Bank, April 7, 2011, www.ecb.europa.eu/press/pressconf/2011/html/is110407.en.html.

92. Ibid.

93. Joe Rauch, "Big Banks Are Government-Backed: Fed's Hoenig," Reuters, April 12, 2011, www.reuters.com/article/us-fed-hoenig-idUSTRE73B3S820110412.

94. Text of Obama speech on the deficit, Washington Wire (blog), *Wall Street Journal,* April 13, 2011, http://blogs.wsj.com/washwire/2011/04/13/text-of-obama-speech-on-the-deficit/.

95. James Politi, "World Bank Sees End to Dollar's Hegemony," *Financial Times,* May 17, 2011.

96. Ibid.

97. Jean-Claude Trichet and Vítor Constâncio, "Introductory Statement with Q&A," European Central Bank, June 9, 2011, www.ecb.europa.eu/press/pressconf/2011/html/is110609.en.html.

98. Ibid.

99. *Statement by the Heads of State or Government of the Euro Area and EU Institutions* (Brussels: Council of the European Union, July 21, 2011), www.consilium.europa.eu/uedocs/cms_data/docs/pressdata/en/ec/123978.pdf.

100. "ECB 'to Act' over Eurozone Debt Crisis," BBC News, August 8, 2011, www.bbc.com/news/business-14439224.

101. James Mackenzie, "Berlusconi Has Ceded Power to ECB—Italy Opposition," Reuters, August 8, 2011, http://uk.reuters.com/article/uk-italy-crisis-idUKTRE7771ZI20110808.

102. "Lagarde Begins 1st Day as Head of IMF," CNN, July 5, 2011, http://edition.cnn.com/2011/BUSINESS/07/05/imf.lagarde/.

103. Jean-Claude Trichet and Vítor Constâncio, "Introductory Statement with Q&A," European Central Bank, July 7, 2011, www.ecb.europa.eu/press/pressconf/2011/html/is110707.en.html.

104. "Highlights—Trichet Comments at ECB News Conference," Reuters, July 7, 2011, http://in.reuters.com/article/ecb-rates-highlights-idINECBNEWS20110707.

105. "Italy—Staff Report for the 2011 Article IV Consultation; Informational Annex; Public Information Notice; Statement by the Staff Representative; and Statement by the Executive Director for Italy" (IMF Country Report No. 11/173, International

Monetary Fund, Washington, DC, July 2011), www.imf.org/external/pubs/ft/scr/2011/cr11173.pdf.

106. Matthew Price, "Fears over Italy's Debt Persist," BBC News, July 12, 2011, www.bbc.com/news/world-europe-14117326.

107. Jean-Claude Trichet, confidential letter to José Luis Rodríguez Zapatero (photocopy), *El País* (Madrid), August 5, 2011, http://ep00.epimg.net/descargables/2013/11/27/2b10649fe77a0775a23fb7eb465ab974.pdf.

108. Claudi Pérez, "Who's in Charge in Spain?" *El País* (Madrid), December 2, 2013, http://elpaís.com/elpaís/2013/12/02/inenglish/1386001836_310579.html.

109. John Lichfield, "Jean-Claude Trichet: The Guardian of the Euro," *Independent* (London), August 5, 2011, www.independent.co.uk/news/people/profiles/jean-claude-trichet-the-guardian-of-the-euro-2332716.html.

110. Jana Randow, Jeannine Aversa, and Scott Lanman, "Central Bankers Race to Protect Growth in 72 Hours of Crisis," Bloomberg, August 11, 2011, www.bloomberg.com/news/articles/2011-08-10/central-bankers-become-tower-of-strength-amid-debt-turmoil.

111. Jeff Black, "ECB Coordinates with Fed to Lend Dollars to Euro-Area Banks," Bloomberg, September 15, 2011, www.bloomberg.com/news/articles/2011-09-15/ecb-coordinates-with-federal-reserve-in-lending-dollars-to-euro-area-banks.

112. Louise Armitstead and Jonathan Russell, "Christine Lagarde: IMF May Need Billions in Extra Funding," *Telegraph* (London), September 25, 2011, www.telegraph.co.uk/finance/financialcrisis/8788223/Christine-Lagarde-IMF-may-need-billions-in-extra-funding.html.

113. Binyamin Appelbaum, "Europe Seeks to Ratchet Up Effort on Debt," *New York Times*, September 24, 2011, www.nytimes.com/2011/09/25/business/geithner-tells-europe-it-must-work-together-on-debt-crisis.html.

114. Armitstead and Russell, "Christine Lagarde: IMF May Need Billions in Extra Funding."

115. Christian E. Weller, "December 2011," Center for American Progress, December 13, 2011, www.americanprogress.org/issues/economy/news/2011/12/13/10825/economic-snapshot-for-december-2011/.

116. "Italy's Sovereign Debt Rating Cut by S&P on Growth Fear," BBC News, September 20, 2011, www.bbc.co.uk/news/business-14981718.

117. "Italy Profile—Timeline," BBC News, December 14, 2016, www.bbc.co.uk/news/world-europe-17435616.

118. Robert Winnett, "Collapse of Euro Could Pose Threat to Peace, Says Angela Merkel," *Telegraph* (London), October 26, 2011, www.telegraph.co.uk/news/worldnews/europe/germany/8851912/Merkel-wins-rescue-fund-vote-after-raising-spectre-of-war.html.

119. www.reuters.com/article/us-greece-referendum-idUSTRE79U5PQ20111102.

120. Helena Smith, "Eurozone Crisis: Greek PM George Papandreou to Resign," *Guardian* (Manchester), November 6, 2011, www.theguardian.com/world/2011/nov/06/greece-george-papandreou.

121. Paola Di Caro, "Berlusconi: impegni vincolanti Se serve metteremo la fiducia," Corriere Della Sera, October 30, 2011, www.corriere.it/politica/11_ottobre_30/Berlusconi-impegni-vincolanti-Se-serve-metteremo-la-fiducia_13100140-02cf-11e1-8566-f96c33d2415f.shtml.

122. Jack Ewing, "European Central Bank, Under New Chief, Cuts Key Rate," *New York Times*, November 3, 2011, www.nytimes.com/2011/11/04/business/global/european-central-bank-cuts-rates-hoping-to-avert-downturn.html

123. "Change of Presidency of the European Central Bank" (press release), European Central Bank, November 1, 2011, www.ecb.europa.eu/press/pr/date/2011/html/pr111101.en.html.

124. Landon Thomas Jr. and Jack Ewing, "Can Super Mario Save the Day for Europe?" *New York Times*, October 29, 2011, www.nytimes.com/2011/10/30/business/mario-draghi-into-the-eye-of-europes-financial-storm.html.

125. "Monetary Policy Decisions" (press release), European Central Bank, November 3, 2011, www.ecb.europa.eu/press/pr/date/2011/html/pr111103.en.html.

126. "Forex—Euro Falls to Fresh Session Low vs Dollar," Reuters, November 23, 2011, www.reuters.com/article/markets-forex-idUSN1E7AM0OR20111123.

127. "The President of the European Central Bank: Mario Draghi," European Central Bank, www.ecb.europa.eu/ecb/orga/decisions/html/cvdraghi.en.html.

128. Leon Mangasarian, "New Greek Premier Papademos Must Save Country's Euro Membership," Bloomberg, November 10, 2011, www.bloomberg.com/news/articles/2011-11-10/papademos-who-took-greece-into-euro-must-now-save-country-s-membership.

129. Catarina Saraiva, "Dollar Status Grows as Foreign Banks Double Deposits at Fed," Bloomberg, November 21, 2011, www.bloomberg.com/news/articles/2011-11-21/dollar-preeminence-grows-as-foreign-banks-double-deposits-at-new-york-fed.

130. "Coordinated Central Bank Action to Address Pressures in Global Money Markets" (press release), European Central Bank, November 30, 3011, www.ecb.europa.eu/press/pr/date/2011/html/pr111130.en.html.

131. Matthew Holehouse, "ECB's Draghi: We Need Fiscal Union, Not Bank Intervention," *Telegraph* (London), December 1, 2011, www.telegraph.co.uk/finance/financialcrisis/8927918/ECBs-Draghi-We-need-fiscal-union-not-bank-intervention.html.

132. Jackie Calmes, "Spotlight Fixed on Geithner, a Man Obama Fought to Keep," *New York Times*, November 12, 2011, www.nytimes.com/2011/11/13/us/politics/spotlight-fixed-on-geithner-a-man-obama-fought-to-keep.html.

133. Zachary A. Goldfarb and Neil Irwin, "US Officials Quietly Cajole European Leaders on Debt Crisis," *Washington Post*, December 6, 2011, www.washingtonpost.com/business/economy/us-officials-quietly-cajole-european-leaders-on-debt-crisis/2011/12/06/gIQAywMxaO_story.html.

134. David Lawder, "Geithner to Add US Weight to Euro Zone Talks," Reuters, December 6, 2011, www.reuters.com/article/us-eurozone-usa-geithner/geithner-to-add-u-s-weight-to-euro-zone-talks-idUSTRE7B50GG20111206.

135. Ibid.

136. Ibid.

137. "Monetary Policy Decisions" (press release), European Central Bank, December 8, 2011, www.ecb.europa.eu/press/pr/date/2011/html/pr111208.en.html.

138. Bloomberg, "Federal Reserve Bank of New York President William Dudley 'Can't Imagine' US Buying European Debt," *Telegraph* (London), December 16,

2011, www.telegraph.co.uk/finance/financialcrisis/8962428/Federal-Reserve
-Bank-of-New-York-president-William-Dudley-cant-imagine-US-buying-European
-debt.html.

139. Ibid.

140. Benoît Cœuré, "Financing the Economy of the Euro Area: The ECB's Role" (speech, Association Française des Tresoriers d'Entreprises, Paris, April 11, 2012), www.ecb
.europa.eu/press/key/date/2012/html/sp120411.en.html.

141. Dominic Rushe, "Markets Surge as Fed and Central Banks Step In to Try to Prevent Credit Crunch," *Guardian* (Manchester), November 30, 2011, www.theguardian.com/
business/2011/nov/30/markets-surge-central-banks-action.

142. "Spain Election: Rajoy's Popular Party Declares Victory," BBC News, November 20, 2011, www.bbc.com/news/world-europe-15809062.

143. "Spain's Reform Example," *Wall Street Journal,* October 29, 2014, www.wsj.com/
articles/spains-reform-example-1414539336.

144. Catarina Saraiva, "Euro Falls Below 100 Yen, 1st Time Since 2001; Aussie, Kiwi Rise," Bloomberg, December 30, 2011, www.bloomberg.com/news/articles/2011-12-30/euro
-trades-near-decade-low-versus-yen-as-european-crisis-weighs-on-growth.

145. Michael Estrin, "What If the Euro Fails?" Bankrate, December 19, 2011, http://www
.bankrate.com/investing/what-if-the-euro-fails/.

146. Maureen Farrell, "ECB Cuts Rates to All-Time Low," CNN Money, July 5, 2012, http://money.cnn.com/2012/07/05/investing/ecb/index.htm.

147. John Lichfield, "Franco-German Relations Cool over Eurozone Crisis," *Independent* (London), June 8, 2010, www.independent.co.uk/news/world/europe/franco-german
-relations-cool-over-eurozone-crisis-1994953.html.

148. Matthias Sobolewski and Dina Kyriakidou, "S&P Downgrades Nine Euro Zone Countries," Reuters, January 13, 2012, www.reuters.com/article/us-eurozone-sp
-idUSTRE80C1BC20120114.

149. "IMF: Global Economy 'in Danger Zone' over Euro Crisis," BBC News, January 24, 2012, www.bbc.com/news/business-16699807.

150. Annalyn Censky, "Bernanke: Fed Will Protect US Economy from Europe," CNN Money, February 3, 2012, http://money.cnn.com/2012/02/02/news/economy/
bernanke_congress_europe/.

151. Ben S. Bernanke, "The Economic Outlook and the Federal Budget Situation" (testimony before the Committee on the Budget, US House of Representatives, Washington, DC, February 2, 2012), www.federalreserve.gov/newsevents/testimony/
bernanke20120202a.htm.

152. Graeme Wearden and Helena Smith, "Eurozone Reaches Deal on Second Greece Bailout After All-Night Talks," *Guardian* (Manchester), February 21, 2012, www.theguardian.com/business/2012/feb/21/eurozone-reaches-second-greece-bailout
-deal.

153. Miranda Xafa, "Lessons from the 2012 Greek Debt Restructuring," Vox, June 25, 2014, www.voxeu.org/article/greek-debt-restructuring-lessons-learned.

154. Ben Bernanke, "2012 Economic Outlook," C-SPAN, February 2, 2012, www.c-span
.org/video/?304151-1/2012-economic-outlook.

155. "Draghi Attacks Bankers over ECB Fears," *Financial Times,* February 9, 2012.

156. Ibid.

157. Ian Traynor, "ECB to Launch Second Wave of Euro 'Quantitative Easing,'" *Guardian* (Manchester), February 28, 2012, www.theguardian.com/business/2012/feb/28/european-central-bank-euro-eurozone.

158. Paul Carrel, "ECB Offers Banks Second, Maybe Last, Mega Funds Fix," Reuters, February 28, 2012, www.reuters.com/article/ecb-ltro-idINDEE81S00K20120229.

159. Richard Milne and Mary Watkins, "European Finance: The Leaning Tower of Perils," IGF, March 28, 2012, www.omegaigf.com/noticiaDetalle.aspx?area=2&cnoti=12912&off=0.

160. Gertrude Chavez-Dreyfuss, "Euro Rises to 3-Week High, May Pull Back Next Week," Reuters, March 23, 2012, www.reuters.com/article/us-markets-forex-idUSBRE82D0IJ20120323.

161. Tom Kington, "Anti-Austerity Parties Ride Protest Vote in Italian Local Elections," *Guardian* (Manchester), May 8, 2012, www.theguardian.com/world/2012/may/08/anti-austerity-italian-local-elections.

162. "'A Political Implosion': Anti-Austerity Parties Win Historic French and Greek Elections," Democracy Now!, May 7, 2012, www.democracynow.org/2012/5/7/a_political_implosion_anti_austerity_parties.

163. "Italy's Sovereign Debt Hits Record High," Deutsche Welle, July 14, 2015, www.dw.com/en/italys-sovereign-debt-hits-record-high/a-18583683.

164. Ben Rooney, "Draghi Says Euro Is 'Unsustainable' Without Action," CNN Money, May 31, 2012, http://money.cnn.com/2012/05/31/investing/ecb-draghi/.

165. Mario Draghi and Vítor Constâncio, "Introductory Statement to the Press Conference (with Q&A)," European Central Bank, June 6, 2012, www.ecb.europa.eu/press/pressconf/2012/html/is120606.en.html.

166. Ibid.

167. "Bundesbank: Germany Walks Fine Line in Euro Crisis," *Financial Times*, June 8, 2012, https://next.ft.com/content/1614cd0a-9f67-11e1-a255-00144feabdc0.

168. Helena Smith, "Athens Descends into Violence as 200,000 March against Austerity," *Guardian* (Manchester), September 26, 2012, www.theguardian.com/world/2012/sep/26/greece-violence-general-strike-austerity.

169. "Monetary Policy Decisions" (press release), European Central Bank, July 5, 2012, www.ecb.europa.eu/press/pr/date/2012/html/pr120705.en.html.

170. Mario Draghi and Vítor Constâncio, "Introductory Statement to the Press Conference (with Q&A)," European Central Bank, July 5, 2012, www.ecb.europa.eu/press/pressconf/2012/html/is120705.en.html.

171. Ibid.

172. Joseph Ciolli, "Euro Falls versus Most Major Peers Before Confidence Data," Bloomberg, July 20, 2012, www.bloomberg.com/news/articles/2012-07-19/euro-set-for-weekly-decline-against-yen-before-confidence-data.

173. Ambrose Evans-Pritchard, "Spanish Debt Crisis Returns as Germany Nears Bailout Fatigue," *Telegraph* (London), July 19, 2012, www.telegraph.co.uk/finance/financialcrisis/9413545/Spanish-debt-crisis-returns-as-Germany-nears-bailout-fatigue.html.

174. "2012 Article IV Consultation with the Euro Area—Concluding Statement of IMF Mission," International Monetary Fund, June 21, 2012, www.imf.org/en/News/Articles/2015/09/28/04/52/mcs062112.

175. Mario Draghi, "Verbatim of the Remarks Made by Mario Draghi" (at the Global Investment Conference, London, July 26, 2012), www.ecb.europa.eu/press/key/date/2012/html/sp120726.en.html.

176. "ECB Signals Resolve to Save Euro," *Financial Times,* September 6, 2012, http://www.ftchinese.com/story/001046436/en.

177. Tony Paterson, "Mario Draghi in Lion's Den: ECB Head Will Confront German Critics," *Independent* (London), September 14, 2012, www.independent.co.uk/news/world/europe/mario-draghi-in-lions-den-ecb-head-will-confront-german-critics-8139962.html.

178. Ibid.

179. Ibid.

180. www.zdf.de/politik/maybrit-illner.

181. Andreas Rinke, "Merkel Wins Support for ECB Bond-Buying Stance," Reuters, September 10, 2012, http://uk.reuters.com/article/uk-eurozone-ecb-germany-idUKBRE8890DY20120910.

182. "Federal Reserve Issues FOMC Statement" (press release), Board of Governors of the Federal Reserve System, September 13, 2012, www.federalreserve.gov/newsevents/press/monetary/20120913a.htm.

183. Julie Haviv and Gertrude Chavez-Dreyfuss, "Yen Posts Worst Week Since February versus Dollar; Euro Falls," Reuters, November 15, 2012, www.reuters.com/article/us-markets-forex-idUSBRE8A70Q320121116.

184. Ben S. Bernanke, "The Economic Recovery and Economic Policy" (speech at the Economic Club of New York, New York, November 20, 2012), www.federalreserve.gov/newsevents/speech/bernanke20121120a.htm.

185. "Federal Reserve and Other Central Banks Announce an Extension of the Existing Temporary US Dollar Liquidity Swap Arrangements through February 1, 2014" (press release), Board of Governors of the Federal Reserve System, December 13, 2012, www.federalreserve.gov/newsevents/press/monetary/20121213a.htm.

186. "Federal Reserve Issues FOMC Statement" (press release), Board of Governors of the Federal Reserve System, December 12, 2012, www.federalreserve.gov/newsevents/press/monetary/20121212a.htm.

187. Jon Hilsenrath and Brian Blackstone, "Inside the Risky Bets of Central Banks," *Wall Street Journal,* December 12, 2012, www.wsj.com/articles/SB10001424127887323717004578157152464486598.

CHAPTER 6: EUROPE PART II: THE DRAGHI MONEY MACHINE

1. Gavin Jones, "Mario Draghi: The Rise of 'Mr Somewhere Else,'" Reuters, April 26, 2011, www.reuters.com/article/us-ecb-draghi-idUSTRE73P4EF20110426.

2. "Mario Draghi: Current Member Biography," Group of Thirty, http://group30.org/members/bio_current/Draghi.

3. "The Changing Role of the European Central Bank" (discussion at Brookings Institution, Washington, DC, November 2, 2011), www.brookings.edu/events/the-changing-role-of-the-european-central-bank/.

4. Landon Thomas Jr. and Jack Ewing, "Can Super Mario Save the Day for Europe?" *New York Times*, October 29, 2011, www.nytimes.com/2011/10/30/business/mario-draghi-into-the-eye-of-europes-financial-storm.html.

5. Though even that was down 29 percent by March 2012 compared to the prior year, and Germany had recorded its lowest growth for a quarter since 2002. Floyd Norris, "Outside Europe, German Trade Surplus Soars," *New York Times*, May 11, 2012, www.nytimes.com/2012/05/12/business/economy/outside-europe-german-trade-surplus-soars-off-the-charts.html.

6. "France's Hollande: Euro Zone Must Ensure Stable Currency," Reuters, February 5, 2013, www.reuters.com/article/us-eu-france-idUSBRE9140DD20130205.

7. "Xi Concludes South Africa Trip," Embassy of the People's Republic of China in the Republic of South Africa, March 29, 2013, http://za.china-embassy.org/eng/znjl/t1027029.htm.

8. Denise Roland, "Merkel Falters on Economic Unity in Eurozone," *Telegraph* (London), April 25, 2013, www.telegraph.co.uk/finance/financialcrisis/10017915/Merkel-falters-on-economic-unity-in-eurozone.html.

9. Elizabeth Pineau, "French Socialists Call for Tougher Stance on Merkel," Reuters, April 26, 2013, www.reuters.com/article/uk-france-socialists-idUKBRE93P14Z20130426.

10. Michael Steen, "Merkel Speech Highlights European Divide," *Financial Times*, April 25, 2013, www.ft.com/content/665e1018-adae-11e2-a2c7-00144feabdc0.

11. Mario Draghi and Vítor Constâncio, "Introductory Statement to the Press Conference (with Q&A)," European Central Bank, May 2, 2013, www.ecb.europa.eu/press/pressconf/2013/html/is130502.en.html.

12. Rajeshni Naidu-Ghelani, "European Banks Haven't Been This Cheap Since 80s," CNBC, May 30, 2013, www.cnbc.com/id/100775405.

13. "The New Sick Man of Europe: the European Union," Pew Research Center, May 13, 2013, www.pewglobal.org/2013/05/13/the-new-sick-man-of-europe-the-european-union/.

14. Heather Stewart, "Eurozone Interest Rates Cut to a Record Low of 0.5%," *Guardian* (Manchester), May 2, 2013, www.theguardian.com/business/2013/may/02/eurozone-interest-rates-ecb.

15. Larry Elliott and Helena Smith, "IMF 'to Admit Mistakes' in Handling Greek Debt Crisis and Bailout," *Guardian* (Manchester), June 5, 2013, www.theguardian.com/business/2013/jun/05/imf-admit-mistakes-greek-crisis-austerity.

16. Ibid.

17. "Mario Draghi Faces Dilemma over Eurozone Inflation Level," *Financial Times*, October 16, 2013.

18. *Greece: Ex Post Evaluation of Exceptional Access under the 2010 Stand-By Arrangement* (IMF Country Report No. 13/156, International Monetary Fund, Washington, DC, June 2013), www.imf.org/external/pubs/ft/scr/2013/cr13156.pdf.

19. Alister Bull and Pedro da Costa, "Bernanke Says Fed Likely to Reduce Bond Buying This Year," Reuters, June 19, 2013, www.reuters.com/article/us-usa-fed-idUSBRE95I05P20130619.

20. Anna Yukhananov, "Update 1—IMF: Greece Making Progress but Must Do More on Taxes," Reuters, May 6, 2013, www.reuters.com/article/imf-greece-idUSL2N0DN0 FO20130506.
21. Marcus Bensasson and Eleni Chrepa, "Greece's Labor Unions Hold General Strike Over Job Cuts," Bloomberg, July 16, 2013, www.bloomberg.com/news/articles/2013-07-16/greece-s-labor-unions-hold-general-strike-over-job-cuts.
22. Matthew Boesler, "Italian Recession Becomes Longest on Record," *Business Insider*, August 6, 2013, www.businessinsider.com/italian-recession-now-longest-on-record-2013-8.
23. "ECB and the People's Bank of China Establish a Bilateral Currency Swap Agreement" (press release), European Central Bank, October 10, 2013, www.ecb.europa.eu/press/pr/date/2013/html/pr131010.en.html.
24. Alanna Petroff, "Europe, China Agree Currency Deal," CNN Money, October 10, 2013, http://money.cnn.com/2013/10/10/news/economy/ecb-china-currency/index.html?iid=EL.
25. Mario Draghi and Vítor Constâncio, "Introductory Statement to the Press Conference (with Q&A)," European Central Bank, October 2, 2013, www.ecb.europa.eu/press/pressconf/2013/html/is131002.en.html.
26. "ECB Establishes Standing Swap Arrangements with Other Central Banks" (press release), European Central Bank, October 31, 2013, www.ecb.europa.eu/press/pr/date/2013/html/pr131031.en.html.
27. Ian Traynor, "Austerity Pushing Europe into Social and Economic Decline, Says Red Cross," *Guardian* (Manchester), October 10, 2013, www.theguardian.com/world/2013/oct/10/austerity-europe-debt-red-cross.
28. Ibid.
29. Ibid.
30. Mario Draghi, "Introductory Statement to the Press Conference (with Q&A)," European Central Bank, November 7, 2013, www.ecb.europa.eu/press/pressconf/2013/html/is131107.en.html.
31. Eva Taylor, "ECB Cuts Rates to New Low, Ready to Do More If Needed," Reuters, November 6, 2013, www.reuters.com/article/us-ecb-rates-idUSBRE9A600O20131107.
32. Fion Li, "Yuan Passes Euro as 2nd-Most Used Trade-Finance Currency," Bloomberg, December 3, 2013, www.bloomberg.com/news/articles/2013-12-03/yuan-passes-euro-to-be-second-most-used-trade-finance-currency.
33. Wanfeng Zhou, "Euro Rises to More Than 2-Year High vs. Dollar; Yen Falls," Reuters, December 26, 2013, www.reuters.com/article/us-markets-forex-idUSBRE9BJ0EF20131227.
34. Phillip Inman, "Euro Plummets After ECB Warns Currency Zone May Need More Support," *Guardian* (Manchester), January 9, 2014, www.theguardian.com/business/2014/jan/09/euro-european-central-bank-unemployment-inflation.
35. Ibid.
36. Ibid.
37. Janet L. Yellen, "Monetary Policy and Financial Stability" (speech, 2014 Michel Camdessus Central Banking Lecture, International Monetary Fund, Washington, DC, July 2, 2014), www.federalreserve.gov/newsevents/speech/yellen20140702a.htm.

38. "Monetary Policy Decisions" (press release), European Central Bank, June 5, 2014, www
    .ecb.europa.eu/press/pr/date/2014/html/pr140605.en.html.

39. Benoît Cœuré, "Assessing the Implications of Negative Interest Rates" (speech, Yale
    Financial Crisis Forum, Yale School of Management, New Haven, CT, July 28, 2016),
    www.ecb.europa.eu/press/key/date/2016/html/sp160728.en.html.

40. Mario Draghi, "Introductory Statement to the Press Conference (with Q&A)," Eu-
    ropean Central Bank, June 5, 2014, www.ecb.europa.eu/press/pressconf/2014/html/
    is140605.en.html.

41. Ibid.

42. Alessandro Speciale and Andre Tartar, "Draghi Seen Delivering $1 Trillion to
    Banks in ECB Offer," Bloomberg, July 14, 2014, www.bloomberg.com/news/
    articles/2014-07-13/draghi-seen-delivering-1-trillion-free-lunch-to-banks.

43. John O'Donnell and Eva Taylor, "ECB Hurls Cash at Sluggish Euro Zone Economy,
    Says Not Done Yet," Reuters, June 5, 2014, www.reuters.com/article/us-ecb-rates
    -decision-idUSKBN0EG1EN20140605.

44. "Eurozone Inflation Slips Further into the 'Danger Zone,'" BBC News, July 31, 2014,
    www.bbc.com/news/business-28583232.

45. Jaime Caruana, "Stepping Out of the Shadow of the Crisis: Three Transitions for the
    World Economy" (speech, Bank for International Settlements Annual General Meeting,
    Basel, Switzerland, June 29, 2014), www.bis.org/speeches/sp140629.pdf.

46. "IMF Executive Board Concludes 2014 Article IV Consultation on Euro Area Policies"
    (press release), International Monetary Fund, July 14, 2014, www.imf.org/external/np/
    sec/pr/2014/pr14341.htm.

47. "Monetary Policy Decisions" (press release), European Central Bank, September 4,
    2014, www.ecb.europa.eu/press/pr/date/2014/html/pr140904.en.html.

48. Ibid.

49. Ian Chua and Cecile Lefort, "G20 Says Nearing Growth Goal, but More Needed
    from Europe," Reuters, September 20, 2014, www.reuters.com/article/us-g20-australia
    -idUSKBN0HE0PD20140921.

50. Jia Lynn Yang, "Jack Lew Had Major Role at Citigroup When It Nearly Imploded,"
    Washington Post, January 10, 2013, www.washingtonpost.com/business/economy/jack
    -lew-had-major-role-at-citigroup-when-it-nearly-imploded/2013/01/10/a913431e-5b6b
    -11e2-9fa9-5fbdc9530eb9_story.html?utm_term=.ab8fe88b2517.

51. "Head of Germany's Central Bank Criticises ECB Stimulus Plan," Reuters, Septem-
    ber 21, 2014, http://uk.reuters.com/article/uk-ecb-policy-weidmann-idUKKBN
    0HG07Z20140921.

52. Stefan Riecher and Alessandro Speciale, "Draghi Sees ECB Becoming More Active in
    Fight for Euro," Bloomberg, September 22, 2014, www.bloomberg.com/news/articles/
    2014-09-22/draghi-says-risks-to-euro-area-economy-clearly-on-the-downside.

53. "Mario Draghi: Interview with Lithuanian Business Daily Verslo Zinios," by Dalius
    Simenas, Bank for International Settlements, September 25, 2014, www.bis.org/review/
    r140926d.htm.

54. "Dollar-Yen Breaches 110 for First Time Since 2008," CNBC, September 30, 2014,
    www.cnbc.com/2014/09/30/dollar-yen-rises-above-110-for-first-time-since-august
    -2008.html.

55. Michael Flaherty and Jonathan Spicer, "US Fed Frets over Strong Dollar, Global Woes: Minutes," Reuters, October 8, 2014, www.reuters.com/article/us-usa-fed-idUSKCN0HX20M20141008.

56. Mario Draghi, statement (at the thirtieth meeting of the IMFC, Washington, DC, October 10, 2014), www.ecb.europa.eu/press/key/date/2014/html/sp141010.en.html.

57. "Euro to Fall Below Parity with Dollar by 2017—Deutsche," Reuters, October 7, 2014, www.reuters.com/article/markets-forex-deutsche-idUSL6N0S214220141007.

58. Mario Draghi, "Monetary Policy in the Euro Area" (keynote speech, Frankfurt European Banking Congress, Frankfurt am Main, November 21, 2014), www.ecb.europa.eu/press/key/date/2014/html/sp141121.en.html.

59. Phillip Inman, "ECB to Spend €1 Trillion on Covered Bonds to Kickstart Euro Economy," *Guardian* (Manchester), October 20, 2014, www.theguardian.com/world/2014/oct/20/ecb-to-pump-one-trillion-euros-into-eurozone.

60. Jeff Black, "ECB Fails 25 Banks as Italy Fares Worst in Stress Test," Bloomberg, October 26, 2014, www.bloomberg.com/news/articles/2014-10-26/ecb-test-shows-25-billion-euro-capital-gap-at-euro-banks.

61. Heidi Moore, "The Fed Has Quietly Ended Its Stimulus. Now the Hard Work Really Begins," *Guardian* (Manchester), October 29, 2014, www.theguardian.com/business/2014/oct/29/fed-quietly-ends-stimulus-hard-work.

62. Pedro Nicolaci da Costa, "Janet Yellen Says Fed Can't Ignore World Economy," Real Time Economics (blog), *Wall Street Journal*, November 13, 2014, http://blogs.wsj.com/economics/2014/11/13/yellen-says-fed-cant-ignore-world-economy/.

63. "Lew Warns of European 'Lost Decade,'" *Financial Times*, November 12, 2014, https://next.ft.com/content/23d79946-6a89-11e4-a038-00144feabdc0.

64. "Dovish Draghi Boosts Hopes of ECB Stimulus," *Financial Times*, November 21, 2014, https://next.ft.com/content/e2bcc510-7160-11e4-818e-00144feabdc0.

65. Mario Draghi, "Monetary Policy in the Euro Area" (keynote speech).

66. Mario Draghi, "Introductory Statement to the Press Conference (with Q&A)," European Central Bank, December 4, 2014, www.ecb.europa.eu/press/pressconf/2014/html/is141204.en.html.

67. "Euro Touches a Nine-Year Low against US Dollar," BBC News, January 5, 2015, www.bbc.com/news/business-30678218.

68. Mario Draghi, "Introductory Statement to the Press Conference (with Q&A)," European Central Bank, January 22, 2015, www.ecb.europa.eu/press/pressconf/2015/html/is150122.en.html.

69. "France's Hollande Says Euro Zone Membership 'Up to Greeks,'" Reuters, January 5, 2015, http://uk.reuters.com/article/us-france-hollande-greece-idUKKBN0KE0H820150105?mod=related&channelName=economyNews.

70. Jochen Hung, "Germany Isn't the Big Bad Boss of Europe," *Guardian* (Manchester), February 5, 2015, www.theguardian.com/commentisfree/2015/feb/05/germany-not-big-bad-boss-europe-economies.

71. Mario Draghi, "Introductory Statement to the Press Conference (with Q&A)," European Central Bank, January 22, 2015, www.ecb.europa.eu/press/pressconf/2015/html/is150122.en.html.

72. Kate Gibson, "Markets Primed for ECB Debt-Buying Splurge," CNBC, January 21, 2015, www.cnbc.com/2015/01/21/markets-primed-for-ecb-debt-buying-splurge.html.

73. P.W., "The Launch of Euro-Style QE," Free Exchange (blog), *Economist,* January 22, 2015, www.economist.com/blogs/freeexchange/2015/01/ecb-makes-its-mind-up.

74. Liz Alderman, "New Leader in Greece Now Faces Creditors," *New York Times,* January 26, 2015, www.nytimes.com/2015/01/27/business/international/after-vote-in-greece-alexis -tsipras-seeks-to-address-debt.html.

75. "Berlin Insists It Expects Greece to Remain in Eurozone," *Financial Times,* January 4, 2015, www.ft.com/intl/cms/s/0/7e0064d4-941e-11e4-82c7-00144feabdc0 .html#axzz3yuL5Bhl9.

76. "Asset Purchase Programmes," European Central Bank, www.ecb.europa.eu/mopo/ implement/omt/html/index.en.html.

77. Brian Blackstone and Ian Talley, "ECB's Draghi Rejects Talk of Greek Euro Exit," *Wall Street Journal,* April 18, 2015, www.wsj.com/articles/ecbs-draghi-rejects-talk -of-greek-exit-from-euro-1429381951.

78. Ibid.

79. Ian Talley and Gabriele Steinhauser, "IMF Official Sees Greek Bailout Needing Several More Weeks of Talks," *Wall Street Journal,* April 17, 2015, http://linkis.com/www.wsj .com/articles/tR2jY?next=1.

80. Blackstone and Talley, "ECB's Draghi Rejects Talk of Greek Euro Exit."

81. Yanis Varoufakis, *And the Weak Suffer What They Must? Europe's Crisis and America's Economic Future* (New York: Nation Books, 2016).

82. "Draghi Says 'Get Used to' Bond Volatility," *Financial Times,* June 3, 2015, www.ft.com/ content/6735194c-09c2-11e5-b6bd-00144feabdc0; John Ficenec, "German Bond Yields Jump After Mario Draghi's 'Volatile' Comments," *Telegraph* (London), June 3, 2015, www.telegraph.co.uk/finance/economics/11649376/German-bond-yields-jump-after -Mario-Draghis-volatile-comments.html.

83. Virginia Harrison and Chris Liakos, "Greece Defaults on $1.7 Billion IMF Payment," CNN Money, June 30, 2015, http://money.cnn.com/2015/06/30/news/economy/ greece-imf-default/.

84. Ivo Oliveira and Paul Dallison, "Varoufakis: Schäuble Will Bring Troika to Paris," Politico, August 3, 2015, updated August 4, 2015, www.politico.eu/article/varoufakis -schauble-troika-paris-madrid-athens-eurogroup-grexit/.

85. Ibid.

86. Anmar Frangoul, "Slap in the Face for Rajoy? Spain Goes to the Polls," CNBC, December 18, 2015, www.cnbc.com/2015/12/18/spain-goes-to-polls-in-general-election .html.

87. Mike Bird, "Italy's Youth Unemployment Just Hit a New Record High—Here's What's Going Wrong," *Business Insider,* July 31, 2015, www.businessinsider.com/italys-youth -unemployment-just-hit-a-new-record-high-heres-whats-going-wrong-2015-7.

88. Ansuya Harjani, "Trichet to Fed: Ignore the IMF, World Bank," CNBC, September 15, 2015, www.cnbc.com/2015/09/15/trichet-to-fed-ignore-the-imf-world-bank.html.

89. "Flash Estimate for the Third Quarter of 2015" (news release), Eurostat NewsRelease EuroIndicators 199/2015, November 13, 2015, http://ec.europa.eu/eurostat/documents/ 2995521/7075215/2-13112015-BP-EN.pdf/b1b2ad4f-32ef-4737-abbe-5dc7b91dd1bb.

90. Matthew Holehouse, "George Osborne Tells Merkel: Give Us EU Reform If You Want to Save the Euro," *Telegraph* (London), November 3, 2015, www.telegraph.co .uk/news/politics/georgeosborne/11973239/George-Osborne-tells-Merkel-Give-us -EU-reform-if-you-want-to-save-the-euro.html.

91. George Osborne, speech to the BDI conference in Berlin, November 3, 2015, www .gov.uk/government/speeches/let-britain-and-germany-work-together-as-partners-for -a-european-union-that-works-better-for-all-of-us-says-chancellor.

92. Steve Swinford, "Angela Merkel Urges Britain to 'Stay in' the European Union," *Telegraph* (London), November 3, 2015, www.telegraph.co.uk/news/newstopics/eurcferen dum/11972490/Angela-Merkel-urges-Britain-to-stay-in-the-European-Union.html.

93. Lotte Jeffs, "The Crush: Mark Carney," *Evening Standard* (London), July 3, 2014, www .standard.co.uk/lifestyle/esmagazine/the-crush-mark-carney-9581450.html.

94. Graeme Wearden, "Bank of England: Governor Carney Has 'No Regrets' After Leaving Rates Unchanged Again—Live," *Guardian* (Manchester), November 5, 2015, www.theguardian.com/business/live/2015/nov/05/bank-of-england-super-thursday -volkswagen-vw-sales-slump-business-live.

95. Mark Carney, introduction to the Bank of England Open Forum, London, November 11, 2015, www.bis.org/review/r151116c.htm.

96. "Monetary Policy Decisions" (press release), European Central Bank, December 3, 2015, www.ecb.europa.eu/press/pr/date/2015/html/pr151203.en.html.

97. Benoît Cœuré, "The Transmission of the ECB's Monetary Policy in Standard and Non-Standard Times" (speech, "Monetary Policy in Non-Standard Times" workshop, European Central Bank, Frankfurt am Main, September 11, 2017), www.ecb.europa.eu/ press/key/date/2017/html/ecb.sp170911.en.html.

98. Rachel Evans, "Euro Climbs as ECB's Mersch Fails to Damp Best Month Since April," Bloomberg, December 28, 2015, www.bloomberg.com/news/articles/2015-12-28/euro -climbs-as-ecb-s-mersch-fails-to-damp-best-month-since-april.

99. James Ramage, "Dollar Rises Against Euro," *Wall Street Journal*, December 23, 2015, www.wsj.com/articles/dollar-rises-against-euro-1450893130.

100. Claudio Borio, Enisse Kharroubi, Christian Upper, and Fabrizio Zampolli, "Labour Reallocation and Productivity Dynamics: Financial Causes, Real Consequences" (BIS Working Papers No. 534, Bank for International Settlements, Monetary and Economic Department, Basel, Switzerland, December 2015), www.bis.org/publ/work534.pdf.

101. Richard Dobbs, Susan Lund, Jonathan Woetzel, and Mina Mutafchieva, "Debt and (Not Much) Deleveraging" (report, McKinsey Global Institute, February 2015), www.mckinsey .com/global-themes/employment-and-growth/debt-and-not-much-deleveraging.

102. "Subdued Demand, Diminished Prospects," *World Economic Outlook Update*, January 19, 2016, www.imf.org/external/pubs/ft/weo/2016/update/01/pdf/0116.pdf.

103. Ibid.

104. Duncan Mavin, "Italy's Banking Fiasco," Bloomberg Gadfly, January 20, 2016, www .bloomberg.com/gadfly/articles/2016-01-20/italy-banking-crisis-could-be-helped-by -paschi-intesa-deal.

105. Mario Draghi and Vítor Constâncio, "Declaração introdutória à conferência de imprensa," European Central Bank, January 21, 2016, www.ecb.europa.eu/press/press-conf/2016/html/is160121.pt.html.

106. Mario Draghi and Vítor Constâncio, "Introductory Statement to the Press Conference (with Q&A)," European Central Bank, January 21, 2016, www.ecb.europa.eu/press/pressconf/2016/html/is160121.en.html.

107. "Federal Reserve Issues FOMC Statement" (press release), Board of Governors of the Federal Reserve System, January 27, 2016, www.federalreserve.gov/newsevents/press/monetary/20160127a.htm.

108. Ann Saphir and Jonathan Spicer, "Fed Again Poised to Cut Longer-Run Interest Rate Forecast," Reuters, September 20, 2016, www.reuters.com/article/us-usa-fed-forecasts-analysis-idUSKCN11Q0EL.

109. Natasha Doff and Rachel Butt, "Emerging-Markets Rise on Fed as Ruble, Ringgit Gains with Oil," Bloomberg, January 27, 2016, updated on January 27, 2016, www.bloomberg.com/news/articles/2016-01-28/emerging-stocks-rise-on-fed-as-ringgit-leads-gains-in-currencies.

110. Communiqué, G20 Finance Ministers and Central Bank Governors Meeting, Shanghai, February 27, 2016, www.g20.utoronto.ca/2016/160227-finance-en.html.

111. Morten Linnemann Bech and Aytek Malkhozov, "How Have Central Banks Implemented Negative Policy Rates?" Bank for International Settlements, March 6, 2016, www.bis.org/publ/qtrpdf/r_qt1603e.htm.

112. "Monetary Policy Decisions" (press release), European Central Bank, March 10, 2016, www.ecb.europa.eu/press/pr/date/2016/html/pr160310.en.html.

113. Mario Draghi and Vítor Constâncio, "Introductory Statement to the Press Conference (with Q&A)," European Central Bank, March 10, 2016, www.ecb.europa.eu/press/pressconf/2016/html/is160310.en.html.

114. Ibid.

115. Ibid.

116. www.chinapost.com.tw/business/europe/2016/03/21/461284/bundesbank-boss.htm.

117. Rebecca Christie and Karl Stagno Navarra, "Draghi Said to Tell EU Leaders 'No Alternative' to ECB Rate Cuts," Bloomberg, March 17, 2016, www.bloomberg.com/news/articles/2016-03-17/draghi-said-to-tell-eu-leaders-no-alternative-to-ecb-rate-cuts-ilwq89vk.

118. Steve Liesman, "Fed Chair Yellen Has a Mini Revolt on Her Hands," CNBC, March 23, 2016, www.cnbc.com/2016/03/23/fed-chair-yellen-has-a-mini-revolt-on-her-hands-as-dissenters-emerge.html.

119. Andrew Mayeda and Mark Deen, "Zhou, Finance Chiefs to Discuss Crisis Planning in Paris Forum," Bloomberg, March 29, 2016, www.bloomberg.com/news/articles/2016-03-29/zhou-finance-chiefs-to-discuss-crisis-planning-in-paris-forum.

120. "Germany Takes Aim at the European Central Bank," *Spiegel Online,* April 8, 2016, www.spiegel.de/international/europe/conflict-grows-between-germany-and-the-ecb-a-1086245.html.

121. "Germany Blames Mario Draghi for Rise of Rightwing AfD Party," *Financial Times,* April 10, 2016, https://next.ft.com/content/bc0175c4-ff2b-11e5-9cc4-27926f2b110c.

122. "Germany's Gabriel Says ECB Policy Expropriates 'Little People,'" Reuters, April 8, 2016, www.reuters.com/article/ecb-policy-germany-idUSB4N12S022.

123. "Communiqué, G20 Finance Ministers and Central Bank Governors Meeting," International Monetary Fund, Washington, DC, April 15, 2016, www.imf.org/external/np/cm/2016/041616.htm.

124. Mario Draghi and Vítor Constâncio, "Introductory Statement to the Press Conference (with Q&A)," European Central Bank, April 21, 2016, www.ecb.europa.eu/press/pressconf/2016/html/is160421.en.html.

125. Mario Draghi, "Interview with Bild," by Kai Diekmann, Nikolaus Blome, and Daniel Biskup, European Central Bank, April 25, 2016, published April 28, 2016, www.ecb.europa.eu/press/inter/date/2016/html/sp160428.en.html.

126. Ibid.

127. Ibid.

128. Mario Draghi, "Addressing the Causes of Low Interest Rates" (introductory speech, "The Future of Financial Markets: A Changing View of Asia" panel, Annual Meeting of the Asian Development Bank, Frankfurt am Main, May 2, 2016), www.ecb.europa.eu/press/key/date/2016/html/sp160502.en.html.

129. "German Current Account Surplus to Hit Record, World's Largest in 2016: Ifo," Reuters, January 30, 2017, www.reuters.com/article/us-germany-economy-trade-idUSKBN15E0W4.

130. "ECB's Villeroy Says Draghi Criticism 'Excessive and Dangerous': Report," Reuters, May 25, 2016, www.reuters.com/article/us-ecb-policy-villeroy-draghi-idUSKCN0YG0KL.

131. Ibid.

132. "Brexit 'Serious Risk to Growth' Says G7," BBC News, May 27, 2016, www.bbc.com/news/business-36394905.

133. Karishma Vaswani, "Brexit Poses 'Major Risk' to Global Growth, Warns Bank of Japan Chief," BBC News, May 22, 2016, www.bbc.com/news/business-36354947.

134. "Germany: Draghi v the Banks," *Financial Times*, May 31, 2016, https://next.ft.com/content/59461c9a-2420-11e6-aa98-db1e01fabc0c.

135. Katie Linsell, Alastair Marsh, and Sally Bakewell, "Draghi Buying Junk Bonds Shows ECB Will Do Whatever It Takes," Bloomberg, June 8, 2016, www.bloomberg.com/news/articles/2016-06-08/draghi-seen-buying-junk-debt-shows-ecb-will-do-whatever-it-takes.

136. "Euro Zone at Risk of Suffering Lasting Economic Damage: Draghi," Reuters, June 9, 2016, www.reuters.com/article/us-ecb-policy-draghi-idUSKCN0YV0M2.

137. Leika Kihara, "BOJ Makes Contingency Plans for Brexit, Sees Dollar Squeeze, Yen Spike as Risks," Reuters, June 15, 2016, www.reuters.com/article/us-britain-eu-boj-idUSKCN0Z11BB.

138. "Federal Reserve Issues FOMC Statement" (press release), Board of Governors of the Federal Reserve System, June 15, 2016, www.federalreserve.gov/newsevents/press/monetary/20160615a.htm.

139. "Fed Chief Yellen's News Conference After FOMC Meeting," Reuters, June 15, 2016, www.reuters.com/article/us-usa-fed-yellen-idUSKCN0Z12BX.

140. Sam Forgione, "Sterling Pares Losses After Hitting 31-Year Low on Brexit," Reuters, June 23, 2016, www.reuters.com/article/us-global-forex-idUSKCN0Z92O8.

141. "Daily Mail Comment: Take a Bow, Britain! The Quiet People of Our Country Rise Up against an Arrogant, Out-of-Touch Political Class and a Contemptuous Brussels Elite," *Daily Mail* (London), June 24, 2016, www.dailymail.co.uk/debate/article-3659143/DAILY-MAIL-COMMENT-bow-Britain-quiet-people-country-rise-against-arrogant-touch-political-class-contemptuous-Brussels-elite.html.

142. "Federal Reserve Is Carefully Monitoring Developments in Global Financial Markets" (press release), Board of Governors of the Federal Reserve System, June 24, 2016, www.federalreserve.gov/newsevents/press/monetary/20160624a.htm.

143. "Statement by Secretary Lew on UK Referendum" (press release), US Department of the Treasury, June 24, 2016, www.treasury.gov/press-center/press-releases/Pages/jl0499.aspx.

144. "Statement of G-7 Finance Ministers and Central Bank Governors" (press release), US Department of the Treasury, June 24, 2016, www.treasury.gov/press-center/press-releases/Pages/jl0498.aspx.

145. Noah Barkin and Francesco Guarascio, "Draghi Sees Brexit Vote Hitting Euro Zone Growth by Up to 0.5 Percent over Three Years: Official," Reuters, June 28, 2016, http://uk.reuters.com/article/us-britain-eu-draghi-idUKKCN0ZE2G5.

146. "Restore EU Trust with Pragmatism, Urges Germany's Schäuble," *Deutsche Welle,* March 7, 2016, www.dw.com/en/restore-eu-trust-with-pragmatism-urges-germanys-sch%C3%A4uble/a-19374908.

147. Shawn Donnan, Gillian Tett, and Sam Fleming, "Lagarde Warns Trump-Style Protectionism Would Hit World Economy," *Financial Times,* July 7, 2016, www.ft.com/content/134aac12-4403-11e6-9b66-0712b3873ae1.

148. "Monetary Policy Decisions" (press release), European Central Bank, July 21, 2016, www.ecb.europa.eu/press/pr/date/2016/html/pr160721.en.html.

149. Shinji Takagi, Donal Donovan, George Kopits, Ling Hui Tan, Nicolas Veron, Sanjay Dhar, Silvia Sgherri, et al., *The IMF and the Crises in Greece, Ireland, and Portugal: An Evaluation by the Independent Evaluation Office* (Washington, DC: International Monetary Fund, Independent Evaluation Office, July 8, 2016), www.ieo-imf.org/ieo/files/completedevaluations/EAC__REPORT%20v5.PDF.

150. Graeme Wearden, "Bank of England Cuts Interest Rates to Ward Off Brexit Recession—As It Happened," *Guardian* (Manchester), August 4, 2016, www.theguardian.com/business/live/2016/aug/04/bank-of-england-interest-rates-stimulus-inflation-report-business-live.

151. Mark Carney, opening remarks at Inflation Report Press Conference, Bank of England, August 4, 2016, www.bankofengland.co.uk/publications/Documents/inflationreport/2016/irspnote040816.pdf.

152. Angela Monaghan and Katie Allen, "Jackson Hole: Yellen Leaves Door Open to Rate Rise Before Year-End—As It Happened," *Guardian* (Manchester), August 26, 2016, www.theguardian.com/business/live/2016/aug/26/all-eyes-on-yellen-as-jackson-hole-kicks-off-business-live.

153. Christopher Condon, "Fed's Regional Bank Boards Increase Pressure for Rate Hike," Bloomberg, August 23, 2016, www.bloomberg.com/news/articles/2016-08-23/eight-fed-district-bank-boards-backed-discount-rate-hike-in-july.

154. Jana Kasperkevic, "Janet Yellen: The Case for an Interest Rate Hike in 2016 Has 'Strengthened,'" *Guardian* (Manchester), August 26, 2016, www.theguardian.com/business/2016/aug/26/janet-yellen-speech-jackson-hole-federal-reserve-interest-rate.

155. Peter Spence, "Currency Wars Pose 'Lose-Lose' Threat After Brexit Vote, Warns ECB's Mario Draghi," *Telegraph* (London), June 28, 2016, www.telegraph.co.uk/business/2016/06/28/currency-wars-pose-lose-lose-threat-after-brexit-vote-warns-ecbs/.

156. Balazs Koranyi and Francesco Canepa, "ECB Hints at Stimulus but Keeps Markets Guessing," Reuters, September 7, 2016, www.reuters.com/article/us-ecb-policy-idUSKCN11D2RN.

157. Mario Draghi and Vítor Constâncio, "Introductory Statement to the Press Conference (with Q&A)," European Central Bank, September 8, 2016, www.ecb.europa.eu/press/pressconf/2016/html/is160908.en.html.

158. Anushka Asthana and Rowena Mason, "David Cameron Quits as MP to 'Avoid Being a Distraction' to May," *Guardian* (Manchester), September 12, 2016, www.theguardian.com/politics/2016/sep/12/david-cameron-to-stand-down-as-mp-for-witney.

159. "Statement from the Governor of the Bank of England following the EU referendum result" (press release), Bank of England, June 24, 2016, www.bankofengland.co.uk/publications/Pages/news/2016/056.aspx.

160. "Markets Too Dependent on Central Banks," *Financial Times*, September 8, 2016, www.ft.com/content/1457ca48-7dbc-11e6-8e50-8ec15fb462f4.

161. Claudio Borio, remarks at media briefing, *BIS Quarterly Review*, September 2016, www.bis.org/publ/qtrpdf/r_qt1609_ontherecord.htm#cb.

162. "Economic Imbalances Risk 'Destabilising' Euro Zone: ECB's Draghi," Reuters, September 26, 2016, www.reuters.com/article/us-eurozone-economy-ecb-idUSKCN11W1MX.

163. Birgit Jennen, "Draghi Goes Head-to-Head with German Critics of ECB Policy," Bloomberg, September 28, 2016, www.bloomberg.com/news/articles/2016-09-27/draghi-goes-head-to-head-with-german-critics-of-ecb-s-low-rates.

164. Ibid.

165. Therese Raphael, "Deutsche Bank's Troubles Touch a Nationalist Nerve," Bloomberg Opinion, October 4, 2016, www.bloomberg.com/view/articles/2016-10-04/deutsche-s-troubles-touch-a-nationalist-nerve.

166. Philip Blenkinsop and Francesco Canepa, "Some Relief for Big-Spending ECB as Euro Zone Inflation Ticks Up," Reuters, September 30, 2016, http://in.reuters.com/article/eurozone-economy-inflation-idINKCN1201I0.

167. Jan Strupczewski and David Lawder, "Finance Leaders Issue Fresh Warnings Amid Deutsche Worries, Pound Rout," Reuters, October 7, 2016, http://uk.reuters.com/article/uk-imf-g-idUKKCN12723Z.

168. Ibid.

169. "ECB Could Hit Inflation Target by Late 2018, Early 2019—Draghi," Reuters, October 8, 2016, www.reuters.com/article/us-ecb-policy-draghi-idUSKCN1280SX.

170. Mario Draghi and Vítor Constâncio, "Introductory Statement to the Press Conference (with Q&A)," European Central Bank, March 10, 2016, www.ecb.europa.eu/press/pressconf/2016/html/is160310.en.html.

171. "Mark Carney: The 'Film Star' Bank of England Governor," BBC News, October 31, 2016, www.bbc.com/news/business-23050597.

172. May Bulman, "Mark Carney to Stay as Governor of Bank of England to Help 'Secure an Orderly Transition' into Brexit," *Independent* (London), October 31, 2016, www .independent.co.uk/news/business/news/mark-carney-governor-bank-of-england-june -2019-theresa-may-philip-hammond-a7389771.html.

173. Zlata Rodionova, "Pound Sterling Falls to Six-Year Low against the Euro," *Independent* (London), October 17, 2016, www.independent.co.uk/news/business/news/pound -value-sterling-drops-euro-dollar-currency-exchange-rate-latest-low-a7366001.html.

174. Hans Bentzien, "Deutsche Bank Poses Greatest Risk to Global Financial System, IMF Says," *Wall Street Journal,* June 30, 2016, www.wsj.com/articles/deutsche-bank-poses -greatest-risk-to-global-financial-system-imf-says-1467239405.

175. Mike Bird, "Understanding Deutsche Bank's $47 Trillion Derivatives Book," *Wall Street Journal,* October 5, 2016, www.wsj.com/articles/does-deutsche-bank-have -a-47-trillion-derivatives-problem-1475689629.

176. Mario Draghi and Vítor Constâncio, "Introductory Statement to the Press Conference (with Q&A)," European Central Bank, January 19, 2017, www.ecb.europa.eu/press/ pressconf/2017/html/is170119.en.html.

177. Piotr Skolimowski, "Draghi Urges German Patience on Inflation as Euro Area Heals," Bloomberg, January 19, 2017, www.bloomberg.com/news/articles/2017-01-19/ draghi-says-ecb-unconvinced-on-inflation-driven-mainly-by-oil.

178. Mark Carney, remarks, in *Inflation Report* (London: Bank of England, February 2017), www.bankofengland.co.uk/publications/Pages/inflationreport/2017/feb.aspx.

179. German parliament.

180. Sahra Wagenknecht (head of Die Linke [Left] Party), email conversation with author, Bundestag, October 8, 2015.

181. Ibid.

182. Mario Draghi and Vítor Constâncio, "Introductory Statement to the Press Conference," European Central Bank, June 8, 2017, www.ecb.europa.eu/press/pressconf/2017/html/ ecb.is170608.en.html.

183. Steven Erlanger and Melissa Eddy, "Angela Merkel Makes History in German Vote, but So Does Far Right," *New York Times,* September 24, 2017, www.nytimes.com/ 2017/09/24/world/europe/germany-election-merkel.html

184. Jack Ewing, "Wolfgang Schäuble, Architect of Austerity, Is Out as Germany's Finance Minister," September 27, 2017, www.nytimes.com/2017/09/27/business/schauble -germany-parliament.html.

CONCLUSION: THE END IS JUST THE BEGINNING

1 Stanley Fischer, "The Low Level of Global Real Interest Rates" (speech at the Conference to Celebrate Arminio Fraga's 60 Years, Casa das Garcas, Rio de Janeiro, Brazil, July 31, 2017), www.federalreserve.gov/newsevents/speech/fischer20170731a.htm.

2. Ibid.

3. Adam Taggart, "It's Time to Get Painfully Honest: Banks Are Evil," Peak Prosperity, on ZeroHedge, March 18, 2017, www.zerohedge.com/news/2017-03-18/its-time -get-painfully-honest-banks-are-evil.

4. Bitcoin, https://bitcoin.org/en/.

5. Rishi Iyengar, "China's Bitcoin Crackdown Forces Exchanges to Close. The Price Is Crashing," CNN, September 15, 2017, http://money.cnn.com/2017/09/15/technology/china-bitcoin-exchanges-prices-crash/index.html.

6. Jeffrey A. Tucker, "IMF Head Foresees the End of Banking and the Triumph of Cryptocurrency," *FEE*, September 30, 2017, https://fee.org/articles/imf-head-predicts-the-end-of-banking-and-the-triumph-of-cryptocurrency/.

7. Ibid.

8. Joseph Stiglitz, "Joseph Stiglitz Explains Why the Fed Shouldn't Raise Interest Rates" (op-ed), *Los Angeles Times*, August 27, 2015, www.latimes.com/opinion/op-ed/la-oe-0827-stiglitz-interest-rates-20150827-story.html.

9. Liz Moyer, "Alan Greenspan: The Bubble Is in Bonds, Not Stocks," CNBC, August 1, 2017, www.cnbc.com/2017/08/01/alan-greenspan-the-bubble-is-in-bonds-not-stocks.html.

10. Evelyn Cheng, "JPMorgan Unleashed: Bank Commits to Largest Buyback Since Crisis," CNBC, June 28, 2017, www.cnbc.com/2017/06/28/jpmorgan-commits-to-largest-buyback-since-crisis.html.

11. Chris Dieterich, "Banks Unleash Record Stock Buyback Plans," Moneybeat (blog), *Wall Street Journal*, June 30, 2017, https://blogs.wsj.com/moneybeat/2017/06/30/banks-unleash-record-stock-buyback-plans/.

12. Thomas M. Hoenig, letter to Michael Crapo and Sherrod Brown, July 31, 2017, http://wallstreetonparade.com/wp-content/uploads/2017/08/earningsandloangrowth_LettertoBankingCommittee_7-31-2017.pdf.

INDEX

Lycurgo C. Querido

Nomi Prins is a former Wall Street executive, journalist, speaker, respected TV and radio commentator, and author of six books, including *All the Presidents' Bankers, Other People's Money,* and *It Takes a Pillage.* Her writing has been featured in the *New York Times, Fortune, Forbes,* the *Guardian,* and the *Nation,* among other publications. She was a member of Senator Bernie Sanders's (I-VT) Federal Reserve Reform Advisory Council, is listed as one of America's TopWonks, and is on the advisory board of the whistle-blowing organization ExposeFacts.

NATION
BOOKS

The Nation Institute

Founded in 2000, **Nation Books** has become a leading voice in American independent publishing. The imprint's mission is to tell stories that inform and empower just as they inspire or entertain readers. We publish award-winning and bestselling journalists, thought leaders, whistleblowers, and truthtellers, and we are also committed to seeking out a new generation of emerging writers, particularly voices from underrepresented communities and writers from diverse backgrounds. As a publisher with a focused list, we work closely with all our authors to ensure that their books have broad and lasting impact. With each of our books we aim to constructively affect and amplify cultural and political discourse and to engender positive social change.

Nation Books is a project of The Nation Institute, a nonprofit media center established to extend the reach of democratic ideals and strengthen the independent press. The Nation Institute is home to a dynamic range of programs: the award-winning Investigative Fund, which supports groundbreaking investigative journalism; the widely read and syndicated website TomDispatch; journalism fellowships that support and cultivate over twenty-five emerging and high-profile reporters each year; and the Victor S. Navasky Internship Program.

For more information on Nation Books and The Nation Institute, please visit:

www.nationbooks.org
www.nationinstitute.org
www.facebook.com/nationbooks.ny
Twitter: @nationbooks